A GENIUS FOR MONEY

A GENIUS FOR MONEY

BUSINESS, ART AND THE MORRISONS

CAROLINE DAKERS

YALE UNIVERSITY PRESS
NEW HAVEN AND LONDON

Published with assistance from the Annie Burr Lewis Fund

For information about this and other Yale University Press publications, please contact:
U.S. Office: sales.press@yale.edu   www.yalebooks.com
Europe Office: sales @yaleup.co.uk   www.yalebooks.co.uk

Set in Arno Pro by IDSUK (DataConnection) Ltd
Printed in Great Britain by TJ International Ltd, Padstow, Cornwall

Library of Congress Cataloging-in-Publication Data

Dakers, Caroline.
  A genius for money: business, art and the Morrisons/Caroline Dakers.
  p.cm.
  ISBN 978–0–300–11220–7 (cl:alk. paper)
  1. Morrison, James, 1789–1857. 2. Businessmen—Great Britain—Biography. I. Title.
HC252.5.M67D34 2011
  338.092–dc23
  [B]
                                                                    2011026892

A catalogue record for this book is available from the British Library.

10 9 8 7 6 5 4 3 2 1

Contents

Illustrations

Acknowledgements

I would like to thank the many descendants of James and Mary Ann Morrison who have given me help in researching this book. The late James Morrison, 2nd Lord Margadale, and his wife Clare first gave me permission to use their archive; Alastair Morrison, 3rd Lord Margadale, and his wife Amanda have continued to allow me access. Their decision to engage a professional archivist, John D'Arcy, helped me considerably. Other family members who have provided materials or shared anecdotes include the Hon. Mary Morrison, the late Hon. Charles Morrison, the late Pamela Gatty, Rhoda (nee Gatty) and the late David Bucknill, the late Nigel Anderson, Lady Ashcombe and her children Henry and Molly Dent-Brocklehurst, Lady Farnham, Rose Sanguinetti, Arthur Carden and Audrey Bryant.

The staff of libraries, art galleries and auction houses, curators of museums and archives, dealers, financial experts, scholars of the period and owners of Morrison houses have generously provided time, information, illustrations and advice. They include: Patricia Allderidge; Marijke Booth, Peter Brown, Desmond Healey, Nora Maas, Orlando Rock, Nick Wilson (all at Christies); Richard Bowden; Brian Allen; Mr and Mrs Barnham; Jean Bray; Charles Brett and Christiana Payne; John Chandler; Jeannie Chapel; Amanda Cammies; Felicity Cobbing; Frances Collard; Michael Darby; Martin Daunton; Francis Dineley; Michael Drury; Caroline Evans; Kathryn Ferry; Simon Fraser; Edwin Green; Jonathan Harris and Bruce Lindsay (Harris Lindsay); the late Reg Harris; Charles Hind and his colleagues at the RIBA; Sarah Hodson; Charles Jones; Susan Kay-Williams and Lynn Hulse (Royal School of Needlework); Nasser D. Khalili and Andrew Keelan (the Khalili

Collection); Ian Leith; Martin Levy; Jeremy Linton; Huon Mallalieu; Jonathan Marsden; W.R. Mitchell; Christopher Newall; David Pearson; Lucy Porten, Charles Pugh and the National Trust staff at Basildon and Hughenden; Martin Postle; Katherine Purcell; Bruce Purvis; Bill Rubinstein; Sarah Rutherford; Colin Ryan; Reg Sawyer; Robin Simon; Margaret Storrie; Canon Gerald Squarey; Adriana Turpin; Jane Wagner; Clive Williams (Basildon); David Wilson; Min Wood.

In addition, the staff of the Beverley Art Gallery; the British Library; the Caledonian Club; the library of Central Saint Martins College of Art and Design; Glasgow University Library; the Guildhall Library; the Hampshire Record Office; Islay Museum; the London Metropolitan Archive; the National Galleries of Scotland; the National Art Library; the Royal Collection; the Royal Academy library; the Russell-Cotes Museum and Art Gallery Bournemouth; Sewerby Museum; Sotheby's; the Wiltshire Record Office.

Attending conferences and giving papers on aspects of the Morrisons has been of enormous assistance, both in testing out my approaches and ideas and maintaining the momentum of research and writing alongside an academic job. In particular, I would like to thank the organisers and fellow speakers at the Nineteenth Century Studies Association conference, 'Money and Myth', at the University of New Mexico, Albuquerque (2011); 'Bloomsday', and other events associated with the Bloomsbury Research project at University College London; the IESA conference on 'Collectors and Collecting', Paris (2010); the National Trust study day at Waddesdon on 'Town and Country Houses' (2010); the International Society of Cultural Historians' conference at the University of Ghent (2008); 'City Merchants and the Arts: the Victorians', organised by the Corporation of London at the Guildhall (2004); the Senior Historians Conference at Cumberland Lodge (2004); 'Wealth and Poverty', the Anglo-American Conference at the Institute of Historical Research (2004); 'Dickens in America', at the University of Massachusetts in Lowell (2002).

I would like to thank the University of the Arts London for awarding me a one-term sabbatical in 2008, also some time throughout the academic year to spend on this project, and a contribution to the expenses incurred giving papers at the Universities of Cambridge, Keele, London, Ghent, Massachusetts and New Mexico. I was awarded a 'Changing Places' grant by the AHRB (now AHRC) to spend a period of time at the RIBA Prints and Drawings Department, and also received a small grant from the AHRB as part of the 'Fashion and Modernity' research project led by Professor Caroline Evans at Central Saint Martins College of Art and Design. The Scouloudi Foundation and the Paul Mellon Centre awarded me small grants to visit Islay and Basildon. I acknowledge the award of a Publication Grant from the Paul Mellon Centre for Studies in British Art to assist with the cost of the illustrations.

This is the third book published by Yale University Press and I would again like to thank all of the team, Robert Baldock, Candida Brazil, Tami Halliday, Beth Humphries and Rachael Lonsdale.

Finally, I would like to thank my daughters Harriet and Madeline for being patient, Nigel Cross for providing perspective at the beginning of the project and reading early chapters, and Neil Burton for reading more than one draft and providing constant, constructive criticism.

Berwick St John and Gower Mews 2011

The Family Tree

Joseph Morrison c.1731–1804 of Middle Wallop — m — (2nd) Sarah Barnard of Somerton c.1761–1803

Joseph Todd c.1767–1835 of Cumbria
1792 (1st) Lucy Plowes of Wakefield d.1798 — m — (2nd) 1804 Laetitia Dann d.1819

Children of Joseph Todd:
- Thomas Todd 1803–68
- Eliza Todd 1806–07
- Joseph Todd 1809–98 m. Maria Glossop
- Emma Todd b. & d. 1811
- Lucy Todd c.1812–90 m. John Downes
- John Edward Todd 1792–1863 m. Jane Downes
- **Mary Ann Todd 1795–1887 m. James Morrison**

Children of Joseph Morrison:
- ?John Morrison b. & d. 1787
- Samuel Morrison 1787–1855 m. 1816 Elizabeth Hillary
- **James Morrison 1789–1857 m. 1814 Mary Ann Todd**
- Maria Morrison 1792–1849 m. 1818 William Cope
- Martha Morrison 1795–

James Morrison **m** Mary Ann Todd — children:
- **Charles Morrison 1817–1909**
- **Alfred Morrison 1821–97 m.1866 Mabel Chermside 1847–1933**
- Frank Morrison 1824–1904 m. 1854 Harriet Grant
- Lucy Morrison 1825–76 m.1856 George Moffatt
- Emily Morrison 1827–54 m. 1850 Capt. John Grant
- Mary Morrison 1830–59 m.1854 Rev. George Goodwin Pownall Glossop
- Henry Morrison 1832–50
- Ellen Morrison 1834–1909
- Walter Morrison 1836–1921
- George Morrison 1839–84 m. Barbara Jane Poore
- Allan Morrison 1842–1880

Mary Morrison m. Rev. George Goodwin Pownall Glossop — child:
- Bertha Glossop 1856–1936

Lucy Morrison m. George Moffatt — children:
- Alice Moffatt 1858–1922
- Harold Moffatt 1859–1945
- Ethel Moffatt
- Hilda Moffatt d.1947

Alfred Morrison m. Mabel Chermside — children:
- **Hugh Morrison 1868–1931** m.1892 Lady Mary Leveson-Gower 1870–1934
- Katharine Morrison 1869–1949 m. 1905 Sir Stephen Gatty
- Dorothy Morrison 1871–1936 m. 1912 Viscount St Cyres
- **Archie Morrison 1873–1934** m. (1st) 1901 Hon Mary Hill-Trevor; m. (2nd) 1920 Dorothy Halton nee Bold; m. (3rd) 1931 Gwendoline Phyllis Talmage

Introduction

In England, personal distinction is the only passport to the society of the great. Whether this distinction arise from fortune, family, or talent, is immaterial; but certain it is, to enter into high society, a man must either have blood, a million, or a genius.

Benjamin Disraeli, *Vivian Grey*, 1826–7

James Morrison (1789–1857) is one of the least known but most extraordinary of nineteenth-century merchant millionaires. The son of a village innkeeper, he was sent to London as apprentice to a haberdasher. There, he proved to be a genius at making money and became the kingpin of textiles and the Napoleon of shopkeepers, creating a business with a turnover in 1830 of nearly £2 million, the equivalent of £200 million today. He invested almost a million (*c.* £100 million) in North American railways, he was involved in global trade from Canton to Valparaiso, and acquired land, houses and works of art to rival the grandest of aristocrats. When he died in 1857 he left his wife and all his nine children fortunes. He turned down the opportunity to buy a title (he considered it a poor investment), so remained a commoner – the richest commoner in the whole of the nineteenth century.[1]

Like a character in Samuel Smiles' Victorian best-seller *Self-Help,* Morrison rose to the top 'by his own unaided efforts and through self-improvement, self-help, abstinence, thrift, hard work, acquisitive drive, innovative flair, and grasp of market opportunities'. On the way he created hundreds of jobs and 'flooded the world' with his goods.[2] He relished the intellectual pleasure in what he called 'the science of business'.[3]

Morrison's 'rags to riches' story is at the heart of this book: his very modern business techniques, his self-education, his election to Parliament as a radical Whig. His achievements illuminate the decades just before the accession of Queen Victoria and the early years of her reign. It was the age of reform, a period of unusual social mobility, the end of slavery and the beginning of empire, with fortunes to be made and lost in textiles, railways, overseas trade and banking. Morrison was part of the circle of political economists who extolled the virtues of free trade, competition and entrepreneurship. London's supremacy as a world city was unchallenged; a 'bottomless pit of consumption.'[4] It was the best time to make a commercial fortune and for a millionaire like Morrison it was also an unprecedented time to acquire great works of art.

Morrison's artistic taste, which developed from nothing in just a few years, was aristocratic and cosmopolitan: along with collectors such as King George IV and the Rothschilds, he shared a passion for luxury and decoration, for tables of Florentine marble, Italian tortoiseshell, ebony inlaid with mother-of-pearl and ivory, and Egyptian porphyry; lacquer bureau-cabinets and boulle furniture; Etruscan vases and classical statues; gold inlay. He took the Grand Tour to Italy, visiting museums and palaces – he called them 'lions' – and artists' studios. He bought paintings by his contemporaries, including Constable and Turner (the latter was a friend and a guest at his houses in London and in the country), as well as collecting Old Masters. The National Gallery in London has two of his paintings, Rembrandt's *Portrait of Hendrickje Stoffels* and Poussin's *Triumph of Pan,* while the Getty in California owns another Poussin, *Un Temps calme,* and Rubens' *Miracles of St Francis of Paolo.* Constable's *The Lock* is in the Thyssen-Bornemisza collection in Madrid. So a major part of this book examines his collecting, the display in his country and town houses, and his patronage of architects and designers.

Like Disraeli's canny tailor Sir Peter Vigo (*Endymion*), Morrison 'had the wisdom to retain his millions, which few manage to do, as it is admitted that it is easier to make a fortune than to keep one'. At his death, his wife and all of his surviving children were left fortunes; four of his sons also inherited their own country estates. While none of Morrison's children were able to match the formidable range of his achievements, his eldest sons did add substantially to the family wealth. Their activities are so important that they form the subject of separate chapters.

The eldest, Charles, though a shy reclusive bachelor was a brilliant financier, investing heavily in South America. By his death in 1909 he had turned his inheritance of one million into fourteen to become the richest commoner of his own generation. Alfred was a connoisseur. Dubbed the 'Victorian Maecenas', he commissioned the architect-designer Owen Jones and a team of talented craftsmen to turn his town and country houses into palaces of art where he displayed the greatest private collections of Imperial Chinese porcelain and autograph letters of the day.

It may seem surprising that the Morrisons are virtually unknown, but there are several reasons for their obscurity. A biography of James Morrison, *Portrait of a Merchant Prince*, was written by a descendant, Richard Gatty. Though serious and competent, only 200 copies were privately printed in 1976 so it never reached a wide readership. Since then economic historians have established the wealth of James and Charles Morrison, and analysed their business practices.[5] Martin Daunton writes: 'The greatest fortune in the textile trades was not made by Richard Arkwright in the production of yarn; it was accumulated by James Morrison ... whose textile warehouse in the City of London supplied the inland trade with its handkerchiefs, ribbons, braids, and fabrics.'[6] But commerce is not a sexy subject. Unlike Rothschild, the Morrison name has no resonance.[7] James Morrison's wealth creation was in part because of the industrial revolution and the explosion in cheap textiles, but he was neither a manufacturer nor an inventor; Arkwright and Wedgwood are better-known names.

James Morrison acquired a very large number of properties, from artisans' dwellings and shops to country mansions, and also commissioned warehouses from his favourite architect J.B. Papworth. As his wealth increased he moved his family from the City of London across the Thames to Balham, then to grander houses in more prestigious locations, all the time adding to his portfolio. It is unfortunate that there is no property still occupied by Morrisons and open to the public on which to base his story.

The textile warehouse in Fore Street, Cripplegate, where James Morrison made his fortune, took a direct hit the first night of the Blitz. The Morrisons' grandest country house was Basildon Park, a fine late Palladian mansion set within a park close to the River Thames. After the First World War it was sold by a grandson, Archie Morrison, along with most of its contents, and is now the property of the National Trust. The Morrisons owned Basildon for almost a century, James Morrison engaging Papworth and David Brandon to complete the interiors and the pleasure grounds, design cottages, farm buildings and a school, and restore the church, but the National Trust's narrative concentrates on the (comparatively recent) post-war occupation by the Iliffes.

Alfred Morrison's London house, 16 Carlton House Terrace, with startling interiors by Owen Jones, was sold by his widow along with a substantial part of his collections. His house at Fonthill was demolished by his eldest son Hugh who commissioned Detmar Blow to design a new house on another part of the estate. Sixty years later this was demolished by his son John Granville Morrison, the 1st Baron Margadale, and much of the contents sold.[8] Fortunately the estate itself remains in the hands of the 3rd Baron Margadale, James' great-great-grandson.

James and his son Alfred were very important collectors and patrons of the arts but the dispersal of their treasures makes it extremely difficult to recreate their collections and assess their visual impact. Many paintings are now hanging in public and private collections around the world but the Morrison provenance is not always acknowledged. A number of James Morrison's paintings from Basildon and 57 (now 93) Harley Street still hang together at Sudeley Castle in Gloucestershire, the property of his descendants the Dent-Brocklehursts, and the house is open to the public. However, visitors are, not surprisingly, attracted by Sudeley's connection with Henry VIII rather than the as yet little-known James Morrison.

There *is* an extensive archive, but even this raises more issues. Though James Morrison refused to 'invest' in a baronetcy, he was sufficiently proud of his achievements to begin ordering his papers in preparation for writing his memoirs: black tin trunks stuffed with correspondence, deeds, Fore Street ledgers, invoices and bills, share certificates, inventories and diaries. He paid a clerk to copy all the correspondence relating to his takeover of his father-in-law's business, and kept his own list of art purchases, including details of how much was paid at which sale. He also kept detailed lists, every six months, of his assets, so that he (and we) can track the steady accumulation of his fortune. Letters from architects, his land agents, parliamentary colleagues, partners in Fore Street, merchants and bankers in London and the United States, were preserved alphabetically, year by year.

All of this provides valuable material for plotting his public and commercial life, what he did and where he went; but personal data are missing. There are virtually no letters between him and his wife Mary Ann or their children. Mary Ann's presence was essential to Morrison's success. Already well read when they married, she was his travelling companion, she provided constant encouragement and support, security and stability, she was his 'helpmeet' in all aspects of his life. But it was probably she, together with Charles (who inherited his father's papers), who destroyed material in the archive. Only odd exceptions have survived, accidentally or deliberately misplaced; Morrison's declaration of love for Mary Ann is such an example, tucked into a Fore Street account book.

The Morrisons were obviously a devoted family. From the parliamentary campaign trail James Morrison wrote home regularly, wishing his children were with him, asking after the youngest, expressing his pleasure in receiving their letters. Orphaned at a young age, sent as an apprentice into a formidable and unknown city, he considered a home as desirable as wealth: 'a state of mind', according to John Tosh, 'as well as a physical orientation'. 'Its defining attributes are privacy and comfort, separation from the workplace and the merging of domestic space and family members into a single commanding concept … home.'[9] The Morrisons' apparent perfect domesticity exemplifies the Victorian ideal. And as Morrison moved his family into ever grander properties he never disposed of anything, so that when his sons grew up he could give them homes from his portfolio of country houses; he also bought property in Middle Wallop, his modest birthplace in Hampshire. He was not ashamed of his roots.

The Morrisons' wealth was legendary in their lifetimes; their land, their country houses and their collections of art were the subject of notice, sometimes envy. James Morrison was also respected in Parliament as a 'practising' political economist and free-trader. His knowledge of textiles, railways and investment in North America was second to none, while his son Charles was an expert on (and made a fortune out of) investing in Canada and Argentina. They provided inspiration for contemporary novelists, from Dickens, Disraeli and Thackeray to Trollope, George Eliot and Henry James, all of whom wrote of the world in which the Morrisons moved and made their millions. In this study, novels are consequently used on occasion to supplement archival evidence, to flesh out the Morrisons.

There is added justification in referencing fiction, as many of the novelists had personal knowledge of the family. Dickens, for example, reported on

James Morrison's political campaigning in Ipswich and stayed at Niagara Falls in the same hotel as Alfred; Disraeli sat opposite James in Parliament and made love to Henrietta Sykes of Basildon; Henry James shared acquaintances with Alfred, while George Eliot and her partner G.H. Lewes shared with Alfred his architect-designer Owen Jones, visited his London home and entertained his young wife.

In their novels excessive wealth, and the desire for it, are mostly linked to excessive and immoral behaviour. Bankers, merchants, industrialists and moneylenders appear as villains (rarely heroes). Dickens' Dombey is typical: 'The earth was made for Dombey & Son to trade in ... Dombey & Son had often dealt in hides but never in hearts.' Our understanding of the period, its *history*, is profoundly coloured by their invented characters. Indeed Henry James claimed 'the novel is history', and the historian Beverley Southgate has recently gone further, suggesting that fiction 'represents and actually embodies some of the widely accepted social mores and intellectual presuppositions of its age'.[10]

In *Self-Help* Samuel Smiles defined the 'use and abuse of money':

Some of the finest qualities of human nature are intimately related to the right use of money, such as generosity, honesty, justice, and self-sacrifice; as well as the practical virtues of economy and providence. On the other hand, there are their counterparts of avarice, fraud, injustice, and selfishness, as displayed by inordinate lovers of gain; and the vices of thriftlessness, extravagance, and improvidence, on the part of those who misuse and abuse the means entrusted to them.[11]

While Melmotte and Merdle are guilty of the majority of Smiles' list of abuses, James Morrison's *actual* life presents a very different model, closer indeed to the 'right use of money'. He was a loving husband and father, hardworking, above all honest, a Cheeryble rather than a Dombey. Disraeli's tailor Sir Peter Vigo is perhaps the closest in contemporary fiction:

He was one who obtained influence over all with whom he came in contact, and as his business placed him in contact with various classes, but especially with the class socially most distinguished, his influence was great. ... He was neither pretentious nor servile, but simple, and with becoming respect for others and for himself. He never took a liberty with any one, and such treatment, as is generally the case, was reciprocated.[12]

Morrison's London and country houses were palaces of art, filled with the physical evidence of his wealth and good taste; he never squandered, only increased his immense fortune, which was shared between his wife and all his surviving children: he was a model millionaire.

❧❧❧

CHAPTER ONE

Middle Wallop

> I was born of humble parents, in a remote county of England. ... I was
> taught the rudiments of no science, except reading, writing and arithmetic.
> But I had an inquisitive mind, and neglected no means of information from
> conversation or books. My improvement was greater than my condition in
> life afforded room to expect.
>
> William Godwin, Caleb Williams, 1794

James Morrison was born in August 1789, most probably at his parents'
home, the Lower George Inn in Middle Wallop, a small Hampshire hamlet
about ten miles from Salisbury. He was baptised on 6 September at St Peter's
Over Wallop.[1] His elder brother Samuel was born in 1787; his two sisters
Maria and Martha in 1793 and 1795.[2]

Over and Nether Wallop are connected by a narrow lane which now
crosses the busy A343 between Andover and Salisbury at Middle Wallop.
The Lower George was conveniently situated beside the crossroads, clearly
visible to travellers approaching from Salisbury. Now, the renamed George
Inn, a half-timbered structure built in 1927, is set further back from the road,
but some eighteenth-century cottages have survived close by.

Most drivers speeding to and from Salisbury barely notice the hamlet;
pedestrians cross at their peril. However, two hundred and fifty years ago,
when the road was upgraded to become the main coach road from London
to the West Country, the increase in coach traffic brought opportunity and
prosperity. The six London coaches passing through each week became
fifty;[3] long-distance and local carriers competed for space. Similar changes

were taking place all over the country as 'foul roads' were transformed into 'motorways', producing a 'sub-economy of inns, ostlers, coaches and coaching services, highwaymen and illicit game-dealers'.[4] The great age of coach travel was about to begin.

The new roads were paid for by tolls collected at turnpikes.[5] Their location could have a considerable effect on local economies, as enforced stops encouraged the establishment of public houses and coaching inns. The Lower George at Middle Wallop, boasting fine bedrooms, the renowned Wallop ale and stabling for sixty horses was just such an establishment. It was opened soon after the turnpike was erected on the Salisbury side of the hamlet; its proprietor was Morrison's father Joseph.

His was the second generation of Morrisons to live in the Wallops. His father George was reputedly a drover from Scotland, who attended the annual fairs in Wiltshire and Hampshire, before choosing to settle in the south with his wife Margaret in about 1720.[6] He was following an established route taken by Scotsmen and women after the Act of Union: 'under post-Union free-trade, Scottish cattle-droving, linen, mining and metal trades thrived. Agriculture and industry were modernised. ... Ambitious Scots anglicised their voices ... disguised their names ... and took the high road south.'[7] The Morrison clan originated from Lewis; James Morrison claimed Scottish descent when standing for election to the Burghs of Inverness in 1840.[8] 'He had travelled in Switzerland and Germany and seen mountains and lakes; but in witnessing those of Scotland he had experienced emotions which he had never felt before, and which he could only account for by believing that there was some mysterious affinity between the present and the past which had stirred up all the Scotch blood in his veins.'[9]

George and Margaret ran a small inn from a cottage which survives (in recent years housing an antique shop), calling it the George. They served the drovers who stayed overnight while their flocks of sheep, sometimes as many as 3,000, rested in pens close by. The sheep were washed, for a fee, in the large sheep-wash situated beside the lane to Nether Wallop, before proceeding to the fairs.[10] These were held annually in unpopulated downland areas close to Andover, Wylye and Devizes; in Salisbury there were sheep fairs fortnightly.[11]

In 1747, a few years after her husband's death,[12] Margaret acquired a lease to their small property from the local landowner, Mr Holloway of Fifehead

Manor.[13] With this security and the help of two of her children Joseph (born
c. 1731) and Mary, she was able to expand the business in anticipation of the
improvements to the road to London. The traffic in carriers was steadily
increasing, and the inn was used for the collection and exchange of goods as
well as for overnight lodging.[14]

When Margaret died in 1767 she left her two farming sons £100 each; to
Joseph and Mary she left the inn, the stock and goods 'equal between them
as long as my daughter Mary shall live single, or if they should not agree to
live together, my son Joseph has to pay my daughter £100, and five pounds
out of the house every year during her life'.[15] At the time, the average income
for an innkeeper was around £100 per annum; an agricultural labourer could
expect £12 10s.; a farmer anything from £40 to £150.[16]

The following year Joseph Morrison married Mary Wheeler of Winchester.[17] He continued to run the 'Old George' for the drovers, local labourers
and 'persons of small means and inferior station',[18] but also took the gamble
of investing in a new establishment across the road, the 'upmarket' Lower
George. Guests were served by 'ostlers, helpers, potboys, and others lounging
about, while waiters flitted to and fro, actively engaged in distributing refreshments, and smart chambermaids popped their heads out of the windows'.[19]

Mary died only five years after their marriage, leaving Joseph with at least
two young children to bring up.[20] Some thirteen years later, he married again.
His bride Sarah Barnard of Somerton in Somerset was younger than him by
thirty years. The Morrisons and the Barnards were well matched; both families represented a similar 'class' in British rural society which included tenant
farmers, yeomen (owners of freehold land), innkeepers, maltsters and
brewers. Joseph's brothers George and John farmed land in Over Wallop; his
niece Margaret had married into the prominent Hillary family, farmers, maltsters, bondsmen and parish clerks, and his sister Mary occupied her own
house, with grounds and an orchard, in Over Wallop.[21] Somerton was a
thriving coaching town, on the main route between London, Exeter, Bath
and Bridgwater.[22] The Barnards had farmed around Somerton for generations; Sarah's mother Sarah Inder was from the nearby market town of
Martock.

The Barnards were also Nonconformists. Somerton was well known for its
mix of Presbyterians, Baptists and Independents and, by the early nineteenth
century, it was the head of the Glastonbury circuit of Wesleyan Methodists.

James Morrison's interest in the ideas of the Freethinking Christians, manifest in his early years in London, would appear to have come from his mother's side of the family. Perhaps of greater significance for him was the confidence, independence and relative prosperity of both Barnards and Morrisons. Through them, he acquired knowledge of trade, commerce and agriculture, and he maintained links with both sides even as his own wealth and influence increased.

In Jane Austen's *Emma*, Emma confesses she finds it difficult to place socially a tenant farmer like Robert Martin; he is clearly distinguished from the agricultural labourers whom he employs, but lacks the education of the professional classes, of doctors, lawyers and the clergy, or the security of his own landed estate. She refers to him as a yeoman, even though yeomen 'strictly' own their own land; she objects to his not desiring her patronage. 'The yeomanry are precisely the order of people with whom I feel I can have nothing to do. A degree or two lower and a creditable appearance might interest me; I might hope to be useful to their families in some way or other. But a farmer can need none of my help, and is therefore in one sense as much above my notice as in every other he is below it.'[23]

Though innkeepers do not feature in the novels of Austen, they were noted during the same period for possessing a similar 'indifference of rank'. 'Each came into continual contact with strangers; each demonstrated the beneficent effect of trade; each lacked the predictable breeding of people of rank or people used to consorting with people of rank. ... Innkeepers and shopkeepers were polite because they sold commodities which in England were in ready supply, which were the subject of intense competition, and the sale of which could be maximised by skilful merchandising. They came to embody one of the most noted features of English life, its supposed indifference to rank.'[24] According to his obituary in *The Times*, Morrison 'was accustomed to say that he was thus launched in life and in the City, with no other means of subsistence than the principles and habits an excellent mother had given him'.[25] The poor writing skills of his brother and sisters suggest that none received much formal teaching as children; his own breadth of reading and sophisticated vocabulary could only have developed during his years as an apprentice and shopman in London. However, growing up among the employees and the customers of the Old and Lower George provided first-hand experience of commerce, and self-confidence.

It also brought news, daily, of a larger world. 'The opening of roads to London was held to be the end of gothic barbarism'.[26] Coachmen and their passengers, aristocratic parties travelling in post-chaises, independent travellers, overnight carriers and long-distance stage wagons all brought and exchanged national and international news, 'the dull roar of a vanishing world, the distant noise of a crumbling society'.[27] The radical writer and poet Leigh Hunt applauded the stagecoach for assisting 'village liberality; for its passengers are so mixed, so often varied, so little yet so much together, so compelled to accommodate, so willing to pass a short time pleasantly, and so liable to the criticism of strangers, that it is hard if they do not get a habit of speaking, or even thinking more kindly of one another than if they mingled less often, or under other circumstances'.[28] No wonder Morrison advised his sons when travelling to listen to their fellow passengers, 'because everyone knows more about at least one subject than you do'.

And the times were hardly dull. Morrison was born in the year the Bastille fell. France declared war on Britain in 1793 shortly after the execution of Louis XVI and Morrison was just nine when Nelson defeated Napoleon's fleet at Aboukir Bay. In December 1800 Nelson passed through Middle Wallop. He was travelling with his mistress Emma Hamilton[29] and her husband Sir William from London to Salisbury, then on to Fonthill as the guests of the notorious William Beckford. The coach was met by a mounted corps at the county boundary just a mile or two outside Middle Wallop, and escorted to Salisbury. After receiving the freedom of the city, Nelson and the Hamiltons proceeded on to Fonthill Splendens for four days of festivities, culminating in a torchlit procession up to the unfinished Abbey. Less than thirty years later, Morrison would be owner of the remains of Fonthill Splendens, purchasing some of Beckford's treasures.

All national and international events were overshadowed for the Morrison children by the death of both their parents in a space of just eighteen months. Sarah died on 17 January 1803; Joseph made his will and died on 7 May 1804, leaving to their children his leasehold estate 'known by the name of the Old George Inn Situate in Nether Wallop held by lease under Sutton Esq & to be equally divided (when Martha 21) and stock and household goods'.[30] The estate was valued at just under £400, so Samuel, James, Maria and Martha could each expect to receive about £100 in 1816, a not inconsiderable sum for the children of an innkeeper.

Samuel and Maria remained with their seventy-year-old Uncle George in Over Wallop and Martha lodged with her Aunt Martha Downton, recently married and living in Pitney, near Somerton. James was almost certainly already living in London, apprenticed to a haberdasher. Stories which circulated when he had become a man of fortune support his arrival in London around 1800 (shortly before the death of his parents), placing him either with relations in Gray's Inn Lane from where he worked for a German furrier's or with a watchmaker and then the Flints of London Bridge, 'great ready-made haberdashers' and early employers of Robert Owen.[31] Morrisons, Barnards and Inders can be found engaged in related trades in the City of London, in Cripplegate and Cheapside, also in Holborn and the Strand[32] – it is more than likely that one or more provided contacts, possibly sharing the apprenticeship fee of some twenty-five guineas.[33]

An apprenticeship in haberdashery was unsurprising, given the proximity of the Wallops to Salisbury, which experienced a revival in cloth manufacture at the end of the eighteenth century.[34] Textiles were at the time the fastest-growing sector of British trade, and fortunes were to be made in all aspects, from manufacture to trade, wholesale to retail.[35] And learning to be a shop-keeper had its advantages: 'Take the drapery trade as it is, where can you see a better? It is light and pleasant, and the members of it are well paid ... its members are housed, and their meals are provided with punctuality, and invariably with liberality, so that there is no real occasion to expend one's salary, except for clothing, and that, with economy, is but trifling.'[36]

So Morrison probably travelled to London in one of the long-distance carriers which frequented the Old George, to make his way in 'the centre of the trade of the whole world.'[37]

CHAPTER TWO

❦

The Todds of Fore Street

Joe Toddyhigh had never been in the capital of Europe before and he wandered up and down the streets that night amazed at the number of churches and other public buildings, the splendour of the shops, the riches that were heaped up on every side, the glare of light in which they were displayed, and the concourse of people who hurried to and fro, indifferent, apparently, to all the wonders that surrounded them.

Charles Dickens, *Master Humphrey's Clock*, 1840

Although the date of James Morrison's birth is not recorded, he made a careful note in different documents of the day he began work as shopman (shop assistant) in the house of Joseph Todd & Co., haberdasher, at 105 Fore Street, St Giles' Cripplegate. 'I came to live with Mr Todd on the 6th of March 1809 at a salary of 40£ pr year.'[1] To be engaged as a shopman, Morrison would have completed an apprenticeship of between three and seven years, followed by at least one year as a journeyman (working for wages). During that time he lost his parents and was separated from his brother and sisters, but in Fore Street he joined an extended family, united by ties of family, affection and commerce.[2]

Joseph Todd had travelled from the Lake District to London in about 1785 seeking his fortune in the textile trade.[3] He first set up a retail haberdashery business at 105 Fore Street, opposite St Giles' Church, possibly with the help of his first wife Lucy Plowes.[4] He acquired a forty-nine-year lease for an annual rent of £60 and opened for business on 30 March 1793.[5] Turnover in the first nine months of trading was £1,488; in 1794 it had increased to

£2,529; by 1805 it was almost £6,000 and he acquired new premises in Cheapside.[6]

The expansion of Todd's business was repeated throughout the capital. London was not just the first city in the world with a population approaching one million, it was recognised at the time as 'the centre of the trade of the whole world, and more ships sail from it in a year than from all other places in the world united. It has fifty times more trade than ancient Carthage, than Venice in its glory; than all the Hans Towns, or Amsterdam could ever boast.'[7] And according to William Pitt, by 1792 four-fifths of Britain's overseas income came from trade with the West Indies, a trade dependent on slave labour.[8]

Sugar was initially the major import; however, by the end of the eighteenth century it was overtaken by cotton. In 1750, 2.8 million pounds of cotton were imported into Britain; by 1790, 33 million pounds were imported, to meet the ever-increasing demands of the Lancashire mills, and in 1800 the figure rose to 55 million pounds. The majority of cotton was grown on slave plantations, not just in the West Indies but also in the southern slave states of North America. These benefited from the invention of the saw gin in 1792, which cleaned short-staple cotton efficiently and cheaply.[9] After the British abolition of the slave trade in 1807, the American plantations increased production; by 1830 slave labour in the southern states was providing three-quarters of the cotton required by British mills.[10]

The increasing imports and development of new industrial technologies enabled ever-faster production which in turn fuelled increasing consumer demand for more varied items. In 1792 almost a million pieces of white cotton cloth were produced in Britain, with 60% sent to printers to be embellished with fashionable designs. By 1797 80% of Manchester's output sold for under 2s. 6d. a yard; 11% sold for a shilling or less – 'the lower class of people were indeed enjoying the fruits of industrialisation'.[11] The range of pure cotton fabrics expanded dramatically.[12]

Much of the finished cloth passed through warehouses in London to smaller retail outlets. The improved communications that had brought prosperity to the Morrisons at the Lower George in Middle Wallop delivered new and fashionable textiles faster than ever before to the whole country. Trade overseas also increased. The Peels, for example, sold their cottons to American merchants through their Liverpool warehouse and through the London house Joseph Peel & Co. based in Cheapside. Cloth was also in demand in Africa, sold by slave traders in exchange for slaves.[13] While Todd remained a small retailer he was peripheral to this cycle; however, the later involvement of his son Thomas and son-in-law James Morrison in the purchase of raw cotton from American plantations placed the family firmly inside the cotton triangle.

For Todd and his apprentices and shopmen, all dreaming of future wealth, the textiles industry provided a number of role models, men whose fortunes brought social position and political power: the cotton spinner Jedediah Strutt, Richard Arkwright, whose water frame transformed cotton production,[14] the mill owner Robert Peel made a baronet and his son the Prime Minister.[15] Todd's neighbours in London were doing well too. Arthur Downes from Shropshire was a merchant, trading with China and India, importing muslins, shawls, rugs and continental ware; two of Downes' children married two of Todd's. Downes sold his imports to the successful Fleet Street linen draper Robert Waithman, who dealt in no 'low goods' but table damask, fine muslins and shawls. Waithman was an active political reformer, becoming an MP, Sheriff of London and Middlesex and eventually Lord Mayor. The 'radical tailor' Francis Place may have bought goods from both Todd and Waithman; as a successful master tailor he eventually earned £3,000 a year and like Waithman he pitched his orders at the wealthier clients.

The location of Todd's business was significant, for most of the important wholesale and retail suppliers of textiles were in the City, around Fore Street, Wood Street and Cheapside. The area was 'in effect a textiles quarter'.[16] It was towards the east end of two great lines of shops 'running nearly parallel', which stretched

> from the Eastern extremity of the town to the Western ... One, lying to the South, nearer the river, extends from Mile End to Parliament Street, including Whitechapel, Leadenhall Street, Cornhill, Cheapside, St Paul's Churchyard, Ludgate Street, Fleet Street, the Strand, and Charing Cross. The other, to the North, reaches from Shoreditch Church almost to the end of Oxford Street, including Shoreditch, Bishopsgate Street, Threadneedle Street, Cheapside, Newgate Street, Snow-hill, Holborn, Bond Street, St. Giles, and Oxford Street. The Southern, which is the most splendid, is more than three miles in length; the other is about four miles.[17]

Todd concentrated his retail business (which remained small) in Cheapside, but his profits were increasingly made in the wholesale market, selling goods to shopkeepers in London and, as the Fore Street warehouse expanded, all over England. Elizabeth Towsey of Chester was a typical client, sending her forewoman on regular visits to the London warehouses to settle bills and order afresh.[18] Robert Owen's employer Mr McGuffry travelled 'frequently to London to make these purchases to supply his regular customers among the high nobility'. McGuffry thrived because he understood the appropriate goods to purchase for his 'local trade'.[19] A draper from Chatham considered Todd's 'a favourite house ... for haberdashery goods and fancy articles [which would] do well on his return home'. He boasted that his account was 'the largest that Todd, of Fore Street, had upon his books, and his great aim used to be to see how much discount he could get each month'.[20] Normally, discount was available at 2½% for cash, monthly payments or net at three months. Francis Place was an exceptional retail customer who carefully manipulated the credit and discount system to his benefit. 'I knew that by purchasing materials at two or three shops, however small the quantities, and letting each of them know that I made purchases of others, each would sell to me at as low a price as he could, and each after a time gave me credit.'[21]

By 1808 turnover was almost £14,000; Todd held leases on 153 and 154 Cheapside, 105 Fore Street and land just behind in Green Lettuce Court.[22] His personal capital had risen to £1,000 and he valued the entire property at £6,000. His wife Lucy had died in 1798 leaving two children, John Edward and Mary Ann. Five years later Todd married one of his shopwomen, Laetitia Dann, from Bexley in Kent and they had a further three children, Thomas, Eliza and Lucy.[23] In 1809, the year Morrison joined, turnover was over £18,000.

According to a contemporary in the drapery business, 'Trade at that time may be said just to have been budding – just about to open out into the wonderful expansion it has since attained.'[24] The impact of Morrison on Todd's business could not be better described: within three years he had helped to increase turnover to £40,663. He was offered a quarter partnership by Todd,[25] but what exactly had he done?

Morrison repeated the approach taken by his father when he chose to invest in a larger inn serving a wider range of customers: he was similarly convinced it was essential to increase the volume of trade but at the same time to expand the range of products for sale. 'As the volume and range of goods available to consumers increased, the profile of a successful shop shifted from one where skill was needed to provide the best stock to one where capital provided a breadth of stock from which customers wanted to choose.'[26] At stocktaking in 1809 the total value of goods for sale was £9,217; in 1813 it had risen to £26,681. Haberdashers dealt traditionally in threads, tape, binding, ribbons and other trimmings but Morrison added fancy items including lace, gloves and hosiery. He also began to stock the goods associated with drapers and mercers: woollen and linen cloth, silks, velvets and other costly materials. Timing was on his side. The warehouse was benefiting from the general improvement in trade following the repeal in 1812 of the 'Orders in Council' which had strangled trade with the continent during the height of the Napoleonic wars.

Morrison also believed in 'small profits and quick returns', realising even small profits could be considerable with a high turnover. And if he could sell goods quickly, offering his suppliers quick returns, he would enjoy 'considerable coercive power over the manufacturer' and be able to buy in bulk on short credit.[27] 'The manufacturer will send his goods to that market, where they will be sure to obtain a ready sale, and that too, generally for prompt payment.'[28] Turnover in 1813 shot up to £64,449, £24,000 more than the previous year.

Morrison developed Todd's practice of not maintaining travelling salesmen; instead employees were expected to have a clear understanding of what would sell through the warehouse.[29] Morrison, in a later conversation with his friend and business partner Sir John Bowring, claimed 'he owed all his prosperity to the discovery that the great art of mercantile traffic was to find out sellers rather than buyers; that if you bought cheap, and satisfied yourself with only a fair profit, buyers – the best sort of buyers, those who have money to buy – would come of themselves. He said he found houses engaged with a most expensive machinery, sending travellers about in all directions to seek orders, and to effect sales, while he employed travellers to buy [from manufacturers] instead of to sell, and, if they bought well [i.e. at the lowest price that could be obtained], there was no fear of his not effecting advantageous sales.'[30] Robert Owen also recognised the significance of such buyers: 'when goods are well and judiciously purchased for a local trade, they almost sell themselves, and give little trouble to the seller; while if they are not bought with judgment, the trouble of sale is greatly increased. The good buyer also is almost sure to gain success in his business.'[31]

The Fore Street house gradually built up strong relationships with manufacturers and customers, researching both new products and market trends; investments were made in staff and bigger, better premises. While Todd financed alterations to the premises in 1813,[32] Morrison and a fellow shopman George Crow went on a fact-finding tour of the manufacturing districts of Derbyshire and Lancashire; on subsequent tours, whether for business or pleasure, Morrison kept careful notes of shops and shopkeepers, the quality of their stock and clientele.

Todd had immediately recognised Morrison's talent for making money. His business acumen was responsible for the increase in turnover and profits; his ideas were driving the company forward. However, Morrison's friend William Cope, who worked in the Cheapside concern, was 'greatly disconcerted' as the two had been planning to set up in business together and had already spotted possible premises, a failed boot and shoe maker's in Fleet Street.[33] He left to join a rival business in Holborn. On the other hand, George Crow and Richard Pearson were simply delighted with the good fortune of their friend; both would become partners and make their own fortunes in Fore Street.

From the few surviving accounts it is clear that Todd was a popular tradesman, known for his honesty and 'straightforward course of industry'. He was the opposite of the fictitious ill-educated proprietor of Tag-rag & Co. in the novel *Ten Thousand-a-Year,* 'a great tyrant in his little way; a compound of ignorance, selfishness, and conceit. He knew nothing on earth except the price of his goods, and how to make the most of his business.'[34] Todd's obituary in Leigh Hunt's *Examiner* praised his 'indefatigable perseverance and well-organised arrangements in all his operations and transactions with tradesmen and merchants with whom he had to deal, [by which], combined with his friendly and liberal conduct towards all persons in his establishment, he ensured their willing and unremitting exertions in prosecuting so extensive a business.'[35]

Working six long days a week in Fore Street, and living on the premises, the young men and women engaged by Joseph Todd inevitably spent much time together as well as mixing with the neighbouring shopkeepers, apprentices, warehousemen and merchants, sharing experiences and ambitions, discussing politics. Todd's eldest daughter Mary Ann returned from boarding school in Hackney in 1809 and started working in Fore Street; the following year her brother John Edward, his apprenticeship completed, returned as shopman.

George Crow, who entered Todd's warehouse in 1812, sent his parents an account of the weekly routine in Fore Street: 'we open shop before seven in the morning and never shut up before nine in the evening and sometimes twelve o'clock, and we have to sleep in the shop. Every night there is five of us, and a son and daughter [Todd's eldest children], three young women and several boys; and six of us sleeps in the shop. Most of the houses have so little room in them. I cannot speak much in favour of London so far ... I never get out except on Sunday.'[36]

The hours kept by haberdashery shops were notoriously arduous. All the goods handled in the day had to be tidied up before the staff could retire to bed. Robert Owen, working for Mr McGuffry in Stamford, remembered retiring to bed at 2 a.m. during the busy spring season. 'The articles dealt in as haberdashery were innumerable, and these when exposed to the customers were tossed and tumbled and unfolded in the utmost confusion and disorder, and there was no time or space to put anything right and in order during the day.'[37] Another draper recalled:

there were no such thing then as *reels* of silk. *Skeins* of silk were laboriously laid singly in sheets of *cap* paper (the ordinary shop paper), and afterwards rolled up for the purpose of being easily drawn out, and finally placed in a holand [*sic*] wrapper, forming an immense bundle, with the heads of the different colours showing themselves in a brilliant variegated mass, from which the customer drew out the shades that were most needed.[38]

Mr Tittlebat Titmouse, shopman in the novel *Ten Thousand-a-Year*, expressed his frustration. 'What a life mine is, to be sure! Here am I, in my eight-and-twentieth year, and for four long years have been one of the shopmen at Tag-rag & Co.'s, slaving from half-past seven o'clock in the morning till nine at night, and all for a salary of £35 a-year, and my board!'[39]

There were diversions close to Fore Street. Lackington's Temple of the Muses, the 'Cheapest Bookseller in the World', in nearby Finsbury Square, offered access to learning for the poorest apprentice or a shopman like

Morrison eager for self-education. The premises boasted a large circular counter in such a spacious room that a coach and four horses drove round it to advertise the opening in 1789. Turnover was prodigious, some 100,000 books a year; Lackington's belief that 'small profits do great things'[40] may have been an inspiration to Morrison; certainly his reading now began in earnest and included the radical writings of Paine, Godwin and Volney as well as the poetry of Goldsmith and Gray.[41] The London Institution was another source of learning, established by City merchants and bankers as a rival to the West End's Royal Institution, with a library and regular lecture programmes. It opened first in Old Jewry in 1805, moving to splendid purpose-built premises in Finsbury Circus completed in 1819.

Morrison's radical leanings and the Nonconformist influence of his mother's family drew him to another group, the Freethinking Christians who believed 'Christianity is congenial with freedom of thought and the exercise of reason'.[42] The 'textiles quarter' had been associated with radicalism for many years: John Milton was buried in St Giles' Cripplegate; the anarchist philosopher William Godwin wrote his life of William Pitt in lodgings in Coleman Street; Grub Street was a warren of old houses notorious for its hack writers; the Revolution Society met in Old Jewry and a branch of the Moral and Political Society met in Cripplegate. The Freethinking Christians first met in Cheapside; they were branded by the government a 'disguised infidel-radical debating club',[43] which was hardly surprising as they denied the divinity of Christ, and rejected baptism, public worship and the marriage service as conducted by the Church of England.[44] Members included merchants, tradesmen, artisans, some of Todd's employees and one of his sons.

By 1813 the Freethinking Christians had moved to the Crescent, Jewin Street, just off Aldersgate Street. Their magazine, *The Freethinking Christians' Magazine, intended for the Promotion of Rational Religion and Free Enquiry*, was printed just off Coleman Street from 1811. It declared 'uncompromising opposition to the political and spiritual tyranny of the established and dissenting churches'; articles were published repudiating pulpit preaching and the payment of preachers; large portions of the New Testament were described as fraudulent, and a piece on the Lord's Supper demonstrated that 'it has no foundation in reason or scripture'.[45]

Within the group Morrison found three men of ability and ambition, Henry Bradshaw Fearon, William Ashurst and John Dillon, who would become lifelong friends and, in the case of Ashurst and Dillon, professional colleagues. Fearon (b. 1770) was never as close as Ashurst and Dillon. He was a partner of Samuel Thompson, founder of the Freethinking Christians. Together they ran a 'gin-palace' at 94 High Holborn. He was also an ardent disciple of Paine and Godwin, and an elder in the Church. In 1817 he visited North America on behalf of thirty-nine families who were considering emigration, to investigate conditions and prospects and on his return published *A Narrative of a Journey of Five Thousand Miles through the Eastern and Western States of America*. Morrison owned a copy of the 'unprejudiced, intelligent and conscientious observations'[46] and no doubt studied it when he began to invest in the continent twenty years later. He also possessed a copy of Fearon's *Materialism and Our Religious Festivals*.

William Ashurst (1791–1855) and John Dillon (*c.* 1792–1868) were exact contemporaries of Morrison and became his closest friends. With only rudimentary education at a dame school, Ashurst had worked since a boy in an attorney's office in Coleman Street, copying legal documents and writing for the newspapers. In 1816 he was articled and in 1821 he was admitted to the Court of the King's Bench. He was a radical through and through: 'Aristocracy is but another name for inequality, as inequality is but another name for injustice. ... Government in this country has grown up *over* the people, not *from* the people. The two great parties – the Whigs and the Tories – have between them crucified the interests of the people.'[47] He also became a friend of Giuseppe Mazzini as well as a deacon in the Freethinking Christians. After becoming solicitor to the Fore Street warehouse he was able to set up on his own in 1822 in Sambrook Court, Basinghall Street. As Morrison's son Walter later recalled, 'my family are the oldest clients of the firm of Ashurst, Morris, Crisp & Co. Indeed my father might claim in some sense to have founded that great firm. My father was making his way as a general merchant in Fore Street, and wanted to find a clever young solicitor to do the work of the firm. Like a good businessman, he was a keen judge of character. He selected Mr Ashurst who from that day did the whole of the business of the firm.'[48]

John Dillon was born in Chelsea, the son of a book dealer, and worked as a librarian for the unorthodox clergyman Charles Symmons of Chiswick and his son John. Symmons wrote poetry, plays and biography, contributed to the *Monthly Review* and supported the Revd David Williams to found the

Literary Fund;[49] his son assisted in translating Virgil. Like Morrison, Dillon had a limited education; however, access to Symmons' library changed his life: 'Originally, from my situation in life, without many of those advantages of Education and mental Culture, which are often the principal aids of literary exertion, I have learned – under, in a great degree, the friendly influence of your Protection, in the stores of your extensive Library, in the personal Intercourse with which you have honoured [me] … something of Books.'[50] Dillon had ambitions to be a writer, but his play *Retribution or the Chieftain's Daughter* performed at the Theatre Royal, Covent Garden, in 1818 received less than ecstatic reviews, even though the actors included William Macready, Charles Kemble and Daniel Terry. It ran for just nine nights, and soon after this Dillon joined Fore Street as a clerk. The decision was a wise one, as he possessed an exceptional ability with figures and rose to become the senior partner. He remained an ardent dissenter, protesting, with his wife Mary Woolley, against the marriage ceremony: 'as servants of Jesus, we worship the one living and true God, his God and our God, his Father and our Father: and disbelieve and abominate the doctrine of the Trinity, in whose name the Marriage Ceremony is performed.'[51]

While Morrison was making friends outside Fore Street, his employer gave up living above the warehouse and moved with his family south of the river to a new house in Paradise Row, Lambeth, close to Lambeth Palace.[52] Todd's merchant friend Arthur Downes had also crossed the river to Lambeth.

The move coincided with a new emotional dynamic at Fore Street: Morrison began to court Todd's eldest daughter Mary Ann. Later, as if nervous of the accusation that his partnership was linked to his pursuit of the boss's daughter, he explained the timing: 'After this agreement [the partnership] had been enter'd into an intimacy commenced between me & Mrs Morrison, but at the time the agreement was signed not the least idea of the kind existed in the mind of any party.'

He was twenty-three when he began to make love to Mary Ann. She was seventeen. She had attended a boarding school in Hackney from the age of four to fourteen, mixing with daughters of merchants and minor gentry. Perhaps the school was similar to Miss Pinkerton's Academy in Chiswick Mall, attended at about the same time by Amelia Sedley, heroine of Thackeray's *Vanity Fair* and the daughter of a merchant.

After her six years' residence at the Mall, I have the honour and happiness
of presenting Miss Amelia Sedley to her parents, as a young lady not
unworthy to occupy a fitting position in their polished and refined circle.
Those virtues which characterise the young English gentlewoman, those
accomplishments which become her birth and stations, will not be found
wanting in the amiable Miss Sedley, whose *industry* and *obedience* have
endeared her to her instructors, and whose delightful sweetness of temper
has charmed her *aged* and her *youthful* companions.[53]

While Morrison's commercial operations were proceeding smoothly, he
began his courtship of Mary Ann in secret, at least from her parents. He carefully preserved some evidence of his feelings, his 'transports', written down on
a sheet of 'unseemly' coarse brown packing paper. Perhaps it is a draft of a love
letter. He was inspired to write after a 'long & lonely walk' back from the Todds'
home south of the river. He had been reading to them his 'favorite Melmoth'
(presumably Samuel Jackson Pratt, 'Courtney Melmoth', a popular author of
sentimental poetry and prose satirised by Byron) on 'enthusiasm'.[54] 'I can thus
in imagination converse with Rosa & feel my heart placid with hope & happy
in Love.' The sentimental language suffuses his address to Mary Ann – he calls
her Rosa – recalling either Rosa Matilda, heroine of the Della Cruscan poet
Robert Merry, or Rosa Matilda, pseudonym of the poet Charlotte Dacre.[55]

He is concerned the approaching partnership will make it more difficult to
declare his feelings: 'The time is approaching when a close application to
business which I have resolved on will leave but few opportunitys [*sic*] of
speaking to her.' But he hopes he has revealed sufficient emotion already for
love to 'bloom'. 'I must therefore leave it to Rosa happy in her kind declaration that her esteem will not diminish.' He is undoubtedly worried about the
response of her father, who is so far unaware of their relationship. 'I hope that
should Rosa hereafter so far appreciate my affections as to render it necessary
to apply to him for his paternal interference he will not be ashamed or afraid
to acknowledge that my principles & my actions will do credit to him by an
alliance – the applause or the censure the enmity or the friendship of the
World will be to me a matter of total indifference – possessing my lovely Rosa
I should possess all the world.'[56]

He and 'Rosa' had been discussing religious belief at some length, but she
apparently feared he did not share her fervour so he wrote at length.

I must declare that few young men pay more attention to the subject than me – ever sensible of a superintending power I have always thought that the happiness of his creatures was the will of the deity & that mankind was left to the guidance of that unerring standard of morality which is implanted in every breast of which we call conscience – a monitor which never fails to agitate the mind after the commission of Vice whilst it diffuses a conscious serenity over the mind on the exercise of Virtue – Reveald [*sic*] religion or Christianity is a comment on this text by rendering us acquainted with that which before was only a matter of speculation – the attributes of Divinity without Christianity is known only by his works – the moral agency of the Word – but as justice was one of his attributes mankind perceived or at least thought they perceived an inconsistency in the triumph of Vice & the defection of Virtue & hence arose the Idea of atheism or the doctrine of chance which supposes the World to have been found by mere accident & that man being a part of Creation was left to Chance also – Christianity explains this mystery by pointing to other Worlds as the place where mankind will receive the merits of his conduct thro life – we should consider Religion as not composed of forms but which teaches us that we never should have absent from our minds that we are moral agents that is beings accountable to God for all our actions This is the essence of Religion.

Mary Ann must have been reassured, and at some point Joseph Todd was made aware of the relationship. He gave his permission for the couple to be married: after all, Morrison was likely to make fortunes for the whole family.

On 6 August 1814, James Morrison and Mary Ann Todd were married at St Mary, Lambeth, by licence.[57] Morrison, like Thackeray's hero Mr Newcome, 'Dick Whittington, and many other London apprentices began poor, and ended by marrying his master's daughter.'[58] There was more good news. His father-in-law agreed to retire in eight years' time (1822), leaving the business in equal shares to his son John Edward and Morrison.[59] 'Years later, looking back [Morrison] used to say that the wedding fees were by far the best investment he ever made.'[60]

CHAPTER THREE

Fore Street and the Textiles Trade

It must be admitted, that Trade tries character perhaps more severely than any other pursuit in life. It puts to the severest tests honesty, self-denial, justice, and truthfulness; and men of business who pass through such trials unstained are perhaps worthy of as great honour as soldiers who prove their courage amidst the fire and perils of battle.

Samuel Smiles, *Self-Help*, 1859

James Morrison expressed his horror of war when he took his family, in 1826, to the site of the Battle of Waterloo:

It must have been a dirty as well as bloody business, think of a lot of men literally stuck in the mud and another set chopping at their heads with large knifes or knocking out their brains with a heavy piece of Iron into their bodies – again think of Nap on one side peeping over a bank at the side of the road to watch the motions of a body of men whom he had sent forward & Wellington squatting behind a small quickset Hedge in a ditch watching the advance of another body which he had sent to meet the French – There are several monuments about the place & all of them say something about enemies of their country – or the human race & about honour, glory, gallantry, youth, virtue, &c &c all of which are lies, or nonsense, when you find it, but without which, it would not be half so poetical as an Irish row in St Giles'. The pursuit of the Prussians after the Battle must have been like the rush of demons from Hell armd with fire & destruction.[1]

In 1815, however, the defeat of Napoleon coincided with a sudden and dramatic increase in the fortunes of the Fore Street warehouse. The turnover the previous year had been £89,420; in 1815 it increased to £243,052 (nearly three times as much) and in 1816 it practically doubled to £465,288. The confidence Joseph Todd had placed in his young partner and son-in-law was proven almost overnight. But what was Morrison now doing?

Overseas trade had been adversely affected during the long years of war with France, and when news of Napoleon's escape from Elba spread through London, some City merchants were also crushed.[2] After Waterloo a period of unprecedented rising wages and falling prices brought more misery to cloth manufacturers,[3] made worse by the ending of the Anglo-American war (1812–14) and an increase in imports of raw cotton from the southern states. Extended production, 'the economics of the use of the cotton gin, and the decreasing cost of transport' meant the price of cotton was also falling.[4] 'Calamitous overproduction' on the part of the mill owners and 'tumbling prices' meant 'excess stocks', 'slimmer profits' and, for some, bankruptcy.[5]

There was a key role for Morrison. 'In this climate, a group of opportunistic London drapers led by James Morrison seized the initiative, establishing a new style of high turnover warehouse. The northern manufacturers never regained the marketing initiative.'[6] The system Morrison developed quickly became known as the 'Todd system' (the Fore Street warehouse was, from the start of his partnership in 1814, renamed Todd, Morrison & Co.) and was followed by other London firms. *The Circular to Bankers*, published on 10 October 1834, provides a contemporary explanation.

These houses were able to establish themselves in this line of business through breaking down of the manufacturers owing to changes in the value of money. When the manufacturers' property began to diminish they made very ready use of the credit being offered to them to obtain their raw materials. They could maintain themselves for years by vending their goods under prime cost at the low-priced warehouses of London. Some bankruptcy cases showed that goods had been sold in large quantities at 25%–30% below the fair ready money price. If goods could be purchased in this manner amounting to say one-fifth or one-seventh of a company's trade and the total trade of the company was worth £1,200,000 to

£1,500,000 this would be an abundant source of profit. This is how the first-established cheap-selling warehouses did it.

James Talcott, a New York merchant who learned his business skills in London, provides further detail concerning the credit system operated by Morrison. The manufacturer was advanced 50% of the fair selling price of goods at interest of 6% while commission on sales averaged 5%. Goods were sold to a large number of retailers (thousands in the case of Fore Street), who were invoiced at 30, 90 or 120 days. 'Altogether, assuming that advances did not run for more than four months, the entire selling cost, including interest and expenses, did not exceed 10 per cent of the selling price, and in many cases was much less. In return, the mill was assured continuity of operation, ample working capital with which to purchase materials and pay its labour, and freedom from credit risk. On the other hand it was a safe and profitable business for the commission merchant [such as Morrison], providing he exercised sound judgement and possessed an intimate knowledge of goods and credits.'[7]

Morrison's decision not to maintain travelling salesmen was continued until incorporation of the business in 1864: 'the house … is the only extensive one of its class that has never had occasion, or deemed it requisite, to be represented in the provinces or elsewhere by travellers or agents of any class'.[8] His buyers, including George Crow, Richard Pearson and his old friend William Cope (who returned to Fore Street in 1817), were much more important, developing specialist areas of knowledge. The strategy was in advance of the times, and not fully developed until department stores in mid-century. 'The wisdom of the modern plan now in vogue [c. 1870], of one man clearly superintending each division, is clearly apparent, by which individual care and judgment is brought to bear upon each section, as it were, answering the best result.'[9]

Morrison was also responsible for introducing fixed prices to Fore Street. Robert Owen claimed Flint & Palmer, where Morrison may have served his apprenticeship, to be 'the first [house] to sell at a small profit for ready money only'.[10] Goods were clearly ticketed and customers who hesitated over the prices or tried to bargain were politely shown the door. The volume of sales at Flint & Palmer (and Fore Street) was so great that a few disgruntled customers made no impact on the turnover. Even so, the practice was regarded with suspicion and distaste well into the nineteenth century: 'putting up prices in windows at all is far from respectable'.[11]

In 1817, Richard Rush, the American Minister in London, wrote of his amazement at the quantity of things for sale and wondered where sufficient purchasers would be found, 'until you consider what multitudes there are to buy; then you are disposed to ask how the buyers can all be supplied'.[12] To meet the demand, Morrison steadily increased the quantity and the range of goods in his warehouse and in 1819 the turnover passed £1 million (£1,025,795), with almost forty shop-hands earning between them a total of £3,000. The house now sold haberdashery, hosiery, gloves, lace, mercery (silks and velvets), fur, woollens, stuffs and fancy trimmings,[13] as it responded to the bewildering range of influences and styles that emerged following the end of the Napoleonic wars. The taste for military detail was hardly surprising, but Tudor dress provided the inspiration for puffed and slashed trimmings, Highland dress and the works of Walter Scott created a wave of 'new' tartans, while classical statuary continued to inspire neo-classical designs.[14]

To understand clearly how the various items for sale in the Fore Street warehouse were combined to form fashionable dress, there is nowhere more informative than Ackermann's *Repository of the Arts*.[15] From 1809 to 1829 the monthly periodical conveyed 'useful information in a pleasing and popular form – to beguile the unlearned into an acquaintance with the arts and sciences – and occasionally to assist even the man of letters in cultivating a taste for both'.[16] Fashionable visitors to the weekly evening receptions at Ackermann's shop, or rather the 'lounge' and 'showroom' at 101 The Strand, could view one another while taking in Ackermann's collection of prints, including work by Turner, John Martin, Rowlandson and Auguste Pugin.[17]

The *Repository* included features on the interiors of shops, the architecture of country houses and suburban villas, 'fashionable furniture', 'The shops of Paris', 'London fashion', reviews of exhibitions, 'patterns of British manufacture ... and where to be bought', advice on how to use fabrics, actual samples of new materials, fashion plates in colour, with descriptions: 'Shoulders, back, and bosom much exposed. Hair in dishevelled curls.' The names and addresses of dressmakers were given next to particular plates: Mrs Gill of Cork Street, for example, was puffed in April 1814, 'to whose taste and invention this work as well as the world of fashion, are under such continued obligations'.[18] The fashion plates and advertisements for new fabrics provided dressmakers with guidance throughout the season. At Fore Street Morrison ensured that everything was available in bulk, from modest thread to luxurious velvets.

Joseph Todd had started out as a relatively modest haberdasher, selling thread tapes, binding, ribbons and other trimmings (white sewing silk was used specifically by stay-makers).[19] Under Morrison, just one part of haberdashery – ribbons and trimmings – was so successful that it was given its own department. By 1816, turnover for the three spring months of March, April and May in cut lengths of ribbons and trimmings was £90,000; by 1824 sales for the year reached over £390,000.[20] Novels of the period frequently present girls fussing over the choice and arrangement of new ribbons to provide instant fashion to tired bonnets and dresses. 'Love' ribbon, for example, was very narrow, while black and white pieces were used for mourning; the rich brocaded gauze ribbon used for bonnets was sometimes a quarter of a yard wide; watered ribbon, sometimes with seals attached, was used for watch ribbons and men's shoes were tied with black double ribbons. Narrow ribbons were also used for edging on chair covers; wider on window and bed curtains. A canny draper in Holborn in about 1822 made a special display of ribbons in his window to attract customers: 'In order to show as many as possible, I placed lines to run along the top of each square of glass in the window … and strung lengths of ribbon on them, passing the end over the line, which we pinned beneath to the block.'[21] Some of the finest ribbon was manufactured at Lyons, so in 1818 Morrison took his wife and their baby son Charles on a visit,[22] presumably to negotiate bulk orders at competitive prices.

The fancy section at Fore Street sold handkerchiefs, ornamental trimming for women's caps, lace, gloves and hosiery. Handkerchiefs were not just for nose-blowing, but an essential fashion accessory for men, women and children. The Barcelona, for example, was a 'twilled square, used for ladies' and children's necks, of plain colours, that were made up in little solid packets, and opened out and cut off singly as they were wanted'. Romals or Romalls were 'a plain silk fabric in neat and small checks, being generally worn by boys', although they could be worn as a headdress. Bandanas were richly coloured silk handkerchiefs with spots left undyed, sometimes described as East Indian, Indian or British. The square neckerchief worn by men 'folded cornerwise, generally with a stiffener inside' was made of plain black silk or satin, or a flowered pattern, while ladies' neckerchiefs could be crepe squares with fringes in white, black, pink, sky and emerald; or plain silk squares with knitted silk fringes; there were also scarves in figured satin or cashmere with borders, the latter sold by the yard, the borders made in Norwich.[23]

Charles Dickens' novel *Oliver Twist* provides an insight into the value and significance of the 'wipe', as Fagin schools his gang to steal handkerchiefs; the fictional account can be verified by scrutinising Old Bailey records. Eight silk handkerchiefs worth 32 shillings were among the goods stolen from Fore Street in 1819 by Richard Harbour, one of the shopmen who slept in the warehouse. He passed the handkerchiefs, stockings, lace, ribbons and a yard of silk to Frances Smith, who cut off the marks identifying the shop. She, however, was spied on by a fellow lodger, William Hamilton (a carpenter and chair-maker), who picked up the marks 'and put them in my pocket. When I found where he lived, I gave them to Mr Morrison, and informed him of everything.' When William Westcoat, the Bow Street 'patrolman', arrived at the lodgings, Smith 'threw herself on the bed and began to cry', but 'between the bed and sacking' Westcoat discovered six silk handkerchiefs. She was transported for fourteen years; Harbour, just eighteen years old, received seven years' transportation.[24] They were more fortunate than Catherine Flanagan (eighteen years old) and Mary Hart (sixteen years) who received the death penalty for stealing 58 yards of lace from Fore Street two years later, although the prosecutors recommended mercy.[25] The young man who stole Joseph Todd's handkerchief from his pocket in 1832 was transported for life.[26]

Handkerchiefs brought together Morrison and John Buonarotti Papworth (1775–1847) who would be his architect-designer for thirty years. Papworth had been associated with Ackermann for several years, contributing prose, verse and drawings to the *Repository of Arts* and designing the premises in the Strand in 1812. His unusual versatility was recommended to Morrison by a mutual friend and radical Alexander Galloway who ran a large machine and engineering business in Holborn.[27] 'Nothing comes amiss to him,' Galloway is reported to have said, to which Morrison replied, 'I wish he could design a pocket handkerchief.' Galloway then wrote to Papworth, 'I have recommended you to a Concern in the Calico Trade, to make some designs for printing' and the architect took up the commission, producing six designs on silk. Papworth's pupil James Thomson recalled, on seeing one of the drawings, 'it was the slightest I ever knew any one to "construct"; but as it proved, it was of great "durability", for from that hour he [Papworth] became Morrison's right hand, to advise, to build, to plant, and to adorn!'[28] The architectural pupil may have found it hard to appreciate the significance of a design for a mere handkerchief, but a manufacturer giving evidence in 1840 to the Select Committee on the Copyright of Designs, commented, 'What is it that makes the trade at all? Is it not the design upon the fabric, and the colour upon it, and the invention of art that is put upon it, if you put more and better of all these things, you will have more trade.'[29] Although Papworth was not actually commissioned to carry out any further work until 1821, the introduction was not unhelpful to Galloway. In 1819 he acquired a large plot of land in West Smithfield, engaging Papworth to design a new factory with a chimney 130 feet high and great iron roofs; Morrison provided a loan of £8,000.[30]

Gloves were another lucrative part of the fancy section. Ladies, in particular, were considered improperly dressed if they left home without gloves. But of even greater significance to a haberdasher, it was 'bad form to wear discoloured, grubby or worn gloves'; paler-coloured fine leather or suede gloves might be worn only once and then discarded.[31] Such customs only increased the Fore Street turnover, and may, because of the high taxes on imported gloves, have encouraged smuggling. Morrison was linked to a particularly ingenious way of defrauding the government of taxes. The foreign exporter packed kid gloves

> in two loads of separate consignments; the one batch consisting of all gloves for the right hand, the other all gloves to fit the left. If both lots were fortunately 'run', well and good, a satisfactory re-union was effected between the separated pairs; but if one lot fell into the hands of the Customs-house officers, and were in due time put up for sale, the possessor of the left-hand gloves would be able to buy up the right-hand gloves that had been captured, and *vice versa*, at the merest trifle, at the Custom-house sales.[32]

Joseph Todd recorded in his diary on 19 April 1811: 'Custom House officers searched the house & found nothing.' This could, however, have been a routine search, and not necessarily evidence that he was guilty of avoiding taxes. On the other hand, Morrison was to be an ardent supporter of the growing movement for free trade led by London merchants. In May 1820, a petition written by Thomas Tooke and presented by Alexander Baring was presented to Parliament: 'that the maxim of buying in the cheapest market and selling in the dearest, which regulates every merchant in his individual dealings is strictly applicable as the best rule for the trade of the whole nation'.[33]

Silk materials, also subject to high import taxes, were located in mercery with all the most expensive and luxurious fabrics. Turnover rose here from £339,335 in 1817 to £429,204 in 1824. There were lustres, fine silk dress materials finished with a sheen made by dipping the fabric in gum and stretching it until dry, and gauzes, thin transparent fabrics made of silk, linen or cotton, with names such as 'celestial blue', 'maiden's-blush rose' and 'turquoise blue stone'. Genteel Miss Matilda, the heroine of Mrs Gaskell's *Cranford*, is attracted to the Cranford draper's when she hears a 'new assortment of coloured silks' have arrived from London; she must decide whether any 'would do to match a grey and black mousselline-delaine that wanted a new breadth'.[34] As the wealthier Elizabeth Grant (in Edinburgh) recalled in 1814, 'my dress and my mother's came from London, from the *little* Miss Stewarts, who covered my mother with velvet, satin, and rich silks, and me with nets, gauzes, Roman pearl trimmings and French wreaths, with a few more substantial morning and dinner dresses'.[35]

Fabrics associated with mourning were known as 'Norwich'.[36] Mourning crape, a lightweight, semi-transparent, black silk fabric, was used for accessories, veils and headdresses: 'every hint of the beautiful sheen and softness of silk was carefully removed by an elaborate process, giving the fabric an extraordinary lugubrious and hard finish'.[37] Bombazine was a mourning fabric used for bodices, skirts and capes; bombazet was the cheaper version made for servants. 'All the fabrics shared the same basic characteristic – a dull, lifeless blackness.'[38]

An often repeated explanation for Morrison's wealth is his cornering of the market in crape for the funerals of various members of the royal family. He certainly did well at times of a royal death, but mourning fabrics were always in demand, and there is no startling growth in sales on the deaths of kings and queens (although he does mark the events in his account books).[39] At the death of the popular Princess Charlotte, daughter of the Prince Regent, in

November 1817, 'the whole kingdom went into deep mourning; linen-drapers ran out of supplies of black cloth; houses and shops were draped in black. Even tramps and beggars tied black rags round their sleeves.'[40]

The only reference in Morrison's correspondence to the significance of mourning for the business was in January 1827. While making an extensive tour of Italy he heard the Duke of York was likely to die. He wrote from Naples to remind George Crow: 'The D of Y will go off I expect either on or before the spring, but this will not perhaps make much difference unless it should fall in March or April – of course after threatening so long every one will have a good stock of black.' Morrison was delighted when he wrote to Dillon the following week: 'the D of Y has died most conveniently – I hope 2 days after[wards] you had no Black left'.[41] If Prince Puckler-Muskau's account is to be believed, no one had any black left: 'The Duke's death seems to be much regretted, and the whole country wears deep mourning for him, with crape on their hats and black gloves. People's servants are put into black liveries and everyone writes on black-edged paper. Meanwhile the Christmas pantomimes go on as merrily as ever. It is strange to see Harlequin and Columbine skipping about the stage in all conceivable frivolities and antics, while the coal-black audience claps and shouts with delight.'[42] By the end of February Dillon gave Morrison the welcome news, 'the shop really ahead! Thanks to D of Y – the warehouse too is his debtor.'[43]

Fore Street began selling shawls in 1817. These were luxury items: China shawls of white, scarlet, crimson and yellow, richly embroidered or plain; rich India shawls and cashmere shawls. George Crow was in charge of the area. One of his staff was William Wilding Edwards, who was found guilty in 1817 of stealing twelve silk shawls valued at £10. He had been employed in Fore Street for nine months. The evidence given at the trial affords an insight into the workings of the house.

> Edwards is to see them [the goods he has sold] entered in the day-book immediately. The day-book is kept in the warehouse on the first floor. There are four day-books, they are placed in different parts of the ware-house. If he sells in the lower part of the warehouse, he must go to the back of the warehouse and put them down. They are all took to that part of the warehouse to be entered; the clerk enters them for him. If a person wants their goods immediately, he is to see them entered. If he sells for ready

money, they are to be entered, but they are sometimes entered after they are delivered, in the ware-house book.

Edwards regularly sold goods to Lewis Levick, who was in the 'jobbing line'. This involved buying items from pawnbrokers, distressed businesses or more regular houses such as Fore Street, then selling on to retailers such as Mr Knott, a Holborn linen draper. On 11 February, Edwards accepted £50 from Levick for a number of items including the shawls, but did not hand over the money or enter the amount in the daybook. He claimed to have left the note on the mantelpiece but later found it missing; however, William Brand, a City marshalman, found the note hidden in the ceiling of the cellar of the warehouse, together with a further £88. Morrison gave evidence in court: 'we have considerable property exposed to the mercy of our servants. I never suspected him before, but always had a very high opinion of him.'[44]

Edwin Chadwick, disciple of Bentham and sanitary reformer, became a friend of Morrison. He recalled Morrison explaining how he became 'the most wealthy and successful merchant of the last half-century':

> The leading principles to which he owed his success in life, and which he vindicated as sound elements of economic science, were, always to consult the interests of the consumer, and not, as is the common aim, to buy cheap and sell dear, but to sell cheap as well as to buy cheap; it being in his interest to widen the area of consumption, and to sell quickly and to the many ... always to tell the truth, to have no shams; a rule he confessed he found it most difficult to get his common sellers to adhere to in its integrity, yet most important for success, it being in his interest as a merchant that any ship captain might come into his warehouse and fill his ships with goods of which he had no technical knowledge, but of which he well knew that only a small profit was charged upon a close ready-money purchasing price, and that go where he would he would find nothing cheaper.[45]

Morrison relished success in all aspects of his life, from watching his warehouse profits grow to buying fine works of art from under the noses of competing collectors. He acquired the knowledge and mastered the skills required for every one of his undertakings and expected his partners to do the same: 'I can't too often inculcate that our superiority does not depend upon any of the accidents of the trade but on ... talent & industry & ... Envy & Power. ... None can approach us in the science of business. ... There is an intellectual pleasure in this.'[46] His closest friends shared this 'intellectual pleasure' in their professions, from the solicitor William Ashurst to the manager of Fore Street John Dillon. But he had no time for staff who lacked commitment to the house. The next chapter will reveal how ruthless he could be when he considered his reputation was being questioned, even if it meant breaking with his wife's family.

CHAPTER FOUR

❧❧❧

James Morrison, 'the Napoleon of Shopkeepers'

The technical marvels of steam engines and spinning-machines are more striking than the mundane activities of merchants and shopkeepers who left fewer visible remains and records, but they are not necessarily of greater economic significance. After all, the greatest fortune in the textile trades was not made by Richard Arkwright in the production of yarn; it was accumulated by James Morrison, the 'Napoleon of shopkeepers', whose textile warehouse in the City of London supplied the inland trade with its handkerchiefs, ribbons, braids and fabrics.

Martin Daunton, *Progress and Poverty*, 1995

James Morrison's promise to his partners was clear: 'I will make your fortune for you if you will undertake not to interfere.'[1] The impressive success of Todd, Morrison & Co. had nothing to do with the contribution of Morrison's brother-in-law and fellow partner John Edward Todd. It had become apparent to Morrison at the beginning of their partnership that his brother-in-law was lazy and not very bright; he revealed 'a want of talent & bad temper, which made him worse than useless to me, he was often very ill & at last so much so as to be unable generally to remain in the Shop and even in Town.'[2] He was also jealous of Morrison's success, and his jealousy eventually caused a rift between Morrison and his father-in-law Joseph Todd. Their dispute coincided, unfortunately, with the serious illness and death of Joseph's wife Laetitia in 1819.

Morrison offered to buy out his brother-in-law and at first his proposal appeared to be acceptable, John Edward expressing himself 'satisfied with the property he was likely to possess'. He could anticipate receiving some £70,000, a considerable fortune.[3] Meanwhile Morrison's father-in-law took out of Fore Street a total of £101,825,[4] and bought two 'gentlemen's' estates south of the Thames, in Twickenham and Molesey.

Morrison immediately offered his most able colleagues George Crow and Richard Pearson partnerships, 'Richard Pearson and his wife having the management of 3 different departments of the business, the purchases and sales of which in the last year alone, amounted to £398,000 and upwards'. As superintendent of the warehouse and shop, Pearson also received 'sufficient meat drink and private apartments in or about the said shop and premises in Fore Street' rent free. Crow, who ran the luxury French silk and ribbon department (Lyons) received a similar salary though without the food and lodging.[5]

No sooner was John Edward Todd's situation apparently resolved, than a new difficulty arose. His half-brother Thomas joined the counting house section of the warehouse and Morrison was forced to promise a partnership if the boy (he was seventeen) should prove 'as useful as another and conform to the hours of business and rules of the house'. Unfortunately Thomas was unwilling to accept the working conditions of his peers. Morrison then offered him special terms: 'I submitted ... that a young man like him with a father of reputed wealth could not be bound as closely to business as a person without such expectations; that it would be absurd and impolitic to attempt it.' His 'attention to the business should only be required from nine in the morning till four in the afternoon' and he should be 'allowed to join any parties at the house of his father, brother or friends'. Thomas, however, was not satisfied. He objected to being under the control of his brother-in-law and left Fore Street. Morrison was disappointed: 'he had cost me much labour to qualify him for the cash'. Thomas' departure, however, provided the opening for John Dillon in the counting house.

While still resolving Thomas' position, Morrison began to carry out extensive work in Fore Street, for 'parts were in a ruinous state and reported dangerous by the surveyor'. 'The roof of the shop was raised, a new skylight added, and a few bed rooms for the shop-women erected, at a part of the premises distinct from those of the men, it being for the interest of the business that board and lodging should be found for all the servants on the premises.'[6] Gas was installed, and a new kitchen and dining room were constructed. Morrison's concern for the welfare of his employees was undoubtedly genuine; however, he also had a very modern understanding of the link between a comfortable working and living environment and increased productivity.

He also turned his attention to the property he had acquired in Grub Street (its name forever linked to the hack writers who lived there) at right angles to the Fore Street premises. He turned to John Buonarotti Papworth, the architect who had provided him with designs for handkerchiefs. Papworth had been gaining a reputation designing London shopfronts and Morrison asked him to design a large warehouse and offices in Grub Street, connected to the Fore Street premises.[7]

Morrison had also acquired a villa in five acres of land on Balham Hill for his growing family and Papworth was commissioned to redecorate the interior. With work going on in his domestic and commercial properties, Morrison took Mary Ann on a series of journeys across England and into Scotland. He kept diaries of these early expeditions and it is possible to see the country through his eyes; in every town and village he looked out for regular and new customers, and for evidence of the affluence of communities. Staying in Woburn on a Sunday, he calculated 'from the appearance of the place we ought to do 150 or 200£ a month'; Northampton offered even better prospects, 'a very large Town & one we ought to do from 300 to 500£ a month at least'. He called on manufacturers and inspected their factories, mixing these business visits with trips to grand country houses, cathedrals and castles, walking over picturesque landscapes and battle sites, and making calls on well-known writers and artists (see Chapter 5).

In the spring of 1823, he took Mary Ann on holiday to Sandgate on the south coast. Passing through Sevenoaks in Kent he noted, 'Good market & has a considerable number of genteel families resident in Town & many splendid establishments in its neighberhood [*sic*]. The Duke of Dorset Marqs. Camden Lords Amherst Stanhope &c. ... we ought to do much more here.' Calling in at 'Knowle', 'an old large & low built House', he declared the Italian and Flemish paintings 'generally bad'. Margate he found 'decidedly a colony from London & may be call'd the fashionable east end. It has lost nothing by ceasing to be fashionable. There is a very large class of money spending people, who never can be so much at home at a watering place as here, this & the steam boats will support & increase it & I should think add to the number & respectability of its settled Inhabitants.'

He liked shops to be 'well conducted' like Jolly of Margate and Hammon & Fritton of Hythe, the latter 'we ought to do all we can with'. However, it needed to be conducted with 'spirit' to avoid its 'dying away'. Lamb of Dover he found 'chiefly fancy a clean neat shop & sells many goods in our way I like this concern.' By comparison, Marsh and Morse in Deal were 'blackguard concerns, ticketing, puffing & lying, here to day & gone tomorrow'. But Deal, until recently a naval port, was suffering in general 'a painful exhibition of the effects of a transition from War to Peace in the Beach Street many of the best houses & shops are shut up & falling into decay, the suburbs are half empty & the other houses fill'd with poor people'.

While it was good to be 'pushing in business', too much attention could be spent on appearance, not enough on the service offered and the purchasing of appropriate stock. At Ashford, Boorman has 'too large & too rich a stock for the place, has 3 expensive dandy hands, besides others, neglects his business, spent 200£ on his shop front ... if he has money will lose it & if not will break'. Location was important. Edwards of Folkestone 'ought to do well' as he is 'building a new house towards the Sandgate entrance to catch the visitors at that place. The houses being so crowded, the streets narrow steep & crooked, that a Carriage can hardly get into the center [*sic*] of the Town.' Sandgate itself, however, was 'too small a place to support a shop worth our notice'.[8]

From August to October, the Morrisons made a lengthy tour of the north of England and Scotland, spending some time visiting factories and mills. They arrived at Manchester, at the home of 'our good friend Mr Worthington' just as it was getting dark, entering the city by 'one of the dirtiest entrances & lined with the dirtiest houses & the most ill taught dirty & ragged children that I have seen'. Worthington provided gossip about the fortunes being made in the city, 'pot Boy Mottram – retired on 70,000' and statistics for the operation of his and other manufacturers' power looms. There were expeditions to the mills of Mr Dyer, Mr Cardwell and Mr Cloggs at Cheadle and a longer visit to the Grants at Bury. Morrison was impressed by the Grants, who, according to Samuel Smiles, were the models for the kindly Cheerybles in *Nicholas Nickleby*:

Mr Grants property extends 3 miles along the Irwell 4 Brothers 3 have houses in different parts of the property, first a Spinning Mill & intended for power looms – next a new one, when finished will be a grand thing, bleaching, dying & printing, the last by machinery cutting blocks also by machinery ... the cottage in which young Peel was born not worth 10£ a year ... dined at Spring side Mr W Grants, all here princely. Band. Hounds, gardens. Houses &c returned Mr D. Grants 12 miles an hour – I saw a piece printed in 1 minte. 58 secds.

In Derbyshire Morrison saw much evidence of the activities of the Duke of Devonshire, a 'good landlord'. They stayed at a 'splendid' inn at Newhaven built by the Duke and admired the church at Buxton, 'like everything here done at the sole expence of his Grace'. By contrast, the Duke of Northumberland, owner of Alnwick Castle, though living on estates worth £94,000 a year, was 'a mere non-entity he attends to no public business does not hunt race or attend to Farming in fact his life seems a total vacancy'.

On returning to London, Morrison received the news that his brother-in-law John Edward Todd was demanding more money, the equivalent of a quarter of the cost of improvements to Fore Street (which were being paid for by Morrison and the Todds). He believed it was unfair that Morrison should reap the benefits and wanted compensation. On Christmas Day, Morrison replied at length to his complaints, refusing to give him any money without engaging a surveyor or barrister to look at the completed work. 'Are you, let me ask, dissatisfied with the management and general results of the business? Are you disappointed at the account of profits which you have derived from my exertions? Are you suspicious, as your notice would seem to imply, of any unfair proceeding in the management of the concern and its accounts in the past or do you anticipate such in the future? If not what is it which you or your advisors would seek for?' Morrison's reputation was being questioned and he was furious: 'I have always and shall always continue to do all that justice and fairness call upon me to do, whatever may be your determination my course will be marked by the same principles and governed by the same feelings.' He was obviously shocked and angered by his brother-in-law's lack of gratitude for being made a very rich man. In all his commercial dealings, he prided himself on his fairness and transparency; John Edward was attacking his character and he, Morrison, wanted nothing more to do with him.

One of Todd's complaints was that Morrison was linking the Todd name to a retail haberdashery shop run in Oxford Street by a former employee,

William Cope. The shop was in reality another of Morrison's investments. His sister Maria had married William Cope in 1818 and the following year Morrison lent them £6,000 to set up business at 337 Oxford Street. The name of Todd was on a board visible in the window, even though the name W. Cope & Co. hung over the door and all the operations were handled in the name of Cope & Morrison. While protesting that his father-in-law knew all about the arrangements, Morrison agreed to remove the offending board. However, he could not refrain from attacking John Edward for dragging his father into the row:

> Failing of success in your own name you now at last try to perpetuate a bitter animosity in the family by involving me in litigation with your father. … In this, as in every other respect, I draw between you and your father a clear line of distinction. … Towards him … I hope to be able to continue to shew that respect which I cannot shew towards yourself. The father of Mrs Morrison has different claims to those of her brother, for whilst it is my wish, and perhaps under the circumstances of our connection, in some degree my duty to seek to disarm him by yielding to caprice, and in some cases even to injustice, towards you I am not called on to observe any such delicacy of feeling.

John Edward continued to demand more money, claiming the accounts of the business were 'imperfect' and 'erroneous'. Morrison was forced to prove how modest the profits were before he had become a partner. 'I only learnt a few days since … that among many untruths which you have lately been busy in circulating among your friends, one is that your father was a man in a large way of business and had a large capital before I came to Fore Street … the best year your father had before 1810 (in which year I went to Fore Street) was £406, and the worst year since I have been a partner (after paying for large alterations and repairs) was nearly 3 times as much as the whole amount of what he had accumulated during the whole time since he had commenced business to the time of our connection a period of 16 or 17 years.' If John Edward really wanted to have the accounts examined, Morrison pointed out that one of Joseph Todd's houses would be needed to accommodate over 700 stock books, ledgers, diaries, parcel books, foreign correspondence, arrears and character books. John Edward responded, describing Morrison's comments as 'evasive, imperfect and insufficient'; he filed a bill of exceptions, then departed to Vienna, where he remained for the next four months.

Morrison then filed a cross bill against both his brother and his father-in-law, and took his family away on a holiday to the West Country, sending Dillon in Fore Street his familiar observations on wages, markets and the landscape. Their route to and from the west would have passed through the Wallops, providing an opportunity to visit his brother Samuel; also to see the famous tower of Fonthill Abbey, only recently sold by William Beckford to a gunpowder contractor.

With Morrison and John Edward out of the way, the row was finally ended through the peace-making of Dillon and Thomas Todd. Joseph Todd agreed to dispose of his remaining interest in the business, together with his freehold property in Fore Street and to retire altogether. Morrison could take over two years early, provided he paid compensation: 'an amount equal to the proportion of the profit which had been realised during the last two years of the formal term of partnership [1820–22]'. A deed of release was drawn up on 19 August 1824. John Edward was persuaded to capitulate, writing a contrite letter on 30 November: 'Sincerely desirous to bring the differences which have so long unfortunately existed between us to an amicable and satisfactory adjustment.' He agreed that he had acted on opinions that were 'erroneous' and said that he 'had no intention to dispute morally the fairness of the accounts or of the balances stated to have been due to me on the 1st August 1823; and that you conducted and terminated our late partnership with perfect satisfaction to all parties, and that your conduct towards me as a partner has been in all respects correct and honourable'. He accepted £663 as the final settlement of accounts (a portion of the money spent by the family on the Fore Street warehouse improvements), adding, 'there had been originally no question but about repairs, and ... the present offer on the part of Jas. Morrison was a handsome one'. He agreed to pay all the legal costs and 'both suits [were] immediately dismissed'; thereafter he and Morrison returned to good relations while he enjoyed a contented 'retirement' in his substantial residence in Russell Square.

Fore Street was now entirely in James Morrison's hands and the house had a new name, 'Morrison & Co'. Victory over John Edward Todd was tempered by the news of the bankruptcy of his other brother-in-law, William Cope. Morrison wrote to Dillon: 'I am very sorry for poor Cope, he will think fortune has a pique against him, remember this & his health & spare him as much as you can, I know he is trucky [sic] & foolish with Fore St.' There is no evidence that Cope was asked to repay the investment in the Oxford Street business and the following year, with further financial support from Morrison, he set sail with his family for a better life in Australia.

Meanwhile Papworth's warehouse in Grub Street was nearing completion and Morrison wrote to inform him that George Crow 'is in raptures with the new Warehouse.'[9] It was five storeys high, five bays wide, with three single doors, one leading to Dillon's counting house. This was specially laid out with different-sized desks (Dillon's was the largest with high and low partitions), a gallery and a bookcase to hold the all-important daybooks. The whole warehouse was fireproofed and had gas lamps fitted half inside and half outside the windows to give light but not obscure the merchandise. (Morrison had acquired shares in the Gas Light and Coke Company in 1821 and on his visit to Scotland had been impressed by gas lighting in the home of Sir Walter Scott at Abbotsford.) The effect of such lighting was noted in the premises of George Hitchcock & Sons, silk mercer, linen draper and haberdasher, of St Paul's Churchyard. 'Here, too, we see on a winter's evening a mode of lighting recently introduced, by which the products of combustion are given off in the street, instead of being let to soil the goods in the window: the lamps are fixed outside the shop, with a reflector so placed as to throw down a strong light upon the commodities in the window.'[10] The total bill submitted by Papworth, including his 5% fee, was £4,251 8s. 11d.

The builder for this warehouse and almost all of Morrison's projects in London and on his country properties was Thomas Burton of Aldersgate Street (later joined by his son Henry). He was a general builder employing craftsmen in all branches of the trade on a daily basis, sometimes as many as 200 and on average 170 men: carpenters, bricklayers, masons, glaziers and painters. Repairs and alterations in the City and the East End of London provided most of his work, but for Morrison he built large warehouses and, in the 1830s and 1840s, carried out extensive work at his house in Harley Street, as well as in Wiltshire (Fonthill) and Berkshire (Basildon). At Basildon he fought off competition from the (now) much better-known firm of Thomas Cubitt.[11]

The trend by haberdashers to build ever bigger, more luxurious shops was noted by Dickens in *Sketches by Boz*:

Six or eight years ago, the epidemic began to display itself among the linen drapers and haberdashers. The primary symptoms were an inordinate love of plate-glass, and a passion for gas-lights and gilding. The disease gradually progressed, and at last attained a fearful height. Quiet, dusty old shops in different parts of town were pulled down; spacious premises with stuccoed fronts and gold letters were erected instead. Floors were covered with turkey carpets, roofs supported by massive pillars; doors knocked into windows; a dozen squares of glass into one; one shopman into a dozen.[12]

Morrison's new premises were even grander, with extensive accommodation for his growing workforce. The top two floors were given over to bedrooms and water closets; a housekeeper was employed to keep some order amongst the male and female employees (some of whom were as young as fourteen). There was a large dining room and a library for the employees, for which, among other items, Morrison ordered two copies of the large paper version of John Britton's *Graphical and Literary Illustrations of Fonthill Abbey Wiltshire*, published in 1823. His care for his employees can be compared to that of the Cheerybles in *Nicholas Nickleby:* 'Everything gave back, besides, some reflection of the kindly spirit of the brothers. The warehousemen and porters were such sturdy, jolly fellows that it was a treat to see them.'[13]

CHAPTER FIVE

The Education of a Gentleman (Part One)

The True Gentleman is one whose nature has been fashioned after the highest models. It is a grand old name, that of Gentleman, and has been recognised as a rank and power in all stages of society.

Samuel Smiles, *Self-Help*, 1859

With complete control of his father-in-law's business, James Morrison was very rich and within the circle of London trade and businessmen he possessed considerable power and influence. He had come a long way from the Lower George at Middle Wallop.

His father-in-law Joseph Todd followed the path of many successful tradesmen early in the nineteenth century by using some of the fortune he acquired from Fore Street to make a tour of Europe in 1823. He also began to collect and commission works of art for his two small estates in Twickenham and Molesey.[1] Morrison, however, was never the conventional successful tradesman, nor was he merely devoted to making money; he was socially and, for a while at least, politically ambitious. He wanted to get to the top of the pile, to what Disraeli called 'the society of the great'.

Disraeli defined 'personal distinction' as the 'only passport' to such society; 'whether this distinction arises from fortune, family, or talent is immaterial; but certain it is, to enter into high society, a man must have either blood, a million, or a genius.'[2] Morrison lacked 'blood', but he was blessed with a million and genius; he made use of both to complete his cultural education and be accepted as a 'gentleman', at the same time working towards obtaining a seat in Parliament. Moving his family from Fore Street to Balham Hill was the first step.

They left the City, William Cobbett's 'monster Wen', in the autumn of 1822. The hills to the south of the Thames were relatively free of pollution and only gradually being built on; they had been a favourite retreat for city merchants since the late eighteenth century.[3] John Ruskin, whose parents moved from Cheapside to Herne Hill the following year, recalled the advantages of the location:

> The view from the ridge on both sides was, before railroads came, entirely lovely: westward at evening, almost sublime, over softly wreathing distances of domestic wood; – Thames herself not visible, nor any fields except immediately beneath; but the tops of twenty square miles of politely inhabited groves. On the other side, east and south, the Norwood hills, partly rough with furze, partly wooded with birch and oak, partly in pure green bramble copse, and rather steep pasture, rose with the promise of all the rustic loveliness of Surrey and Kent in them.[4]

Balham Hill began to be developed in the mid-1770s, a mixture of terraced properties, porticoed and bow-fronted town houses and rustic cottages. Balham House on the west side of the hill was built for a silk mercer and later became the home of Sir Arthur Helps, Clerk of the Privy Council; Bedford Hill House was occupied by Richardson Borradaile, MP, an East India merchant and chairman of the Hudson Bay Company. Transport to London improved as the population increased, and by the 1830s seven rival operators ran coaches to Charing Cross, the Strand and Gracechurch Street.

Morrison acquired five acres of land from Thomas Puckle of Devizes, the major landowner who had already developed the east side of the hill with properties for modest businessmen and shopkeepers. There were two houses on the property, both by the local builder John Loat. The larger became the Morrison family home; the smaller was let. The total cost was £5,000, paid for with the increasing profits from Fore Street.[5] The Morrison establishment included three live-in servants, three horses for riding, a four-wheeled carriage and two two-wheeled carriages, one cow, some ducks and a small flock of sheep. A similar property on Balham Hill advertised a few years previously was 'calculated for a family of the first respectability'.[6]

The only image of the exterior of the house that survives is a drawing by J.B. Papworth indicating the addition of a porch to the front of a solid three-storey Georgian property.[7] Papworth was brought in to work on improvements soon after the Morrisons moved in, the engineer Alexander Galloway again acting as go-between: 'My friend Mr Morrison wishes to see you some morning soon at his House on Balham Hill, near Tooting, as he has some matters on which he wishes to consult you.'[8] Papworth already knew the area; he worked on Park Hill, Streatham, for William Leaf, founder of a rival textile firm,[9] and he carried out small additions to the Ruskins' house on Herne Hill.[10]

Papworth was more than builder and decorator: under his guidance and through his introductions, Morrison extended his knowledge of the arts, refined his taste and acquired a reputation as a serious collector. As Papworth's pupil James Thomson wrote later, 'from [Morrison's] room in the east, to his picture gallery in the west, everything requiring either judgment or taste, [Papworth] directed for some thirty years'.[11] The lawyer Matthew Hill, who would become a close friend, recognised the significance of Morrison's aesthetic education. '[He] began doubtless by studying the logic of facts, but he enlarged his knowledge by books and was an excellent political economist. He had given himself an aesthetic training and obtained through the study of works of art, much the same ... modes of thought – as the regularly educated obtained from their classical studies and from general literature.'[12]

Morrison's self-education was continuous and extensive, and he expected his employees to take a similar interest in improving their skills and knowledge. 'Use your long evenings in gaining the [French and Spanish] languages,' he urged James Croft, 'you can do nothing without them – and especially the french.' He admitted of himself, 'I don't know what to do – when I have nothing to do'; when travelling in Britain or on the continent, if he was unable to visit a factory or a museum he would read newspapers, novels (Scott was his favourite) or poetry. 'I pick up everything on my route,' he wrote, 'all that I can scrape up relating either to mind or matter.'[13]

His tour through England and Scotland in 1823, during the tortuous negotiations with John Edward Todd, was not taken without extensive preparation. His library contained key books including Carlisle's six-volume *Topographical Dictionary of England, Wales and Scotland* (1808), Britton's *Cathedral Antiquities of England* (fourteen volumes, 1814–35) and *Fine Arts of the English School* (1812), Pyne's *Royal Residences* (1819) and Dugdale's *Monasticon Anglicanum* (six volumes, 1817–30). In Neale's six-volume *Views of the Seats of Noblemen and Gentlemen in England, Wales, Scotland and Ireland* (1819–23), he could study examples of 'our national taste for whatever is beautiful in nature, or classical in art ... that happy union of splendour and comfort'.

He and Mary Ann stopped frequently to take in historic buildings and picturesque views. A walk through Dovedale turned into an unpleasant scramble in the rain – 'we came out of the Dale muddy to our knees & our feet & legs soak'd in water'. Mary Ann was four months pregnant (Frank was born on 24 January 1824) and felt unwell for much of the tour. To her husband, however, even in the pouring rain, the Lake District was the 'finest landscape I have ever seen or fancied'.

The works of Robert Southey, the poet laureate, were in Morrison's library, and they called on the celebrity author at Greta Hall, Keswick, where he kept house for his own family and that of his sister-in-law Sara Coleridge (her poet husband was permanently absent). Byron called Southey 'the only existing entire man of letters';[14] though he was working on his *Book of the Church*, he was able to give Morrison a total of six hours of conversation across two visits. Morrison jotted down page after page of opinions, references, recommended reading on religion, North America, cooking, history, science, philosophy, the education of girls, politics ('we are sleeping on gunpowder') and lawyers ('certainly an evil').[15] While Morrison was flattered by the time given to him for conversation with the poet laureate, Southey was interested in both his guest's wealth and his spiritual state. He wrote to the Revd Nicholas Lightfoot: 'the most interesting stranger who has found his way here is a Somersetshire [his mother's home county] man – Morrison by name, who, at the age of two or three and thirty, and beginning with little or nothing, has realised some £150,000 in trade. ... This person is well acquainted with the principal men among the Freethinking Christians; he likes the men, but sees reason to doubt their doctrine. He seems to be searching for truth in such a temper of mind that there is good reason for thinking he will find it.'[16]

Equipped with Southey's reading list, Morrison turned his attention to the more general improvements in education, science and the arts he observed for himself in the northern industrial cities. He found in Manchester's new museum a 'good collection of Birds & Insects only just commenced – Manchester will shew herself as a fine patron of Science & the arts in the next age.' Liverpool was bursting with new buildings, 'the Docks very grand full of ships ... Tobacco warehouses – Warehouses 11 stories – Wellington assembly rooms ... Botanic Garden ... Corporation very Rich & use their riches in Docks, in magnificent buildings & in markets – improving streets &c – private charities equally grand. Blind asylum – new Hospital ... Guildhall & Exchange, the first belonging to Corporation – has a beautiful set of Rooms ... fine Public Market.'

He was less impressed by some of the country houses visited, or some of their owners. At Harewood, only the gardens, the vegetables and fruit were worth commenting on, and at Hamilton Palace, where the Duke of Hamilton was adding new rooms for his growing art collection, Morrison noted, rather condescendingly, 'all improving & will soon boast of a grand exhibition'. However, while Morrison liked the Duke's Hobbema and the 'celebrated Daniel in the Lions den by Rubens' he also noted a ' "bad" Snyder'. At Lowther Castle, as yet unfinished,[17] the outside, with its 'noble ascent & fine terrace', contrasted with the inside, 'low & gloomy & the ornaments I think far inferior to Fonthill'; at Raby, Morrison noted that the Chinese drawing room was 'bad', the Billiard Room 'common' and bedrooms decorated in 'execrable french style'.

He was most critical of Alnwick Castle and its owner, the Duke of Northumberland. The Morrisons had to make their visit at eight in the morning as the family was in residence but found the breakfast parlour 'cold & naked, man just putting the things on the Table'. The grey and white library was also 'cold & naked', with a 'tasteless small collection of books all on the Tables childish'. Morrison noted, pityingly, that the locks had been taken off all the pistols in the armoury in 1817 'for fear of the Radicals storming the castle & carrying of[f] the Arms'.

The cultural confidence apparent in Morrison's 1823 journal had been acquired over a very short period of time, through reading, conversations and travel with Mary Ann, political and economic debate with Joseph Todd's circle of tradesmen and merchants, and with close friends such as John Dillon (who was busy building his own library and art collection) and his solicitor William Ashurst. His knowledge of the arts was provided by Papworth's artistic circle, visiting exhibitions and attending lectures.

He never expressed shame about his modest roots, maintaining close relations with his brother Samuel in Middle Wallop and his sister Martha who had moved to Bristol to live with their uncle George Barnard. But he was eager to learn. A comment made on the death in 1823 of the political economist David Ricardo could easily be applied to Morrison. 'His education had been of a very commonplace kind, and he had to educate himself and to acquire that stock of knowledge which is indispensable for a man who lives in good society, and more particularly in the society of well-informed persons.'[18] All his life Morrison continued to acquire the publications of friends and acquaintances from Dillon's play *Retribution* to the political economics of John Ramsay McCulloch. He wrote to Dillon in 1826, en route to Italy, 'I shall look after ... spinning & statues – ploughing & painting – shops & cathedrals – weaving & geology – botany & bibliotheques (have I spelt it right).'

The Royal Academy, located in Somerset House since 1780, was the major but not the only place where Morrison could study contemporary art. The British Institution for Promoting the Fine Arts in the United Kingdom had opened at 52 Pall Mall in 1806 with the Prince Regent as its President. A small circle of collectors and connoisseurs administered the gallery, which showed the work of living artists but also Old Masters lent from private collections (some in the country houses visited by the Morrisons). *The Times* dubbed it the 'favourite lounge of the nobility and gentry'.[19] The National Gallery opened in 1824 at 100 Pall Mall, formerly the home of John Julius Angerstein, whose collection had been bought by the government.

Through Papworth, Morrison would also have gained access to private galleries, such as Sir John Leicester's in Hill Street. The opening in 1818 attracted a crowd of 'beauty and fashion, the chief nobility and gentry, the distinguished members of the legislature and of the learned profession, the taste and educated mind of England'.[20] Leicester owned a number of fine Turners (one of which Morrison later bought), but Morrison also visited the artist's own gallery at 47 Queen Anne Street. It was far from conventional: 'against the wall there were heaps of dirty frames, and stacks of dusty pictures, with their faces turned inward. As for the sofa, it seemed dangerous to your future peace to rest on it. The drawing-room was peopled with filthy tailless cats.'[21]

Within a decade Morrison would be sufficiently confident to purchase Old Masters; however, like many new collectors of the period he began with contemporary works, many purchased at the Royal Academy Summer Show, choosing artists from Papworth's circle. He was also sufficiently confident to commission works, beginning in 1824 by asking Papworth's friend, the well-known portrait painter Henry William Pickersgill, to paint five portraits, of himself, Mary Ann, his father-in-law Joseph Todd, and his new business partners John Dillon and George Crow.[22] Pickersgill depicted him as a gentleman of fashion and culture, soberly dressed and holding a book; Mary Ann is wearing a dress made of luxurious satin-silk in the most up-to-date style. Her portrait was hung in the Academy in 1825. Pickersgill's *Portrait of a Gentleman* was also shown, though if it was of Morrison, the subject preferred not to disclose his identity in the catalogue.

At the same time Morrison commissioned a bust of Mary Ann from the sculptor William Behnes, who in addition painted a delicate portrait of three-year-old Alfred.[23] Morrison also acquired the work of the animal painter Robert Hill, the enamel painter Henry Pierce Bone and the artist George Barrett. 'I like Barrett's drawings so well,' he wrote to Papworth, 'that I would buy another or two, if different to those I have and very exquisite. I hope you have your eye on anything likely to suit me.'[24]

Morrison's most surprising and exciting purchase of 1824 was initiated by Pickersgill, who encouraged him to buy a painting by his friend John Constable.[25] *A Boat Passing a Lock* is one of Constable's finest works.[26] Constable was pleased by the hang, the reception and the sale: 'My "Lock" is liked at the Academy, and indeed it forms a decided feature, and its light cannot be put out, because it is the light of nature, the mother of all that is valuable in poetry, painting, or anything else where an appeal to the soul is required … I sold this picture on the day of the opening for one hundred and fifty guineas, including the frame, to Mr Morrison.'[27] It was lent to the British Institution exhibition 'Living Artists of the English School' the following year, suggesting Morrison was keen to show off his good, indeed advanced, taste.

Visiting Paris in August, Morrison commisioned another portrait of Mary Ann, from the court painter Lizinka de Mirbel. The couple visited the Louvre to see a mixture of British and French art, '2000 pieces & most of them bad tho perhaps quite equal to ours, if our three exibitions [*sic*] were united … here are pictures by Sir Thos Lawrence, Prout, Fielding & Constable. Horace Vernet appears, by far, the best artist in France.' The same year Morrison had expressed his irritation to Papworth for missing a Prout in

London: 'I was too late again for Prout. I could not go in time, and if I had I should have rather had your judgment than mine.'[28] He bought *The Ducal Palace Venice* at the Royal Academy in 1826.[29]

Morrison's relations with Turner seem to have begun in 1824 when he visited the artist's gallery to discuss a drawing. He wrote a number of notes to Papworth: 'I am very anxious about Turner. If I get very good things I shall become attach'd to the Arts.' 'I call'd on Friday on Turner; he seems in a queer humour about the Drawing; and at that moment I think I increased his acidity by breaking abruptly into his Gallery with a party, <u>where he was painting</u>, but where I had never found him before; he was very civil, but in the course of conversation ask'd why it was sent to him. I could only refer him to you. He has no objection, he says, to its being exhibited. What say you? Should I allow it?' 'I almost fear to call on Turner, at least in the hope of getting him to alter the Drawing, but you know the man.'[30]

There is no record of Morrison owning a drawing by Turner unless it is the watercolour *Rise of the River Stour, Stourhead (The Swan's Nest)* which he purchased in 1825.[31] About this time – the exact date is unknown – Morrison also acquired one of Turner's largest works, *Thomson's Aeolian Harp*,[32] exhibited since 1809 in the artist's gallery, a Claudian interpretation of the Thames at Richmond.

Morrison was invited to his first Royal Academy dinner in 1825, and would continue to attend the prestigious annual event most years until 1845. It was an honour. He mixed with the artists whose work he liked and in some cases already owned, including Turner, Constable, Pickersgill, Henry Howard, William Hilton, David Wilkie and William Collins. He had just commissioned Collins to paint a work, *Fisherman's Farewell*, for 350 guineas. When shown the following year the reception, according to Collins' son Wilkie (the novelist), was 'most brilliant ... among all his productions, none had hitherto more powerfully vindicated his claim to be considered a figure-painter as well as a landscape-painter than this picture, which continued, during its exhibition, to be a centre of attraction to all classes of visitors ... extraordinary truth and nature of the figures, of the perfect absence of any artificial refinement on the one hand, or exaggerated coarseness on the other, in the different personages composing the fisherman's family.'[33]

At the dinner Morrison had the opportunity to see and perhaps speak to magnates such as the Earl of Egremont, patron of Turner, and the Marquess of Lansdowne; members of the Tory and Whig parties including Canning, Peel and Palmerston; fellow collectors and connoisseurs such as Thomas Baring, MP, George Watson Taylor, MP of Erlestoke, Thomas Hope and the small number from similar modest backgrounds such as Robert Vernon.

Morrison's cultural education did not stop at the fine arts. Through Papworth and his circle of manufacturers, tradesmen and dealers, Morrison acquired a thorough appreciation of contemporary and historical design, encompassing furniture, furnishings, porcelain, glass, jewellery and clocks. Though now little known, Papworth was one of the most prolific and versatile designers of the period. 'No man of the time presaged more clearly the dichotomy of mid-century taste – on the one hand eager interest in and understanding of new materials and processes, and on the other love of eclectic ornament under the spell of prevailing historicism.'[34] He made use of a bewildering range of styles: Greek, Italianate, Gothic, Egyptian, Chinese, Etruscan, Tudor and Jacobean. However, he worked with a number of manufacturers capable of producing work for him of the highest quality, thus avoiding the ridiculous excesses of the fictional character Mr Soho created by Maria Edgeworth in her novel *The Absentee*. Mr Soho, the 'first architectural upholsterer of the age', is engaged by Lady Clonbrony to fit up her London apartments for her gala. In his conceited, dictatorial tone, he proposes a different theme for each apartment, including a Turkish tent, with 'SERAGLIO OTTOMANS, superfine scarlet – your paws – griffin – golden – and golden tripods, here, with antique cranes – and oriental alabaster tables', and an Egyptian effect with 'MOON CURTAINS, with candlelight draperies … out of the common completely. And of course, you'd have the *sphinx candelabras*, and the phoenix argands.'[35]

Three firms were closely associated with Papworth and, through him, with Morrison, for the next thirty years: Morant, Snell and Seddon. George Morant & Sons, 'house decorators, carvers, gilders & picture frame makers', had worked to designs by Papworth since 1808. He also designed their shopfront at 88 New Bond Street, and their house in Hendon. Morant was a great 'encourager' of contemporary art, and a member of the first council of the Art Union of London; the next generation of Morants and Papworths cemented their friendship through marriage.[36] William and Edward Snell began making furniture designed by Papworth mostly in the French Empire style in the early 1820s. He also worked on their business premises at 27

Albemarle Street, their 'factory' in Belgrave Road, Grosvenor Basin and their houses in Berkeley Square and Portland Place. For Balham, the Snells made new pieces of furniture but also altered furniture and furnishings brought from the Morrisons' first home in Fore Street. Their first account for March to September 1825 was over £650; Morrison was a very important client.

The furniture-making firm of George Seddon was the best known of the three, employing hundreds of craftsmen in Aldersgate Street, in the City of London (and neighbour to Morrison's builder Thomas Burton). The size of the business can be assessed through insurance policies: in 1818 the stock was insured for £10,000 and in 1830, following an extensive fire, a claim was made for the loss of £1,500 worth of mahogany alone.[37] George IV was the most prestigious and probably the most unreliable of their clients; by 1830 he owed the firm £200,000 for furniture made for Windsor Castle. Papworth designed extensive premises in the Gray's Inn Road for George and Thomas Seddon following the fire of 1830, with separate areas for packing, joiners and bedstead-makers, polishers, veneerers, carvers and gilders, Japanners, turners, upholsterers and cabinetmakers.

A letter from Morrison to Papworth in 1823 provides an example of how a commission could develop. Morrison wanted a chair 'easy to sit in and yet not heavy. Remember it is a room constantly in use, and it is of the greatest importance that the chairs be comfortable. Can't you unite novelty, elegance, and the comfort of a lounging chair. The one shown us at Snell's was neat and pretty, but we have seen many very like it, and it would not be easy to the back.' Letters also reveal Morrison relying on Papworth's taste: 'choose a paper for the [Balham] Library at Morant's, the patterns and colours I must say nothing about, I am so bad a judge of these things.' 'I am afraid you sometimes hesitate about ordering or buying these kind of things [a frame] without first consulting me or Mrs M.; we would much rather leave it to you to do just as you please, and shall always be obliged by your buying anything which you think will suit us.' 'I regret very much being obliged to trouble you so frequently – but I do so only in matters of Arts, and you have brought all the trouble upon you by leading me into temptation.'[38]

Morrison's cultural education proceeded alongside his emerging political ambitions; both made possible by the increasing profits from the Fore Street warehouse. His attempts to become a Member of Parliament on a radical ticket were supported by his wife and father-in-law, his partner John Dillon, his solicitor William Ashurst and business acquaintance Alexander Galloway. Galloway had been imprisoned in 1799 for his role as assistant secretary of the London Corresponding Society and Ashurst was a friend of Mazzini and Robert Owen.

The Peterloo Massacre of 1819 had revealed the harsh measures of which Lord Liverpool's government was capable (eleven were killed and over 400 wounded) and Morrison had joined Joseph Todd in a number of activities organised by the City of London and critical of the government. These included subscribing to provide relief to the destitute, attending meetings in favour of free trade and contributing to campaigns to ensure the continuing election of the MPs Burdett, Waithman and Alderman Wood. Burdett had been fined and sentenced to three months' imprisonment for his public remarks about Peterloo. William Ashurst was probably wise to keep his most extreme opinions to himself:

> Government in this country has grown up *over* the people, not *from* the people. The two great parties – the Whigs and the Tories – have, between them, crucified the interests of the people. ... If the House of Peers may be called the house of incurables, the House of Commons may be called the house of wordy twaddlers – spouters of dead verbiage – men who meet to bury the nation's business under a mass of words, to postpone the days of the people's emancipation from rigmarole and extravagance.[39]

The City had sided with Queen Caroline when she returned to London in June 1820 to claim her rights as queen (Alderman Woods' son was the Queen's chaplain) so it was hardly surprising that money was raised to help the families of two 'Queenites' killed during the demonstrations which occurred during her funeral procession through London the following year.[40] Contributing to the appeal, Morrison found himself in the company of celebrity critics of Liverpool's ministry, including the philosopher Jeremy Bentham and the MP Joseph Hume. In 1822 he became a member of the general committee of the British and Foreign Philanthropic Society (its aim to provide permanent relief for the labouring class) along with the Irish MP Thomas Spring Rice, supporter of Catholic emancipation and anti-slavery, and Robert Owen, the founder of the idealistic mill settlement of New Lanark. Bentham had shares in New Lanark; when Morrison visited Southey in the Lake District in 1823 the poet laureate believed he was 'bound to New Lanark, with the intention of vesting £5000 in Owen's experiment, if he should find his expectations confirmed by what he sees there'. Though the Morrisons spent some time with Owen seeing his social experiment at first hand, no money was actually handed over. Morrison also considered investing in James Hamilton of Dalzell's co-operative at Motherwell, an eccentric scheme which envisaged a new world populated by 100 unmarried tailors who, in a special ceremony, would select their wives from among 500 girls. Again Morrison did not part with his money: the potential return was too risky.[41]

Morrison's financial independence and political persuasion were made clear during the winter of 1823 when he subscribed along with the Whig grandees the Marquess of Lansdowne and Lord Holland, William Wilberforce, Joseph Hume, and William Haldimand, MP, merchant and director of the Bank of England, to a fund for Spanish refugees fleeing from persecution by the despotic Ferdinand VIII. Morrison was one of the most generous subscribers and the following year he joined the committee together with Joseph Fry, Zachary Macaulay, Queen Caroline's lawyer Henry Brougham and the merchant John Bowring.

Bowring may already have known Morrison. His father was in the woollen trade in Exeter[42] and from 1817 he ran his own business in Cheapside shipping herrings to France and importing wine. From this period, however, they became close, sharing political views and business deals, Bowring on occasion causing Morrison embarrassment and financial loss. He was a member of Bentham's circle, which included the tailor Francis Place and James Mill (father of John Stuart Mill), who worked in the India Office and would become a close acquaintance of Morrison when he was eventually elected to Parliament.

While there is no evidence Morrison attended Bentham's famous dinners, he did carefully preserve an example of his writing. It is a lively piece from about 1784 in which Bentham attacks the government of the day; it was probably given to him by Bowring when he was editing Bentham's works for publication. Whether Morrison kept it with such care because of the significance of its opinions, the fame of the author, or the personal reference (in the first sentence) to their shared lack of education, there is no way of knowing. 'I have not so much of the Ball room etiquet in me. ... I am a staunch friend

to reform, my mind is pregnant with its purest sentiments, and my heart
will not shrink from the attempt to accomplish it; we have many obstacles
to surmount The Road is Ruggy [*sic*] and the Dangers extreme, but an
abundance of Good can not be accomplished without the chance of some
misfortune.'

Morrison was close enough to Place by 1824 to be discussing publishing
tracts for working people.[43] Though his proposal was not developed, he
became a regular subscriber to the Society for the Distribution of Useful
Knowledge, joining the committee at the invitation of Brougham.[44]

Bowring, Hume, Galloway, Brougham, Lansdowne, Edward Ellice, MP,
William Haldimand, Bentham, Macaulay and Thomas Spring Rice were also
all involved with raising funds to support the Greek War of Independence.
Bowring became Honorary Secretary of the London Greek Committee
which was formed in 1823. Morrison, for once, is not included among the
subscribers. Perhaps he was not as confident as the *Morning Chronicle* about
the commercial advantages of an independent Greece 'with liberal laws in the
Peninsula and in Greece, the commerce of Europe may be increased to an
unbounded extent, and the prosperity of mankind in a proportionate degree
promoted.'[45]

He *was* involved, however, in the founding of London University. The
original proposal for a 'great London university' was made in 1824 by
Thomas Campbell, author of the popular *Pleasures of Hope* (1799), who then
wrote an open letter to Brougham, published in *The Times*, February 1825.
The intention was to establish a university for students of all religious persua-
sions (or none); at Oxford and Cambridge undergraduates still had to
confirm they were members of the Church of England. Brougham chaired a
meeting on 4 June at which a committee was appointed, and in August eight
acres of land was acquired in Bloomsbury for £30,000, paid for by Isaac
Goldsmid, John Smith and Benjamin Shaw.[46] The first council included
Brougham, Hume, James Mill, Lansdowne and others well known to
Morrison. The immediate need was capital, at least £150,000, and members
of the council sought funds from within their circle. Morrison agreed to buy
fifty £100 shares; his partners George Crow and John Dillon also bought
shares.

It was hardly surprising that Morrison was by this time being considered
by the radical wing of the Whigs as a parliamentary candidate. His

'networking' was successful. As an independently wealthy man he could pay for his own campaign (unlike Francis Burdett who needed the efforts of Place and City friends to raise a subscription for his election expenses), and as a businessman with proven commercial skills his knowledge was invaluable to the party.[47] Dover was proposed, with the Russia merchant and pro-free trader Charles Poulett Thomson (future Baron Sydenham) standing for the other seat and, most important, the political backing of Joseph Hume.

Bowring wrote to Morrison on 28 July 1825 full of encouragement and flattery: 'you would really & truly be of great value to the popular cause', particularly if the next Parliament develops a 'liberal commercial policy'.[48] The electorate at Dover was under the influence of the Conservative Duke of Wellington who was Lord Warden of the Cinque Ports, and the radicals there had first asked Hume, a strong candidate, to stand. He was unwilling to give up his seat in Scotland but recommended Morrison and Thomson 'as Gentlemen possessing ample independence of fortune, having habits of business, and professing principles that will induce them, on all occasions, to support every Reform in the State that is likely to promote the Prosperity of the Country, and the Happiness of the People'.[49]

Hume, red-headed, dour and pedantic, was known as the 'Apothecary'. He had made a fortune in the Bengal service of the East India Company before working with a clothing company producing army uniforms (he was linked, like so many radicals, to the textiles industry). In Parliament, he was regarded as leader of the radicals, attending every debate, 'a sort of animated fixture ... he always filled his pockets with [pears] ... ate them in the house as substitute for dinner'.[50] Though never a popular figure he was a rigorous advocate of free trade and defender of public economy. He appealed to Morrison for his 'industry and determination in ferreting out the facts which were uncomfortable to the political establishment but vital in the formation of radical reform programmes'. Moreover, although interested in social reform he was 'a capitalist, concerned in the investment of money, the manufacture of goods, and the safety of British commerce overseas'.[51] They became friends.

Hume was especially known for developing an effective network of communication outside Parliament, with 'those open to radical influence through correspondence with individuals and political associations in the country, organizing press handouts, choice of candidates, and tactics at elections'.[52] He helped Morrison and Thomson draft their letter to the

Independent Freemen of the Town and Port of Dover: 'Our public Conduct will be guided by the Endeavour to produce the greatest Sum of Happiness to our fellow Men and fellow Citizens. The Cause of Civil and Religious Freedom, the Reform of Abuses, the Retrenchment of unnecessary Expenditure, and every Measure likely to promote the general Prosperity, will have our ardent Advocacy and Support.'[53] Even a song was composed in honour of the candidates and circulated in printed form:

Men of Dover! Men of Dover!
Throw the Warden's Party over:
Who's the Knave, and who's the Fool
To be led by Liverpool?

Men of Dover! you inherit
All your Father's glorious spirit!
Break the Warden's slavish chain
Never to be link'd again!

Men of Dover! shall he tell you
He can buy and he can sell you?
He shall see, and he shall rue,
What a Freeman's will can do!

Ye have found and ye shall lead 'em
Men who will achieve your Freedom:
MORRISON and THOMSON see –
Crown them both with VICTORY![54]

The pair were duly selected as candidates and on 27 September 1825, at a meeting held at the Beehive Tavern, Leadenhall Market, they received the congratulations of the Freemen of Dover resident in London. Hume, 'the wise and indefatigable and unchanging friend of the people',[55] was thanked for finding the candidates. Everyone agreed to work as hard as possible to get them elected. Morrison was described to the gathering as 'a man of business like themselves, who by mere force of talent and intellect had raised and directed one of the most extensive businesses which this Kingdom or perhaps the world, could produce. When such a man in the prime of life was willing to direct his powers to the public service, he was certainly deserving of Support.'[56] His wife, Mary Ann, who gave birth to their first daughter Lucy just two days before the meeting, may have held a different opinion regarding who needed support.

There was, in the end, no election in 1825; instead a financial crisis rocked the City. When the London bank Pole, Thornton & Co. crashed on 12 December, forty-three provincial banks were dragged down.[57] Speculation in new joint-stock companies had offered huge returns, but many were mere 'bubbles', as the Duke of Wellington had foreseen: 'the greatest national calamities will be the consequence of this speculating mania, that all the companies are bubbles invented for stockjobbing purposes & that there will be a *general crash*'.[58] On 14 December Morrison wrote to Papworth: 'All the people in the City you know are at this moment terror struck like a City surprised by an Earthquake. You can hardly expect one to bestow a thought on vertu or pictures. The finest picture in the world to-day would not have obtain'd 100 sovereigns on the Exchange.' He, however, rode out the storm with ease, buying up bankrupt stock for Fore Street and continuing to add to his art collection.

By the following spring Morrison was having second thoughts about fighting an election at Dover. While announcing in the press that ill health prevented him from standing,[59] a letter from Dillon suggests he was worried about finding the several thousands of pounds required for election 'expenses', or bribes, at Dover. He had only just finished paying off his father-in-law for the Fore Street business, but Dillon explained that he would have to pay up front on the day Parliament was dissolved. 'Mr Bowring called at 2 o'clock. The sum named is to be paid on the dissolution of Parlt. & not on the death of the present member. Parlt is to be dissolved May 5th.' Poulett Thomson did gain a seat, but only at 'great financial cost'.[60]

Instead Morrison decided to take Mary Ann on a Grand Tour. A gentleman's education was not necessarily completed by obtaining a seat in Parliament, but an extensive tour through Europe was essential. The Morrisons planned to begin their Grand Tour in July. However, the chance suddenly arose to fight in another constituency. A resident of Great Marlow in Buckinghamshire, which returned two MPs, had asked Thomas Wooler, editor of the radical paper *Black Dwarf*, if he could find a candidate at the last minute to stand against the father and son Owen and Thomas Peers Williams. Wooler approached Morrison, who agreed and Ashurst sent a clerk down to promise his immediate attendance. His first visit was reported in *The Times* on 13 June, his 'eloquent speech' greeted with 'rapturous applause'. Excitement was whipped up by the prospect of a very rich man of 'unexceptionable character' becoming their MP. 'He is the architect of his own immense fortune, and his disposition to benefit the town and the public is on a par with his extensive means.' Morrison was apparently 'promising to support zealously and constantly whatever measures have for their object the happiness and prosperity of the people to strengthen the securities of good government – to obtain the prompt, the cheap and effective administration of Justice – to extend the benefits and the blessings of Commerce'.[61]

Morrison returned on the final voting day, the horses were removed from his carriage so that it could be drawn through Marlow by his supporters and he made another speech: 'Whatever the result of the pending contest, he would oppose the interests of Messrs Williams on every future opportunity, by all constitutional means in his power, until the borough of Great Marlow was completely emancipated by the thraldom under which it had been so long oppressed.'[62] He was himself the victim of such 'thraldom', forced to spend the night at the Red Lion Inn in Wycombe, as the local Crown Inn was closed to any opponent of the Williamses, father and son.

The result was close, considering Morrison was accused of being an atheist (he had expressed his own views on religious liberty too strongly for many Anglicans); bribery and threats on behalf of the Williamses were also extensive. Morrison received 122 votes, his opponents 127 and 144. Ashurst investigated the votes cast, discovering, for example, Mr Wethered bribing the wife of Philip Pearce for her husband's vote, John Creswell suddenly finding the money to pay his rates (and gain the right to vote) only on the morning of the election, and William Westbrook and Wildsmith Badger among a number not qualified to vote at all.[63] According to *The Times*, Morrison had encouraged electors not to give 'plumpers', or both their votes to one candidate, but to divide their two votes between him and the Williams son, 'and his liberality thus left him in the minority'. After their victory the Williamses began a campaign of eviction of any of their tenants who had voted for Morrison, to the horror of *The Times*. 'Feudal tenure is the only tenancy now in Marlow; yes, in the 19th century, in the year 1827'.[64]

Place's comment on the members of the new Parliament, including the Williamses, was damning:

> The elections have now closed and the degraded people have as usual returned a set of miscreants to the house of Commons, but this is to no very great extent their fault. They have no choice. Very few indeed are the places for which any man can hope to be returned without spending a large sum of money, and those who are willing to spend large sums of money simply to enable them to serve the country are still fewer. … Thus it happens that a large majority of those who compose the house of commons are as little qualified and as little worthy to sit in a house which should really represent the people as it is perhaps possible to collect together in any way. When some years ago a member said that if the first 688 men that crossed Westminster Bridge were brought into the house these would be as wise and as honest a set as then composed the house, he did not exaggerate the matter.[65]

Morrison and Mary Ann meanwhile finalised the arrangements for their first European tour.

❧❧❧❧

CHAPTER SIX

The Education of a Gentleman (Part Two): The Grand Tour

Is a man tired of Life in England? Let him fly to Lake Maggiore.
Morrison to Dillon, 12 October 1826

The Morrisons were quite a party when they left London for the continent in July 1826: James and Mary Ann, their eldest and youngest children Charles and Lucy, Mary Ann's twenty-year-old half-sister Lucy Todd, Miss Smith, daughter of a neighbouring haberdasher from Fore Street, and Maria, the Belgian maid, who 'gets on admirably & talks french with the washer women'. Lucy was less than a year old and still being nursed; Charles, who was almost nine years old, was to be left at a school in Geneva run by Mr Tapfer for a year's immersion in European languages. Their other children, Alfred and Frank (aged five and two), remained behind in the care of the Danns in Bexley.[1]

The itinerary was not unusual: from Brussels through Germany and Switzerland to Italy with extended stays in Geneva, Venice, Rome, Naples and Florence, returning through Switzerland and France, remaining a couple of weeks in Paris before crossing the Channel from Calais to Dover. Visitors to the continent had been increasing steadily since Waterloo, with some 45,000 crossing from Britain each year.[2] The Grand Tour was no longer exclusive to the aristocracy and gentry, although a family party like the Morrisons needed considerable funds to pay for their carriage, hotels and guides, not to mention the purchase of souvenirs. Morrison spent £400 in the first two months alone, so the whole eleven months abroad may have cost over £2,000. This was modest compared to the expenditure of Mr Lambton (created Earl of Durham in 1833), encountered first at an inn at Vevey. Lambton was already 'in possession [of the inn]', wrote Morrison. 'Vevay too small to hold two great men we therefore order'd a dinner & horses', and they carried on to the next town. Morrison heard of Lambton again in Rome: 'the bankers here [charging interest to supply money] chuckle at so good a customer: he spends £1,500 a month.'[3]

Neither a journal nor a diary survives; however, Morrison wrote regularly to two of his employees. Dillon was now his senior partner and financial manager of Fore Street and James Croft was a young member of staff working for his new mercantile venture which operated out of King's Arms Yard, off Coleman Street. Morrison specifically asked for the letters to be preserved. 'Keep my letters apart – they will be part of my journal & I may want them when I return.'[4] He wrote with a purpose, providing commercial information to be acted on while he was abroad (for example urging Fore Street to cash in on the death of the Duke of York), but he also included commentary on the state of Europe, its culture and politics.

Perhaps he intended his 'journal' to be the basis of an autobiography, to be added to the correspondence from the acrimonious takeover of Fore Street which he had ordered to be copied for him by Ashurst's office. Certainly the letters from his Grand Tour provide significant insights into his family life, and his reactions to sites and scenes; the opportunity to get 'inside' the man, to live with him for almost a year. Morrison's engagement with everything he sees and everyone he meets is infectious; he would have been a stimulating travelling companion.

The letters to Dillon are intimate. He was a close friend and the most trusted of his partners, and in the correspondence Morrison reveals the personal side of his character, from affection and concern for his family (Lucy's teething, the receipt of a first letter from Alfred) to a growing awareness of and pleasure in exercising the power and influence associated with commercial success. He had obviously been left exhausted in body and mind by his electioneering, and his prolonged and unpleasant row with his brother-in-law, but he could share his state of health with Dillon, writing from Geneva on 16 September, 'I am altogether better in health and I hope shall return somewhat improved in mind also.' He wrote again, on 2 October, 'my mind was sick & suspected at home – it has now recover'd & I am in the humour for activity again – many things become interesting.'

Dillon could be trusted with almost anything, as Morrison acknowledged: 'I am much obliged ... to you in particular for the extra-official matters which you attend to for me.' The voters of Great Marlow, for example, required regular attention, in case another general election was called. Morrison wrote from Schauffhausen on 24 August, on hearing Owen Williams was unwell. He hoped he would not die 'this year. I like travelling too well to wish to return before the time I originally fixd.' Dillon was advised to spend £100 in the constituency, 'a little personal attention'; however, Morrison was surprised to hear that in his absence he had apparently proposed the establishment of a Co-operative Society and a 'Blue Club'. He wrote from Rome on 9 December with Christmas approaching, asking Dillon to spend another £50 or £100, to prevent 'opening the door to another person ... the great object is to keep the thing alive'. Turkeys were sent to the most important electors.

Morrison learned on his travels that his connection to Wooler, editor of the *Black Dwarf*, had been too radical for the constituency. He met a captain and his wife also travelling in Europe and reported their conversation: ' "Why", said the lady, "are you the gentleman that was at Marlow? Ah! I heard of you. We lived there and know Miss Wethered: her father would not have opposed you had you not been so violent a radical. But Tom [Williams, MP] is a great ass, and you will certainly get in next time." '[5]

Dillon also helped over the embarrassment caused to Morrison by his offer of financial support for the creation of London University. Having agreed to purchase £5,000 worth of shares, Morrison was suddenly being asked to pay up. However, he had just made the final payment to his father-in-law for Fore Street and spent liberally at both Dover and Marlow. As he explained now to Dillon, the political significance of supporting the university was uppermost in his mind: 'To you I need not point out the policy & even necessity with reference to the future of my standing well with such persons as compose the Council – that I must not appear to do that reluctantly which I had offer'd freely & particularly that if I am to take the responsibility of paying 5,000£ I ought to receive all the glory to which I am entitled.'[6] He had been flattered when approached personally by Henry Brougham for a subscription. 'I was at that time very busy, or very idle, & did not (fool as I was!) see a single person on the subject & merely replied that understanding myself as only pledged to the advance of 1250£ I consented – at that time I had a general impression that one fourth of the capital was all they had proposed to expend.' He now asked Dillon to arrange a meeting with Brougham to see if it would still be possible to pay in instalments.

Another embarrassment for Morrison was his commercial relations with John Bowring and Alexander Galloway who in 1826 were being accused of malpractice in connection with the second Greek loan. Galloway had accepted the commission to provide six steam engines for ships which would be part of an expedition led by Lord Cochrane against the Turks. Unfortunately none of the engines were completed on time.[7] Galloway was accused of deliberately delaying the work because one of his sons was supplying weapons to the Turks and another, based in Alexandria, was in the pay of the Pasha of Egypt.[8]

Morrison found himself defending Galloway 'against the Greeks' but also becoming increasingly suspicious of Bowring. It would appear money he had lent to Bowring for the Greek cause had been used by Bowring's own trading company. Morrison was in danger of being tainted by the same scandal. 'He is bound ... to return it as early as possible & at any reasonable sacrifice even the destruction of his business especially if that has (as it evidently has) been supported by my money. ... There are two things to attend to – settle the ac/t & take care that he acts & that others understand him to act only as my agent.'[9] Morrison was quick to react when he considered his reputation at risk.

He had become commercially involved with Bowring through his new enterprise in King's Arms Yard. Soon after Morrison became sole owner of Fore Street he set up, under his own name, an import and export concern.[10] A warehouse in Queenhithe was rented, and credit was provided by the Quaker bill-broking firm Overend, Gurney & Co. (which already supported Fore Street), Samuel Gurney becoming a close friend from this time.[11] Morrison's feckless brother-in-law William Cope was given another opportunity to make a living as a company agent taking a mixed cargo (including hosiery) from King's Arms Yard to Australia.

Morrison was not unlike Dickens' Gradgrind in *Hard Times* in his search for 'facts, facts, facts'. His gathering of information was voracious: 'I don't know what to do – when I have nothing to do.' He read widely before setting out on his tour; his library contained books on European economic and political history, studies of the landscape, the language and local customs as well as architecture and the fine arts. His impressions of St Peter's in Rome, for example, would appear to have been influenced by two books in his library, the Revd John Chetwode Eustace's *A Classical Tour through Italy made 1802* and Joseph Forsyth's *Remarks on Antiquities, Art and Letters during an Excursion in Italy in the Years 1802 and 1803*. Eustace wrote of St Peter's filling the eye 'and the imagination with magnitude, proportion, riches and grandeur', while Forsyth warned the English visitor that St Peter's might seem disappointing when compared to St Paul's. However, 'greatness is ever relative. St Paul's is great, because everything around is little. At Rome the eye is accustomed to nobler dimensions, and measures St Peter's by a larger scale.' Morrison wrote to Dillon on 30 November 1826: 'we visited St Peters a second time this morning in a fruitless search after its magnitude and grandeur about which we have heard so much & which every body tells us we shall yet find. Either St Pauls is as good (if not better) or we shall find St Pauls different when we return.'

He was not afraid to voice his own opinion, and on many occasions cut through the sometimes sanitised image presented to tourists at popular sites. At Waterloo, for example, he was affected by the horror of war: 'a dirty as well as bloody business ... there are several monuments about the place & all of them say something about enemies of their country – or the human race & about honour, glory, gallantry, youth, virtue etc etc, all of which are lies or nonsense'. At Herculaneum he wondered about the inhabitants: 'they were I suspect, voluptuous, dirty & lazy. History shows us only the armour that glitters in the sun afar off when we cannot see the animal which bears it – the admiration for the ancients is very irrational if it is not cant.' On the other hand, his understanding of the sublime in literature and painting provided him with the appropriately romantic response to the mountains of Switzerland, 'some of the most beautiful & most terrible scenes ... in the solitude of such a place & hearing only the sound of the distant avalanches or witnessing as we did one close to us a man forgets everything else'.[12]

Morrison called historic sites, ruins, churches, palaces and collections of art 'lions'. The term was originally used to refer to actual lions housed in the Tower of London, but by the eighteenth century it could be applied to any significant site or object. In Bologna, for example, the lions were 'glorious pictures'; in Verona there were 'lions without number', including the amphitheatre, churches, collections of pictures, antiquities, tombs and relics. The

Morrisons did their best to see everything: we 'workd till 6, dined & [worked] again till 9'. Sometimes, however, they succumbed to a surfeit of lions, and took a day off. In Geneva, for example, Morrison confessed 'the next day was an idle one, the ladies like a ship from a long cruise in bad weather wanted refitting they went a shopping & Charles & me fed the fish from the bridge'.[13]

Time and time again Morrison realised all was not as it first appeared: debt, corruption and poverty lurked behind the most magnificent facades. The interiors of the Venetian palaces had been stripped of many of their paintings, sold to British collectors; at Como he found 'all that comes from the hand of man an extraordinary mixture of dirt and elegance, of fine shaped buildings seldom finished, and with the inside half a palace and half a barn'. After visiting a palace in Karlsruhe in which only a couple of rooms had been furnished, he compared the profligate German princes to drapers, for 'they always undertake too much, & like them are rarely in a condition to pay 20/- in the pound'. Throughout Italy he was struck by the general poverty, and the contrast with the England he had travelled through three years before. There was no point as yet, he wrote to Dillon, in developing trade with Fore Street.

> You must recall it is only in capitals or largest purely commercial towns (of which there [are] only 3 or 4 in Italy) that any thing could be done – the peasants here <u>as in all other countries</u> wear home made things the men for the want of native cloth wear principally sheep skins – there is no gentry, scarcely any thing worthy to be calld a middle class – except the merchants & priests – Even in the principal towns, such as Ferrara, you look in vain for a decent shop & in Rome the very best is not equal to a very middling very inferior one in London – indeed more business can be done in Exeter or Plymouth than in all the papal dominions in our way.

He summed up Italian trade as no more than 'an old man collecting rags & skins at the doors of dirty cottages – or buying a few shillings worth of silk from a miserable peasant – or higgling with a poor fellow about a sack of corn which he has brought on the back of a donkey from the mountains'.[14]

Only the Jewish communities revealed energy and skill: they 'have all the money & do the business'. In Mantua, for example, Morrison commented on their power, 'in a fair way to eat up all the xians. Of 5 Silk Merchants (the only

trade here) 4 are Jews & they are too the principal Bankers.' But he also observed
the restrictions under which they were forced to live. 'The Pope is doing all that
he can to kill them by suffocation or to force them away. … In the popes domin-
ions [they are] obliged to live in certain parts of those towns (where they exist
in considerable numbers) & at 6 oclock the gates (built with money rais'd from
the Jews) are closed & at some religious fetes they are shut up for 2 or 3 days –
they are besides subject to all sorts of indignity – the great ones have generally
left the country.' The branch of Rothschild's established in Naples by Carl
Mayer in 1821 had become independent, and escaped such ignominious
restrictions; invited to one of their receptions, Morrison observed it was the
Baron 'who really commands here, both Court, Exchange and fashion.'[15]

In Rome, the Morrisons tried to combine visiting lions with renewing their
acquaintance with contemporary art, but their interest in the latter prevailed:

> we don't get on very fast altho we work very hard – as we [are] constantly
> turn'd from the regular road which people follow in seeing the Lions at
> Rome, by something interesting in Modern Art &c – in painting they are
> far, very far behind us & as for printing generally before as in Sculpture –
> the merit of this is entirely owing to Canova who has changed the style of
> Sculpture as completely as Scott has novels – but Thorwaldsen has
> exceeded him & the rivalry thus excited will in all probability produce one
> who will excel both.[16]

Again, it is clear from Morrison's comments that he was not one to be
taken in, even by artists, when he was considering parting with his money.
The production of art in Italy was a thriving commercial concern: 'there is
trade in Art here & Art in their trade. Canova's studio is litterally [*sic*] a
manufactory of Venus' & Thorwaldsen is little better – works are made in his
studio & sold as his which he perhaps never saw.' He had invitations through
Papworth and Pickersgill to call on the sculptor John Gibson from Liverpool,
whom he discovered working on a commission for his banker friend
Haldimand; also Charles Eastlake who worked in Rome between 1816 and
1830 and was elected Associate of the Royal Academy *in absentia* just after
Morrison left Italy (Morrison bought his *Escape of the Carrara Family* at the
Royal Academy in 1834).

Eastlake and Gibson were particularly friendly to the Morrisons: 'we have seen [them] often they are very polite & useful in matters of modern art'. Morrison consequently commissioned the sculptor John Henning, living in Bloomsbury, to make one of his plaster tablets of the Elgin Marbles (to a scale of 1:20) to be sent as a gift to Gibson: 'the same that he done [*sic*] for me last year – tell him [Morrison advised Croft] to let it be a good one which I dare say he will be anxious to do when he hears the name of Gibson.'[17]

After visiting David Wilkie's studio Morrison agreed to buy *The Confessional* for 150 guineas. The completed painting arrived in London after the Morrisons' return with a letter from Wilkie asking for the outstanding £57 10s. and offering its companion *The Pifferari* for the same price 'which if agreeable to you my Brother [handling Wilkie's affairs in London] also has it ready for delivery'.[18] Morrison declined and the painting was snapped up by the Prince Regent.

The Morrisons attended a number of balls, dinners, performances of music and opera as they travelled through Europe, and although they obviously enjoyed the experiences, an element of guilt, of the need to make jokes about such frivolity, can be found in the letters home. In Naples, for example, they managed to get an invitation to the 'Ball of the Nobility' even though merchants and bankers are 'rigidly excluded, but of course it never occur'd to them to formerly exclude a "Haberdasher" and therefore I got in'. There was an element of 'dressing up', as Morrison confessed on going to a masked ball held in Rome by the French Ambassador during carnival. 'I am to appear in a long Buff silk gown trim'd with rose color'd sattin! I never thought I should come to this – and in a mask too ... Wilkie, R.A. tried to dance – I did not.'[19]

An invitation to a ball at the Villa Torlonia could not be refused. The Princes Torlonia were the most successful bankers in Rome, administering the finances of the Vatican; Giovanni Torlonia's magnificent villa housed a first-class collection of classical sculpture.[20] 'Behold me', wrote Morrison, 'at ½ past 9 – in a domino (just like an old womans hooded cloak) of puce gras de naples (the pattern piece I had bought at St Luccia) trim'd with crimson ribbon Vandyked & in a black mask ... dancing in every room ... [next day] knockd up, this raking wont do, a man had better serve behind a counter than in the fashionable ranks, provided he shuts up at 8.'[21] As a mere apprentice and then shop assistant, Morrison had worked six days a week and shut up shop nearer midnight; Dillon would appreciate the joke.

Although Morrison's letters from the Grand Tour are packed with descriptions of amusements and cultural observation, the underlying message is one of personal success and the increasing awareness of commercial power. In Ancona, on 15 November 1826, Morrison reported meeting tradesmen in skins 'very anxious to do business with us, and in this as in other instances I have had proofs that my name is known sufficiently & in a very short time would be current'. In Rome a couple of weeks later he wrote, 'our House begins to be known & merchants every where are anxious to do business'. In Naples he found an inefficient Exchange 'full of merchants – and all the business done is not half Fore St!' He felt sufficiently confident to buy a huge consignment of Puglia lambskins, writing gleefully to Croft that 'all the Neapolitan skins are under my thumb'. To Dillon he added that Fore Street 'has been much talkd of as a wonder'. He and Mary Ann were offered boxes for the opera by Rothschild and were introduced to two gentlemen, one of whom exclaimed ' "Oh! Morrison Ah I have heard much of that name." '

By the spring of 1827 he had met, discussed commercial transactions with and been entertained by the principal financial houses in Italy, Demidoff in Florence, Torlonia in Rome and Rothschild in Naples. The dinner the Morrisons attended at the Villa San Donato in Florence, home of Nicolas Demidoff, was the most sumptuous. The Demidoffs were flamboyant Russian industrialists, ironmasters, fabulously rich from supplying weaponry to the Imperial armies. Nicolas had a passion for eighteenth-century French painting – Boucher, Greuze, Fragonard – which he shared with the Marquess of Hertford.[22] Dillon was sent a description on 23 March 1827:

About 40 sat down at 7 – present only one English besides ourselves, the Marquis of Huntley [George Gordon, 9th Marquess of Huntly] – nearly all of them stars Garters or Ribbons & constituted most of the Haut ton at present in Florence – everything was served on Gold & it was altogether one of the most splendid entertainments which I have ever seen – all the family were particularly polite & even kind. Mrs M was handed in, & sat by, the late Austrian Commander in Chief at Naples ... we were invited to go afterwards to Lord Burghersh's party [eldest son of Earl of Westmorland] ... but I thought one assembly of this kind enough for one night ... you will think I fear I am on the 'road to ruin' – but these are rather tasks than pleasures.

Morrison concluded: 'I cant too often inculcate that our superiority does not depend upon any of the accidents of trade but on talent & industry & consequent economy and power.'

The journey home was leisurely. On a stay in Paris they attended a French court of law, heard a eulogy by Cuvier at the Institut Français, and visited both Sidney Smith and James Fenimore Cooper. George Crow met the party at Rouen but the Channel crossing was rough and Mary Ann, now pregnant again, was unwell (Morrison was always seasick).

From a hotel in Brighton Morrison sent a brief note to Dillon: 'I write this the last of my correspondence on the Grand Tour.' He had specific requests, including the most recent copy of the *Quarterly Review* and his favourite biscuits. Also, Mr and Mrs Pearson were invited to dine on Sunday at Balham Hill, Dillon the following night. Work would begin again in earnest. 'None can approach us in the science of business, independent of success and profit. There is an intellectual pleasure in this.'

CHAPTER SEVEN

⚜

Into Parliament

On 7 July 1827, only a few days after returning from his European Tour, Morrison attended the sale at Christie's of the collection of Sir John Leicester, 1st Baron de Tabley. He bought Turner's painting *Pope's Villa at Twickenham*. Leicester's offer to sell his collection to the nation to form a 'National Gallery for British Art' had been turned down by the Prime Minister four years before, to the disappointment of many artists. William Collins wrote to David Wilkie on 9 July:

> his executors determined to sell by auction his collection of pictures in Hill-street. The artists in general, but more particularly those who had pictures in the sale, were more than bilious. Turner and Sir Thomas Lawrence did everything in their power to induce the executors to put it off; but they were bent upon turning the pictures into money immediately.[1]

Morrison, however, now owned three paintings by Turner. *Pope's Villa* was an exceptional work. John Landseer's 1808 review captures the unique atmosphere: 'in the scene before us, the Thames flows on as it has ever flowed, with silent majesty, while the mutable and multifarious works which human hands have erected on its banks, have mournfully succeeded each other; and not even the taste, and the genius, and the reputation of Pope, could retard the operation of Time, the irksomeness of satiety, and the consequent desire of change.'[2] Pope's villa was demolished by order of its new owner, who was irritated by the cultural tourists seeking entry; the scene would have chimed well with Morrison, just returned from touring the ruins of Europe.

Two weeks after the sale, Morrison attended a public dinner at Great Marlow in a bid to revive his political ambitions to be the radical candidate for the constituency. It was a jolly affair: 'business dismissed its care and infirmity its crutch on this joyous occasion: and bands were parading and light blue silken flags with constitutional mottos floating in all quarters of the town'. Toasts were drunk to the King, the Duke of Clarence, the Army and Navy, the House of Commons, the People 'the only source of legitimate power' and Morrison 'the firm and zealous advocate of public freedom'. Morrison then toasted the 'Free and Independent Electors of Great Marlow' and 'Charles Poulett Thomson and the Reformers of Dover'. His companions included John Bowring (they had presumably resolved their financial differences) and a new friend, Matthew Davenport Hill; they toasted Canning, the government and 'the Liberty of the Press.'[3]

Hill and his three brothers were in the process of starting a school, Bruce Castle, in Tottenham, north London, following the innovative ideas put into practice by their father at Hazelwood School in Edgbaston. Morrison was an early supporter of the venture, which was underpinned by ideas of representative democracy and competitive capitalism; he and his Todd brothers-in-law, John Dillon and William Ashurst, all sent sons to the school.[4] He remained close to Matthew Hill, who left education for the law and penal reform. Ashurst and Rowland Hill formed a famous alliance to reform the postal service.

With no likelihood of a general election Morrison largely ignored Great Marlow, apart from commissioning Papworth to build a couple of cottages and thus maintain favour with the electors. Instead he turned his attention to expanding business in Fore Street and King's Arms Yard, increasing his portfolio of property and cultivating the useful circle of politicians, landowners and bankers whom he had already met through the part he played in founding London University.

The economic crises affecting the country at this time, especially the slump in textiles, appear to have had no impact on Morrison's commercial activities. Foreign competition in particular had a disastrous effect on the British hosiery trade and on the manufacture of gloves and lace, consumers preferring French trimmings, haberdashery, fine linen collars and cuffs. For Morrison, however, cheaper foreign goods meant a higher turnover, and as an importer through King's Arms Yard, he could respond immediately to demand. Following news from James Croft in August 1827 that 'I have sold all the skins [for gloves]', he replied: 'you must write to all our men soon & especially Naples & Sicily to look about them & see what they can do next year'. The turnover in Fore Street for 1829–30 reached almost £2 million (£1,883,391), with the highest sales in Manchester goods (cottons), ribbons and mercery. The annual salary bill for 150 employees was £10,000.

Morrison relied increasingly on his friend the Quaker banker Samuel Gurney to provide credit and to hold deposits of surplus cash. Overend, Gurney & Co. was regarded as an exemplar of Quaker probity, Gurney himself enjoying a reputation for 'unimpeachable integrity'.[5] The firm lent Morrison the money to buy out his father-in-law Joseph Todd, to purchase shiploads of skins for the glove-makers of Yeovil, to invest in town and country properties (for example £16,500 for part of Wallasea Island and some of the finest oyster beds in the country), to pay for new warehouses in Fore Street and Grub Street and to cover election expenses. Between 1827 and 1832 Morrison took £350,000 as income from Fore Street, using part to increase his capital in the business to £300,000 but also paying back Gurney a total of £150,000.

Morrison was a very modern tradesman in recognising the connection between the physical appearance of his warehouses and his customers' confidence in the business. Papworth's new commission was to provide a front for the ramshackle houses that made up numbers 103–107 Fore Street. Thomas Burton was again engaged as the builder; the project cost £5,500. According to Papworth's son, the intention was to bring the shopfronts 'into unison to form a whole [thus presenting] a business-like facade'. 'Great taste' was exhibited 'in the details and in the difficulties attending the arrangement of the doors and windows'.[6] Behind the new facade a family home was created for Dillon, including four bedrooms and a library decorated with blue-striped wallpaper.

The next project was a warehouse in Grub Street adjoining the premises already built by Papworth and Burton in 1824. A further warehouse or 'packing room' was built on the site of Greyhound Yard to the rear and, in 1834, the Fore Street premises were again improved at a cost of £6,000. When completed, the property was complex, with entrances on Grub Street and Fore Street, and incorporated two counting houses, accommodation for staff and areas devoted to specific goods such as hosiery, mercery, gloves and silk. With Morrison engaging specialist buyers, his 'house' was beginning to look rather like a department store.[7] And conveniently, in 1830, Grub Street was renamed Milton Street 'to escape its notorious connotations of literary hackwork'.[8] In a letter to her son Charles, Mary Ann provides a description of a visit with the family:

> We have to-day been giving a treat to the little girls, it being your Father's day in the City he invited us to accompany him and Lucy has I think been quite happy for she has found many friends who have supplied her with scraps of finery besides having a good game of play in the warehouses with the baskets the latter much to the taste of Emily who sometimes forgot to hide her rosy face when spoken to by a stranger.

Morrison's continuing financial success and his recognised ambition to become a Member of Parliament on a radical ticket led, not surprisingly, to an invitation to attend meetings of the Political Economy Club. The club had been founded in 1821 by Thomas Tooke, its members (a maximum of thirty-five at any one time) a cross-section of bankers, civil servants, lawyers, writers and university men interested in debating economic matters. At Morrison's first visit on 5 May 1828, topics debated included lowering taxation and paying off the national debt.[9] Morrison became a regular visitor and was elected in 1834.[10] The comments of a fellow member provide a snapshot of how Morrison was perceived at the time. He 'bought and sold anything in the shape of manufactured goods, English and foreign, always increasing in importance and prosperity, till his warehouses were like a palace and his fortune princely [and] he is a well-informed, clever man'.[11]

Members and their guests were all known to Morrison. He was proposed for election by John Ramsay McCulloch, the first Chair of Political Economy at London University (who became one of his debtors); he was seconded by the lawyer Walter Coulson, editor of the *Globe* and Bentham's secretary. Other members included the MPs Charles Poulett Thomson, Henry Warburton, and the Whig grandee Viscount Althorp, all three serving alongside him on the Council of London University. The club, the university and, eventually, Parliament welcomed Morrison for his practical economics and commercial flair.

George IV's death on 26 June 1830 triggered a general election and Morrison decided to try once more to win a seat. He had heard from Great Marlow in May: 'my friends think there is a chance of my fighting the battle successfully this time'. However, he was not so optimistic and engaged an agent to find a safer seat. Isaac Sewell had trained as a solicitor, but 'practised' as a broker in mortgages and parliamentary seats from a room above a Nonconformist meeting-house next to Salter's Hall in the City of London. Before looking for a suitable seat for Morrison, Sewell helped him purchase his first large agricultural estate at Cholsey in Berkshire (1,200 acres costing £50,000) and negotiated Morrison and Samuel Gurney lending a large sum of money (£190,000 at 5%) to the Marquess of Headfort, an Irish landowner struggling with inherited debts. Morrison had already lent small amounts of money to tradesmen, but his financial relationship with Headfort and other landowners and politicians (including the future Prime Minister Earl Grey) gave him an unprecedented and intimate knowledge of the precarious finances of the upper classes.

Sewell's proposed safe seat for Morrison involved his lending a large sum of money to another Irish aristocrat. Whereas Headfort was a family man who was burdened with the debts of his father, William Pole-Tylney-Long-Wellesley, nephew of the Duke of Wellington, was a notorious rake possessing, it would seem, no moral scruples. He 'employs his time at his toilet, in the lounge of Bond Street, or in the ring of Hyde Park in the morning; and in Fop's Alley, at the Opera-House, or in voting away the people's money in the House of Commons in the evening'.[12] Eight years before, after spending a large part of his wife's fortune, he had fled to the continent to avoid his creditors and then eloped with the wife of a captain in the Coldstream Guards.[13] To obtain a seat in Parliament again, Long-Wellesley needed an injection of funds and Sewell came up with a cunning plan.[14] He proposed that Morrison lend money to Long-Wellesley which would buy both of them seats. St Ives in Cornwall (population 4,776) had two seats, which, according to the son of the late Sir Christopher Hawkins, could be secured through the purchase of his estate. Morrison lent Long-Wellesley the deposit of £2,000 plus an additional £40,000 to buy Hawkins' estate in return for a mortgage and one of the seats.

Morrison went down to St Ives late in July to meet the electors. Once again the horses were removed from his carriage which was drawn into the town by his supporters. 'The carriage was preceded by a band of music, and the party proceeded slowly through the different streets. Opposite Burgess's Hotel, Mr Halse's band etc. came up [Halse was the Tory candidate], and the opposing parties cheered most lustily, but no other hostile movement was made. The Mayor, it appears, has ordered that the bands shall cease playing at nine o'clock each evening. "All is gay at gay St Ives".'[15] On 4 August, Morrison came top of the poll with 217 votes, Long-Wellesley was second with 181. Halse received 152 votes as his purchase of a majority of shares in the St Ives Consol Mine influenced some of the electors with links to the mine. Sewell was furious that Halse received any votes at all, as Hawkins had assured him both seats were secure. 'It appears from the state of the poll that only <u>one</u> seat can fairly be called marketable as the other must be fought for.'[16] Morrison, however, was now a Member of Parliament and the holder of yet more Irish mortgages worth some £42,000.

Morrison called himself an 'independent Member' and in a later election speech he spelt out his manifesto: '[He] attacked slavery, the monopoly position of the East India Company and the large number of offences that carried the death penalty. He wanted reform of the tithe, the Bank and the Poor Law and the provision of a school under the control of the state in every village. He supported increased pay for the resident clergy, equalisation of the income of bishops and the removal of sinecures in both Church and State. He advocated colonial reform and an end to all monopolies.'[17] In Parliament he was immediately recognised for his commercial expertise and welcomed into the group of opposition MPs interested in trade and finance led by Lord Althorp who supported free trade but also genuinely believed the commercial classes should actively participate in government. At the same time Morrison lent Earl Grey, the leader of the party, £8,000 at the favourable interest rate of 4%.

The Tories, led from the Lords by the Duke of Wellington, remained in power until November. The King then invited Earl Grey to form a government. Althorp became Chancellor of the Exchequer and Leader of the Commons. While still in opposition Morrison had been invited with Poulett Thomson and the more moderate Thomas Spring Rice to attend a meeting at Althorp's rooms in the Albany to discuss the implications of reducing a number of import duties and their deliberations formed the basis of Althorp's first budget.[18]

Morrison spoke twice in February 1831 in support of Althorp's budget, addressing issues from his personal experience. On 7 February he concentrated on textiles. As far as he was concerned the reduction of taxes was always of economic benefit:

> The silk-trade had been very much benefited by having been opened, there were more persons now employed at Manchester in the silk-trade than at Spitalfields, and there was not one weaver unemployed in the latter place, neither was there one in the workhouse, which was unexampled. The advantages of free trade were also proved in our woollen, linen, and leather manufacture, all of which had been improved by foreign competition. In the woollen manufacture, a new branch of trade had been created by the introduction of light French articles which had been speedily imitated and given employment to thousands.

Free trade, he continued on 15 February, 'could not fail to be advantageous to this country'. 'Commerce could never long continue safe, farmers could never have any security for their capital, nor landholders any certainty of their rents, until the present Corn-laws were altered ... the importation of silks from Lyons could not injure, but must benefit the country. The consequence of it had been a vast improvement in our silk manufactures.' Less than five years before, while travelling through Europe, he had written to John Dillon about the impact of free trade in Switzerland, 'you see the competition of different countries always in full play ... a free trade – really a free trade would give to England the market of the whole continent'.[19]

Morrison was an MP from 1830 to 1837 and again from 1840 to 1848, but he made few speeches and never accepted (if he was ever offered) a position in government. He was a listener by nature and though he relished his commercial success he never pushed himself forward in a public arena. In their own speeches both Althorp and Poulett Thomson acknowledged Morrison's 'great practical knowledge' and 'enlightened observations'.[20] However, Morrison sought election to Parliament not to exercise political power but rather to acquire the status it conferred on him as the 'Napoleon of shopkeepers'.

His wife Mary Ann had another view of the effect of a seat in Parliament. She wrote to their sons Charles and Alfred apologising for the lack of the carriage to convey them home from school. 'The lateness of the hours at the House of Commons renders it necessary for your father nightly'.[21] To her relief, Morrison's election was followed by two major changes in family life: he first bought a small country estate in Wiltshire, then Balham Hill was let and he bought a town house in Harley Street. His metamorphosis from the son of a country publican to a member of the ruling classes was complete.

CHAPTER EIGHT

❦❧

Fonthill

Men who have made their fortune in trade are ... covetous of land which for them is the one sure passport to social consideration.

George Brodrick, *English Land and English Landlords*, 1881

During the summer of 1829 Morrison rented a country house for his family. The Pavilion at Fonthill in Wiltshire was just twenty-five miles from his brother Samuel in Middle Wallop, and the extensive grounds provided his children with the opportunity not only to ride and shoot, but also to row, sail and fish on a large and picturesque lake. The holiday was such a success that Morrison decided to purchase his own country estate; with his election to Parliament in 1830 he also decided to let Balham Hill and buy a town house closer to both Fore Street and Westminster.

Morrison had in mind a particular country property which was much larger than the Pavilion – Basildon Park in Berkshire. The grand Palladian mansion designed by John Carr overlooked the Thames Valley; surrounded by extensive gardens and parkland, the estate, including fourteen farms and the villages of Lower and Upper Basildon, comprised nearly 4,000 acres. He would have seen the particulars when the owner, Sir Francis Sykes, first tried to sell it on 23 September 1829 at the Mart in the City of London. Sykes wanted £100,000, too much for Morrison or, it emerged at the auction, anyone else. When Sykes again tried (unsuccessfully) to sell his estate, Morrison expressed his fondness for the property to his architect Papworth: 'for me I have seen nothing like Basildon ... such a House and such a situation! What a casket to enclose pictorial gems.'[1] However, his assets in 1830 amounted only to about £460,000; Sykes' asking price of £98,000 was, for the moment, still beyond Morrison's reach. He decided, instead, to buy the Wiltshire estate which had given his family so much pleasure and which was, fortunately, for sale. Compared to Basildon, Fonthill Park was a modest property, comprising just over 1,000 acres including the lake. Morrison agreed to pay £35,000, and a contract was signed on 1 October 1830.

Basildon Park may have been the property Morrison desired but Fonthill came with a much more interesting provenance: it was a surviving part of one of the most infamous estates in the country. Morrison was buying into the extraordinary story of Fonthill and its eccentric owner, William Beckford, dubbed 'England's wealthiest son' by Byron.

The Pavilion was the remaining west wing of Fonthill Splendens, a Palladian mansion built in 1755 for Alderman Beckford, twice Lord Mayor of London, and the 'third generation of a family of buccaneering sugar poten-tates'.[2] Splendens was almost entirely dismantled early in the nineteenth century by the alderman's son William as he created the fantastical Fonthill Abbey, on the hill above. William Beckford was a larger-than-life figure, bisexual, reclusive, author of *Vathek*, collector of important works of art, boulle furniture, Renaissance goldsmiths' work, Japanese lacquer, fine books and *objets de vertu*.[3] He was the subject of endless gossip; country neighbours and London society eagerly speculated about the activities of the eccentric collector, his general factotum Gregorio Franchi, a Turkish servant Ali Dru and the dwarf Pierre de Grailly behind the seven-mile-long and 12-foot-high wall which he built around the inner part of the estate.

Beckford's Gothic abbey attracted most attention. He began the project with his architect James Wyatt in 1796; the tower was projected to reach 300 feet to rival nearby Salisbury Cathedral. In 1800 he orchestrated a dramatic torchlit viewing of the unfinished abbey (the tower had by then collapsed twice) for the nation's hero Nelson, accompanied by his mistress Emma and her husband Sir William Hamilton.[4]

By 1806 the tower was completed, rising to a height of 270 feet, though still encased in a 'spider's web of scaffolding'.[5] It entered local lore: 'The Tower's clear as glass tonight: the weather won't hold' or 'It'll be hot by mid-day: the mists are down on Fonthill Tower.'[6] And it could be seen on a clear day from the highest point on the turnpike road between Middle Wallop and Salisbury.

Most of Beckford's income was derived from the family sugar plantations. With the abolition of the slave trade, falling revenues, the loss of uninsured ships and lavish spending on the Abbey and its contents, he was forced in 1822 to sell up and move to Bath. He stage-managed his departure to dramatic effect. The auction at Christie's was announced for 17 September and 7,200 catalogues, each including an entrance ticket, were sold. Some 600 or 700 people visited daily to gawp and wonder; many were 'quality' from London.

The antiquarian John Britton and the bookseller and printer John Rutter were engaged by Beckford to produce lavish illustrated descriptions of the whole estate so it was possible for a wide circle of people to study the collection; Morrison subscribed to two large paper editions of Britton's *Graphical and Literary Illustrations of Fonthill Abbey* for the new library in Fore Street. He also acquired his own copy of Rutter's *Fonthill Abbey* and would appear to have visited (it was, after all, close to his brother); on his trip to Scotland in 1823 he noted that the ornaments at Lowther Castle were 'far inferior to Fonthill'. He was developing a taste for the furniture and furnishings preferred by Beckford (they both loved crimson and gold), hardstone vessels and paintings (particularly the work of Dutch artists).

Beckford postponed the Christie's auction to 8 October (thus allowing more entrance tickets to be sold) but meanwhile negotiated the private sale on 5 October of the estate and some of the contents for £300,000 to John Farquhar. The Christie's sale never took place; Phillips auctioned many items from Fonthill the following year in a sale that lasted thirty-seven days.[7] Beckford decamped to Bath and Farquhar moved into the Abbey.

Farquhar had made his fortune in Bengal where he was the sole contractor of gunpowder to the British government. At Fonthill he continued to exercise his business skills, charging £5,000 a piece for the two Parliament seats of the rotten borough of Hindon and building a cloth factory beside the picturesque lake.[8] He also permitted J.P. Neale to produce a new publication, *Graphical Illustrations of Fonthill Abbey The Seat of John Farquhar Esq.*

On 21 December 1825 the tower of the Abbey collapsed in on itself. Wyatt's contractor had failed to lay the foundations according to Beckford's specifications.[9] Public interest was so great that John Buckler's drawing of the ruined building was printed for mass consumption.[10] Farquhar, who slept through the incident, was said to have remarked, 'now the house is not too big for me to live in'. Beckford apparently commented: 'Well it has shown more civility to Mr Farquhar than it ever did to me. He has had it but one year, I had it twenty-seven, and in that time it neither bowed nor curtsied.'[11]

Farquhar immediately decided to sell the entire estate: the Abbey estate to his neighbour John Benett MP of Pythouse and the Park estate to his nephew George Mortimer. However, he died before either his purchase of the estate from Beckford or the sales to Benett and Mortimer were completed. This did not stop Benett advertising for sale parts of the Abbey including 'the splendid range of plate glass and painted windows ... stone architraves, mullions and Gothic Ornaments'; doors and stained glass found their way to the Pavilion.[12]

Farquhar was a bachelor and left no will, so his several nieces and nephews became claimants to his property.[13] Morrison's purchase of the Park estate from George Mortimer was not clear-cut, and Mortimer's untimely death in 1832 made the legal situation even more complicated. The final settlement was made on 6 December 1838.[14]

Sir Richard Colt Hoare and Lord Arundell, local landowners and the authors of *History of Modern Wiltshire* (1829), were dismissive when they described the Park estate: '[the] magnificent mansion, once the seat of science, hospitality, and comfort, but now reduced to one small fragment; its fine transparent lake, disfigured by an unseemly cloth manufactory erected on its banks; its pleasure grounds neglected'. Rutter pointed out the disadvantage of a public road 'running close to the mansion [the Pavilion] between it and the lake, [which] destroyed entirely that privacy and quiet so admirable in a country residence'. The site of the Pavilion was 'very low, and ... subject to frequent fogs'.[15] Isaac Sewell warned Morrison that the estate was 'too distant from town for you as a residence'.[16] The coach to London took eleven hours.

Morrison was hardly enthusiastic himself when he wrote to Papworth inviting him to visit in the summer of 1831. 'You will like to see this wretched specimen of bad taste and the ruins of one of the finest in the kingdom in what remains of the Abbey.' The production of woollen cloth had ended but the factory buildings beside the lake were extensive: the mill was six storeys high and 105 feet long, its machinery driven by three waterwheels; a further building of five storeys contained a press room, weaving rooms and a drying-house. Papworth wrote to his wife soon after he arrived at the Pavilion:

all day yesterday we were at business, except a ride to the Abbey after dinner – it is a RUIN! – and not capable of inspiring any other than painful thoughts of the instability of human affairs – and high towers. ... Fonthill is a beautiful place ... not the refined place it has been reported to be. Gravel walks are in themselves beautiful if well disposed. None are here, however, – no, not one – the place is for the feet of Horses and not for those of Man – as if none were worthy to traverse it but such as have the privileges of a Centaur.[17]

Both Morrison and Papworth were reflecting on the negative aspects of the estate. The sale particulars, however, claimed that 'if Elysium can be contemplated upon earth, the claims of Fonthill will be irresistible', and indeed the landscape of the estate was and still is an arcadia. Mrs Andrew Stevenson, wife of the United States envoy in London, described her approach when she visited the Morrisons in 1836:

The approach to the Pavilion is through the village of Fonthill Bishop, & some fine woodland brings you to the entrance lodge a building of considerable elegance. Tradition ascribes its design to Inigo Jones, that great master of English architecture, it was built in the time of Charles the 2d. On passing the Lodge a wide & extensive lawn opens upon you adorned with plots of flowers & rare shrubs. Trees of every graceful form which lead the eye by fine gradations to those distant clumps of massy foliage which surround the lawn on two sides, on one of which is the church of Gothic architecture just showing itself through the trees, on the other is a gentle undulation rising from the back of the house, and cut into walks which wind up amidst flowers and shrubs to a very pretty summer house from whence you command a most beautiful & extensive view – but the most striking object is the Lake winding in front of the house looking like a broad deep river & covered with swans who proudly floating on their glassy Empire give life and animation to the scene.[18]

Classical references abound at Fonthill: stone from the estate quarry was used to build a hermitage (which contained a stone hermit), caves and a rustic tunnel. Beckford wrote a prose-poem 'Satyr's Range', transforming the woods and grottos 'into a place of water nymphs, sly satyrs, altars for holy sacrifice, and finally a home for the great god Pan himself'.[19] On the other hand, John Britton thought the estate presented 'most diversified, picturesque, beautiful, and romantic scenery' and was reminded 'alternately of Poussin and Ruysdael, of Salvator and Wilson, of Gainsborough and Turner'.[20]

Morrison's own Turners were not dissimilar. *Rise of the River Stour at Stourhead, The Swan's Nest* was painted on a neighbouring estate. The lake at Fonthill was carefully designed to give the impression of a long reach of a sizeable river, similar to the Thames in the Claudian *River Thames at Richmond, Thomson's Aeolian Harp.*[21] But the strongest link is between Turner's 'serenely pensive' painting of the demolition of Pope's Villa beside the Thames at Twickenham and the ruined state of Beckford's vision at Fonthill. John Landseer reviewing *Pope's Villa* in 1808 wrote: 'At such a time the mind willingly enthralled by a certain feeling of melancholy pleasure, is instinctively led to compare the permanency of Nature herself with the fluctuations of fashion and the vicissitudes of taste.'[22] By purchasing Fonthill Park, Morrison was buying, literally, the landscape of his Turners.[23]

Though initially dismissive of Fonthill, Papworth accepted the commission from Morrison to transform house and park. He began with essential work to the Pavilion, writing on 14 March 1832, 'this is a very busy day here in matter of pipes drains bills and other very needful matters for your immediate or rather early comfort & of a sort that needs the eye of carefulness that no more should be done than needful'. He concluded, 'Mr Combe [*sic*] & myself have been very fully employed'.

Papworth's visits were brief, and he relied on James Combes to oversee much of the work, directing stonemasons and carpenters. Combes came from a long-established Tisbury family of farmers, mill owners and dissenters. His father John Coombes [*sic*] 'a man of property',[24] was an enthusiastic improver and amateur water engineer, and had been regularly consulted by the local gentry on land improvement and drainage. James Combes took up land management as an occupation, becoming surveyor, valuer and land agent for Morrison and other landowners, including the Earl of Pembroke at Wilton. In 1834, he was a commissioner tasked with enclosing common and waste land in the parish of Tisbury. The role of agent or steward was only just becoming professionalised; their significance as the main instrument in the rationalisation of technology and tenure was to be profound. 'A good agent was a man who improved the agricultural practice and value of an estate, who was self-effacing enough to channel all public credit to his employer, and who cultivated the expected reciprocation of respect between the landlord and the community.'[25]

Combes' annual salary of £100 from Morrison was supplemented by remuneration from the Earl of Pembroke and other neighbouring estate owners. His correspondence with Morrison reveals the appropriate flattery and familiarity. 'Your speech', he wrote in February 1834, 'in seconding the address is thought highly of in this part of the country.' Remembering to send some rooks to London to bake in a pie, he added, 'I can recollect hearing Mr Todd say he was particularly fond of young Rooks.'

His links to the community were invaluable to the nouveau riche Morrison, his local knowledge of particular use in the distribution of charity and the eviction of tenants.[26] It was Combes who helped Morrison plan his first social event at Fonthill, a reform 'festival' to be held in the summer of 1832, immediately after the passing of the Reform Bill. The immediate locality would be affected quite considerably by reform: the notorious pocket boroughs of Hindon (170 eligible voters) and Old Sarum (eleven eligible voters and three houses) would lose all their seats (two each); both Shaftesbury and Wilton would lose one of their two seats.[27]

Combes took a leading role in the planning of the party, knowing the taste of his neighbours much better than Morrison, but also suggesting ways his employer could save money. Their close relationship was based on these factors: Combes providing clear information yet understanding a rich man's concern with value for money. He wrote at length on 22 June 1832:

> I think yours is a very good scheme in making a kind of a Reform festival, nor do I think that it would be disagreeable to any of the neighbouring Gentry, unless it prompts them to do the like, which some of them can ill afford. ... Your proposed method of doing it is very good – if you do not take on Tisbury I would certainly recommend you to confine it to <u>Fonthill Gifford</u>, seeing that you have a much greater quantity of land in Tisbury ....
>
> In Fonthill Gifford I suppose there would be nearly 400 to supply (children inclusive) therefore the probable expense for these alone would be as follows –

400 lb of Beef or Mutton	10.10.0
100 Gallons of Flour	5.10.0
100 Gallons of Beer	8.0.0
200 lb of Raisings	5.0.0

This to be cooked by the parties at home –

I think the better way would be to give Bread Cheese & Beer on the Terrace, this would please even the Women much better than Tea, and be attended with less expence – Calculating 200 to be present the expense of filling these would be nearly as under –

40 Gallons of Bread	3.0.0
100 lb of Cheese	2.10.0
100 Gall. of Beer	8.0.0
Tobacco Pipes £c	2.0.0
This exclusive of Fire works and musicians if any –	44.10.0

Combes added, on 6 July, 'if you choose to have fire works (which would be considered a grand thing here) there is an excellent person at Bath for these things'.

There is little evidence surviving to convey the external appearance of the Pavilion when Morrison acquired it, nor do we know much about the alterations made by Papworth. The sale particulars described it as an Italian villa of 'unpretending character', 'full of comfort'. The ground floor consisted of an entrance hall 'fitted up in Marble', two drawing rooms 'finished in Oak' with folding doors of oak salvaged from the Abbey and 'completed in the Gothic taste'. The ceiling of the library 'humbly imitated the one at the Abbey', stained glass from the Abbey had been used in the dining-room windows and the walls were hung with tapestry. There were eleven 'best bedrooms', four dressing rooms and a billiard room, as well as ample accommodation for servants, and the usual offices.

The most essential building works and interior decorations were completed by the summer of 1835. In April, Charles wrote to his mother from university in Edinburgh, 'I hope I shall see the improvements at Fonthill before very long'; in July, on arrival at the house, he wrote that 'the buff bed has arrived, & will be ready tomorrow. The Library wants nothing but curtains, which in this sunny weather would be very desirable.' His brother Frank also wrote:

'Mother your bedroom will be the drawing room which Charles used to study in. Susan wishes to know which room she should get ready for Father's dressing room as Father's dressing room will not be ready.' Lucy, aged ten, added, 'Susan will be glad when some one comes down to coock [*sic*] for us as she has been very poorly and she bake[s] all our bread.'

There are few clues with which to identify the contents of the Pavilion; bills rarely distinguish between Morrison's properties, and no inventory was made of Fonthill at his death. Glass was brought from Joseph Todd's house in Lancaster Place and both the Snells and Seddons made pieces of furniture to designs by Papworth using luxurious materials and expensive woods. The Seddons' curtains for the drawing room were of green cloth trimmed with gold, designed to hang below 'Oak Gothic Canopies' of matt and burnished gold; scarlet and white curtains of cloth, lace and tapestry hung in the dining room; the curtains in the library were of cinnamon and gold; Chinese pattern paper was hung in at least one of the bedrooms. Morrison had acquired a magnificent Louis XV ormolu-mounted ebony, tortoiseshell and brass-inlaid boulle library table.[28] Crimson and gold prevailed, as did highly ornamented tables with tops of coloured marbles,[29] bronze statuettes, Etruscan vases and antique marble urns.

In the summer of 1836, Papworth was desperately trying to engage Alexander Roos to paint the ceilings, writing to Morrison on 29 July: 'Mr Roos is not in town, he is expected on Saturday – so soon as he comes I will endeavour to arrange with him – he would dine with your upper servants on the domestic table – I will arrange his remuneration & let you know all about it.' He wrote again in September: '... there is no hope of getting Roos this year & Lambelette and all the decorative men I know are engaged at least for three weeks by works at the several Theatres – perhaps we shall do, therefore, best to finish the plainworks & leave the arabesque ornaments for another time.' Roos was famous in the 1830s for his 'Pompeian' interiors, based on first-hand knowledge of Pompeii (which the Morrisons had visited in 1827).[30]

Whoever finally carried out the work, Mrs Stevenson was impressed: 'The house is indeed a cottage as Mr Morrison called it ... altho' it contains twenty-six rooms some of them very rich, tastely and beautiful beyond any thing I have seen except in the Palaces of the Nobility ... Mrs Morrison told me that the ceilings of my chamber, dressing room, and the one adjoining had cost 800 pounds.'[31] Beckford, however, expressed disapproval when he rode over from Bath. Charles reported to his parents the memorable visit:

I don't know whether you have heard that Beckford came over from Bath some days ago to look at his old residence. He recognised the swans, disapproved of the new portico & other embellishments on the side of the house, & asked whether Mr Benetts new building at the Abbey was not intended as workhouse for the use of the Poor Law Commissioners.[32]

Combes' letters rather than Papworth's provide details of works on the estate with regular protestations about the difficulties of carrying out instructions within budget. As Combes' son later accused his father of mishandling the Fonthill accounts, Combes may have been covering up his own shortcomings. A letter written on 10 March 1834 is typical:

The work on the Park is going on and I hope it will very near be accomplished by the end of the month, the situation at the Terrace is a more heavy job than I anticipated, I will not swear that I shall get all the labour of this alteration, Draining and filling up the swamp, and making the new road into Little Ridge [east side of lake], making up the Islands at the Pond head &c for £100, but if I am to be confined to that sum, some part must go unfinished, the Islands was a thing which we never thought about until the Pond was lowered and it would be a pity to let such an opportunity be lost.

Lowering the lake became an annual event from 1834 when special sluices were installed. A thousand people came to watch the operation the first year, when three tons of perch and a ton of eels were taken out. Trout were put back but perch and tench were distributed locally to the poor. A ton of fish was also sent to London to be sold at Billingsgate Market. Combes provided the details, recommending the Fonthill carp to Mrs Morrison. 'Mr Bowles of Shaftesbury who is a great Carp eater says the Fonthill Carp are of a much better flavour than any others he has ever tasted.'

To Combes, all architects were a nuisance. In March 1838, for instance, he wrote to Morrison, 'Mr Papworth should be here in April and the sooner the better for he is sure to make a mess when he comes, and if he comes in the

Hot weather whatever he does will look bad all the summer.' However grudg-
ingly, Combes finally had to admit that Papworth's overall concept for
Fonthill was an improvement. The architect had already been much employed
in the design of gardens and garden furniture; his *Rural Residences* (1818)
and *Hints on Ornamental Gardening* (1823) had contributed to the populari-
sation of the Picturesque style in gardens.[33] At Fonthill he repaired and
added to existing features, opening up vistas, improving the Morrisons'
enjoyment of their pleasure grounds. New retaining walls with vases were
added to the north side of the gateway, ending in large piers. The boathouse,
at the north end of the lake, was repaired – Pevsner described it as a flooded
'crypt of nave and aisles'[34] – and a new waterfall created close by. Combes was
impressed, though he tried to persuade Morrison it was his idea: 'Mr P is
much pleasd with the new waterfall and so in fact is every one that has seen
it this I always told you would be a great improvement, and the effect
produced is quite as good as I anticipated – The view from the House north-
ward is totally changed, I never saw a greater difference in a landscape.'[35]

Papworth designed a new gateway for the south entrance, and a picturesque lodge of stone and thatch which was taken by the gardener. It was a
favourite destination for the Morrison children's walks. The family increased
steadily during their occupation of Fonthill. Emily was born just before the
purchase of the estate, in 1827, Mary was born in 1830, Henry in 1832, Ellen
in 1834, Walter in 1836, George in 1839 and Allan in 1842. In 1840, the
thirteen-year-old Emily wrote to her mother: 'our walks ... to the lodge
where we saw the gardener's child a very pretty boy of only one year and four
months old but who can run almost as well as Doll [Walter aged 4] and who
makes a variety of sounds between the unintelligible chortles of the latter and
the screams and cries of our dear Georgy [aged one].' Job the gardener was
talented, supplying a luxurious range of foods from the enclosed ten acres of
fruit and vegetable gardens, with hot houses and green houses 220 feet long:
grapes, apricots, cherries, apples, pears, cucumbers, french beans,
broccoli, onions, parsnips, potatoes, bags of sage and thyme, and butter from
the dairy herd.[36]

Dismantling and demolishing the cloth factory which disfigured the
southern end of the lake was a major undertaking. Until 1829 two hundred
workers had been employed to manufacture super-fine woollen cloth and
kerseymere, and some had lived in the twenty-four cottages available to the

workers. The intentions of Farquhar and Mortimer had been admirable: every workman living in the new cottages was allocated a portion of land 'in order that he may accustom his family to the cultivation of the soil'[37] and would not be solely reliant on work in the mill. However, the experiment had lasted only a couple of years before the mill shut down. Morrison's brother Samuel came over from Middle Wallop in July 1832 to remove useful doors and windows, while Papworth planted trees to hide the remaining buildings from the Pavilion.

The local clergy held their annual missionary meeting in one of the buildings for a number of years, to the irritation of the dissenting Combes. 'The Missionary Meeting was yesterday, a great many people attended, Mr Harben was so unreasonable as to ask me to open the fences at the Pond head, that the carriages may drive there and set down the quality, this I refused.'[38] Combes used his position of trust at Fonthill to persuade Morrison to sell a field to the Tisbury dissenters to build a chapel when Lord Arundell, a Roman Catholic, refused 'from an illiberal feeling towards Protestant dissenters'.[39]

Beckford's grottos and tunnel had become overgrown and damaged, so Papworth set Combes and his workforce to clearing, repairing and replanting in order to provide a pleasure ground for the Morrisons. The children must have thought they were in fairyland. A long passageway, the 'dark walk'[40] lit at intervals by round spyholes, went under the public road and opened out into a wooded dell above the lake. Here a hermitage had been constructed below a rocky, artificial cliff, and after repairs had been completed early in 1837 it was once again possible to use the fireplace for picnics.

From the landing place on the west side of the lake the Morrison children set out in boats designed by Papworth. The *Lucy of Fonthill* was first on the water in 1831. Safety was an issue and Combes advised Morrison, 'you must always have some one about the Quarry [on the east side] this man ought to be the Ferryman and so row the children over, he could always be call'd by ringing a Bell'.[41] A new, safer boat with a coppered bottom was ordered in the spring of 1839, as 'the young Ladies have taken to row themselves of which I [Combes] am very glad as it makes them all much more independent, they certainly ought to have a safe Boat and not run any risk of being drowned'. Combes made sure to point out his importance: 'I was uneasy about the young Ladies last year many times have I watched them 'till they Landed'.[42]

Papworth created a grand landing stage on the east side of the lake, complete with large stone spheres on pedestals. A walk along the east bank led to the first of three grottos. Close to the lakeside, it was designed, again, for picnics. It was reached through dark winding passages leading to the surprise view. Beckford had described the effect: 'A broken arch opened to your view the broad clear expanse of the lake, covered with numerous aquatic fowl, and weeping willows adorning its banks.'[43] Above, there was a cold bath grotto which Combes restored: 'We have made the two small ponds to hold water above the Rock where the Bath is, made it fall out of one into the other, and carried it from thence into the Bath in the Rock which we have reclay'd and made to hold and is now full of water, and from thence carried it thro' to the Grotto, this makes the Rock & Grotto quite lively to what it has been for many years past.'[44]

The third grotto, cut out of the hillside above, was actually twin caves, connected at the back by a narrow passage; this was Beckford's Cave of the Satyrs, but Papworth found new occupants. He attended the final sale, in July 1843, of the Coade stone factory[45] in north Lambeth, and recommended a number of items for Morrison's properties. The sculptor John Bacon produced a number of allegorical and mythological figures to be used as moulds for the production of pieces which could be up to nine feet in length. One particular item caught Papworth's eye, an enormous display piece:

At Coade's in the Belvedere Road there are works that would suit your objects – some for indoor and some out. ... The Polyphemus Acis and Galatea in the third days sale – This will probably be sold for a small sum – for its taking down removing & repair will be a considerable draw back to biddings for it – The Giant would certainly perform well over the coverd way at the Landing, Fonthill and the Acis and Galataea [sic] in the Cavern of the Rookery.

On discovering the sea nymph Galatea and her lover Acis embracing in their secret grotto by the sea, the giant Cyclops Polyphemus, hopelessly enamoured of Galatea, hurled a huge rock down on the couple. Acis was crushed to death but had the consolation of being transformed into a river. The trio cost sixteen guineas at the Coade sale.[46]

Papworth turned the quarry area, dug to build Fonthill Splendens, into a haven for birds and animals, where the Morrison children kept pet deer and peacocks. He also designed special houses for pigeons and bees. Combes supervised the planting of 'Fern, Tuscan, Adders Tongue' and the safe delivery of the animals: 'The Ducks arrived quite safe, and are now with the other Curious ones in the Paddock in the Quarry, we did not pinion them there is no danger of their flying away. The large White South American Geese are nesting, one is now sitting with 10 Eggs, I am pleased at this, these are the only ones of the sort in England so 'tis said, I have heard that they are delicious to eat.' He also recommended buying deer from the Marquess of Buckingham: ten couple 'for 40 Guineas I don't think we shall do better, they are fine fallow Deer Black & Spotted'. Not all deliveries of live produce arrived intact, however: 'A Poultry basket was brought here this day from the North Devon [coach] containing 1 brace of Ducks. ... The basket was broken and the Ducks got out, one of them the Guard saw get out when the coach was coming down Fonthill hill, but could not stop the Horses soon enough to catch it. ... It may probably find its way to the Lake.'[47]

The Morrisons used Fonthill regularly from June to December. Morrison's diary entries in the 1830s and 1840s record gentle walks through the estate with his family or with Combes, launching the children's yacht, the potatoes being dug up and the lake lowered, occasional expeditions to Longleat and Stourhead, to his brother's family in Middle Wallop or to the Isle of Wight, and the constant arrival and departure of sons and daughters from schools and universities. Some names recur every year, members of his and Mary Ann's families, partners in Fore Street, a few politicians including Joseph Hume and his family, Sir John Easthope, owner of the *Morning Chronicle*, and its editor John Black, and the lawyer and educationalist Matthew Hill. Visiting artists included Henry Pickersgill, Papworth (a regular guest), and William Collins who stayed for a few days in 1834. Collins was a practised country-house guest. His 'gracious manner ... most gentlemanly bearing [and] cultivated understanding' were noted in his obituary in the *Art-Union Journal*, 'exciting the esteem and respect of all with whom he came in contact'.[48] Dinners were given and accepted among a small circle of land-owners and clergymen: the Groves of Ferne, the Seymours and Stills of East Knoyle, the Wyndhams of Dinton and the Benetts of Pythouse.

Letters from the children suggest their annual summer exodus to Wiltshire was a rural idyll:

We have unpacked this morning & put the school room in order. All our books arrived quite safe. Mary's bird quite enjoyed the ride & chirped all the way. When we got in [at nine o'clock last night] Esther had baked some excellent bread & we made a very good tea of mutton chops & eggs. It rained so on Saturday that we could not get out in the morning but after dinner we rowed on the water. Fonthill looks beautiful it is to my eyes far prettier than any thing we saw at Matlock or Chatsworth. The bank leading to the summer house has been cleared. ... We have seen a few of the deer but the mowers being in the field they do not come near enough for us to see much of them. To day we have been to church.[49]

But Fonthill was also a backdrop to the complex financial negotiations which took place during the late 1830s over the creation of Morrison's merchant house, Morrison, Cryder & Co., followed by his taking on the agency of the Bank of the United States. The 'strong prejudices in favour of us Americans' which Mrs Stevenson enjoyed with the Morrisons were extended to bankers, merchants and politicians, including George Peabody, William Shepard Wetmore and, on 11 October 1839, the Secretary of State, Daniel Webster. There was nothing showy about a stay at Fonthill:

The usual breakfast hour is about half past nine, when everybody drops in, as they are ready. The breakfast consist[s] of a variety of cold bread – dry toast – and excellent butter, with eggs on the breakfast table – on the side table is every variety of cold meats, to which the gentlemen help themselves, and the ladies who wish for any. The servants disappear after bringing in the urn and coffee, and everybody helps themselves. When the meal is over, everyone moves off to the library, drawing room, or their own apartments, as fancy or inclination dictates. Those who choose to walk in the grounds, or row on the lake do so. Mrs Morrison and myself generally rode the pony phaeton until after lunch, when the real business of the day commences. About two o'clock the horses and carriages are at the door for some previously arranged plan of amusements and about six the family assemble in the drawing room, dressed for dinner etc. Coffee is handed after dinner, and is followed almost immediately by tea, the usual hour for retiring is between eleven and twelve. I have become accustomed to these hours altho' I cannot say I like them.[50]

Morrison used a fortune made in London to create a new estate in Wiltshire for himself and his heirs, building new cottages and repairing old, extending the Pavilion, filling it with fine furnishings and paintings, restoring Alderman Beckford's pleasure grounds. However, the Wiltshire labourers whom he employed were some of the poorest in the country. William Cobbett took one of his famous rides close by only three years before Morrison first stayed in the Pavilion: 'The labourers here *look* as if they were half-starved ... For my own part, I really am ashamed to ride a fat horse, to have a full belly, while I see their poor faces present me nothing but skin and bone while they are toiling to get the wheat and the meat ready to be carried away to be devoured by the tax-eaters.'[51]

Shortly after Morrison signed the contract to purchase Fonthill there was a crisis across the country. The general election in the summer (when Morrison was first elected MP for St Ives) left the Duke of Wellington leading an unstable Tory government and the Whig opposition demanding reform. Disturbances had begun in July in north-east Kent, then spread across the south through Hampshire and Wiltshire. Letters 'signed' by Captain Swing were sent to owners of agricultural machinery threatening to destroy their machines and demanding that agricultural wages be raised. Wiltshire saw the most actions in court against the machine-wreckers – 339 – with 152 men convicted and 151 transported.

The 'Pythouse Battle' which took place on 25 November just a few miles from the Pavilion remains one of the most famous of the Swing riots. John Benett's threshing machines at Pythouse were the focus, his labourers, according to Lord Arundell, the poorest and most oppressed in the entire country. A witness account of the dramatic finale was recorded in 1883:

the mob they made for the plantation, but some on 'em did vight wonderful and they had all manner of iron bars and great sticks and all sorts. But the cavalry they did lay about 'em wonderful – they smashed 'em about awful. ... Mr Benett, he did beg of the cavalry not to fire, he said he didn't want no man killed, but there, they did fire, lots on 'em. Mr Wyndham [of Dinton Park] he did command 'em – and then they surrounded 'em and took 'em all, and we had to get our farm horses and wagons and take them to Salisbury – and the blood did trickle out of the wagons the whole way to Salisbury.[52]

Benett was senior magistrate, the chief prosecution witness and foreman of the jury: fourteen men were transported to Van Diemen's Land (renamed Tasmania in 1856), and two were imprisoned with hard labour. Morrison's radical friends in Parliament Joseph Hume and Henry Hunt led the plea for a pardon on 8 February 1831 but Benett's account ensured that they failed. He had, after all, been hit on the neck by a stone 'and knocked senseless' and his threshing machines at Pythouse Farm and Linley Farm had been destroyed.[53] Morrison was concerned enough for the fate of the men to note in his diary on 3 December 1833: 'Fonthill men not surrendered by Govr of Van Diemen's Land' and two years later he was asking Benett to join him in giving help to the wives and families of the Fonthill convicts. The men were finally pardoned in 1836.[54]

So what did Morrison do to help the labourers once he was settled at the Pavilion? The populations of Fonthill Gifford and Fonthill Bishop were declining: in 1831 they numbered 442 and 211.[55] He gave annual gifts of money, faggots and meat to both the poor and the old. Each winter Combes reminded both Mary Ann and her husband of the harsh conditions, before presenting a list of names for their consideration. 'The 2 last days has been the coldest we have had, we have now a considerable fall of snow,' he wrote to Mary Ann in January 1837. 'My heart bleeds for the poor creatures who are half naked, half starved and without firing.' Combes also made sure Morrison knew how grateful the villagers were:

> It was very affecting to hear the expressions of gratitude uttered by these poor old creatures towards you scarcely any of whom had ever seen you. Many of them I found in Bed to keep themselves warm the others shivering over a handful of hardly lighted coals – The old blind man declaimed (as soon as I put the half crown in his hand) 'May Mr Morrison and all his family have those beautiful words of our Redeemer address'd to them at the last day' 'come ye blessed of my Father receive the Kingdom prepared for you from before the formation of the world'.[56]

Morrison was encouraged by Combes to give through him rather than the Church of England. Combes wrote, for example, in December 1838: 'Last Winter when you directed me to give £5 to the Tisbury Coal Subscription, Mr Webber began by refusing all the Catholics (which are a numerous sect in Tisbury) and if I had not accidentally heard of it and threatened to withdraw your subscription the poor Catholics would have had none.'

The Morrisons also supported a schoolteacher in Fonthill Gifford and built a school, designed by Papworth, at Fonthill Bishop. Papworth produced a number of plans in 1838, 'on as economic principle as may be desirable', and voluntary contributions from the community paid for the building.[57] Mary Ann's efforts in Fonthill Gifford earned her the title 'Lady Bountiful' from her American guest Mrs Stevenson:

> She pays from her own private purse twenty guineas a year to a school mistress to teach the poor children of the Parish, besides hiring a room, paying for fire, books, working materials etc. and clothing all who are not able to get decent garments to attend school in. She took me to her school and to visit with her the cottages of the poor. ... Mrs Morrison says she hopes in a few years to be able to ameliorate the condition of her parish but Mr Beckford has left her much to do.[58]

Morrison's accounts for 1835 reveal the school costs were over £47. Miss Lucas was appointed schoolmistress, supervising some fifty children for £5 10s. a quarter. Her task was undoubtedly lonely and she encountered some resistance from her pupils, as she explained to Mary Ann who had ordered some shirts to be made by the girls: 'I am very sorry to say that the Shirts are not finished scarce any of the great Girls has been at School lately the two best workers has left the School altogether and the other girls I cannot get to attend sometimes once a week.' Mary Ann provided leaving prizes and treats at each end of year. But village education in the 1830s was as haphazard and dependent on charity as it had been when Morrison was growing up in Middle Wallop.

The general condition of the labourers improved little in Morrison's lifetime – he would not pay higher wages than his neighbours. In Parliament, in 1834, he supported his party's reform of the Poor Law which established the system of workhouses later vilified by Dickens. Combes provided him with plenty of evidence that the scheme was, in practice, both unfair and cruel. 'Several of the labourers of Fonthill Gifford are order'd to walk so many miles a day between Fonthill and Hindon, as a punishment for being out of work' (4 May 1836). 'The magistrates of the Hindon Division has [*sic*] refused to exonerate any of the labourers in Fonthill Gifford from the payment of Poor Rates for their Cottages. The poor fellows and families are now half starved out it is impossible for them to pay' (5 April 1840).

Van Diemen's Land offered opportunities for some and Morrison followed many landowners in encouraging labourers and their families to consider emigration. Combes reported in 1835 the offer of financial support from the parish to Charlotte Macey to join her husband who had been transported to Van Diemen's Land after the Pythouse battle; however, she refused to leave Fonthill. As Combes noted a few years later, the labourers 'says they had a right to be here, and to live from the land'.

Unlike his neighbouring landowners, Morrison was able to provide opportunities in the textiles trade through his own haberdashery business, as Combes remarked, 'it being such a good place to even get a young man forward'. Penuel Cross was one such young man sent to Fore Street in about 1836 at the age of sixteen. His widowed mother Betty Cross ran the Boot Inn in Tisbury (her sister Anna Maria was married to James Combes, hence the recommendation). By 1841 Penuel had completed his apprenticeship and was a 'warehouseman'. Morrison's links with trade offered the chance of making a real fortune in London.[59]

Morrison's eventual holding consisted of Fonthill Pavilion and Park, the neighbouring estate of Berwick St Leonard, Place Farm, acquired from Lord Arundell, and a few additional outlying acres, a total of 3,254 acres; the value increased from the purchase price of £35,000 to over £82,000. He had managed to acquire land which even William Beckford had failed to grasp, as Combes pointed out:

> This River [flowing from Fonthill Lake down to Place Farm] is the place where the Ducks and Geese go to feed in the Evenings, where numbers of them used to be shot, I have myself 20 years ago kill'd 2 or 3 Couple in an Eveng. This was always Mr Beckfords greatest annoyance, and he would at that time have given almost any money to have been put into the position in which you now stand, but Lord Arundell would never sell the land to him.[60]

The estate provided Morrison with a position in the country, confirmed when the Whig grandee, the Marquess of Lansdowne, Lord Lieutenant of Wiltshire and owner of the Bowood estate, recommended his appointment as a magistrate in 1836. Only the year before, Melbourne was resisting making tradesmen magistrates. He wrote to Lord John Russell: 'I always admitted a man's being a trader – to be an objection to his becoming a Magistrate. ... The notion was that manufacturers would not be considered impartial judges in cases between the working men and their employers. You may certainly say the same with respect to the Country Gentlemen in disputes between farmers and their men and also upon the Game Laws; but after all Country Gentlemen have held, and still do hold a higher character than Master Manufacturers.'[61] He was persuaded, and on 5 February 1836 Morrison 'call'd on Lord Lansdowne at his request. Offer'd to put me in the Commission of the peace in the most handsome manner.' Mary Ann added, when writing to her son Charles, 'He told your father he must come over to Bowwood [*sic*] next season to see him & was very kindly & friendly in his manner.' A few days later, Morrison was presented at court by the Marquess, and Mary Ann was describing to Charles Lady Lansdowne's 'At Home':

> A brilliant assemblage of rank, everyone except two gentlemen in full court costume or military. The ladies as they appeared at the Drawing Room only discarding their trains: there was a magnificent display of diamonds and feathers ... I met a few persons I knew; was introduced by Mr Gordon who paid me a visit with Miss Benett [of Pythouse]. A few of our principal artists, Rogers the poet who has invited your father to go and see his pictures. Your father I think knew half the gentlemen in the room and had much shaking of hands. Altogether it was a very gratifying evening.

Morrison 'took the Oaths & qualified as a Magistrate' on 31 October 1837. The patronage of Lansdowne went further; in 1840 Morrison was made Deputy Lieutenant of the county.[62]

Fonthill was a financial and social asset: an investment to be nurtured and increased, to give Morrison status and authority. He would have appreciated receiving Combes' letter of 30 May 1837: 'Fonthill begins now to look very fine, some Gentlemen were here from London last week and went from here to Stourhead, when they returned they told me that Stourhead was not worthy to be compared to Fonthill.'

CHAPTER NINE

❧❧❧❧

57 Harley Street

Mr Merdle [of Harley Street, Cavendish Square] was immensely rich – a man of prodigious enterprise; a Midas without the ears, who turned all he touched to gold. He was in everything good, from banking to building. He was in Parliament, of course. He was in the City, necessarily.

Charles Dickens, *Little Dorrit*, 1855–7

Mary Ann Morrison confessed to her eldest son Charles early in 1831 that she found her husband's responsibilities as a Member of Parliament a trial. Committee duties 'obliged him to be in town by half past ten in the morning [and] detained him until the Speaker took the chair'. Much worse, however, were the late sittings. He always needed the carriage so that 'it very rarely occurs to be at my disposal', and he rarely returned to Balham before midnight, often two or three o'clock in the morning.

> This is no small trial to his health which hitherto has been (considering the amazing change in his habits) wonderfully good. I have sat up till his return with the exception of two nights when not quite well, but my politeness is giving way and I believe I shall no longer continue to do it … I am sure I shall tire of this House of Commons – it is a great drawback on domestic comforts. With a home in town it might be rather less objectionable.[1]

Three months after writing to Charles, her prayers were answered: a house had been found.[2] James Morrison bought at auction, for 4,700 guineas, the remaining fifty-eight-year lease of 'a capital town mansion, desirably situate

No. 57, on the west side of Upper Harley Street, Cavendish Square.[3] The house (later renumbered 93) remained the property of the family until the death of Charles Morrison in 1909.

Number 57 Harley Street was one of the largest houses in the road, with a ground rent of £21 12s. per annum. It was built in 1783, probably by the first lessee John White, surveyor, architect and builder to the Duke of Portland, the owner of the estate.[4] The Portland estate was a fashionable eighteenth-century development that attracted members of the aristocracy and gentry, Members of Parliament, wealthy merchants and bankers. William Beckford of Fonthill rented 6 Upper Harley Street from 1811 to 1817; number 57 had belonged to a Lincolnshire gentleman, Bateman Dashwood esquire. Other close neighbours of the Morrisons included the Duke of Dorset; the Barons Boston, Churchill and Grantley; the Chairman, Deputy Chairman and three directors of the East India Company and the American banker Timothy Wiggin. Morrison's parliamentary friend Joseph Hume lived close by in Bryanston Square.

Nineteenth-century novelists frequently criticised the architecture of the Portland estate. Disraeli, for example, found it timid, insipid and uniform, 'all those flat, dull, spiritless streets, all resembling each other, like a large family of plain children.'[5] Dickens was similarly dismissive of the area, associating it with some of his most damaged and disreputable characters. The merchant Paul Dombey lived 'on the shady side of a tall, dark, dreadfully genteel street in the region between Portland Place and Bryanstone Square'. The house was 'of dismal state … as black a house inside as outside.'[6] The Podsnaps' home (in *Our Mutual Friend*) was nearby, 'in a shady angle adjoining Portman Square', its contents 'massive', 'hideous' and 'corpulent'. 'Everything was made to look as heavy as it could, and to take up as much room as possible.'[7] Dickens was most critical of the 'expressionless, uniform' houses in Harley Street, where the 'immensely rich' swindler Merdle resided:

Like unexceptionable Society, the opposing rows of houses in Harley Street were very grim with one another. Indeed, the mansions and their inhabitants were so much alike in that respect, that the people were often to be found drawn up on opposite sides of dinner-tables, in the shade of their own loftiness, staring at the other side of the way with the dullness of the houses.[8]

But these houses were all about the inside, the 'front stage', which was the principal, sometimes the only indication of the proprietor's wealth, taste, character and standing.[9] The particulars of 57 Upper Harley Street emphasised its suitability for a 'family of the first consequence with a large establishment'; it was up to Morrison to decorate the rooms in the appropriate fashion.

The usual team was engaged: Thomas Burton, William and Edward Snell, Thomas and George Seddon, George Morant plus Leschallas for the 'colouring', all working to Papworth's direction and design. Estimates for essential work came to £3,980, almost as much as the house. Burton's building works came to slightly over £1,000; Leschallas' 'colouring' was the considerable sum of £791; Morant's painting and papering was almost £500; furniture made by the Seddons and Snells amounted to over £1,000.[10]

The house was ready for occupation by the end of 1832, coinciding nicely with Morrison's return to the first reformed Parliament, though no longer as the independent MP for St Ives. He had consistently voted in favour of the Reform Bill but realising St Ives would lose one of its seats he had engaged the wily broker Isaac Sewell to find another. Sewell quickly made contact with his acquaintances among 'the leaders of the Independent party' in Ipswich, writing to Morrison, 'Mr Alexander the Ipswich Banker who is a great & powerful Supporter of the reform question has been with me ... they want Merchants.' Ipswich was an ideal constituency. With a population of over 20,000, it would continue, post-reform, to elect two MPs; also the 'leading men ... had been or were engaged in some trade or profession', hence the support for Morrison. His wealth was also of significance; the Tories had been successful at the 1830 election in part because they were richer than the opposition candidates.[11]

Morrison was probably relieved that abandoning St Ives would make his relationship with his fellow Liberal MP Long-Wellesley merely commercial. Long-Wellesley's attempts to seek control over his children forced his uncle the Duke of Wellington to intervene and the children were made wards of court. When Long-Wellesley removed his daughter, the Lord Chancellor Henry Brougham locked him in the Fleet Prison for contempt of court. He then invoked parliamentary privilege but his plea was rejected by the Committee of Privileges of the Commons. 'The vast property he had acquired by marriage and all that came from his own family, was squandered;

and, after many years of poverty and profligacy, he subsisted on a weekly pension from his relatives, the late and present Dukes of Wellington.'[12]

All went well for Morrison at Ipswich at the general election in July 1831. He received the highest number of votes, 468, with his fellow Liberal, the lawyer Rigby Wason coming second. One of their opponents, Captain Robert Fitzroy, lost any chance of being elected when he spoke out in favour of rotten boroughs, declaring, 'let well alone'.[13] He forged a rather different career, taking command of HMS *Beagle* and setting sail for the Galapagos Islands with Charles Darwin on board. As usual, Mary Ann was less than thrilled with her husband's success, writing from Balham to Charles:

> I have this morning received a letter from your Father stating his great success at Ipswich. ... I have not the slightest idea when I shall leave home. Your Father told me the day he started he should want to sit a whole week on his green sofa when he returned – this is my gain in Election's many deprivations and disagreeables of all kinds.

At the next general election in December 1832 Morrison again came top with 599 votes. He and Mary Ann moved into their newly decorated town house immediately after.[14]

Over the next six years Morrison spent a further £12,000 buying works of art, porcelain, marbles and bronzes for his town house; by the end of his life he valued the house and its contents at £46,000. After viewing the collection in 1854, Gustave Waagen declared 'the specimens of costly plate, vases, objects in ivory ... Raphael-ware, and other tasteful objects, all quite in keeping with the other works of art in this fine collection'.[15]

Papworth worked on 57 Harley Street and Fonthill at virtually the same time. While he concentrated in the country on creating a picturesque landscape to be enjoyed by the family, for the town house he designed interiors to represent and reflect Morrison's position as a merchant millionaire and reforming MP. It was in London rather than the country that Morrison entertained members of the Cabinet, leading bankers and economists, Royal Academicians, and his business partners from Fore Street and the United States of America. The style and detail of the decoration, the quality of workmanship applied to the fittings in the library and gallery, and the choice of works of art, furniture and decorative objects reveal his sophistication as well as his wealth; albeit on a small scale, he was joining the ranks of major European collecting dynasties including the 3rd and 4th Marquesses of Hertford, the Rothschilds and the Barings, not to mention individuals such as George IV, the 3rd Marquess of Lansdowne, William Beckford and George Watson Taylor. And he achieved this position in the few years he had been married to Mary Ann.

The most lavishly decorated rooms were on the ground and first floors: the rooms seen by visitors to the house. The ground floor in the sale particulars comprised a dining room, library, and a gentleman's dressing room or morning room with a bath 'with pipes &c as fixed and Sofa covering it' and water closet. Papworth used a quantity of reds and crimsons in both the dining room and the library: scarlet curtains with 'rosetts & pendant tassels' for the dining room[16] and crimson trimmings on the library curtains. The Seddons made an eight-foot ottoman for the library covered with crimson cloth and trimmed with crimson silk rosettes, and a similarly covered pedestal.[17]

The dining room, with two windows opening on to Harley Street, already contained a black marble chimneypiece with a looking glass above. To increase the height of the glass 'by additional head', the Snells used 'raffle leaf, & frieze relieved by buhl, buhl up the pilasters &c finished in mat and burnished gold'. The Seddons sold Morrison a set of mahogany dining tables over five feet wide and 16 feet long 'of rare and curiously mottled wood' on 'four massive turned and carved legs and castors'. In a letter to Papworth, they made sure he – and of course Morrison – understood the quality of the tables and the generous deal they were offering: 'We think it so desirable to please Mr Morrison that we will consent to take Eighty guineas for the beautiful dining table although we feel assured that you are aware they are worth much more money.'[18] Only a small number of paintings were displayed in the dining room, including the Pickersgill portraits of Morrison, Mary Ann and Joseph Todd.

In the library much time and money (almost £400) were spent by the Seddons making a lavish 'suite' of bookcases of 'very fine rosewood highly polish'd enclosed by panel'd doors and pilasters, fitt'd with patent locks, fill'd with silk and richly ornamented to design with carved rosettes scroll ornamental handles and knurl'd [sic] mouldings the whole fitted to 12 Antique Sienna scagliola pedestals deep black and gold plinths and surmounted by yellow Antique Sienna scagliola slabs'.[19] They also made a matching marble-topped table, five feet long, 'supported by truss brackets richly carved in foliage & other ornaments'. The Snells provided Spanish mahogany spindle-back chairs covered in green morocco; the silk inside the bookcases was also green.

Morrison formed his library with the same attention to detail he applied to his business transactions; there is no sense that he bought books 'by the yard' or simply to impress. There is almost always a reason behind his collecting. For example, he amassed a large number of topographical studies of Great Britain, Europe (particularly France), North America, India and China, all countries of which he had personal cultural or commercial knowledge. His library also reveals his keen interest in art and architecture, as well as containing books by or connected with friends and acquaintances, including his partner John Dillon's play, his Freethinking Christian friend Henry Fearon's travels in North America, as well as political economy texts by McCulloch, Bentham and Joseph Hume.

Morrison may not have studied classical languages, but the objects displayed on the bookcases and pedestals were mostly classical in age and reference, including Etruscan vases, antique busts and bronze statuettes. He was emulating the aristocratic and cosmopolitan collections he had seen in London and touring Britain and Europe.[20] At Lansdowne House, for example, where Morrison and his wife attended a reception, they would have seen George Dance the Younger's decorations of the library with an Etruscan border, Egyptian marbles incorporated in the chimneypiece and Grecian statues displayed in niches next to the books. Visiting the museum at Naples in 1840, Morrison's son Charles wrote to his mother (who had visited the museum herself in 1827),

I have given you this long story about the Etruscan vases because I thought, as you have a set of them in Harley St & at Fonthill it wd be interesting to you to have yr recollection of the collection here refreshed, or to be acquainted with anything in it wh may be new to you. If I recollect right, the most valuable of yr vases, wh is one of the oldest class, has a figure on whose shield is the device of the 3 legs – if it be so, you will appreciate it better now that you know the importance of that circumstance in the controversy concerning the origin of the art. At all events I think that vase as curious as any of those in the Museum here – & the other vase wh is placed on the bracket in the library at Fonthill, quite as fine & bold in form as any that I have seen today.[21]

There were more Etruscan vases in the luxurious gentleman's dressing room situated to the rear of the ground floor. The room was decorated in primrose and light blue, with a chimneypiece of black and gold marble, elaborate fitted furniture, and double doors leading to the lavatory and bath.

The 'front drawing room' on the first floor, with three windows opening on to a balcony overlooking Harley Street, was transformed by Papworth into a gallery for Morrison's growing art collection. The design for the gallery ceiling is painted with washes of brown, blue and orange which may indicate the final colours, and the mouldings and cornice were lavishly gilded.[22] The curtains were an elaborate confection by the Snells of green and crimson silk damask and brocade silk lace.[23] Ranged around the walls were cases with scagliola tops and pedestals of bright *verd antique* scagliola on plinths of black and gold. The lighting was a challenge. Papworth explained to Mary Ann his experiment of hanging four '3 light lamps' rather than the usual '4 light lamps' and not simply hung from the centre of the ceiling: 'I want to benefit the pictures & yet light up the room adequately … giving more diffused & ample light than a Centre lamp … it will be somewhat of a novelty.'

Mary Ann found the gallery space sufficient to hold fifty people when she gave a party early in 1837. Her daughters were home from school (they were boarders at the Misses Fennings, Edwardes Square, Kensington), she hired a pianist and gave 'an elegant supper … I found the gallery when clered [*sic*] a very good sized room for that number.' Charles, who was away at university, received the details: ' Henry [aged five] looked lovely in a green velvet dress with a white satin pleating in front and lace ruff this you will think my vanity & folly my daughters also were quite to my satisfaction in simple white muslin and dear Walter had his share. I know if I were telling you these things, instead of writing them, you would say Mother Mother, still I must tell you my weakness.'

The back drawing room opened into a conservatory and a 'very elegant boudoir' (with a water closet) which eventually became a schoolroom as the family continued to expand. The drawing room was awash with colour: the cornices and pilasters were painted in sepia, red and yellow; the walls covered by Morant with panels of cinnamon silk and blue striped silk tabouret.[24] Morant also provided gilt ornaments and mouldings over the windows and doors and a further 60 feet of burnished gold moulding.[25] A decade before, Morrison had commented on the drawing room at Raby Castle: 'very rich' with 'blue striped tabberet [sic] ... lined with crimson'. The finishing touches in Harley Street were provided by the purchase of a spectacular looking glass originally at Erlestoke Park in Wiltshire, home of George Watson Taylor.[26]

Watson Taylor (1771–1841), married to a Jamaican heiress, had acquired lavish treasures for his house in Cavendish Square and his country mansion, but the slump in his income following the abolition of slavery forced the sale of both his houses. He shared his source of income and his taste with William Beckford, and had earlier bought items from the Fonthill sales.[27] Papworth acquired the mirror, together with two 'unfinished ebony and mosaic console tables and a pair of *verd antique* urns at the Erlestoke sale, then persuaded Morrison to pay £70 for a red marble chimneypiece by Richard Westmacott:[28] 'The Chimney piece (& I mention it with great deference) is one that with a very little work would make a very suitable addition to the Earlstoke [sic] Glass & accord with your Drawing Room.'[29] Gustave Waagen noted the frame of the mirror when he visited Harley Street as 'unique of its kind, consisting of a series of enamels, forming two pilasters reaching to a considerable height on the walls. It is said to have belonged formerly to Marie Antoinette, and was purchased from Mr Watson Taylor.'[30] Morrison recorded a different provenance in his diary 'J. [of] Bond Street told me our drawing room glass was made for Watson Taylor by De La Haute of Paris, that it is all modern.'[31]

The fittings in Harley Street combined Papworth's designs with the making skills of the Seddons and the Snells. They would be expensive, as the Snells warned Papworth: 'Mr Morrison must notice that in working to your designs, the forms, the moldings, and the quantities of materials, are totally different from articles which are prepared by Upholsterers to meet the market.' Papworth in turn made sure his patron understood (and would pay for) original designs: 'it is quite clear to me that for many things in the way of Furniture we must be altogether new in design & material – all art is open to us & many materials subservient to its uses that have not been (henceforth) freely combined in creating an effective object.'

With increasing confidence, Morrison was also inspired, coming up with ideas and commissions related to pieces he already owned: 'I send you a writing desk as a specimen of Buhl work, and I want you to design for me merely the case of an Inkstand for the Gallery [in Harley Street]. I should think it may be in Turtle or Tortoiseshell, or Ebony, inlaid either with brass or pearl, and with gilt or silver ornaments – pray try your best.'[32] He was concerned to find or make the very best work, writing to Papworth in 1833, 'we are only anxious now that we have so many things that you should occasionally raise the standard a hole or two. We must decide on looking out only for the superlative very soon.'[33]

Morrison's growing collection of British watercolours hung in the drawing room, including Turner's *Swan's Nest (Stourhead)* and Samuel Prout's *Venice*. Morant made new 'sweep' frames, 'handsomely ornamented' in burnished and matt gold for Harding's *Grecian Landscape*, Copley Fielding's *Shipwreck* (also called *A Storm with a Vessel in Distress*),[34] Mackenzie's *Milan Cathedral* and Papworth's two drawings of Mary Ann and her children. Morant also reframed Constable's *Lock* after Papworth called on the artist: 'I have seen Mr Constable – who will let me know what he will allow for the frame if you choose to have a new one – he will clean & varnish the picture in the room.'[35] Papworth routinely sent Morrison descriptions of pieces he had seen in 'antique' furniture shops, and paintings coming up for auction or on display in exhibitions.[36] On 16 May 1832, for example, he recommended to his friend James Ward: 'the Cows in the Shed is perhaps the best of his small size extant – this will give you an opportunity to judge & choose between that & the milking – provided you decide to take any.' Morrison bought *The Milk Maid*.

The decision to create a formal gallery in his London house followed Morrison's acquisition in 1831 of his first Old Master painting, Claude Lorraine's *The Rape of Europa*, which cost him the considerable sum of 1,000 guineas.[37] About the same time Morrison acquired one or both of his small intimate Watteaus, *Fête Champêtre* and *The Guitar Player*. Constable, Turner or Wilkie, all three admirers of the French artist, could have brought his work to the attention of Morrison, while Turner had 'discovered' Claude Lorraine.[38]

Dutch genre paintings were admired by Turner's circle and Morrison began to build up a considerable collection. Their 'apparent transparency, simplicity and directness', their 'undemanding subject-matter and charm, the sheer virtuosity of their illusionism, even their modest and intimate scale' appealed to some of the wealthiest and cosmopolitan collectors, including George IV, the Barings,[39] Beckford, the Hertfords, the Marquess of Lansdowne and Sir Robert Peel; Morrison had seen examples in Knoyle House, the home of his Wiltshire neighbours the Seymours, and in the Mayfair town house of his banking friend Abraham Robarts.[40]

In 1835 he went to Christie's to view the collection of Lord Charles Townshend with Peter Norton, by this date his regular buyer at auctions in London and the country.[41] Morrison liked Berchem's *Archway or Drinking Fountain* best, and paid 760 guineas at the auction. He also bought Teniers' *Cowhouse* for 675 guineas. Peel was at the same sale, successfully bidding for a Ruysdael.[42] The same year Morrison acquired Cuyp's *Sunny Landscape* (also called *Landscape with Figures*) for £399. Aelbert Cuyp was particularly admired by Turner as a painter 'to a judgement so truly qualified, [who] knew where to blend minutiae in all the golden colour of ambient vapour'.[43] Dickens chose Cuyp for a less worthy purpose. In depicting, disparagingly, the interior of Merdle's Harley Street house, he used a Cuyp landscape with cows to convey the appearance of both Merdle and his government guests:

Mr Tite Barnacle ... and Mr Merdle, seated diverse ways and with rumi-
nating aspects, on a yellow ottoman in the light of the fire, holding no
verbal communication with each other, bore a strong general resemblance
to two Cows in the Cuyp picture over against them ... Lord Decimus
composed himself in the picture after Cuyp, and made a third cow in the
group.[44]

Peter Norton helped to acquire two of Morrison's finest paintings, Parmigianino's *The Virgin and Child with St John*, and Poussin's *Landscape with a Calm*. The Parmigianino was previously owned by Watson Taylor and cost Morrison 600 guineas,[45] while the Poussin had belonged to a jeweller Thomas Hamlet, and cost £451 10s.[46] Morrison would have seen Poussins in the Louvre and in the collection of the Hoares at Stourhead.

Morrison maintained close relations with the Royal Academicians, whose taste was informing his own acquisition of Old Masters. He and Mary Ann had met Charles Eastlake in Rome and in 1834 bought his *Escape of Francesco Novello di Carrara, with his Wife, from the Duke of Milan*. Eastlake was now living close by in Upper Fitzroy Street, and asked permission the following year to engrave the painting for Finden's *Royal Gallery of British Art*.[47] Their relationship continued over the years: he was invited to dinner in Harley Street and in 1854 he brought together Morrison and Gustave Waagen over a 'plain dinner' in Fitzrovia.

Other artists dined at Harley Street, mixed up with Morrison's partners from Fore Street, Mary Ann's extensive Todd relations, Wiltshire neighbours and American business partners. David Wilkie and George Jones dined together with the Whig barrister Henry Bellenden Ker, a fervent supporter of popular education and the appreciation of art.[48] Pickersgill sat through an evening of readings from romantic literature with John Dillon, Morrison's solicitor W.H. Ashurst, Joseph Hume, MP, and the Cryders, new merchant friends from Philadelphia. Turner joined members of the Todd family and the vicar of Fonthill. Invited to Pickersgill's house in Soho Square the night before the Royal Academy dinner in April 1836, Morrison found himself among friends: the painters Turner, Jones, Clarkson Stanfield, Charles Robert Leslie, the sculptor Sir Francis Chantrey and the collector Robert Vernon (whose house had been improved by Papworth).

The guest list for Mary Ann's 'at home' on 30 January 1839 confirms their own artistic circle: painters (Pickersgill, Eastlake, Collins, Turner, Jones, Stanfield) and sculptors (Chantrey); architects (Owen 'Alhambra' Jones and Papworth); the President of the Royal Academy, the antiquary John Britton and the librarian of the British Museum. The 'Burton' included in the list must be their own builder, Thomas Burton. Soon after the party, Morrison began sitting to Chantrey, who sculpted his bust in an appropriately classical pose.

Morrison was, however, more than a collector. Motivated in part by commercial gain (he was convinced that better design led to more sales) he took an active part in Parliament in promoting public access to art and founding the first Government School of Design. This, together with his less successful attempt to regulate the management of railways, is the subject of the next chapter.

CHAPTER TEN

❦

In Parliament

Morrison launched his campaign for both a 'national collection' of art and a school of design from his position as member of the 1832 Select Committee on the Silk Trade.[1] He wrote to Papworth:

> We shall some day get a Gallery, and that soon, for our National Collection, and I want, and will try hard, to get also a School of Design. For this purpose I think our 'Silk Committee' would be a good opportunity to open the subject to Parliament. ... Would you like to give your opinion before the Committee? Our deficiency in selecting and combining colours, and in design, as compared with the French, may be seen well at Howell and James's [haberdashers], and the remedy is to teach drawing as a profession for this purpose. France must continue to lead fashion so long as she has this advantage over us. Perhaps you would think of some other artists who may be induced or would like to attend.[2]

The committee's official role was to 'examine into the state of the silk trade, and to inquire what effects have been produced by the changes in the law relating to it since the year 1824'.[3] James Deacon Hume, Secretary of the Board of Trade (not to be confused with Morrison's friend Joseph Hume), had then drafted the bill repealing prohibition on foreign imports of raw and thrown silk; Morrison, in 1832, was concerned to prevent any return even to moderate protection. He engaged John Bowring, his old, sometimes irritating, business acquaintance who was a respected expert on foreign manufacture, to research the state of the silk industry in Lyons 'from the mulberry man to the exporter' and discovered from him that 'the impetus which foreign demand and foreign competition (the most efficient of all sources of improvement) has given to the cultivation of silk is very remarkable'.[4] J.D. Hume was invited to dinner in Harley Street before giving evidence in support of continuing free trade: 'our weavers are now enabled to produce fancy goods ... fully equal, and as regards some sorts, superior to the quality of goods made in France'. Cheaper silk was reaching 'every class of the community'.[5]

In Parliament Morrison extended his argument about the allure of fashion to gloves, challenging the idea that distress in the glove-manufacturing districts of Yeovil and Worcester was caused by the importation of French gloves. In his opinion fashion played a more significant part. The preference for kid gloves (made in Yeovil) had contributed to the collapse of Worcester's production of beaver gloves; however, the Worcester manufacturers' unsurprising response – a shift to the manufacture of kid gloves – had resulted in the collapse of business in Yeovil. Even worse, both kid and beaver were now threatened by the new fashion for cotton gloves, just like the pair he was wearing and which he proceeded to flourish in the air to the amazement of the House. Opposition MPs were quick to accuse him of having a personal interest in cheap foreign imports but he stuck to his argument. The export of English gloves to North America had also been adversely affected by fashion, as the French style was preferred.

Many Whigs shared Morrison's commercial interest in improving design, including his Dover colleague Charles Poulett Thomson, now MP for Manchester and Vice-President of the Board of Trade, William Ewart, the radical utilitarian MP for Liverpool, Lord John Russell, Paymaster of the Forces and Joseph Hume, who specifically attributed the relative success of French textile designs to the quality of teaching at the Lyons School of Design. Their views were echoed by the influential Tory member of the committee, Sir Robert Peel, himself made rich by textiles: 'Peel acknowledged our general ignorance in design was the reason of our inferiority'.[6]

Morrison returned to his hobby horse, the need to improve British design education, the following year, during a debate on the establishment of the Soane Museum in Lincoln's Inn Fields. While fervently supporting Soane's gift to the nation, Morrison was worried by the suggestion that the British Museum might be given control of access. His experience was rather different

1 Henry William Pickersgill, *James Morrison*, 1824.

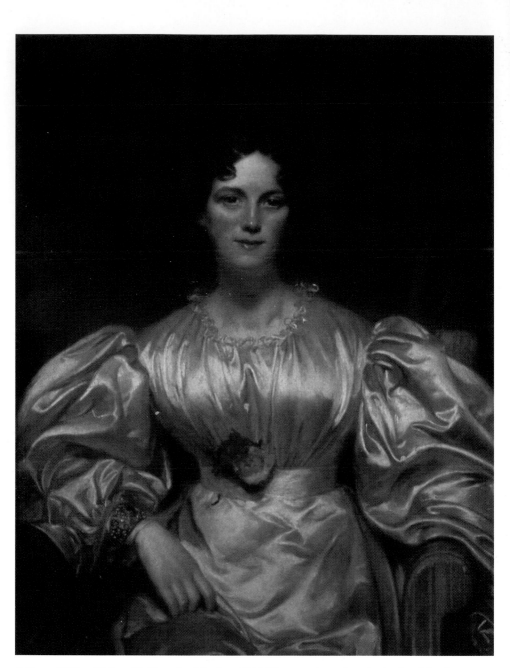

2 Henry William Pickersgill, *Mary Ann Morrison*, 1824. The portrait was hung in the Royal Academy Summer Show in 1825, the first year James Morrison was invited to the prestigious annual dinner.

3 The Lower George Inn, Middle Wallop, *c.* 1910. The view is looking towards Andover and London; the Old George Inn run by James Morrison's grandparents, was in a cottage to the left of the coach road; the sheep pens were to the right.

4 Thomas Hosmer Shepherd, *Fore Street and St Giles's Cripplegate, c.* 1830. The Fore Street warehouses are to the right (approximately).

5 Fabric plate from Ackermann's *Repository of Arts* for February 1810, showing actual samples of new materials.

6 William Brockedon, *John Buonarroti Papworth*, 1824.

7 J.B. Papworth designed extensive new premises for George and Thomas Seddon in the Gray's Inn Road, *c.* 1830, with separate areas for packing, joiners and bedstead-makers, polishers, veneerers, carvers and gilders, Japanners, turners, upholsterers and cabinetmakers.

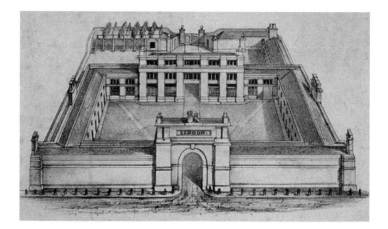

8 John Constable's *The Lock* was purchased by James Morrison from the Royal Academy in 1824 for 150 guineas including the frame.

9 J.M.W. Turner's *Pope's Villa at Twickenham* was purchased by James Morrison from Sir John Leicester, 1st Baron Tabley, in 1827.

10 William Collins, *The Fisherman's Farewell*, commissioned by James Morrison in 1825 for 350 guineas, shown at the Royal Academy in 1826.

11 J.M.W. Turner, *The Rise of the River Stour, the Swan's Nest*, watercolour, purchased by James Morrison in 1825.

12 J.B. Papworth, design for warehouses in Milton Street (formerly Grub Street). The warehouse on the left was completed in 1824; the warehouse on the right was added *c*. 1830–2.

13 J.B. Papworth, design for warehouse in Fore Street, *c*. 1828–30 when turnover reached almost £2 million.

14 Henrik de Cort, *Fonthill Splendens*. The Palladian mansion was built in 1755 by Alderman Beckford but mostly demolished by his son to build Fonthill Abbey.

15 The Pavilion, the remaining west wing of Fonthill Splendens, which James Morrison bought in 1830.

16 Beckford's Fonthill Abbey in 1823. The tower collapsed two years later.

17 The Rev. C. Harbin, *Ruins of Fonthill Abbey – from the Bitham Lake, Oct.1 1845.*

18 J.B. Papworth, *Emily, Charles and Lucy Morrison*, c. 1831. In 1831 Charles would have been 14, Emily 4 and Lucy 6 years old.

19 57 Harley Street was acquired by James Morrison in 1832. The dining room was on the ground floor, with two windows opening on to the street; the front drawing room on the first floor was transformed by Papworth into a gallery.

20 Claude Lorraine, *The Rape of Europa,* 1667. This was the first Old Master acquired by James Morrison in 1831 for 1000 guineas.

21 Peter Paul Rubens, *The Miracles of Saint Francis of Paola, c.* 1627–8, oil on panel, unframed 97.5x77.2 cm, framed 128.3x97.2x9.2 cm. This was the first painting James Morrison bought, in July 1838, from William Buchanan.

22 Nicolas Poussin, *Landscape with a Calm (Un Tem[p]s calme et serein)*, 1650–1, oil on canvas, unframed 97x131 cm, framed 125.7x160.7x7.9 cm. Purchased by James Morrison in 1836 from the jeweller Thomas Hamlet for £451.10s.

23 Aelbert Cuyp, *Sunny Landscape* or *Landscape with Figures*. Purchased by James Morrison in 1835 for £399.

24 The entrance front of Basildon Park, now the property of the National Trust. James Morrison bought the estate in 1838 for £97,000, including timber.

25 Francis Chantrey, *James Morrison*, commissioned by James Morrison in 1839 for 200 guineas.

26 The Pink Drawing Room, Basildon Park.

27 Luini, *Flora*. Purchased by James Morrison in 1846 for £772 from Sir Thomas Baring and believed to be by Leonardo da Vinci. Displayed in the Pink Drawing Room until replaced, probably by Charles Morrison, with Greuze's painting of a young girl.

28 The Central Staircase Hall, Basildon Park.

29 J.M.W. Turner, *Thomson's Aeolian Harp*, 1809. The date this was purchased by James Morrison is not known, but it is assumed to be around 1825.

30 The Octagon Room, Basildon Park. Papworth had the walls covered in purple fabric and thick bands of gilt papier-mache ornament placed in the angles of the room. Green china crackle vases from Beckford's 1845 sale are displayed on the chimneypiece carved by W.G. Nicholls to Papworth's design.

31 William Hilton's *Comus with the lady in the enchanted chair* or *Una bound by the spells of Comus* hung above the chimneypiece. Exhibited at the Royal Academy in 1823, but bought by James Morrison from Christie's in 1841.

to that of Alexander Baring (later 1st Baron Ashburton, famous for crossing from the Whigs to the Tory benches to earn his family the title 'See Saw Barings)[7] who claimed that application to the librarian of the museum always facilitated entry 'for any gentleman who came there for any purpose connected with science or art'.[8] Morrison addressed the House: '[he] was aware that it had been stated that there were 123 days in the course of each year on which the public were admitted [to the British Museum], and supposed therefore his own applications must have been peculiarly unfortunate. Within the last two years, however, he had made at least a dozen attempts to obtain admission, but had always called upon a wrong day.'

Even worse than his experience, manufacturers from the north of England visiting London 'for the purpose of obtaining information' would find entry virtually impossible.

At this season of the year [spring], a vast number of persons interested in the manufactures of the country come to the metropolis for the purpose of obtaining information, and on their account he would, if possible, have the British Museum opened every day in the week during the months of April, May and June. It was not enough that upon application to the public officers of the establishment those persons might obtain admission, because all persons who know anything of the institutions of this country must have experienced how repulsive it was to make applications to public officers when any difficulty could be thrown in the way of granting the required favour.

He then linked entry to the museum and 'information' to the general lack of education in the 'higher branches of art' which would make Britain competitive. 'This country was very deficient in the means of teaching the higher branches of art, and much needed some institution similar to those which were found on the Continent. He doubted whether the public money could be expended so beneficially in any other way as by establishing schools for teaching art and science.'[9]

Finally, in 1835, Morrison's ideas came to fruition. The government set up a select committee to inquire 'into the best means of extending a knowledge of the Arts and the Principles of Design among the People (especially the Manufacturing Population) of the Country; also to inquire into the

Constitution, Management and Effects of Institutions connected with the Arts'.[10] The chair was Morrison's fellow MP William Ewart, members included Bowring, Peel, Lord John Russell and Poulett Thomson. Evidence was taken between July 1835 and August 1836. Just before, on 30 May, Mr and Mrs Ewart sat down to dinner in Harley Street with the Todds, the vicar of Fonthill, Mr and Mrs Williams (Williams was a partner at Fore Street so particularly interested, like Morrison, in the commercial significance of design) and Turner. 'JMW Turner presents his respects to Mr & Mrs Morrison and he will with very great pleasure wait upon them on the 30 of May (Saturday week) at ¼ before 7 oclock.' Ewart was not a supporter of the Royal Academy approach to art education, preferring the teaching methods adopted in Germany and France, so discussions with Turner, RA, would have been lively.

Papworth gave his evidence on 21 August. A month before he had read a paper 'On the benefits resulting to the manufactures of a country from a well directed cultivation of architecture, and of the art of ornamental design' to the one-year-old Institute of British Architects of which he was Vice-President.[11] He presented similar evidence to the Select Committee. 'There is a class of Artists called Pattern drawers, employed by Calico printers, Paper stainers, Silk manufacturers, Carpet makers, and many others. These rarely express any power of imagination, or good drawing, and for their resources depend greatly upon Articles introduced into England from Foreign markets.' Thus 'Manufacturers lament exceedingly the want of adequate assistance for their purposes.'[12] Morrison, described as a 'Purchaser of Manufactured goods home and abroad, through the agency of James Morrison & Co.', spoke to the committee on 30 July: 'I have found generally that we have been very much superior to foreign countries in respect of the general manufacture, but greatly inferior in the art of design.'[13]

Gustave Waagen, in his role as Director of the Royal Gallery in Berlin, was invited to give evidence by the committee, which believed he could 'contribute usefully to resolving the perceived crisis surrounding the quality of British design which, in turn, was seen as inhibiting the marketable qualities of British goods'. He described the Prussian institutions and their far superior 'instruction of the manufacturing population in the Fine Arts'.[14] The architect C.R. Cockerell, a friend of Papworth, linked the decline of decorative arts to the 'introduction of mechanical art' but also to the 'absence of taste' in those commissioning work, the employers 'who have not had the means of forming a good taste, and who have not had the wealth, during the last half century of taxation, war and dear living, to encourage those secondary arts which are expensive in this country'.[15] He was repeating the point Morrison had made in 1833 regarding manufacturers' inability to access resources such as the British Museum. In France, for example, 'the extreme accessibility of their museums, libraries and exhibitions, have [*sic*] greatly tended to the diffusion of a love of art, as well as of literature, among the poorer classes'.[16]

The Select Committee Report was published in August 1836 and Poulett Thomson was given the task 'in consequence of the present low condition of art in this country' of establishing the first School of Design in Ornamental Art, with a grant of £1,500.[17] Morrison was in regular contact with Poulett Thomson as he formed the council overseeing the school. H.B. Kerr, Eastlake, Chantrey and Cockerell were among the seven who attended; Papworth was appointed part-time director.

Papworth took up his post on 14 April 1837 on an annual salary of £250. The school opened on 1 May in Somerset House, occupying the rooms made vacant by the move of the Royal Academy into the National Gallery's new building in Trafalgar Square. Papworth designed the furniture, purchased equipment, selected the teachers and appointed his son as librarian and secretary on an annual salary of £70. Donations began to come in for the library and teaching collection, including four casts of the Alhambra from Owen Jones; on a visit to Paris in 1843 Kerr bought French wallpapers and bronzes. In 1857 the school moved to South Kensington; its final transformation was into the Royal College of Art; its library (now the National Art Library) and its teaching collection became part of the Victoria and Albert Museum.[18]

Though Papworth was replaced as director within a year, Morrison, his patron, can claim to have made a major contribution to the country's art and design education and the campaign to open and create more museums for the public. Otherwise, however, Morrison's first period in Parliament was hardly the beginning of a glorious political career.

He started off well enough. His knowledge of the textile trade and his financial independence (he was sufficiently rich to fight for his seat without the aid of party funds) were advantages in the reformed Parliament and invitations came from high places. He was one of sixteen dinner guests at the house of Lord Palmerston, the Foreign Secretary, early in the session. He was sufficiently impressed to list all of the drinks consumed, including sherry, Madeira, champagne, hock, hermitage, port, claret, porter and ale. A couple of weeks later he dined with the Hon. Edward Stanley, Secretary of State for Colonial Affairs.

Attending and giving evidence to the Select Committee on Manufactures, Commerce and Shipping, which met during May and June 1833, was a relatively civilised affair, and, in January 1834 he was asked by Lord Althorp, Chancellor of the Exchequer, to second the address at the opening of Parliament. However, he was worried that such a speech would inevitably signify his support for all government policies, thus compromising his preferred position as an 'independent'. He sought the advice of James Mill, then called at Downing Street where he was 'kindly received & much flattering talk. Lord A [Althorp] went so far as to say he would undertake to omit anything in the address which I objected to.' Morrison was still not convinced, so he again called on Mill whom he found 'very strong in favour, never knew it consider'd as pledging a man to general support or as in the slightest degree fettering his independence'. He was forced to admit there was 'no hope of escape!'

The speech itself was mostly uncontroversial: he claimed imports and exports were improving; that eight years of free trade had been beneficial to the silk trade. However, his comments on Irish manufacture managed to enrage the Irish nationalist MP Daniel O'Connell. While the north of Ireland was improving, Morrison stated that manufacture 'could not be established' in the south, 'where agitation and outrage prevailed'. And he condemned moves to form an Irish Parliament. O'Connell responded with a direct attack on Morrison. 'There was a species of free trade which was useful to the millionaires, who, from their command of capital could be content with small profits. Such men might profit by free trade, while many small dealers would be annihilated by it.'[19] Immediately after he spoke, the Rt Hon. James Abercromby, MP, congratulated Morrison: 'I had said in two short sentences what had hurt OConnells feelings more than any thing that had been said in that House.'[20] Unfortunately the animosity did not end there and O'Connell made another personal attack in Ipswich in front of Morrison and his electors a couple of years later.

Morrison's speech also precipitated the playing of an unpleasant practical joke on his family. Mary Ann warned their eldest son Charles to look out for a letter, apparently signed by their solicitor William Ashurst, which claimed that Morrison was dangerously ill, having suffered an apoplectic fit directly after making his speech. Both Morrison's brother Samuel and his father-in-law Joseph Todd received copies of the letter, begging them to come immediately to Harley Street. The first the Morrisons knew about it was when Samuel turned up on their doorstep in the middle of the night, in a state of great agitation, having travelled all the way from Middle Wallop. Mary Ann added: 'so far from any calamity having happened, your father is daily receiving congratulations on the success [of the speech]'.

Morrison's enthusiasm for the Commons blew hot and cold, and like Mary Ann he preferred being at home in the evening with his family. His diaries contain frequent entries lamenting his having to endure speeches that 'lasted the whole of the evening'. When Althorp urged him to publish the 1834 speech he again sought advice from his partner Dillon, the political economist McCulloch and Coulson of The *Globe* before deciding against. Instead he chose to display his achievement privately, sending copies to a list consisting of family, his lawyer and his architect, Fore Street partners, a number of close bankers, Wiltshire neighbours, Members of Parliament, economists and Robert Southey.[21]

Morrison lacked an assured public voice and disliked the heckling of the Commons. He preferred to debate with like-minded individuals, over dinner or at the Political Economy Club (later at the Reform Club). His close circle comprised some of the most advanced radical thinkers of the day: economists, philosophers, politicians and statisticians, including Nassau Senior, Edwin Chadwick, James and John Stuart Mill and Joseph Hume, who pushed reform of Parliament, local government and the Poor Law. He was on Robert Owen's visiting list. Owen dropped in for breakfast on 26 June 1833 to lobby him and presumably try to raise money: 'the world soon to be altered', he optimistically informed Morrison, 'provincial machinery about to be set up everywhere'. Morrison also brought together tradesmen, merchants and bankers to discuss free trade and overseas investment.

He was in Fonthill when the Palace of Westminster caught fire on 16 October 1834. The King dismissed Melbourne's government the following month (Melbourne had replaced Earl Grey in June) and a general election was called. Neither Morrison nor his parliamentary ally Joseph Hume were particularly enthusiastic about standing. Hume confessed he would like to retire 'but could not do so while the Tories were in the field'. Morrison went to Ipswich in December 'to <u>decline a seat</u> in the next Parliament, but the Committee could not find another man who would have done as my successor; and neither Whigs nor Radicals in London could assist them. I am therefore <u>of necessity</u> in the thick of it.'[22]

His fellow candidate Rigby Wason suddenly fell seriously ill, leaving him 'all the speaking to do'. He wrote on 5 January 1835 from Ipswich to Mary Ann: 'our majority remains about 80 and we have nothing to fear but bribery, of which our friends are a little afraid ... don't be surprised if we are beat – every effort is made by our opponents to pick up a single Vote – and to reduce our promises ... Now I am in it I shant like to be beat – but if I am I shall feel more happy when I get home with you & the children.' He was right to fear bribery, for the Tory candidates Robert Dundas and Fitzroy Kelly won, to the surprise of all, by a narrow majority. The *Suffolk Chronicle* described the methods of the Tory electioneers: 'bribery, the most open, intimidation, the most glaring, oppression, the most galling and coercion, the most abominable.'[23] Morrison's son Charles was more philosophical: 'Father will now have an excellent opportunity of going to bed early, improving Fonthill, & philosophizing upon the mutability of political dignities, & the fickleness of public opinion.'

Charles also asked 'how did it happen? ... did the Tory candidates come in by bribery?' Mary Ann replied, 'we hear the [Tory] fund at the Carlton Club is or was two million ... Simms, our tailor, came on the outside of a coach from Kent with a man who had just received forty pounds. Intoxicated with his success he said he minded not how soon the King died or a change of Ministers, that he might get another as good a bribe.'[24]

Morrison and Wason had been gathering evidence of bribery in Ipswich throughout the election and presented their petition to a committee of the House of Commons. Some of the individuals they required to be questioned had disappeared to the continent and taken false names before warrants could be served. However, Morrison's solicitor Ashurst and his clerk managed to round them up to face questioning from the committee, the petition was successful and the two MPs were found 'by their friends and agents guilty of Bribery and Corruption.'[25]

The by-election in June was reported by Charles Dickens for the *Morning Chronicle*. Morrison's young son Alfred, who joined his father and brother

Charles in Ipswich, later described seeing 'the bright figure of the young Dickens, who had been sent down specially by Sir J. Easthope – then proprietor of the *Chronicle* – to report the speeches; he came into the Committee Rooms at the White Horse to consult about forwarding the speeches to town'.[26] Dickens had also covered the earlier general election in Suffolk and Essex and found plenty of material to use for the Eatanswill election in *Pickwick Papers*.

Charles Morrison provided a description of the lively reception given by the Liberals of Ipswich on his father's return for the by-election. Once again the horses were removed from Morrison's carriage, half a mile from Ipswich:

a number of Flags, devices, &c went before us, with a band of music, of which nothing but the drum was audible; there was abundance of green boughs, & of course deafening shouting. Various popular houses were cheered, as Mr May's; unpopular ones were groaned at, & here & there a window was broken, but not half a dozen I should think in the whole town. In addition to the usual demonstrations, they kept firing off guns or pistols: & I fear the magistrates talked of calling out the police to stop the firing. ... We made the circuit of the town, as I suppose & were then brought back to the marketplace, where a <u>rostrum</u> adorned with boughs, had been erected out of the 2nd floor of a grocer's. The multitude assembled beneath. You know that I am an exceedingly bad judge of numbers, but from a very rude kind of calculation I supposed there were from 3 to 4000 present. Father then made a short speech. Mr Wason followed & made a rather longer one, in which he certainly did not mince the matter. He mentioned all the names now so familiar to the Committee, Cooke, Clamp ... & told some anecdotes to them. Father had attributed the chief honour of our success to Wason, for his perseverance & activity. Wason did not decline the praise, but said that if he had been the more liberal in personal activity, Father had supplied the <u>money</u>. The mob of course received both with sufficient enthusiasm.[27]

Back in Parliament, Morrison took the initiative on 17 May 1836 in introducing a railway bill proposing that the state intervene in the running of railways: he moved 'a resolution relative to the periodical revision of tolls and charges levied on railroads and other public works'.[28] He believed Parliament 'should have the power to examine into the whole management and affairs of each [railway] company, to correct what may have been amiss in the former, and to fix the rates of charge for another period of years'. Above all he wanted to protect the public. 'When peculiar privileges, and a substantial monopoly, are conferred on any set of persons, the public interests ought always to be secured against their abuse.'

On this occasion Morrison allowed his speech to be published, sending personal copies to the usual mixture of family, Fonthill neighbours, journalists, bankers, Fore Street partners, economists and merchants.[29] He also chose as the question for debate at the Political Economy Club 'Is it desirable that Railroads should be made a strict monopoly for a fixed number of years?' However, his pride in his speech and confidence in winning over Parliament were misguided. He had been successful in manoeuvring his colleagues towards the founding of a school of design (and giving Papworth the job of director) but on this occasion he misread the commercial implications of legislation which might affect the vested interests of a large number of MPs. He was accused of damaging confidence and threatening the value of railway shares. 'By the mere introduction of [his bill] a panic had been created throughout the country.' 'Doubts were entertained in high quarters as to the advisableness of interfering with new undertakings, by which capitalists might be deterred from embarking in them.'[30]

At the same time he was attacked in public by the Irish MP Daniel O'Connell. Radicals in Ipswich invited O'Connell, who was touring the country complaining of injustices to Ireland, to address a political dinner in the town. Morrison and Rigby Wason, the two sitting MPs, could not turn down their invitations, as Morrison explained to his son Charles: 'I am sorry O'Connell is going to Ipswich, but I could not help it. They asked me to a dinner, and I of course accepted. They were at liberty to ask any other person: it was their affair, not mine.' The crowds that assembled in the town reflected all political opinions and O'Connell chose to use the opportunity to attack both MPs: 'If having elected your representatives they voted against free institutions for Ireland and against your rights and privileges, when they came for re-election you would tell them you had had enough of Morrison's Pills and Wason's Black Draughts.'[31] *Morison's* Pills were of course invented not by James Morrison, but by the quack James Morison, but his reputation in the constituency was seriously damaged. Meanwhile in the House of

Commons there was a 'flare up' over his proposal to regulate the railways, and, after a 'murderous' attack, he withdrew the bill.

He was more successful outside Parliament as a member of the committee which founded the Reform Club. The first meeting was at 14 Carlton House Terrace, the home of his friend Edward Ellice, on 8 February 1836; the aim to create an alternative to Brooks's, the traditional Whig club, which continued to block the membership of radicals. 'Talent, not birth, was the key to membership' of the Reform, and the club was so successful it became the preferred 'rendezvous of Whigs, Whig-Radicals, Radicals, Ultra-Radicals, Chartists, et hoc genus omne.'[32] It was home from home for Morrison, with members including Dillon, Ashurst, George Crow and Alexander Galloway, Henry Fearon, Henry and Richard Dann (relations of Mary Ann's step-mother), the businessmen William Downes and William Leaf, M.D. Hill, Frederick Hill and the banker Abraham Robarts; Christians, Jews (Lionel Rothschild), dissenters, industrialists, architects, writers.

The club's palatial building in Pall Mall, designed by Charles Barry, was opened in 1841. The interior design provided another familiar reference point for Morrison with plenty of gold. It was significant as club and building: 'a private institution which has shaped the political history of this country, housed in a building of rare beauty and major architectural significance. The origins of modern party politics; the transition from Whiggery to Liberalism; the Renaissance revival in High Victorian architecture – all these themes are embedded in the club's history.'[33] Morrison was a member for life.

He maintained some commitment to Parliament for a while longer. In December the *Suffolk Chronicle* reported a speech in which he defended his record as a radical:

He had voted for the abolition of military flogging and the reduction in the newspaper tax. He repeated his arguments in favour of the ballot. He opposed tithes, which he expected soon to be abolished, and he objected to episcopal membership of the House of Lords. He had supported the reduction in the use of the death penalty. He suggested some alterations to the existing corn law was necessary. While he favoured the introduction of the Poor Law into Ireland, which he believed would end starvation there, he regretted that outdoor relief had been refused to those of good character.[34]

Nevertheless, by the time the next general election was called, following the death of William IV on 20 June 1837, Morrison had decided to leave Parliament. He was no longer confident of the support of the Ipswich electors and the Whig government would discover it had lost the support of the country.[35] His son Alfred wrote to Mary Ann from Edinburgh, 'I heard it very gravely stated the other day … that Father was too wise a man to trust himself in an Election for Ipswich & that the Tories were going to walk over the course'.

In the end Morrison was absent from the Commons for only three years. However, since 1836 he had been deeply committed to a completely new venture, which was already threatening to wipe out a large part of his fortune. His complicated commercial relations with America would dominate his and his family's lives for many years.

CHAPTER ELEVEN

'The American Project'

> Credit has bought our land, built our cities, cleared our fields, founded our
> churches, erected our colleges and schools.
> The Governor of Ohio, 1837, in Bodenham, *History of Banking*, 2000

In 1833 James Morrison was forty-four years old. He was an MP in the reformed Parliament, respected by the government for his knowledge of trade and finance. He and Mary Ann and their seven children moved between their luxurious town house in Harley Street and the picturesque Fonthill estate in Wiltshire. He was worth about £700,000, of which £300,000 was invested in his Fore Street business. His income for the year comprised £66,000 from Fore Street plus £19,000 made up of rentals from agricultural estates and properties in London, interest payments from mortgages and loans and a small number of investments.[1] This was a large income, more than most aristocrats' and the equivalent in today's money of almost £8 million. He delighted in hearing of the power of Fore Street on his European travels, jotting down in his diary flattering remarks made by government ministers and aristocrats. 'Lord Hatherton told me at Brook's that the Countess & Duchess of Sutherland had lately said to him that she wish'd her Grandson (Lord Stafford) was my partner.'

He could have chosen to enjoy a life of comfort and ease, buying more art treasures, travelling in Europe with his wife and children, attending meetings of the Political Economy Club and the council of London University. His American friend Mrs Andrew Stevenson certainly thought, after a visit to Fonthill, that he had every right to feel content with his lot: 'Mr Morrison is a Member of Parliament, immensely wealthy, which of course gives him what all men covet, power, & influence, & when to this you add health, a well regulated mind & temper, with the most perfect domestic happiness & prosperity, I think you will admit he has nothing more to desire in the world. His manners are very pleasant & amiable, his conversation sensible & entertaining, & he has strong prejudices in favour of us Americans.'[2]

Instead he undertook a new project which he knew to be highly risky: he formed a merchant bank[3] with an American partner, John Cryder. Commentators at the time marvelled at the state of the American economy, 'prosperous beyond example', but the downturn that followed was 'rapid and alarming'.[4] Morrison found himself caught up in a major financial crisis which overwhelmed merchant houses and individuals on either side of the Atlantic and would last from 1836 to 1841.

In trying to work out why Morrison was unnaturally rash, the question arises as to whether he simply wanted more money, if not for himself then for his family. The terms of his lengthy will confirm he intended to leave each of his children their own substantial inheritance (daughters as well as sons), so he needed to find new sources of wealth. Did he also relish taking on the established merchant banks like Barings? The nickname in the City for his own newly formed bank, Morrison, Cryder & Co., was 'Over-Baring'. On the other hand, was he perhaps bored by merely running Fore Street and buying property and convinced (like many British investors) that the American venture was a safe bet? David Kynaston, historian of the City of London, observed:

> Even Morrison, one of the shrewdest businessmen of the age, underestimated the dangers involved. Three were paramount: dependence on the continuing buoyancy of American trade; the problem in the pre-telegraph era of granting acceptance credits to traders beyond the realm of personal knowledge; and the increasing tendency of London houses to grant 'open credit', in other words accepting bills of exchange unsecured by invoices or bills of lading.[5]

Two men encouraged Morrison's early interest in investing in North America, both fellow Liberal MPs with a background in trade and finance. John Easthope, MP for Banbury, rose from modest clerk in a provincial bank to become a wealthy stockbroker, magistrate, Chairman of the London and South-Western Railway Company and the Mexican Mining Company. In 1834 he bought the failing liberal newspaper *Morning Chronicle* for £16,500 and in 1841 he was made a baronet.[6] In January 1833 he persuaded Morrison to buy shares in the Canada Land Company (he was a director) and by 1836 Morrison's holding was worth over £3,000.

Edward Ellice, MP for Coventry, was brother-in-law to the Prime Minister Earl Grey, government whip and joint Secretary to the Treasury. He had even closer ties with Canada than Easthope. His father had founded the Hudson Bay Company and he personally owned Beauharnois Seigneur, a large estate near Montreal. In March 1833 Ellice described the opportunities on the Beauharnois estate, Morrison taking notes: 'population 9566 – of which Catholic 6529 Protestants of all kinds 3037 – some years ago it would have been difficult to collect 5000 bushels of Potatoes – in 1830 – 147,000 bushels. [Ellice] thinks 75,000 bushls of wheat. The wool of their sheep forms the winter clothing of nearly the whole of the Canadian Country population – everything is done by hand & all at home ... 12 British schools, 7 Canadian.' Morrison's notes failed to mention the political dimension to the settlement, British emigrants being encouraged to settle to swell the numbers of English-speakers and reduce the power of the French Canadians. Easthope's company had a similar political agenda.

The hearings of the Select Committee on Manufactures, Commerce and Shipping, lasting through May and June 1833, provided Morrison with more detail about the potential for investing in North America. The American banker Timothy Wiggin, when asked 'Is it easy for a man without capital, but with good character and conduct, to embark largely in business in the American trade?' replied, 'I think there never was a time when he could do it with more facility than now.'[7] Joshua Bates, partner at Barings,[8] spoke of the ideal location of London for such trade: 'There is no place in Europe where such an assortment of goods can be collected together ... any person wishing to begin an operation to a distant country must, I think, begin it here.'[9]

While Morrison was addressing Parliament in January 1834 about the positive state of British exports, including the sale of iron to build American railroads, he borrowed from Samuel Gurney £20,000 to buy stock in Pennsylvania, the state which was the most advanced in building railroads.[10] In February he bought $50,000 of New Orleans City Bonds and 200 shares in the New Orleans Canal & Banking Co.; in May (with advice from Easthope) he invested £10,000 in the New Jersey Canal & Railroad Co. These were not insignificant amounts (though Rothschild's had bought 4,000 shares in the New Orleans Canal & Banking Co. the year before) but in January 1835, immediately after losing the election at Ipswich, Morrison began to consider a much larger and riskier investment opportunity. Gurney, whose firm was already a major promoter of American state securities in London,[11] introduced him to the American businessman John Cryder, who asked Morrison whether he would invest a substantial amount of capital to join him as a partner in a new 'house'.

Cryder was the first of the group of American merchant bankers with whom Morrison worked closely over the next decade (Peabody remains the most famous). Based in Valparaiso with William Shepard Wetmore and Richard Alsop, Cryder had done 'all the English and American business of the old Chilean city [Valparaiso]'.[12] He then followed Wetmore to Canton to trade in tea (the East India Company lost its monopoly of China tea in 1833), Alsop returning to Philadelphia as their principal agent and also establishing his own bank, which continued to deal with Chile: 'it was notorious for many years, that Alsop & Co, every five years, made a profit of over a million of dollars'.[13] Morrison heard from Cryder that his business in Canton and Valparaiso in the year October 1833 to October 1834 had earned almost £300,000, while he believed their dealing in American stocks could produce a profit of £5,000 per annum. Meanwhile Morrison asked around his banking acquaintances to find out more about his potential partner. Timothy Wiggin's trading house was one of the few significant Anglo-American houses in the City; he was also a neighbour of Morrison in Harley Street and had made a fortune in textiles in Manchester.[14] He assured Morrison that Cryder was well educated as a merchant and a person of high character, 'understands he has about 25,000£ he had little to begin with at Canton but believes he will get a fortune'.

Discussions were lengthy and coincided with the parliamentary investigation into bribery at the Ipswich election. Morrison suggested 'that an experiment might be made for a year', then in May both agreed to do business only with 'large & first rate houses'. Recommending that Morrison charge the house a rate of 4½% interest on his capital investment, Gurney also agreed to provide credit up to £100,000 and to arrange through the Rothschilds the availability of credit across Europe. An agent was hired to work in India, Richard Alsop became the company's agent for 'consignments, credits, and securities' in Philadelphia and Francis J. Oliver in Boston.[15] Wetmore was the essential link at the Canton (tea) end. In London Morrison did his best to negotiate with the East India Company which still exerted control over the Canton exchange even though its monopoly had ended.[16] He called on Sir James Carnac, a director of the company and a Harley Street neighbour, and also on his friend James Mill at India House 'about security of goods from Canton'.

Cotton was the other major commodity traded by Morrison, Cryder & Co. At the time the southern states of America were enjoying a cotton boom;[17] between 1815 and 1840 cotton production increased from 100 million to nearly 1,000 million pounds; by 1840 exports had reached $3.5 million.[18] Morrison had heard at the 1833 Select Committee of the profits to be made. Gabriel Shaw, of Thomas Wilson & Co., handled silk, wool and cotton on a commission basis. Giving evidence at the committee, he testified that 'a party shipping cotton from the United States to England upon his own account, is deriving a profit of from five to ten per cent at this moment'.[19]

The role of the port of Liverpool was key. The receipts from the sales in the port (where three-quarters of the cotton came from America) were 'the most important single item in the American international merchandise accounts'. The 'Liverpool cotton market registered the world demand and supply, it also reflected the outlook for trade in cotton cloth and the speculative sentiments of cotton speculators and so-called cotton dealers.' According to one New York politician writing in 1837, 'The fall of one penny per pound in the price of cotton is equal to a diminution of means to meet engagements of Ten Millions of Dollars.'[20] Coincidentally Mary Ann Morrison's half-brother Thomas Todd was in need of a job, after losing much of his inheritance speculating in textiles. He was set up in Liverpool with £6,000 from Morrison, his role to handle the sales of the consignments of cotton in which Morrison, Cryder & Co. had a financial stake. Todd was to be 'quite independent of us [Morrison, Cryder & Co.] and we independent of him, to do business with him at Liverpool & he with us as long as mutually beneficial'. Todd's position (and the company's) was strengthened further when he joined Jackson's of New Orleans and Philadelphia, which had 'good connexions [with] planters who are considerable shippers of cotton'; the business was renamed Jackson, Todd & Co.[21]

Morrison, Cryder & Co. opened for business on 1 January 1836. An office was taken in Broad Street and a bank account opened at Robarts. Cryder's capital investment was almost £75,000, Morrison's almost £200,000 including £80,000 worth of American stock. At the time, £100,000 was a large amount of capital for a British merchant bank.[22] Morrison, Cryder & Co. immediately became one of the elite group of seven Anglo-American houses which together financed almost the whole of American trade: W. & J. Brown & Co.; Barings; Lizardi & Co.; Timothy Wiggin & Co.; Thomas Wilson & Co. and George Wildes & Co. Brown's was the largest with seven partners and capital of £1.2 million; Wildes the smallest with four partners and capital of £200,000. All sought to gain a 'market share in the financing of transatlantic trade'.[23]

For the first six months all went well. Morrison's sound credit rating and his network of professional colleagues and acquaintances in textiles, banking, credit and Parliament, were of great significance. He was trusted, like Disraeli's Mr Vigo, the tailor in *Endymion* who became an MP, chairman of a railway company and extremely rich. Vigo 'bought estates, hired moors, lavished his money, not only with profusion, but with generosity' but, even more like Morrison, he 'could command no inconsiderable amount of capital, and he had a following of obscure rich friends who believed in him, and did what he liked'.[24] Dinners at Harley Street were used by Morrison to share confidences and test the market as he brought together directors of the Bank of England and private bankers, interested MPs and members of the government, suppliers of credit, his partners from Fore Street and his new American friends. Women were not excluded and Mary Ann Morrison was particularly close to Wetmore's sister, and to the wives of Joseph Hume, John Cryder (also a Wetmore) and the American Minister in London, Andrew Stevenson. Even Papworth joined the circle, working on Cryder's house in Regent's Park.[25] When Charles and Alfred were travelling in North America a few years later these contacts were invaluable.

Agents dropped in for breakfast at Harley Street on their way to and from Canton, Calcutta and Chile. The correspondence of Morrison, Cryder & Co. reveals details of the shipments in which the house invested, and their response to fluctuating prices and demand.[26] For example, Messrs Filter &

Delmerins in Paris received instructions in March 1836 to select French goods to the value of £10,000 'best adapted to the Markets of Chile & Peru'. The 'barque *Valparaiso*' was en route from America with cotton and tobacco for Liverpool from where it would sail to Bordeaux to pick up the selected luxuries before again crossing the Atlantic. 'As silks are enormously dear we agree with you as to substituting other articles likely to do better ... the Eau de Cologne, Porcelaine, Looking Glasses, saddles, Cuckillos Flamingoes ... 1000 Boxes Claret would not be amiss probably, and do you think some imitation Spanish Brandy might answer, now that none can be had in Spain.' Meanwhile the *Rosedale* was on its way from Canton via Singapore with 'green Teas the prospect for which is improving here [in London]. Green Teas will no doubt be run up high in China by reason of the large demand for the U States, here, they are gaining reputation fast.'[27] The more familiar teas imported from Canton and Hong Kong were orange pekoe, black leaf pekoe, campoi, bokea, congou and gunpowder. They were prone to damage: 'gnawn by cockroaches' appears regularly in the reports. Raw silk and silkworm cocoons were also vulnerable on the long sea voyages from Canton and Calcutta to London: reports listed 'worm eaten', 'sea damaged', 'mildewd', 'stained'.

Morrison, Cryder & Co. was also dealing in American state securities. The stock was attractive to British investors (including Morrison, who steadily increased his personal holding), appearing to be safe, with high interest rates often promptly paid. Their fierce promotion in London by 'financial inter-mediaries' including Overend, Gurney and the Anglo-American houses only added to their desirability.[28] However, there were risks attached, recognised by contemporaries on both sides of the Atlantic. An American politician writing at the time observed:

The rage for speculation in lands is great and hitherto has proved very lucrative to the adventurer. The mania for rail roads is without any bounds, there is scarcely a former bye path that is not converted into a rail road. It is marvellous to think where capital for such extensive operations can be procured, no doubt it proceeds from the facilities afforded by numerous banking institutions. But should a revulsion take place in the money market (an event very probable) it may be expected that a serious reaction must follow.[29]

On 11 July 1836, the administration of President Jackson issued the Specie Circular which permitted only specie (gold or silver) to be used to buy public lands.[30] When Americans, without sufficient supplies of gold themselves, turned to the Bank of England, the Bank, worried about its own diminishing gold reserves, raised its exchange rate.

For Morrison, the first sign of trouble coincided with the mauling of his railway bill in the Commons (see Chapter 10). He noted on 13 July, 'Cryder finds money getting scarce! Told him he must write Alsop [in Philadelphia] again not to enter into any engagements which would require shipment of bullion.' On 26 October, the Governor of the Bank of England summoned the partners of all the Anglo-American houses to explain his policy of maintaining gold reserves and not supporting their supplying of credit to America:

> The sentiments of the Court of Directors that the extensive Credits hitherto given to the Bankers of the United States and others, either as open Credits or in anticipation of the Sale of States Securities in this Country, are objectionable so far as the Bank of England is concerned in the issue of Bank Notes, and to request the concurrence of such houses in checking that system, which they deem to be prejudicial to the currency of the country.[31]

Morrison was in Fonthill, so missed the meeting at the Bank of England, but the effects were clear. Suddenly there were no buyers for American securities:

> The long period of American expansion, with an inflow of foreign goods and capital paid for by the issue of more and yet more stocks, was halted abruptly when the European investor lost interest and confidence in these securities. In the crisis that followed, American merchants found themselves unable to remit the huge sums owing to their European creditors, and brought down not only their own houses but the houses of their creditors as well.[32]

At first only small banks collapsed. Morrison noted the closure of the Agricultural and Commercial Bank of Ireland, Foster & Co. of Carlisle, and the merchant house of Douglas Anderson & Co.[33] His son Charles, an undergraduate at Cambridge, had no idea of the threat to his father's merchant bank: 'I am glad Broad St continues prosperous. Shall be glad when I come up to learn how the monied world has got on, as I am here in the midst of a set, who know no more of what passes there than of the politics of Timbuctoo.' The same month, December, Morrison made a settlement on his wife as if he anticipated problems ahead.

With the New Year the situation deteriorated rapidly: the price of cotton fell[34] and Richard Alsop wrote to Morrison from Philadelphia: 'pressure increasing, the blow up terrible … do as little as possible'. Three of the Anglo-American houses, Wiggin, Wilson and Wildes, known as the '3 Ws', had the most business tied up in America so were under the greatest threat and on 10 February 1837 Morrison repeated Cryder's words: 'Gurney had just told him G. Wildes & Co must go!' A plan was immediately hatched by the other houses to save Wildes. Morrison offered £10,000, Barings £20,000, then Gabriel Shaw at Wilson's proposed 'we should form an association (all the Houses) to accept for parties buying goods – as all!' And Morrison called on the Governor of the Bank of England to say 'the Bank must interfere … promptly'.

On 18 March Morrison wrote down exactly how much he was worth, how much in debt: 'my liabilities were less our debts less suspicious or dangerous our capital was one third of our acceptances & my personal property equal to the whole amount'.[35] There followed almost daily meetings and dinners with bankers, American merchants and politicians, as all the time he waited nervously for the packet boats to arrive in Liverpool with funds. Morrison's diary entries make painful reading: 'even the tea sale is going bad', 'why is the Money so tardy'; 'can breathe again in the city'; 'anxiously waiting for packet boats'; 'joy in the city'; 'news very blue, absolute Panic'. Joshua Bates of Barings writes to him on 21 May, 'Has known the business in US all his life & has been in London 16 years, never knew such a state of things before.'[36] The following day, when two more banks failed, Morrison seems to despair: 'god knows when this is to end!!' But after twenty-four hours he writes, 'in better spirits today – one sometimes sees the same things with the sun on them & at other times in shade, how different they appear!!'

On 30 May Morrison wrote: 'News from US horrible the Bank deliberating on the W's – and all consternation dismal forebodings no sleep all night.' He continued, 'Rascal [a packet boat] in at Liverpool news horrible second edition of the "Times" [published] just as the Bank met to decide on the W's – if this Packet had been a day later or the Times correspondent less vigilant the Bank would probably have done it but this destroyed everything, after 3 days discussion they decided no, & on morning 2 June they all stop'd!!' All three of the 'Ws' closed. Bell & Grant, Gowan & Marx followed, and with 'universal distrust as far as respects American Houses' Morrison decided to seek assistance from the Bank of England.

The 5th of June was a 'horrible day' as he was forced to take the deeds of his properties to the Bank and apply for a loan. The banker Glyn later commented: 'It must have been a bitter step.'[37] He asked for £350,000 but was offered only £300,000: 'Freshfield wish'd me to lower the amount or increase the security – I could do neither.' He finally received £325,000, an enormous loan for one individual.

On 9 June Morrison collected the first £100,000 from the Bank: 'another black day seeking comfort but finding none – these trials must be a warning to me as long as I live. ... The last ten days has been like a horrid dream! All the W's are gone and with them many others, indeed, as far as respects the American Houses, one looks about to see who is left standing, not who has fallen, the list is a brief one now!' However, he was aware of his unique position: the textile business in Fore Street provided real security, as Dillon was able to show when he drew up details of their trade from 1822 to 1836, 'a kind of epoch in the business.'[38] 'All who had not resources out of business like myself or opulent friends like Barings are gone. ... We shall of course lose & that I fear considerably, but we shall soon make it up.' Typically, Morrison could see the future financial advantages: 'A few of us must have all the business hereafter.'[39] But he was badly shaken, as he admitted to Richard Alsop, writing on 17 July: 'we shall pray for & hope for remittances out of the £300,000 owing us chiefly by dry goods people ... my independence has not been touched. Mr C [Cryder] has behaved extremely well during the whole time, he knew those who were indebted to us & I did not, the stake was an awful one for both but a life hitherto of constant prosperity has made me but ill prepared for the trials we have had to pass through.'[40]

The year 1838 brought renewed confidence as the 'British shouldered the heavy load of dead canals, railroads, state bonds and mortgages on deflated land.'[41] When Morrison took the decision 'no credit without security & no cash advances' he was repeating the views of Joshua Bates of Barings: 'We come to the conclusion that the present system of credits is one of extreme hazard, & that we should use great caution – not to keep goods on hand but to sell as fast as consignments arrive, & to cultivate our rich correspondents while we throw off the doubtful.'[42] Negotiating the extension of his partnership with Cryder, Morrison stressed that any new business had to be based on respectability and security. 'No scheming institutions & rag tag & bobtail dry goods people'. He was finally applying the standards which had stood him in such good stead in haberdashery.[43]

As business rallied,[44] Morrison – never one to miss an opportunity to increase his portfolio of investments – turned his attention from America to something more reliable: a large gentleman's estate and mansion in Berkshire. He had desired Basildon from the moment he first saw it, in the summer of 1830 (see Chapter 8). The grand Palladian mansion had been designed by John Carr in 1776 for the wealthy 'nabob' Sir Francis Sykes (1732–1804).[45] Sykes had survived Siraj-ud-Daula and the Black Hole of Calcutta to make a fortune of £700,000 with the East India Company in Bengal. He died, however, before the interior of Basildon was completed and his son and grandson (the second and third baronets) lacked the health, wealth or interest to complete Carr's designs.[46] The third baronet, also Sir Francis, raised a mortgage on the property when he came of age but used the money to fund an expensive lifestyle following the Prince of Wales' Carlton House set. In 1829,[47] he failed to sell the 'noble' estate (shortly before Morrison bought the Fonthill estate as 'second best') so the mansion was let in its unfinished state to a series of tenants including Byron's friend Sir John Cam Hobhouse.

Sykes put it on the market again in 1838 following the social disgrace of his 'headstrong, wilful and passionate' wife Henrietta.[48] Both the baronet and society had tolerated Henrietta's affair with the novelist and rising politician Benjamin Disraeli, conducted in part at Basildon. However, Sykes' discovery of his wife and the artist Daniel Maclise 'in flagrante delicto' (Maclise had completed a family portrait shortly before) was the final straw; Henrietta was barred for ever from society.[49]

Morrison first visited in July 1838 while inspecting his estate at Cholsey. He tried out the brand-new Great Western Railway which had opened from Paddington as far as Maidenhead the previous month. Construction was continuing through to Steventon, passing between Basildon Park and the

River Thames, with stations at Pangbourne, Goring and Wallingford Road. Morrison appreciated the fact that Basildon would be less than an hour from the capital (his shady lawyer Isaac Sewell had pointed out a decade before that Fonthill was too far from London).

> We shall soon not want a Town House. In three years all the best Physicians will recommend a ride in a steam carriage an hour before dinner as much better than a ride in the Park, and my cards will run thus; Train off at 6; dinner on table 7 precisely; return steam up at ½ past 10; carriages to Paddington at ¼ past 11; Brunel and 50 miles an hour![50]

Mr Washbourne, Morrison's agent at Cholsey, sent him news of interested parties. 'A person from Tewkesbury has been looking over Basildon.' 'I now hear Mr Benyon de Beauvoir is not likely to buy … Mr Fuller Maitland is now spoken of as being desirous of it.'[51] At the auction the property was 'bought in' at £79,500 but then a Mr Thomson emerged with an offer of £78,000. Washbourne wrote: 'if you lose the chance of buying it now the opportunity may never again offer', and Morrison immediately sent his agent James Combes over from Fonthill. Combes' letter by return was a powerful influence:

> If you now let this property slip you will in my opinion hereafter regret it –
> I have been thinking a good deal about it lately probably another such an opportunity for your making a Political interest may never occur during your life or the lifetime of your Sons, therefore if you want Political power <u>buy it</u>, for you will never obtain it at a cheaper Rate – You will never obtain political power without paying for it in some shape or other, but if you do not want such power, <u>then let it go</u> for land will never produce an income like other investments. … Basildon with Cholsey remember confers a great County interest, as well as a Borough one.

Morrison, who by now had been out of Parliament for a year, took Combes' advice, and the following day travelled cross-country to Basildon with Mary Ann and his two eldest sons.[52] In the evening he wrote to Washbourne 'with instructions to close at the price ask'd if he could not do better'.

Morrison signed the contract with Sykes' solicitor John Lake on 14 September. He would pay £76,000 plus a further £21,000 for the timber.[53]

Washbourne wrote from Cholsey: 'I am very glad to hear you are so well pleased with the purchase and whether a good bargain or otherwise in point of value, I cannot but consider it a very desirable acquisition to your Berkshire Property.'[54] Back in Wiltshire, the purchase attracted local comment. On a visit to Pythouse, Morrison found Mr Benett 'cordial in talking about my buying of Basildon – had 2 or 3 good offers for the [Fonthill] Abbey. Would I buy the Terrace?' With the purchase of Basildon Morrison was recognised to be a very rich man indeed.[55]

His elevated position was confirmed by the offer of a baronetcy the following year for a 'mere' £5,000. The offer came through Isaac Sewell, who had organised the financial arrangements with the Duke of Wellington's even more disreputable nephew Long-Wellesley for 'buying' a parliamentary seat at St Ives. 'I shod not have troubled you with any communication had I not been applied to within a few days past by a most respectable party with the offer of a Baronetcy & wch is to be had for a pecuniary consideration – no other condition – but £5000 is the Sum – is it worth your acceptance?'[56] Sewell continued in a second letter, Morrison having expressed doubts about the offer: 'there is no mistake about it – your name wod be at once accepted, and known as your property & principles are, the whole wod be accomplished without requiring the remotest pledge from you ... Shod you take the dignity you must make up your mind how you will be gazetted – whether of Fonthill or Basildon.'[57] Morrison discussed the subject with Abraham Robarts, a close banking friend: 'Robarts told me his father declined a Baronetcy chiefly at his mothers instigation he also declined one from Lord Grey.'[58] A baronetcy, unlike a peerage, did not come with a seat in the House of Lords. In Disraeli's novel *Sybil*, set in 1837, Sir Vavasour Firebrace, who is obsessed with obtaining a peerage, makes it perfectly clear a baronetcy is not worth the money. 'A baronetcy has become the distinction of the middle class; a physician, our physician for example, is a baronet ... and I daresay some of our tradesmen, brewers, or people of that class.'[59] Morrison was rich enough to buy Basildon and confident enough to turn down such an unimportant title – and did so.

When Morrison took the chair at the Political Economy Club on 6 December 1838 to discuss Nassau Senior's question 'What is the natural limit to the accumulation of capital?' he may have wondered what the limit might be for him. As usual he calculated his worth in his diary – just over £1.2 million (in today's values some £100 million). However, a few days later, he received a letter from his son Charles in Cambridge; he had decided not to attempt the examination for an honours degree.

> I write to you rather than in answer to my Mother, because I owe you the disagreeable explanation, wh must be the principal subject of this letter. I shall not distinguish myself at all in the Degree Examination, & have indeed for the last 3 weeks resolved not to go out in Honours at all. I am very sorry for this, as it will disappoint you – & this feeling with [the] extreme repugnance I have felt to do anything has prevented me from writing till now.

Charles had won prizes at Edinburgh University but at Cambridge he had been dogged by crippling migraines and difficulties reading, and now realised he 'cd not be the first man of my year', indeed 'I saw more clearly that I shd only get into that worst of all positions for a man's future prospects, a position of respectable mediocrity.' Urged by his father to take the examination, 'I took 2 Tutors, took to early rising, regular diet, regular exercise, & gave up everything but the subject wh I had to read for the Examination. I kept it up for about a month pretty well – but felt from the beginning that there was something wrong in my head, wh prevented me from making the strenuous exertion of the various faculties by wh I cd alone master a subject or retain it in the memory. At last my old head-ache came back – & I then abandoned everything.' James Mill had warned Morrison years before against sending Charles to Cambridge: 'it might spoil him for commerce'. Charles' description of his physical and mental state suggests a complete breakdown:

> I am now I think in a worse state than I have ever been – because tho I feel no pain, I am sensible of a drying up of the current of ideas such as I never before experienced, together with a strange sinking of my spirits, a sort of dullness of all sensations & feelings, wh is I suppose, what physicians call hypochondria. I did not give up the attempt to read till I felt the <u>impossibility</u> of doing so with any effect & am now waiting in a state of perfect inaction, till the power of my mind returns. For the present inefficiency of the latter, & the state of my nerves, eyes, & general health I am very much annoyed, & shd be as much alarmed, did not I make equanimity my

principle. ... This ends the first act of my life – & it is better that the curtain shd fall at once, than leave me to stammer & blunder thro the last speech. When it rises again, it must be with entirely new scenery & acting, & a very different audience, or it were better it shd not rise at all.[60]

In November 1839 Charles left for Italy, with no date set for his return.

Charles' collapse was a setback for Morrison, who had told Cryder he planned to remain in business for no more than three years, buying Charles in as an equal partner. Now, he went ahead on his own, setting up a new merchant house (after all, he had other sons to recruit into the business). He wrote in his diary on 1 January 1840: 'began the Broad St concern in my own name. I meant it as JM & Son but to please C [Cryder] I relinquish'd the Son for the present'. Not only Cryder had objected. Charles wrote from Italy on 12 January, 'it is better that my name is not on the doors of yr new Counting House ... . there wd have been no use in giving me the character of a merchant till I can support it'. On 3 February James Morrison & Co. moved to 62 Moorgate Street. Gabriel Shaw, formerly employed at the collapsed Anglo-American house Thomas Wilson & Co., became manager for a share of the profits.

Confidence in North America was slow to return, so with business quiet Morrison was persuaded to stand again for Parliament. A relatively safe seat in Scotland was about to become vacant so in the company of his backer Edward Ellice, Morrison embarked on an exhausting journey to Inverness (it was still winter in the north) to present himself to the electorate. Arriving at Edinburgh he expressed relief to Mary Ann: 'all 4 rooms ready at our old Hotel how comfortable after travelling more than 400 miles 32 hours sitting in a carriage to find a clean room & a good fire & a good bed (altho a hard mattress)'. He reached Inverness at 2.30 in the morning: 'after a ride of 21 hours the moon & the snow made it almost as light as day – I am here 600 miles from home, half the distance between London & Rome.'

His speech was reported in the *Inverness Courier*:

He had travelled in Switzerland and Germany and seen mountains and lakes; but in witnessing those of Scotland he had experienced emotions which he had never felt before, and which he could only account for by believing that there was some mysterious affinity between the present and the past which had stirred up all the Scotch blood in his veins.[61]

While his reference to his 'Scotch blood' was politically calculating rather than genetically accurate, at least one banker called him the 'wiley Scotchman' in a private letter, suggesting he may already have drawn on the Morrison ancestry.[62] He was genuinely attached to the country (sending his elder sons to Edinburgh University), he found the people 'quiet & reasonable in their politics & all are very kind to me', the mountains 'glorious', the trout from Loch Leven 'beautiful'. He confessed to Mary Ann, 'I wish'd I had had you all on an open carg. in the highlands yesterday – it would have been … surprises to all – although Doll [Walter] would have blink'd at the cold a little & Dibs [George] nose would have turn'd blue.' As always, he was missing his wife and children: 'how I should have liked to have turn'd out all the young ones to have a good run to day by the sea side'.

While Morrison was still in Scotland, the sitting MP for Inverness and the Burghs applied for the Chiltern Hundreds. Morrison remained to fight the by-election and defeated the Tory candidate. He described the occasion for his daughter Ellen and, through her, his baby son George:

My dear Ellen

I was going to write this to your little brother George, because altho he is a very little boy now[63] he may some day, when he is a man, become a Member of Parliament himself, but as it will be a long time before he will be able to read this and you can read now I write this to you instead of him and beg you to keep this till you are an old woman.

I was at 12 oclock to day proclaim'd Member for this district of Burghs before a great crowd of people in the Market Place the opposite windows being full of ladies and little girls and boys, and I had to make a long speech to them. We had flags, a band of music and every body was very happy. … I am now the Representative in Parliament for 4 Burghs, or Towns. One of them is Fortrose in the County of Cromarty, another is Forres in the County of Moray or Morayshire. Nairn is in the County of Nairn. You will find all these places on the Map of Scotland. The principal Town of the four is Inverness and there the Election takes place.

This City, for I think they call it a City, is a beautiful place or rather in a beautiful situation. The sea comes up close to it and there are mountains cover'd with snow near it and some of the finest Lakes or Lochs as they call them here are in the neighbourhood. The battle of Culloden was fought about two miles from the town. Macbeth murder'd Duncan in a castle close by the Town, and there are some fine old places which are call'd Vitrified forts.

Your affectionate father

J Morrison

Setting off for London, he sent a note ahead to Mary Ann: 'Let the Carriage be at the station on Monday morning when the Mail train arrives & Mrs Cameron up to open the door & shew me how much George is grown.' Morrison's love of his wife and family was intense. He disliked lengthy night sittings in Parliament which deprived him of evenings at home and he had been away in the north for a month.

On his return to his merchant house in Moorgate Street Morrison found himself being tempted, once more, to invest in an American venture, exhilarated perhaps by his success in Scotland. The charismatic Samuel Jaudon, agent for the Second Bank of the United States, was visiting London and the continent seeking new sources of credit. He approached Morrison to see whether his house would take on the agency of the bank, previously handled by Barings.

The Second Bank of the United States (BUS), based in Philadelphia, had been under a federal charter from the American government from 1816 to 1836, then under charter from the state of Pennsylvania. Nicholas Biddle retired from the presidency of the bank in 1839 but still wielded influence in Congress. The bank was America's largest business enterprise[64] and at the height of Biddle's power his influence had been comparable to that of the American President.[65] Jaudon, operating in London as the bank's agent, had been marketing 'whole rafts of American securities since 1838, on the back of an apparently recovering economy',[66] and by 1839, $200 million of American securities were owned in England.[67] Jaudon had been on business and social terms with Morrison and Cryder since the beginning of 1839, and the house had handled a large number of his American securities.[68]

Morrison was suspicious of a closer relationship, as he explained to his son Charles, who was still in Italy, but making a gradual recovery, in part through following his father's financial dealings:

Everything in the U.S. continues as bad as possible ... Most of the dry goods men have lost all they had, and now the Banks are suffering awfully ... The planters [cotton] and Banks in the South are alike bad. I have been very much pressed by Alsop and by others to take the Bank [of the USA] ac/t, but I have finally decided to adjourn the question to the Autumn. I have done this because her credit is now so low that it would be a bad time to begin; because my arrangements here are not ripe; and finally because I cannot help doubting Jaudon's cordiality in the matter.[69]

Morrison was more confident when agreeing a loan to Jaudon of £100,000 at the advantageous rate of 11%. As he explained to Charles, 'I am doing well with the capital'.

On 11 September Morrison and Jaudon drew up a further agreement, Jaudon depositing bonds and securities to the value of just over half a million pounds to secure advances in cash from Morrison.[70] Charles doubted the immediate realisable value of the securities. The Reading Railroad was possibly one of the better investments: 'if this RR escapes from the financial embarrassment out of wh it is now struggling into perfect life, & if it can really get the great mass of the coal traffic at a profit, its success will be fully established within less than 2 yrs.'[71] He would have preferred his father to pay back the money he had borrowed to purchase the Basildon estate.

Meanwhile, and to the surprise of the whole Morrison family, Alfred declared that one year at Cambridge University was sufficient. Instead he wished to join his father and pursue a career in the City. This spurred Charles to agree to be formally involved, the house was quickly renamed Morrison, Sons & Co.[72] and Morrison agreed to take on the agency of the BUS.

Alfred, new to both business and American politics, was hopelessly optimistic: 'should we be connected in any way with the U.S. Bank, which will most probably be the government bank, we should in that way be immediately connected with the U.S. government.' The Morrisons hoped that with the Whigs in power in America (President Harrison and Vice-President John Tyler) there was a real chance the BUS would again be chartered as a government central bank. On 23 January Morrison signed an agreement with the BUS to provide credit of about £700,000 (the equivalent of $3.77 million)[73] against BUS securities valued at £2.75 million. To raise such a large amount

Morrison borrowed, in turn, from Brown, Shipley & Co. and Denison & Co.[74] The *Morning Post* reported the event in terms flattering to Morrison:

> The new agency commences with a deposit in its hands of the sum of 750,000£ sterling to face the drafts which are to be passed upon it from the United States, the cash having been realised out of a portion of the mass of those American securities with which the United States Bank imprudently encumbered itself. The transfer of the agency to a house of the well known opulence of that of the possessor of the Fonthill and other valuable estates is an arrangement which is undoubtedly calculated to aid the concern most materially in extricating itself from its embarrassments.[75]

But the arrangement lasted for less than a fortnight. On 4 February the BUS finally collapsed, unable to meet its interest payments or the demands for gold. The total losses to foreigners holding shares in the BUS at the time has been calculated as $25 million.[76] Morrison was left owing thousands to his fellow bankers and owed thousands by the BUS.

When Charles wrote to his mother from Rome on 15 April he was unaware of the seriousness of the situation:

> If that affair [the BUS] & our connection with the Institution generally is managed on our part with dignity, & ended profitably, it will be a great thing, not so much for the profit, wh, to Father at least, is of little consequence, as for the display of his <u>power</u>, & the removing whatever bad impressions may remain either in U.S. or in the City from the early mismanagement & obscure termination of the old house under Cryder.

On 19 April Morrison scribbled in his diary: 'this & tomorrow the heavy Bank days'. And a couple of weeks later, once he had grasped the true situation, Charles wrote with grave concern:

> I have been very uneasy with the thought that principally for my sake and Alfred's you had increased your interest in America securities by so immense amount ... by far the greater part of your colossal fortune now rests mainly on the value of America stocks, that is on the good faith and ability to pay off the State governments ... I hope you will have an

opportunity of getting clear again of the Yankees. ... It will then be the time for Alfred and myself to consider whether we ought to consent that for the sake of giving us an occupation and some thousands a year of profits, you should bring your splendid and solid fortune within the sucking of that gulf of foreign loans and foreign speculation which has swallowed up so many millions and tens of millions of English capital.

Although Charles could not help but express a pride in his father's gamble, 'the Yankee ought to regard you as a great national benefactor for having protected in various ways such an amount of their stocks at such a time'.

The impact on the American economy was disastrous: 'work stopped on railways and canals, people were thrown out of work, banks closed their doors, and depression settled over the western part of the US'. In Britain, investors saw their securities rendered worthless. 'In 1839, $200 million of American securities were owned in England, and by 1841, when the Bank of the United States failed, $120 million of these were in danger of suspension.'[77] 'Since the States had depended on the Bank of the United States for loans to meet interest payments, since most states could no longer borrow abroad to pay the interest, and since the returns on the underlying investments were virtually non-existent, in 1841 and 1842 eight American states and one territory stopped interest payments.'[78]

Though retired, Nicholas Biddle was considered personally responsible by the banking community.

[The BUS, by its] reckless loans to unprincipled and wild speculators [had been] a curse to the steady and honest Merchant and Tradesman who can only regret its disastrous end on account of the loss and suffering it may bring on many a widow and orphan. ... If Mr Biddle could live a century longer and devote all his talents and energies to good he could not repair the evil he has occasioned.[79]

Americans in London were cut, including Morrison's friend George Peabody who was refused admission to the Reform Club because 'he was a citizen of a nation that did not pay its debts'.[80] The Revd Sydney Smith, Canon of St Paul's, had bought 'safe' securities in the state of Pennsylvania which was now defaulting on interest payments and he confessed an extreme reaction whenever he met anyone from that particular state:

> a disposition to seize and divide him – to allot his beaver to one sufferer and his coat to another – to appropriate his pocket handkerchief to the orphan, and to comfort the widow with his silver watch, Broadway rings, and the London Guide which he always carries in his pockets. How such a man can set himself down at an England table without feeling that he owes two or three pounds to every man in the company, I am at a loss to conceive. He has no more right to eat with honest men than a leper has to eat with clean.[81]

In the summer of 1841, the BUS finally assigned its securities 'to provide for the payment of sundry persons and bodies corporate which the Bank is at present unable to pay'.[82] Morrison's portfolio was valued at £1 million. Charles was reassured, writing on 3 June: 'I no longer feel any uneasiness about the BUS affair, since I have understood the particulars – still I think it is a question worth a serious consideration, what proportion of your fortune you ought to leave dependent on the security of such a nation as the Yankees, whether by investment in stocks, by acceptances, bonds or in any other shape.'

That question was to be decided in part by Charles and Alfred, who set out to North America to represent Morrison, Sons & Co. during the lengthy liquidation of the BUS. They were eventually successful in achieving a final settlement, though not until June 1843. Their travels are the subject of the next chapter.

CHAPTER TWELVE

❦

Letters from America, 1841–1845

Alfred Morrison left Liverpool on 5 October 1841 on board the steam packet
Columbia, reaching Boston three weeks later.[1] It was a rough crossing and
Alfred compared his experience confined in the fore cabin with forty passengers, 'all the hatches & doorways closed', to being incarcerated in the Black
Hole of Calcutta. Most of the passengers were French Canadians and
Americans returning from their European travels; also agents of Liverpool
cotton houses, 'a gambling set'. Alfred's companion was the wealthy China
merchant William Shepard Wetmore, one of his father's closest business
associates. Alfred also made use of a letter of introduction from his father to
another passenger, Lord Morpeth, who had been Chief Secretary for Ireland
until defeated in the general election.

Alfred was just twenty-one years old. He had only spent one year in
his father's merchant house under the watchful eye of Gabriel Shaw but
he was to investigate and attempt to realise the assets assigned to Morrison
Sons & Co. following the liquidation of the Bank of the United States. The
responsibility was considerable. Morrison and Shaw wrote regularly with
advice but communication with London took several weeks, sometimes
months, so Alfred often had to take decisions for himself about which
securities to sell to pay off his father's enormous loan (£700,000, including
£250,000 borrowed from Overend, Gurney & Co.) and which to keep.

Charles, recovered from his mental and physical breakdown, reluctantly
crossed the Atlantic in May 1842 to join Alfred, but his better financial brain
brought their tortuous negotiations to a satisfactory conclusion, leaving the

Morrisons with almost £1 million tied up in comparatively safe North American investments.

Before the Civil War North America was not often visited by the 'cream of English society'; it was not part of a European's Grand Tour. However, the 'human, material and cultural traffic between the two countries' was gradually increasing, as British businessmen in search of profit were taking to the steamboats and railroads criss-crossing North America.[2] James Morrison's Freethinking Christian friend Henry Bradshaw Fearon had travelled across the continent in 1818 to provide information for thirty-nine families considering emigrating and wrote *Sketches of America. A Narrative of a Journey of Five Thousand Miles through the Eastern and Western States of America.* Fanny Trollope's popular two-volume *Domestic Manners of the Americans* was written slightly later, based on her unsuccessful attempt to build a life for herself and her children in Cincinnati between 1828 and 1830. The criticisms in these and other accounts of the United States were similar, with a focus on slavery and spitting. There was general agreement, however, that the opportunities for 'getting on' were considerable.

Exactly three months after Alfred, Charles Dickens crossed the Atlantic on the *Britannia*. They visited many of the same sites, staying in the same hotels and even meeting up at Niagara Falls, so Dickens' observations are particularly interesting to read alongside the letters of Alfred and Charles. Unlike the Morrisons he found little to celebrate, and both *Martin Chuzzlewit* and *American Notes* deeply upset many Americans. His opinion was clear: 'I think it impossible, utterly impossible, for any English man to live here, and be happy.'

While little survives of the correspondence *to* Alfred and Charles, their parents kept most of their letters, comprising some quarter of a million words. Alfred wrote regularly to his parents, to Charles and to Gabriel Shaw at Morrison, Sons & Co. and after Charles arrived they shared the correspondence. Mary Ann usually received the more colourful letters describing scenery, the people and the architecture; Charles sent his father page after page of financial analysis. Sir John Easthope agreed to publish some in his newspaper, the *Morning Chronicle*, to the embarrassment of Charles, who wrote to his father from New York: 'It matters little one way or the other, whether my authorship is known in London – but if it becomes generally known here it may do some harm, in as much as in scribblg those papers I did not take time to pick expressions sufficiently respectful to the dignity of the Starry Republic.'[3] Their point of view is unique. They were immensely rich, both educated at the universities of Edinburgh and Cambridge with extended visits to Europe, and brought up in luxurious houses hung with fine paintings. Their father was a Member of Parliament, Justice of the Peace and Deputy Lord Lieutenant of Wiltshire. However, they appreciated the significance of commerce, which had after all provided the family fortune, and like their father they were committed to free trade.

They had impressive contacts, including the Secretary of State Daniel Webster, Andrew Stevenson, Minister in London, as well as merchants and bankers who were also some of the wealthiest men in the country. When the Governor of Ohio commented in 1837, 'Credit has bought our land, built our cities, cleared our fields, founded our churches, erected our colleges and schools',[4] he could have added it was James Morrison who supplied some of the credit. Webster had received a letter a few months before Alfred's arrival assuring him that Morrison was labouring hard in the Commons to make 'some advances towards an alteration in our Import duties in the spirit in which we talked over this subject when I had the pleasure of seeing you in London and in Fonthill'.[5]

Alfred first realised he was in a 'new world' when he booked into the Tremont House in Boston, a hotel 'unlike anything to be met with in England'. 'The custom is to live in public, eat in public and sleep too, for I observed that most of the rooms had more than one bed in them. Breakfast is served at eight and dinner at two, and at least two hundred persons sat down at each meal.' Dickens declared the hotel 'a trifle smaller than Finsbury Square'[6] and retreated to a private room to have dinner, avoiding the crowds which Alfred noted 'loafing about and doing nothing else but smoke and spit'.

Alfred was impressed by the 'respectable' men he met in Boston, 'several persons who belonged to a class that I have seen few specimens of in England – most of them either were in or had retired from business, and were more free from prejudice and better-informed than two-thirds of the House of Commons'. At one dinner party he met Joseph Story, the first professor of law at Harvard Law School and Judge of the Supreme Court in Washington, the historian George Bancroft and the historical painter Washington Allston. 'Their conversation was quite as interesting as that of the same class of persons would be in England, and they had none of the intolerable Yankee drawl and prosiness.'[7]

From Boston, Alfred and Lord Morpeth were taken on a tour of Lowell's famous textile mills, a popular destination for visiting Europeans. They were given special treatment and accompanied by Nathan Appleton himself, the founder of textile manufacturing in America. By 1850 six-storey brick mills lined the river for a mile; six miles of canals drove the waterwheels of forty mills, powering 320,000 spindles and almost 10,000 looms and providing employment for over 10,000 men and women.[8] Dickens also did the tour and was impressed by the girls employed in the mills, not 'degraded brutes of burden.'[9] Alfred noted the unusual process: 'I saw cotton spinning, weaving and printing, all these generally carried on in the same concern, carpet-making and machine making.' As the beneficiary of Fore Street, Alfred would not have agreed with Dickens' indictment of America as a 'vast counting house.'[10] When Charles Morrison visited Lowell in April 1843 he provided his father with a lengthy analysis of the mills including the education and dress of the girls, 'cotton stuff of sober colours & small patterns', the advantages of cheaper cotton wool from the southern states and water power instead of steam; above all, the virtues of the New Englander: 'quick, ingenious, argumentative, scheming, inquisitive, perpetually eager to better his condition, throwing himself with equal ardour into every pursuit he turns to, his ordinary pursuit money-making, but capable of devoting himself to other objects, the labors of the missionary, the studies of the man of science, the dreams of the artist with equal fervor.'[11]

In New York Alfred stayed in another 'barrack' of a hotel, the Astor House, with accommodation for three hundred, plumbing on the upper floors and gas lighting in the public rooms. Room and board, including four meals, was $1.50. The hotel, on the fashionable western side of Broadway, had opened in 1836.[12]

Like other British visitors, Alfred was always comparing the cities and towns he visited to their equivalents in his own country. New York he considered closest to London, with 'altogether the air of a metropolis'. Charles agreed it 'has more the air of a great city', and compared Broadway to the boulevards of Paris. However, Alfred found Wall Street, 'the Lombard Street of N York', a 'very strange looking place'. It had been rebuilt after a major fire in 1835.

It is an irregular street & not a broad one but contains the oddest & most incongruous mixture of architectural designs that I have ever seen. The buildings are principally occupied by banks & large companies & their great object seems to have been to erect a front which should compete with that of their neighbours – the prevailing taste seems to be classical & the result is that you see a row of classical fronts & porticoes of them of different proportion & size & neither of which harmonizes with the rest – you observe every order of architecture except Attic – Doric, Ionic Corinthian & sometimes a little mixture of Egyptian – These fronts are generally out of all proportion to the size of the buildings. ... The Americans I should say spent a great deal of money on their buildings, public & private but generally I do not think they spend it well – There seems to be no originality in their architecture, their buildings are all copies.[13]

While Alfred dismissed the architecture, Dickens disliked the money-making: 'Some of these very merchants whom you see hanging about here now, have locked up money in their strong-boxes, like the man in the Arabian Nights, and opening them again, have found but withered leaves.'[14]

Alfred had the opportunity to study the homes of his father's wealthy business partners and was struck by Wetmore's house in Waverly Place, newly furnished and full of 'Chinese curiosities ... very beautiful'. Wetmore's domestic arrangements were also of interest. He kept a Chinese servant who used to wait on him in Canton, 'as vigilant & faithful over his master's property as a house dog. He speaks very little English – & it is a laughable thing to hear W pattering the Canton dialect to him – this dialect being a broken sort of baby's English, mixed up with some outlandish words.' The forty-year-old merchant was a widower and 'determined to be married' again. However, as Charles later commented, 'having passed all his younger years as a mercantile adventurer abroad, & having lived for years at Canton shut up in factories, where no lady was to be seen, he has become an experienced judge of almost every article of commerce, from diamonds to cotton wool, but women are a kind of goods of wh he knows nothing'.[15] Consequently, he had to be rescued on several occasions from the clutches of fortune hunters by his anxious female relations. Charles' assessment of his final choice, Miss Rogers, the daughter of a failed Salem merchant, as 'a regular flirt', was correct. Once married, and in possession of a small fortune, she embarked on an affair with her husband's coachman. 'He [Wetmore] bore the trial like a hero. Instead of making a town talk, he quietly flung over it the veil of charity and silence. No one ever heard what became of his wife or his coachman.'[16]

Early in 1842, Alfred made an extensive trip south to Philadelphia, Washington, Richmond and Charleston. In Philadelphia (the headquarters of the BUS) he stayed with his father's close business associate Richard Alsop, and again noted the taste of one of the richest men in the city,[17] spotting in his collection 'a few things in the way of pictures & furniture which I shd. like very well to see at Basildon'. Alsop also had a trotting horse 'which I should like very much to exhibit in England'.

Alfred compared the design of the bank, 'built on the plan of the Parthenon' and being copied all over the country, to the practices of its former director Nicholas Biddle. 'His taste in architecture has found imitations just as his crooked courses have found followers & the country is now suffering under the effects of both.'[18] Dickens wondered at the sight of the door tight shut to 'the Tomb of many fortunes, the Great Catacomb of investment'.[19]

Alsop accompanied Alfred to Washington where he was introduced 'as everybody else is introduced' to the President, John Tyler.[20] Alfred found him shabbily dressed and the White House pretty shabby too with worn furniture. 'You may imagine', he wrote to his mother, 'how strange it appeared to me to be received at the door by a dirty negro in slippers & with a coat worn out at elbows & to be ushered into a room which reminded me very much of a provincial assembly room.'[21] Visiting Washington the following year Charles dismissed the Capitol as 'the hugest monument of bad taste wh it has been my fortune to survey … . the capitals of the columns are a most unfortunate variation of the Corinthian, the principal portico is no genuine portico at all, & the whole exterior presents a singular combination of meannesses into one great failure.'[22] Dickens, on the other hand, without the benefit of the Morrisons' extensive cultural education, found it 'a fine building of the Corinthian order'.[23]

In Richmond, Alfred (and Dickens) visited the tobacco factory and heard the slaves singing. 'Some one of them constructed a rude verse containing an allusion to another, or perhaps to myself who was standing by personified as Massa William & this was followed by a chorus which struck me as being very musical & if the allusion was successful by the loud laugh which is peculiar to the negro.' He continued: 'The only production of Richmond are negroes & chewing tobacco, both of these articles the importance of which is unknown in England. ... Negroes are raised in Virginia, Maryland & I believe S Carolina for the South just as cattle are raised in Scotland for the pastures of the South of England ... they speak of the negroe pens & the Southern drovers.' He then explained to his mother that he 'made a rule never in any way to allude to or discuss the subject & as an Englishman it was particularly necessary to observe caution'. His travelling acquaintance Lord Morpeth had apparently been received with 'coolness' in the South because it was known that he had attended an Abolition Fair in Boston. Alfred, as the representative of Morrison, Sons & Co. with numerous investments in the slave states, discovered quickly that he had to observe a neutral position (although he and Charles towards the end of their stay attended an abolition meeting at Lowell and heard speeches by William Lloyd Garrison, Collins and the black abolitionist Charles Redmond).[24] On a train taking him further south towards Charleston Alfred encountered a regular slave trader, 'a perfect brute of a man' and feared for all those in his power. Dickens also met a slave trader on board a train: 'the black in Sinbad's Travels with one eye in the middle of his forehead which shone like a burning coal, was nature's aristocrat compared with this white gentleman'.[25]

Alfred was able to cover vast distances on the railroads, in many of which Morrison, Sons & Co. found themselves reluctant shareholders.[26] The first successful run of an American steam locomotive was made on 24 August 1830, and construction had increased at a dramatic pace, from 3,328 miles in 1840 to 8,879 miles in 1850. However, Alfred discovered that the experience of travelling was as hazardous as some of the stock, constructed with little regard to safety, comfort or duration. He tried the sleeping arrangements between Weldon and Wilmington: 'shelves are suspended three deep from the sides of the carriage; they are just such as might be used for displaying crockery. ... I passed a most villainous night. Fortunately I am not troubled with the nightmare but if I were I am very sure that a dingy foul smelling RR car with a bed of torture consisting [of] two hard boards with the victim between them & the upper one supporting a stout, hardbreathing man wd for some time be the leading feature in my dreams.'[27] Travelling from New York to Philadelphia a few months later, Charles was equally unimpressed: 'only one line of rail, apparently no very large capital laid out either on the construction of the road itself or the accessories – & the rate of travelling is not good'.[28] It was unfortunate that his train ran over a cow. Dickens was struck by the segregation of passengers by gender and colour, the noise and the limited conversation – politics, banks and cotton.[29] Such conversation would not have troubled the Morrisons.

Dickens' horror of slavery prevented him from travelling further south than Richmond: 'My heart is lightened as if a great load had been taken from it, when I think that we are turning our backs on this accursed and detested system.'[30] Alfred was driven by the business interests of his family and found the indolence induced by Charleston's warm climate fascinating. 'The verandahs of the hotels are filled by groups of men occupying more chairs than you wd. think it possible for one man to make use of, indolently smoking & at intervals taking a pull through a straw or tube at the julep beside them. The men in the streets with their broad brimmed straw hats & linen jackets – cantering quietly along on horses shew little of the restlessness & go ahead principle of the Yankees.' He added, 'all labor [was] performed by negroes'.[31]

James Morrison was keen to hear from his sons about the possibilities of further investment in North America, and both Alfred and Charles replied with dire warnings of the consequences of such action. Alfred, for example, advised against setting up an investment trust:

> The opinion of all men who have resided long in this country is that there is no <u>security</u> in this country & it is the opinion which I have been for some time gradually coming to myself – Everything is constantly changing & fluctuating, you may be safe for one year & you may then suddenly awake & find your property swept away; you shd. never place implicit confidence in any man here; they are all too clever … I wd never advise any Englishman who does not know the country & people thoroughly to invest a dollar in America. Notwithstanding Taxation & Chartism I wd. still advise him to stick to the three per cents.[32]

Investment in America had to be for the long term. Interest returns of 6% and 7% looked attractive but were rarely paid. Alfred also gave a perceptive analysis of the future power and 'warlike spirit of the Americans'. 'For purposes of defense & in a just war this I believe is the most powerful country in the world. ... Every man in the country might I believe in two months be made as good a soldier (I think rather better) as any in the world.'[33]

In the spring of 1842 Alfred took an extensive trip from New York to Buffalo primarily to investigate the value of mortgages and other securities of Duer & Co., which claimed to be worth $1.2 million. His father had meanwhile received a depressing letter from J. Robertson, President of the (liquidated) Bank of the United States. 'Under all circumstances, and from every view we can take of the condition of this Bank, or its prospects, we find it impossible to meet our engagements to you, or to make even any partial remittances. We therefore think it best to recommend to you, and we do it in the most earnest manner, to continue to exercise forbearance towards us, and to hold on to the Stocks which have been pledged to you. They cannot be sold now, but at ruinous prices; and would fall short of the debt due to you.'[34]

Alfred meanwhile enjoyed the landscape, appreciating the opportunities for farmers, particularly in the western part of New York State. Travelling to Albany on the Hudson River (on the *Troy*, the 'finest steamboat on the river'),[35] he passed the military academy of West Point, the home of Washington Irving and enjoyed views of the Catskill mountains, 'like the Jura as seen from Geneva'. In July, to escape the summer heat of New York, Charles retreated to the Catskill Mountain House (he also invested in a $12 broad-brimmed Panama hat 'made of a peculiar straw or rather reed, & said to last a man's lifetime'). The Catskills were only just being developed for tourists, following the opening in 1825 of the Erie Canal which connected Buffalo on Lake Erie with Albany on the Hudson; artists were also capturing the as yet unspoilt scenery.[36] Twenty years later, when he was building up his own collection, Alfred bought a number of paintings of the area by the major artist of the Hudson River School, Jasper Francis Cropsey.

He could hardly believe that the settlements he passed were only a few years old:

The whole line of country from Buffalo to Albany is filled with thriving towns & villages – In order to understand fully the force of the word prosperous as applied to towns it is necessary to come to America; the contrast between the surrounding country & these mushroom towns, the activity & respectable appearance of the people – in the case of the women the elegance of their dress – & the immense displays of goods & provisions which you see in every store do not exist at all in the old world. Utica, Syracuse, Oswego & I am told still more Buffalo & Rochester are really wonderful places when it is considered that 25 or 30 years ago not a home existed on the spots which are now covered with manufactories.[37]

At Niagara, Alfred was not disappointed by the falls, in particular the Horseshoe, 'the grandest thing which I have ever yet seen'. He described for his mother the impact of watching the sunset from a rock overhanging the fall, 'an event in a man's life-time'.

The hotel had few guests, but he noted one in particular: Charles Dickens. 'Boz was there but did not see visitors; in this his conduct was considered too aristocratic; the poor man has been hunted from place to place & I suppose thought that at Niagara he wd. be able to hide his head for a day or two, but he was mistaken & one or two deputations of farmers came to have what the Indians call a <u>talk</u> with him – I hope he will take his revenge upon them by writing a book.' Alfred was dismissive of the novelist's knowledge of the country: 'if he does [write a book] it will be worth nothing as he can have seen nothing of the country or people'.[38]

Alfred, unlike the novelist and his own brother, was always keen to try different experiences, however physically uncomfortable. To study the potential of Duer's investments in Grand Island, on the Niagara River, he stayed with a family of Mormons in a 'genuine log cabin', sleeping under 'woollen homespun blankets', fighting off bugs, and eating pork with 'apple sauce ... made by boiling down in sweet cider to a jelly apples & intermixing spices such as cloves'. He shot an eagle, walked through miles of swamp and admired oaks 'which would compare with the oak at Basildon'. He concluded, however, that the land was a 'dead weight ... the timber is magnificent but there is no demand for it ... I wd not at present touch Gd Island with a pitchfork.'[39]

Charles confessed to his parents his 'horror of responsibility'; nevertheless, his father expected him to take control of his American portfolio, selling off stock at the highest price he could obtain, either through a Wall Street broker or at auction, while investing in safer enterprises on behalf of Morrison, Sons & Co. His passage across the Atlantic on the steamer *Acadia* cost £40 10s. (wine was £1 extra and the steward's tip was 10 shillings). The crossing was miserable. 'I mitigated the violence of the seasickness & especially the actual vomiting by remaining quiet in my birth [*sic*] – but there was quite enough to confirm me in a resolution never again to go out of sight of land in a steamboat without an exceedingly good reason.'[40] He stuck to his resolution: once back in England he never travelled abroad again though he lived until he was ninety-two.

The brothers met at Jones Hotel in Philadelphia at the end of May 1842. Charles wrote to his mother that Alfred was in 'very good health … the principal alteration in his appearance is that he's very much freckled, & looks older & more manly. He has got a prompt, decisive manner, wh has I suppose been taught him by travelling & doing business among this sharp race of men.'[41] With Charles taking the lead, the brothers tried to grasp the essentials of railroads, canals, coal, farming, cotton, gas and even the water supply for New York without much help from the 'cut-throats' and 'crooks' they encountered. 'I am thoroughly sick & disgusted', Charles wrote to his father in November, 'to find that there is not in this country one man, who acts single-mindedly & jealously for our interests, when we employ him or when he volunteers his services.'[42]

Railroads were a source of constant anxiety. The Bank of the United States owned a quarter of the Philadelphia and Reading Railroad, as well as part of the Philadelphia, Wilmington and Baltimore Railroad. At the end of June 1842 the Morrisons sold these securities for just over £200,000. They then bought back £130,000 in the Wilmington line under their own name, Charles confident the return was genuinely 6% and that there was a sinking fund (their holding was later reduced to £87,000). They loaned the Reading line £40,000, eventually holding $311,000 worth of bonds and $459,000 in notes and, much to their relief, business began to pick up the following year.[43] Charles described to his father watching a train 'with one Engine 100 coal cars, containing about 330 tons coal, the same Engine having taken the empty cars up the day before. … As you may suppose, the train appeared very long – & as I saw it first emerge from under an Archway, the Engine showing itself first, & drawing out the string of cars one after another until it seemed that there wd be no end to the chain, the effect was singular.'[44]

Alfred investigated the future of the Hazleton Company (coal), concluding that 'a few thousand dollars carefully administered to such a company … wd produce a wonderful effect'. With his father's authorisation, Charles then went ahead and bought $75,000 of shares in the Hazleton: 'I have become a coaldealer, a trade wh I certainly had no idea of engaging in when I came out here.' The brothers had less confidence in the Morris Canal and Banking Company which had been created to pay for a second outlet for Pennsylvania anthracite, the Bank of the United States again owning a quarter interest. Land was bought next to Hazleton but Alfred discovered the one vein of coal was not worth working, and that the canal was dug only four feet deep so locks were unable to take boats carrying more than 25 tons of coal. In 1845 the Morrisons listed their holding of bonds as worthless.

Returns from farm mortgages turned out to be rather different to the British model. After going over Alfred's report of the properties he had visited in New York State, Charles explained to their father (who was expressing impatience with the slow return of funds) that he could not expect to receive large sums of money within a specific time: 'the whole mass of yr investments, advances, commts [commitments] here must be looked on as stuff the time of realization of wh is altogether uncertain'.

The farmer may for a very long time find it inconvenient to pay it [the mortgage] off, & not think it necessary to make a great exertion to do so. When a man enters on a lot of wild land in the Chatanque lands or any similarly managed tract, he usually has very little capital, wh he exhausts in paying up a certain proportion of the purchase money (the rest remg as a mortgage) & clearing a few acres of land, & settg up a log house. In the following years he goes on clearing the land a little at a time, building barns, replacing the log house by one of frame or brick, stocking his farm &c &c in this way a long course of years may elapse, during wh the man may find more urgent or more profitable uses for his money than paying off the mortgage, & may find it quite enough to meet the interest. It is only when his farm is fully cultivated, supplied with buildings, & stocked, his house well furnished, & his own & his wife's wardrobe filled too, that he will begin to have money to spare. Yet during the whole of the time the ultimate repayment of the mortg may be considered certain – because every stroke of the man's hatchet, or nail driven in to the buildings, adds to the value of the land, & therefore even if no part of the purchase money had been pd originally the <u>improvements</u> wd form a growing margin to secure the seller or holder of the mortgage.[45]

Charles advised his father to expect nothing from America but rather to pay off everything he owed in England, 'after that it will be time enough to buy land, &c, when you have an actual surplus to invest'. 'After all what is the use of lendg money with one hand, if you have to borrow it with the other. It is annoying to reject opportunities of purchase of land nr Basildon or in other desirable situations – but it is much more annoying for a man with a million & a half to have to go to the Browns, Dennisons & Gurneys for a renewal of loans, & for his house to have its means & liabilities so nicely balanced, that even a call on it for £5000 may be very disagreeable.' Charles was concerned at his father's lack of 'ready cash', 'every £1000 wh you realize being absorbed immediately in the great gulf of cash advances & investments in anticipation of yr income'. Convinced that in the end the United States offered the possibility of large profits, he suggested it would be wise to keep £100,000 always available for a tempting investment opportunity, a view he maintained throughout his long and successful life as an investment banker, though he increased the figure to half a million pounds.

On 1 September 1842 the brothers took part in a little bit of Anglo-American history. They were guests at the dinner given at the Astor House in New York for Lord Ashburton after the signing of the Ashburton Treaty which settled a long-lasting dispute over the border between the States and Canada. Congratulating Webster on his appointment as Secretary of State, James Morrison had referred to the strained relations between Great Britain and the States but was reassuring: 'the wish for peace is not only general but universal among us'.[46] On 19 April 1842, Alfred had written at length to Charles about relations between the countries. He also believed war could be avoided: 'all sensible men, as far as I have been able to observe, agree in the main with Ld Aberdeen [Foreign Secretary] as to the principles asserted by our governments on the subject of the right of Search.' He was referring to the treaty signed by Britain, Austria, France, Prussia and Russia agreeing to reciprocal rights to search ships suspected of carrying slaves. The United States regarded the treaty as a threat to its commercial activities, slaves being essential for the production of cheap cotton and sugar, but agreement was finally reached for a joint cruising squadron off the coast of Africa. Alfred was more concerned by the *Creole* case, and the 'Boundary question': 'if we cannot gain our point by arbitration we had better pay for the territory at once & make a great merit of the concession – it wd be a set off to the Creole case.'

The *Creole* was an American brig carrying tobacco and slaves in October 1841 from Virginia to New Orleans. Nineteen slaves seized control, killing a slave owner. They sailed into British-owned Nassau where the mutineers were imprisoned and the slaves not involved in the uprising liberated. The Americans demanded that all the slaves be handed back. Compromise was reached with the extradition of the mutineers and the payment of compensation for the freed slaves.[47] In the end Alfred was optimistic about relations. 'Tyler though weak is I believe honest & with Webster, on whom the matter principally depends, success in the negociations with Ld Ashburton is the trump card with which he hopes to recover his waning popularity.'[48]

The Astor House dinner was also the subject of some controversy, as the toast to Queen Victoria was cheered with gusto, but the toast to President Tyler was met with ominous silence. Charles explained to his mother what had really happened:

> The fact was that this being the first toast of the evening [to Tyler] we did not know what the etiquette for the evening was to be & when the name of the [President] was given out, quietly rose from our seats & repeated the words drank our wine & sat down again, supposg we had done all that was proper. When the next toast 'the Queen' was given we rose again – & this time, hearing the signal given from some part of the table '3 times 3' proceeded to make a noise accordingly with equal innocence of intention … The quickness with wh this story of an insult offered to the Prest by the Whigs of NY has been spread, & the importance wh has been attached to it is characteristic. The fact is that the Americans are in a state of chronic electioneering excitement … You will also read something of an outrageous insult offered to the reporters at the dinner, the effect of wh was that at a certain stage in the proceedings they all felt themselves obliged to walk off, & leave subsequent speeches unreported. I cd not for some days learn what this outrageous insult had been – but was at length informed that it had consisted in not giving them any dinner.[49]

While Charles remained in New York staying with Wetmore, Alfred travelled north in the autumn of 1842 by way of Lake Champlain (the setting for Fenimore Cooper's *Last of the Mohicans*) to Upper Canada. He was to

investigate the worth of the Morrisons' relatively small investments in the
Canada Land Company and the Beauharnois Seignory. Alfred stayed in
Toronto with the Commissioner for the Canada Land Company, a relation
of Sir John Easthope (who as director of the company had persuaded
Morrison to invest). He was confident the land (150,000 acres) could be
profitable 'if the Province remains quiet. The shareholders may get a large
profit, every thing depends of course upon the quantity of land which can
be sold every year.' The Beauharnois Seignory was riskier: 'Lower Canada is
not the favourite resort of [British] emigrants, owing to its French inhabitants.' The Seignory had been the property of Morrison's friend and fellow
MP Edward Ellice. However, Alfred and Charles were critical of Ellice,
discovering he had sold the property for the inflated price of £150,000
rather than taking a personal interest. He should have 'gone to reside there
for a few years, & turned his cleverness & activity from political intrigue to
the improvement of the property, & the management of the population
upon it, he mt have made a splendid property of it – or if *you* [James
Morrison] had bought the whole from him, & sent Alfred or myself to reside
upon it, you might have made a great profit.'[50] Charles, however, was keen to
encourage his father to buy Canadian land because 'you do not go beyond
the protection of British law – good land, as yet uncultivated, & lying
along the great channel of the St Lawrence, & within half a day's journey
of the Capital of Canada ought one wd think to advance in value as rapidly
as in almost any other locality in N America'. So while the Morrisons
withdrew from Beauharnois, they increased their holding in the Canada
Land Company. And in 1848, independently of his father, Charles joined
a brand new venture, the Trust and Loan Company of Upper Canada (see
Chapter 16).

Alfred arrived at Kingston, Upper Canada, with a letter of introduction
from Lord Stanley to the newly appointed Governor General Sir Charles
Bagot. 'I cd. not have been there at a better time,' Alfred wrote. 'The
Legislature was in session & the excitement caused by the change of ministry
& in fact the whole policy of the country was very great'. Bagot had been
given the task of creating the first efficient ministry for the country, bringing
together representatives from the French and English provinces. The newly
created House of Parliament met for the first time on 8 September 1842, just
before Alfred arrived. Invited to dinner, Alfred found Bagot 'very cordial

[expressing] opinions which I think a Governor General never should express & which convinced me that he was not the most discreet man in the world'. (It would appear that Lord Stanley agreed and Bagot was forced to retire.) James Audubon the naturalist was a guest,[51] Alfred also met the new Attorney General Lafontaine, 'in fact Prime Minister'. He liked the French population, 'probably as happy and contented a race of people as can be found on the face of the Globe'.[52]

In November the brothers prepared to travel south to New Orleans, 'to extract cash or cotton'. Charles required a new wardrobe and sent his mother a lengthy diatribe on the subject of New York tailors and bootmakers, fashion in general, and the effeminate behaviour and unhealthy appearance of the young men of the 'upper classes' he encountered:

> They persist in pinching me up within clothes made on the American pattern wh is an awkward imitation of the French. The Americans have no notion of anything substantial or comfortable – thin soled boots with extravagant high & tapering heels, coats buttoning very tight to make the waist look small, & nondescript vestments with a fancy cut & velvet trimmings instead of great coats, are the only style they know anything of. As all the young men here who have any pretension to fashion lead a town life all the year round, having no idea of such rough employments as hunting & shooting, walking in the mud or travellg on the top of a coach, their tradesmen have no experience in dressing them for any useful purpose.[53]

Once on his way, however, he cheered up. He was specially impressed by the efficient slaughtering of pigs in Cincinnati, sending his mother a lengthy and graphic description: 'in twenty four hours from the time when the fat hog walked into Cincinnati from the interior of the State, he is travelling down the Mississippi in a barrel at the rate of 14 miles an hour, on his way to feed the West India slaves. If Adam Smith had visited Cincinnati, he wd. have quoted the packing of hogs as there practised, as an illustration of the division of labour, by the side of the manufacture of pins'.[54] On the muddy waters of the Mississippi, he managed with the provisions of a 'gentleman passenger': two rolling towels and two pieces of yellow soap.

Alfred (unlike Dickens) found travelling by steamboat 'the most luxurious mode of travelling to be met with anywhere'. He was struck by the gambling: 'three men actually played for certainly twenty consecutive hours & when we left at Natchez they had begun again for the second night after a few hours rest & from what I know to the contrary continued to play until they reached New Orleans'.[55] During the night, the brothers passed 'the ill fated city of Cairo' renamed Eden by Dickens in *Martin Chuzzlewit*.

'Heyday!' cried Martin, as his eye rested on a great plan which occupied one whole side of the office. ... Heyday! what's that?'

'That's Eden,' said Scadder ... .

'Why, I had no idea it was a city.' A flourishing city, too! An architectural city! There were banks, churches, cathedrals, market-places, factories, hotels, stores, mansions, wharves; an exchange, a theatre; public buildings of all kinds down to the office of the *Eden Stinger*, a daily journal; all faithfully depicted in the view before them.

'Dear me! It's really a most important place!' cried Martin, turning round.

'Oh! It's very important,' observed the agent.

'But, I am afraid,' said Martin, glancing again at the Public Buildings, 'that there's nothing left for me to do.'

'Well! It ain't all built,' replied the agent. 'Not quite.'[56]

Earlier in the year the brothers had investigated Cairo for its investment potential. Not as gullible as Chuzzlewit, they asked one of their agents Mr Wylie to visit. 'He landed at Cairo, & walked over the site with Holbrook's agent. Has the worst possible opinion of the scheme. There are a few houses, & an hotel, wh professedly pays $1200 rent but as the landlord has now hardly any custom, he certainly does not pay it. Wylie thinks that if a large town is to grow up in that neighbourhood, it will probably not be at Cairo, wh is so very unhealthy, but either on the Kentucky or the other side of the river, a little below the junction, where there is some comparatively high ground.' Alfred passed by again the following year. 'Nothing can be conceived more miserable than the appearance of Cairo. There are no signs of new buildings springing up & the old ones all look out of place. ... The sight of Cairo wd. almost break the heart of any man who was either deeply interested himself or who had induced his friends to invest in the concern.' Dickens' Eden nearly killed Chuzzlewit and his loyal companion Mark Tapley.

In New Orleans, the brothers stayed at the St Charles Hotel, 'perhaps the largest building in America' but owned by a bank, so consequently unprofitable. Charles was struck by the nature of the Creole population, a quiet race apart from their fondness for duels '& as the object here is really to kill, or at least disable your antagonist, the combatants in a duel with pistols being allowed a certain time to take aim, & the small sword being often used instead of the pistol, a good many lives are lost'.[57] Alfred decided the American population in the city were the 'scum of the Union; any man who has lost his character in other parts of the country would have a fair start in N. Orleans ... No man comes to N Orleans for the purpose of residing in it. He visits it as Englishmen visit Calcutta to make money & return home.' Above all, he realised, 'every man's soul is absorbed in cotton'.[58]

The New Orleans Gas Light and Banking Company, known by the Morrisons as the Gas Bank, was their main subject of scrutiny. It was one of a number of improvement banks chartered by the State of Louisiana in 1835 to construct and operate gas street lights in New Orleans and five other towns.[59] Acquired by the Bank of the United States, it was now included in Morrison's assets and he hoped it could be sold for $1 million. To his disappointment, his sons managed to acquire just over half a million dollars in cash, the rest in bonds and shares, but as Charles explained, it was better to take what was on offer in the extraordinary financial climate.

> When you have an immense property like the Gas Bank debt wrecked in a
> climate wh kills you with yellow fever during one half the year, & wastes
> you with a warm damp atmosphere during a great part of the other half, if
> you attempt to go to its rescue – a troop of pirates plundering it, & every
> man whom you employ for its protection ready to fall to & join the plun-
> derers – the best course you can adopt is to make haste & get together as
> much of the most valueable & portable part of the cargo as you can carry
> & run off with it.[60]

Morrison had little justification in criticising his sons; he was himself encoun-
tering problems investing in consignments of cotton through Jackson, Todd

& Co. in New Orleans (the firm Mary Ann's half-brother worked for in Liverpool). His need for quick returns affected his judgement and he regularly ignored Todd's advice, selling too soon or too late. In December 1842, for example, his profit on a consignment of cotton was a mere £64 11s. 4d as he refused to wait until prices rose.

From Tallahassee, in early 1843, Charles wrote to his father a sixteen-page letter analysing cotton production and the economics of the slave plantations. He had had an interesting debate with the planters over what they regarded as the capital necessary to determine their profit. Including 'feeding, clothing & lodging the stock of negroes acquired for the cultivation, the wear & tear & interest of money on the tools & machinery' was clear enough to him, 'but the planter adds two other items, larger than any of the foregoing, viz interest on the purchase money of his stock of negroes, & interest on the purchase money of his land, both being reckoned at the rates of the good times before '37'. Alfred provided the political context in a letter to his mother:

> To hope that the planters will abolish slaves is to suppose that they will voluntarily make beggars of themselves; if the slaves were free they wd immediately become small proprietors & the plantations wd become worthless; the cultivation of cotton wd cease because the price of labor wd be too high & it cd be produced at a cheaper rate in other parts of the world. Until the population becomes far more dense or whites supply the place of the blacks the abolition of slavery wd produce nearly a total destruction of the south.[61]

By May 1843, Charles could write 'our affairs here seem at last to be moving with some security'. They had received $56,000 from the Gas Bank, $130,000 from the sale of Kentucky stock and, on 1 July, $200,000 from the Commercial Bank of Natchez. On 29 June an agreement was signed between Morrison, Sons & Co. and the BUS under which the former accepted the remaining securities it held in full satisfaction of all claims against the Bank. The general economic situation was improving too. Daniel Webster wrote to Joshua Bates at Barings in November, 'There is no kind of doubt, that the President will be able to communicate to Congress a very favourable state of things regarding our public finances.'[62] The budget balanced in the following spring.

Charles returned to England in the summer of 1843. Alfred, after spending from May to October in England, returned to complete transactions and indulge in more travelling. He at last managed to get to Cuba in the spring of 1844. He stayed in Havana with James Robb, President of the Gas Bank, who was trying to bring gas to Cuba. Alfred thought Robb might be the man to look after their investments in the southern states, particularly as he would be visiting England to order gasometers and pipes. Mary Ann received a colourful picture of Cuba, from cockroaches and scorpions to cock-fighting and cigar-rolling:

In Havanna you wd find the greatest collection of doubtful characters to be met with in any spot on the globe … . the blacks are to the whites frequently in the proportion of forty or fifty to one. This is of course a very alarming state of things particularly as perhaps two thirds of the negroes are imported slaves, speak but little Spanish & their recollections of their wrongs are quite fresh. The insurrections of negroes are numerous, but people do not like to speak of them. … The slave trade continues to as great an extent as ever, within the last ten days it is a matter of common gossip that some 2000 slaves have been landed within a few miles of Havanna … . [in the docks] the negroes mostly work half naked at least one half of them are imported slaves. Many of them unlike the slaves in the Southern states in America are immense men & shew a development of muscle which delights me. You can tell the Africans by the marks or scars on the face or arms – many of them are beautifully tattoed [sic] on the body & some have their teeth jagged like a saw.[63]

Alfred sent his father a thousand of the best cigars he could buy, but discovered he needed to send a minimum of 100 pounds in weight to get through English customs. Jackson (of Jackson, Todd) added a further 7,000 in New Orleans. 'This may I fear give you a larger quantity than you wish for … [however they] might be kept for years, improving all the time'. Alfred described to his mother the manufactory of Cabaius, an old lady who was reputed to produce the best cigars in Cuba. She 'is very fat & is always dressed in white muslin with satin slippers; she superintends her own workmen – the lady herself who generally has a large cigar in her mouth, sits in a large chair, surrounded by half naked negroes who are making the cigars

& at one end of the building you see the female slaves cooking & washing, tame pigeons & fowl run about the hall which is very large & covered with a large old fashioned wooden roof; the whole scene, *lady & all*, must I think be peculiar to Cuba.'

For Charles and Alfred, the time spent in North America was seminal. Alfred had given up university for a mercantile career but his experiences dealing with 'cut-throat' Americans proved he was not suited to business. Charles made it clear to their father: 'I have great misgivings as to a partnership between myself & Alfred'. ... I do not think he will become a working man of business ... . nothing but necessity will induce him to become the inmate of a countinghouse [with its] botheration & confinement ... Alfred does not value money, & does like his ease.' If he were reduced to poverty, Charles thought, Alfred would be willing to work, but given his advantageous position he had no desire whatsoever to make his own fortune. 'I shd have to mount guard during his hours of duty as well as my own. This with the large development of combativeness in Alfred's head, altho it is now generally latent, & my dyspeptic irritability, wd certainly lead to wrangling.'[64]

Charles' situation was the opposite. He recalled that before he had gone out to America his father had 'first proposed the question to me that it is desirable for me to be a man of business, & to make a fortune for myself'. After struggling with illness and depression at university and living in exile in Italy, he had proved to himself how efficiently he could deal with, indeed relish, 'botheration and confinement'. He had learned how best to 'make a business' of investments: 'The rich men in the country (I mean all those who succeed in continuing rich) make a business of their investments – have an office, keep accounts, become Directors in a Compy whenever they invest in its Stock, spend the hours of business in Wall St & such places, know of everythg wh is stirring, & as far as possible do everything themselves.' He noted the pitfalls: 'the sons of rich men [in the States] hardly ever turn out well. Either they fall into habits of idleness dissipation & expence, & so squander away their father's earnings, or they are poor creatures only fit to be their father's clerks, & incapable of taking their place.'[65]

And he had advice for his father as a 'man of large fortune'. He should invest one-third in the United States, with a return of 5% to 7%. Charles also suggested a spread across states, cities and companies; New York he considered a particularly strong opportunity.[66] He went on: 'it appears certain that our family has no business in speculation – you have uniformly been successful both in business & in investments, where you went on the present & certain value alone – & I believe as uniformly unsuccessful in everything of a speculative nature.'[67] It was a perceptive observation which Charles would follow in building up his own fortune.

CHAPTER THIRTEEN

ಲ⁄ಕಾ೪

Basildon: Papworth's Last Commission

I passed there [Basildon] in '34 & '35 some romantic hours ... the house a Palladian palace.

Disraeli, Hughenden Papers

Shortly before Charles and Alfred left for North America to safeguard their father's investments and ensure he had the means to repay his debts, Morrison engaged his architect and designer J.B. Papworth to turn Basildon into a comfortable family home that also displayed his increasing and significant collection of paintings and furniture. Unlike shiploads of tea, American railway stock and bales of cotton, the Basildon estate appeared to be a sure investment.

The estate was, according to the 1829 sale particulars, 'situated in one of the most fertile and picturesque parts of the county, and commanding, on all sides a vast variety of grand and beautiful scenery'.[1] The park overlooked the Thames Valley, and was separated from the River Thames (and the church of Lower Basildon) by the road from London to Reading and Oxford, and the newly constructed Great Western Railway.

Benjamin Disraeli's connection with Basildon has already been mentioned (Chapter 11); his passionate love affair with Henrietta Sykes took place shortly before Morrison bought the estate. In his later novel *Endymion* Disraeli compared the wealthy of the period in which he was writing, 1869–70, to the 1830s:

The great wealth then, compared with the huge society of the present period, was limited in its proportions, and composed of elements more

refined though far less various. It consisted mainly of the great landed aristocracy, who had quite absorbed the nabobs of India, and had nearly
appropriated the huge West India fortunes. Occasionally, an eminent
banker or merchant invested a large portion of his accumulations in land,
and in the purchase of parliamentary influence, and was in time duly
admitted into the sanctuary. But those vast and successful invasions of
society by new classes which have since occurred, though impending, had
not yet commenced.[2]

As Disraeli suggests, Morrison was unique among his generation of tradesmen
(rather than bankers) in acquiring so much land by himself. None, from such
a modest background, could match the size and value of his portfolio which,
by 1838, included property in London, Middlesex, Essex, Kent, Wiltshire,
Buckinghamshire, Berkshire, Suffolk, South Wales and Cornwall.

At Basildon Morrison was attracted by both the house and its situation,
close to London but 'in one of the most admired, healthy, and desirable Parts
of Berkshire'. He noted the convenience in his diary: 'coach from two oclock
train [from Paddington] puts down passengers & leaves parcels at our gate at
about 6.'[3] By contrast, the journey from London to Fonthill took twelve
hours by coach.

The house is one of John Carr of York's finest works. It is faced with warm
golden Bath stone, symmetrical, with a three-storeyed block in the centre
connected by low stone wings to the two-storey pavilions on either side
(containing the kitchen and the laundry). On the east-facing garden side the
central block projects out from the wings, with views of the terrace and the
valley beyond; on the west front the Ionic columns of the portico are thrown
into sharp relief against the dark background of the loggia.[4] Inside, the principal (first) floor was intended by Carr to contain a series of interconnecting
reception rooms for the grand entertainments that were a regular part of
country-house life in the eighteenth century. However, his client, Sir Francis
Sykes, ran out of money before the interior was completed. Only half of the
main rooms were decorated, and many lacked plaster ceilings, mouldings,
complete door furniture and mantelpieces. On visiting in September 1839 to
assess the condition of the property, Morrison's builder Thomas Burton
commented: 'it is much to be regretted that Sykes could not find the where-
withal to finish the rooms for you, it would have saved you somewhere about

£1000'.[5] The stable block was in danger of collapse, the roofs of the two wings needed new slates; even the turret clock was broken. The pleasure grounds and park had been neglected and many of the cottages on the estate were unfit for habitation.

With the power of the novelist, Disraeli completed Basildon by transforming his mistress Henrietta Sykes into the heroine of *Henrietta Temple* who rescues Ducie, her father's 'dingy and desolate villa', to create 'a temple worthy of the divinity it enshrined'.[6]

> There is not on the banks of the Brenta a more dingy and desolate villa than Ducie appeared when we first came, and as for the gardens, they were a perfect wilderness. She [Henrietta] made everything. It was one vast, desolate, and neglected lawn, used as a sheep-walk when we arrived. As for the ceilings, I was almost tempted to whitewash them, and yet you see they have cleaned wonderfully; and, after all, it only requires a little taste and labour.

Morrison turned to the ever-obliging Papworth, who immediately approached his regular team of builders and craftsmen, although on this occasion Morrison also obtained a rival quotation from Thomas Cubitt. Burton and Cubitt submitted estimates on 13 April 1840. Burton's was accepted; his estimate of £4,086 was £164 less than Cubitt's (his final bill was closer to Cubitt's at £4,200). The work took several years, and the Morrisons continued to make Fonthill their country home until 1846.

The priority for Morrison was to see Basildon made a home for his large family (his eleventh child was born in 1842 when Mary Ann was forty-seven years old); but it was also to be a 'casket' to enclose his 'pictorial gems'. In addition, he wanted to restore the pleasure grounds and park and make the estate profitable. Papworth, who turned sixty-five in 1839, was taking on a complex project, his responsibilities ranging from new designs for plaster ceilings and marble floors, curtains and wall coverings, to planning the planting of the pleasure grounds and designing new cottages and farm buildings. Also he had to contend with a client who was liable to bursts of extreme anxiety brought about by the complex financial negotiations with the Bank of the United States, then the delay in news from his sons in North America. Would Alfred and Charles be successful in restoring his losses?

Papworth began with essentials, including supplying an efficient hot-water and heating system, digging new external drains and cesspools, improving the internal sanitation and fitting a system of bells for communication and security. This was particularly important, since the house was to be empty for several years until the work was completed. He recommended an alarm bell on top of the house: 'an Alarm bell is an outward & visible sign to Thieves, that precaution is taken against them, & they have respect to it – on this principle Bankers & Goldsmiths display Fire arms in their shops – even Fire – it is said – never occurs in a House that displays a row of Fire Buckets.' He added by way of advice: 'Nothing of this would I say before Mrs Morrison but I feel it my duty to say so much to you.'[7]

When he turned his attention to the surrounding grounds, Papworth put himself in the position of the family and their guests, considering the initial approach to the house, the views from the windows, the creation of attractive walks. He enlarged the lodges either side of the main entrance with the intention to impress. Known as the Oxford Lodges – situated on the London to Oxford road – they were based on the Athenian Tower of the Winds, with lavish decorations. The piers of the gates were topped with huge baskets of fruit crowned with pineapples and held aloft by putti, a design Papworth based on the ornaments on the Flowerpot Gate at Hampton Court.[8] He also added walls to flank the lodges: 'I have agreed for the wing walls right & left of the Lodge for 45£ the stone work – they will give great effect to the Lodges making the whole length about 137 feet – & you can carry beyond it if you should so desire.'

Although the house required a grand setting Papworth proposed to Morrison that it should not sit isolated in an expanse of lawn but blend with the landscape and plantations.[9] 'My object is to increase what it has there already – extending the Grass – without too much affecting the appearance of the Hanging wood, & to leave clumps & good trees – singly, or otherwise, as Park furniture & embellishments. Oaks & Elms, Ash & Hollies & as many Thorns as possible should be preserved … it is better to cut down too little than too much at once.' He imagined Morrison looking out of the library window towards the downs, taking in the 'distant landscape' through 'valuable peeps' through the trees and shrubs.[10]

At Fonthill Papworth had created a paradise for the young Morrisons, repairing Beckford's follies, adding a waterfall and a landing stage, designing boats, turning a quarry into an enclosure for deer and acquiring statues to lurk inside the caves and tunnels. At Basildon, his approach was slightly different. From his portfolio of designs for garden furniture he provided 'a simple shelter from Rain & for resting in the field', a thatched 'umbrello' at the centre of a rose garden and a thatched summerhouse. He also planned shady walks through shrubberies and rides across the park taking in views across the wide Berkshire downland; appropriate for older children some of whom, by the late 1840s, were entertaining their prospective husbands and wives.

Basildon presented a new challenge for Papworth, in the form of negotiations with the 'Western Railway' contractors and Mr Brunel. As soon as the contract to buy Basildon was signed, Papworth was calling at the company offices to discuss the effect of the railway on the estate. He thought the company's proposed work at Pangbourne Bridge, for example, was 'highly objectionable & this I fully & satisfactorily pointed out'. He proposed a decorative 'frontispiece' to add to the parapet of the bridge and designed a pretty cottage which would be seen both through the arch of the bridge and from trains passing over: 'if properly placed it will be very picturesque and attractive to the Railroad passengers'.[11]

Planting to screen the railway line from the estate was essential, with Morrison probably having to bear the cost. As Papworth explained: 'the Act of Parlmt gives to the contractors power to finish them [the embankments] by Turfing or Planting – the first is least costly & will probably be adopted'. Papworth's position as go-between was not helped by Morrison losing his temper with the navvies. Diary entries by Morrison reveal how he ended up in court, being sued by the contractors for harassment. He noted on 27 September 1840, 'Ordered rail road men to stop throwing up the bank'. On 30 September he wrote, 'Men still at work. McDonald [in charge of the navvies] telling them not to mind me', and on the next day: 'Men stopped [by Morrison]. Hammond and McDonald at the house. Scene. Turned McDonald out of house.' The case was heard the following year, Alfred writing pompously to Charles, 'Father is to be brought into court in a few days for assaulting a niggling specimen of a surveyor ... we are sure to win. Thesiger is engaged and he is instructed to thunder as much as his brief will permit of, and if possible demolish this little man.'

If Alfred looked forward to 'some rare fun' in court, the incident revealed that his father's increasing tendency as he entered his fifties to lose his temper, to suspect he was being cheated and to worry about finances (even though the value of all his property amounted to some £2 million) was becoming worse. One sad consequence was the end of his long and productive relationship with Papworth. Although Papworth had never been as busy, he was increasingly troubled by the ailments of old age. He worked from his home in Bloomsbury with the assistance of pupils and, as he grew older, his two sons John Woody and Wyatt. However, according to Wyatt, the 'effects of very cold weather while practising in Landscape Gardening' began to affect his sight. At the same time he was juggling work for Morrison with a number of other commissions. While dealing with Fonthill, Harley Street and Basildon, he also worked for Lord Lucan on his country and London properties, he designed a new country house (Ornhams Hall) in Yorkshire for George Crow, Morrison's retired partner in Fore Street, and carried out a number of small commissions in and around London.[12] A letter to Morrison written on 12 August 1839 conveys his typical schedule:

> On Thursday, it is most likely that I shall be at Laleham to see Lord Lucan the last time before his departure for Ireland – it will be a day of crowded business but I hope to get to Staines on that night on my way to Bassildon [*sic*] – from Staines I imagine it will be easy to get to the Rail Road (Gt Western) early in the morning – & thence to Twyford & [by coach to] the Crown at Reading by about 11 o'clock … . sleep at the Crown & then your gig could fetch me early in the morning – say 8 o'clock – this would give a long day.

From the beginning there were a number of problems at Basildon which angered Morrison but over which Papworth had little control. Morrison took his family to the house for a short visit over Christmas 1840, but Burton's plasterers were unable to complete their work before their arrival and the bell hanging was unfinished. Then the new hot water system blew up. One of Morrison's servants accidentally emptied the system so the boiler caught fire. Morrison was so angry he considered taking Messrs Smith, the supplier of the system, to court, but his solicitor Ashurst calmed him down: 'I understand that one of your domestics burnt the bottom of the boiler out by turning off a supply which ought to have been turned on. If so, this fact, judiciously mixed up by a skilful counsel with matters having no relation to it, &

a Jury of Tradesmen would lose you the Verdict.'[13] On New Year's Day Alfred wrote from Basildon to his brother Charles (still on the continent): 'We have left Fonthill some time and have been here ever since – that is in person but not in name as, should anyone take the trouble to call, it would be a question of whether a chair could be found for him to sit upon – the house being not half finished and not at all furnished.' Basildon was 'in a wretched condition'.

Morrison's few surviving letters to Papworth from this period reveal his increasing impatience. 'Will you tell me whether Mr Simpsons men are clear'd out – whether the men have finished the lodges, what remains to be done at the Cottages – Whether you have mark'd all the timber that is to be cut – Whether you have done any thing more with Mr Hilliard about felling the beech – What you have done with the man in Oxford, the bank, the measurement of my timber here [Fonthill] & at Basildon – and also about the Keeper.'[14]

In responding Papworth is forced to provide explanations for endless minor problems. The local men were not sufficiently skilled to complete his 'peculiar and particular' park wall of brick and flint, so there was a delay until Henry Burton (who had taken on the work when his father fell ill) and 'some London hand' were engaged. There were insufficient local men to work on several building projects at the same time, then a cottage collapsed before it could be repaired, forcing Morrison to spend more money rebuilding. Papworth's plans for planting were frequently misinterpreted; he wrote, for example, that he had 'never proposed planting at the top or crown' of the hill. Similarly his proposal for the ice well 'seemed quite understood and no other drawing … could have been necessary', but still the plans were misunderstood. Burton's letters to Morrison are similar in tone: 'I will use all exertion to remove your annoyances. The doors *shall* all be down & hung this week … . the Library was done. … The glass has been sent to day.'[15] And it took him months of cajoling to receive final payment for his work.

The situation worsened at the beginning of 1844. Morrison had received information, in the form of a spiteful letter, possibly from one of his tenant farmers or even the Basildon land agent Mr Simmons, questioning the amount of time Papworth was spending on site at Basildon and Fonthill, so he demanded an account of all his work up to the end of 1843 and copies of all his plans. Papworth was not well but replied with a general defence of his impossible situation:

As I have neither a proper plan of the estate shewing the nature of the ground, nor any assistance at Basildon, I cannot I dare say do all that you require of me. The works are done without the personal control that only can enable me to try to fulfil your wishes, and in doing without this I find my reputation in jeopardy.[16]

According to Papworth's son, the relationship finally foundered over the building of the new stables and coach house and Papworth's refusal to hand over his design. Carr's original stables had been close to the house, but Papworth considered they interfered with the views from the loggia on the west front, and proposed their demolition.[17] The new stable block was planned at a distance from the house, close to the kitchen garden, with generous accommodation for horses, carriages and servants. When Morrison demanded to know why there had been little progress, Papworth replied that all that had been agreed was the 90-foot-square space to be staked out ready to build a platform. It was Morrison's changes that had caused the delay, as Papworth tried to explain:

two years ago the place for the Great Stables was well considered, and that 20ft at least lower down from the Ice well left as a mark was as I considered the better place. ... Perhaps I was wrong in yielding too readily to your wish to save a great tree. ... I am not aware of anything like vacillation of purpose in my arrangements.[18]

Papworth continued to work on designs for the stables and his last surviving letter to Morrison dated 21 March gives no hint of their dispute. However, by June the architect Charles R. Cockerell was at Basildon sketching his idea for a new stable block. There is no explanation as to why Cockerell was approached (he was a friend of Papworth's), although Morrison would have known of his work as architect of the Bank of England. However, it would appear Papworth had been sacked.

Papworth retaliated by suing Morrison for an unpaid bill of £224 2s. Morrison then asked Ashurst to investigate all the architect's charges and time spent at Basildon, Fonthill and Harley Street. By the spring of 1845 Ashurst had discovered no discrepancy in the accounts: 'I understand that you expected they would be found to differ materially, but they do not.' Then a 'disinterested architect' was engaged to view all Papworth's works 'for which he seeks to recover fair compensation'. Meanwhile Morrison and Ashurst did their own calculation of Papworth's correct total fee (5% commission), and discovered he should have received £2,500, not the £2,000 already paid. It would appear Papworth had a case after all and in June he was offered 1,000 guineas as compensation. This he turned down.

Why Papworth refused is a mystery: hurt pride, anger, sadness that the trust of such an important client was lost, increasing blindness. The dispute dragged on. More petty details were gathered by Ashurst: 'some of the items charged in one year or in one plan are not charged in another – for sometimes we found this to be the Case several times in Harley St.' Also Papworth appeared to have charged for designs that were not completed: 'P never gave Healey designs for any thing but a single fender ... I bought grates ready made'. 'Simmons says P gave no design for his house – he marked it out & P alter'd it a little.'

A suit was brought against Papworth and in April 1846, after scrutinising the accounts supplied by both sides, Sergeant Manning, counsel on the western circuit, declared against the architect.[19] At the same time Cockerell sent in his bill for his drawings and a model of the Basildon stables. Papworth's health deteriorated and he eventually retired from practice. He was presented on 25 January 1847 with a silver inkstand inscribed by friends from the architectural profession and his former pupils; Cockerell made a speech in his praise. He replied, explaining he was 'exhausted with the efforts of a most active and anxious life, and nearly blind'. He died on 16 June.

Morrison's behaviour towards Papworth appears indefensible and no documents survive to prove otherwise. He could be ruthless in business but his falling out with Papworth still seems small-minded and insensitive. Another architect completed Basildon. David Brandon (a neighbour of Papworth's in London) was engaged to restore Lower Basildon Church in 1846 and he took on the remaining work at Basildon as well as extensions to the Pavilion at Fonthill.[20] However, his contribution to Basildon was minimal. Morrison's vision of the house as a 'casket' to enclose his 'pictorial gems' was largely realised for him by Papworth.

The unpleasant ending of the long and amicable relationship with Papworth coincided with Morrison's final years in the House of Commons. Here, too, Morrison's conduct was far from exemplary, and he ended up being examined by a Special Committee of Inquiry, accused of abusing his position as chair of a select committee.

Morrison's earlier campaign proposing government controls over the railway companies (see Chapter 10) found fresh support in the 1840s from the Prime Minister Sir Robert Peel and the President of the Board of Trade, William Gladstone. Alarm during the height of the railway 'mania' led to the passing of the Railway Regulation Act of 1844 which was meant to impose some central control over railway charges. However, the Act was watered down as Peel and Gladstone came under pressure from the railway directors 'now becoming organized to resist any changes affecting their interests'.[21]

At the time Morrison criticised the government for its timidity; he then returned to the subject the following year. His political patron the Marquess of Lansdowne wrote in support. 'I have long entertained the opinion that it is most desirable that the publick ought not to concede all property in railroads in perpetuity to companies without any reserve of future power to the state.'[22] Morrison's subsequent speech to Parliament was powerful. He was eloquent in his support for the railways: 'Life is absolutely lengthened to us all by this rapid mode of transit; space and time are almost annihilated.' When he and his wife Mary Ann travelled to Scotland in 1823, it took the stagecoach two days and nights to reach the border; twenty years later the same journey by railroad had been reduced to some twelve hours. There was a personal element to his words, as he emphasised the power of the railways to educate the whole population: 'Communication will take place with all parts of the country. There will be no districts to which the light of knowledge will not have penetrated; new ideas and improvements in arts and science, will quickly be communicated from one end of the country to the other; old prejudices, narrow feelings of bigotry and hate will wear away.' From his position as both a businessman and the owner of agricultural estates, he welcomed the role of the railways in breaking down the geographical and intellectual divides between town and country. 'The whole community will be on the same level as to knowledge and civilization. All parts of the country, all sections of the community, will be mutually known to each other, and the collision of thought and feeling will raise the whole people in the scale of civilization. Their intelligence and their morality will be alike improved; and then, indeed, we shall see that this application of its power is one of the greatest benefits yet conferred by steam upon mankind.'[23]

Unfortunately a major section of the population was denied access to these benefits: the labouring classes. But if prices were reduced, they would 'be enabled to leave those parts of the country in which wages are low, and proceed to those in which wages have been permanently higher, or where a greater temporary demand exists for labour'. Morrison's major proposal was consequently to ensure the railways offered 'the cheapest means of transport in the world'. And he applied exactly the same approach as he had taken so successfully in Fore Street. 'Upon the true principles of mercantile science, it will be found that in railways, as in all other mercantile speculations, large profits are most surely attained by a large trade brought into existence by low prices.'

Morrison's speech was made to an almost empty House on the evening of the last day before the adjournment for the Easter vacation.[24] However, he continued to lobby for change by publishing a pamphlet, *Observations illustrative of the defects of the English system of railway legislation, and of its injurious operation on the public interests; with suggestions for its improvement*, in February the following year, which was favourably reviewed in *The Times*. His comparison of British and French railways was based – as was all his evidence – on personal experience. His major investments in railways apart from North America (see Chapter 12) were in France, some £153,000 by 1847.[25] He thought the French system far superior: 'every railway shall, after a greater or less number of years, become the absolute property of the state', including his own Paris to Rouen line. 'They will then, if worked for revenue, constitute a property compared to which the largest treasure amassed in former times by any sovereign or state shrinks into insignificance.' Also, unlike in Britain, the French government took the initiative in deciding on which railways to construct, with the intention 'to give as perfect a communication between all parts of the kingdom as its wealth and populousness will permit'. Not so in Britain. The following month, on 19 March, Morrison proposed that a select committee be set up 'to inquire whether, without discouraging legitimate enterprise, conditions may not be embodied in Railway Acts better fitted than those hitherto inserted in them to promote and secure the interests of the public', and the House was persuaded.[26]

Morrison was offered and accepted the chair. However, even though some members were his friends, the committee was not weighted in favour of regulation. Joseph Hume was the only certain ally. Sidney Herbert, MP for Wilton, was his Wiltshire neighbour but also chairman of the South Western

Railway; his old friend Sir John Easthope was a major investor in railways, Charles Russell was Chairman of the Great Western Railway and George Hudson, MP for Sunderland, was better known as 'the railway king' (and as the model for the fictional swindlers Melmotte and Merdle).[27]

Hume tried to help him, explaining it was vital to 'make up your mind as to the several points you wish to establish – the evidence by which to establish them & the object you aim at by establishing them.'

> The enquiry you have undertaken and the end in view – <u>the benefit of the community at large</u> – will have many shrewd & ready opponents whose interests are against you, & whose efforts will be great to stop the measures you have perhaps contemplated. You should get some person who is accustomed to look at evidence, to whom you must unfold your whole case plans & objects, that they may assist you to select the strong & important facts for the Committee & for the public as you must bear in view always that the final and the most critical tribunal is the public.[28]

The committee met twenty-seven times, sitting two or three times a week, but Morrison was increasingly anxious (his uncomfortable dispute with Papworth was also proceeding through the courts), and taking Hume's advice, he wrote to Edwin Chadwick on 29 July. 'I wish I could induce you to look over confidentially the Evidence & papers and advise me upon them. I suspect the Evidence will be found deficient.'[29] There is no evidence that Chadwick helped him and when the first report was presented to the Commons on 7 August, although it was seconded by Hume, only one proposal was accepted: to set up a Department of the Executive Government for the 'Superintendence of railway business'. Following on from this the Chancellor of the Exchequer proposed appointing a railway board.[30]

Meanwhile, and apparently undaunted by the rejection of much of the report, just three weeks later Morrison presented a second version to Parliament. He had put back all the ideas that had been rejected by the House, including proposals that full accounts of companies should be placed before Parliament and lines should be run privately for only a specified number of years. *The Times* published the report on 28 and 29 August, offering Morrison its personal congratulations. It was 'perfect in all its parts and wants but life to make it a most important production'.

Unfortunately – and to Morrison's embarrassment – *The Times* had published what was in effect only a draft report. Even worse, apart from a clerk, Morrison had been the sole member of the Select Committee to attend the meeting at which the draft report was 'presented'. He wrote immediately to *The Times* explaining their mistake but the newspaper continued to give support: 'In our estimation the paper loses nothing of its importance in losing its official stamp. The arguments remain the same: the information is not less valuable; the facts are equally true.' The editor John Delane sent a personal note to Morrison: 'I hope you will think the error as to your non-Parliamentary report now sufficiently remedied. Its very authentic appearance misled me and I fancied, for it was quite impossible to keep up with the last fortnight's legislation, that it must have been at some time approved and received.'[31]

However, the damage was done. Morrison's integrity was questioned. While Parliament was in recess over the winter he escaped with his family to Italy but the following spring, just before he returned from abroad, Lord Granville raised the status of the report. Then Morrison's ally Joseph Hume appeared to turn on him confirming that he (Hume) had been given no opportunity to approve the draft and that Morrison was quite simply inexperienced. As far as Hume was concerned, 'This was the first [Select Committee] he [Morrison] had presided over & it would be the last'. John Dillon, now senior partner in Fore Street, was furious with Hume for criticising Morrison and with Morrison for escaping to Italy. He tackled Hume in the Commons, suggesting he correct the 'erroneous report in the house'. But he also wrote to Morrison on 20 March: 'to speak plainly (& I write very hastily) you have offended your friends in the house by your absence – they would have you (reasonably enough) give up every object in life to fight the parliamentary battle'.

On returning to London, Morrison had to face a Special Committee of Inquiry set up to inquire into the '*Printing of a document purporting to be the report of the Select Committee on Railway Acts, 1846, 1847 (236) xii*'. To his relief the committee found that 'this irregularity of the proceedings appears to have arisen purely in mistake'. An inexperienced clerk had placed the draft with documents approved for publication while Morrison was out of town. However, Morrison chose not to stand at the general election in the summer. Instead he brought together all his speeches and the Select Committee report into one document, published the following year, in which he spelt out his serious criticism of the development of the railway network in Britain.

> In the history of no country, has there been such a bare-faced sacrifice of the public interests for the benefit of private associations, who, without any efficient restraint or restriction have been suffered to monopolize, and for their own selfish purposes to employ the means of communication of a great industrial nation.[32]

He would have appreciated the notice of his friend the political economist J.R. McCulloch in the fourth edition of his *Principles of Political Economy*, published in 1849, on the 'culpable inattention' of the country's legislation with regard to railways and the 'great ability' of James Morrison in pursuing the subject.[33] He also received a supportive letter from Edward Strutt, member of the first railway board: 'Many thanks for your pamphlets which I have read with much interest. You are certainly entitled to the merit of having been the first to foresee the importance of the Government taking up the question of Railway legislation, & I have always wished that more regard had been paid to your warnings.'[34]

Basildon was Morrison's solace. The next chapter provides a detailed description of the house during his occupancy, its opulent decorations, luxurious furnishings and its outstanding collection of art.

CHAPTER FOURTEEN

⑊⑊⑊

Basildon: 'What a Casket to Enclose Pictorial Gems'

On the whole, we may safely affirm that nobody enjoys life in so noble and varied a manner as Englishmen of the higher classes of society, who rejoice not only in greater wealth, but in a more general intellectual cultivation, than their fellow-creatures. If we consider the fine works of art with which they are surrounded, the opportunities of musical enjoyment, the free use of all the treasures of literature which their admirable private libraries afford, their residence at the most delightful country seats, their travels into the finest parts of Europe, and, finally, the varied and interesting social intercourse which they command, you will agree with me that they have not much left to wish for.

Gustave Waagen, *Treasures of Art in Great Britain*, 1854

In 1847 Morrison retired (or retreated) from Parliament to the splendour of Basildon and the company of those he loved the best, his wife and children. Basildon was above all a family home and Mary Ann's last child, Allan, was still only five years old. The house was sufficiently large to accommodate in comfort all their eleven children from infants to young adults. None of the Morrisons' children had left home; none was married. Charles, the eldest, was thirty in 1847 and the only one with a career. Since returning from North America he had followed his father's advice 'to be a man of business, and to make a fortune for myself'. But he never left his parents' home, moving between Basildon and Harley Street. Alfred was shifting restlessly between a career in the army and Parliament, filling his time hunting, learning Italian and irritating his father; he even contemplated becoming a Roman Catholic.[1]

He was living up to Charles' analysis: 'he does not value money & does like his ease'. Frank, twenty-three in 1847 and the only son who did not go to university, was revealing an unfortunate interest in music halls and actresses.

While Basildon brimmed over with family activity, children's games, sport and lessons, its internal appearance, the furnishings and furniture, the works of art, the *objets d'art* and the extensive library, conveyed a very different message. Morrison, born in a village inn, apprenticed to the haberdashery trade, had acquired not only a fortune, but an education and such sophisticated taste that he was able to choose paintings, sculptures and furniture of the highest quality for all his houses. Though his background was trade and commerce, he could emulate the aristocratic and cosmopolitan collectors of his day; he had joined Waagen's 'higher class' who 'rejoice not only in greater wealth, but in a more general cultivation, than their fellow-creatures'.

Basildon is no longer owned by the Morrison family. James Morrison's grandson Archie sold it with most of the contents shortly after the First World War. It is now the property of the National Trust and presents an interior constructed by the Iliffes who restored it after the Second World War.[2] Only one room gives visitors an understanding of the grandeur and luxury that the house would have conveyed in the 1840s and 1850s. Consequently this chapter will explain in some detail how Morrison acquired his treasures and attempt to provide an impression of the interior when occupied in the mid-nineteenth century.[3]

Right up until his dismissal Papworth was advising Morrison on picture sales, and providing the Seddons and the Snells with designs for furniture and furnishings to enrich Basildon. He suggested to Morrison the possible adapting or 're-arrangement' of pieces of furniture, including cabinets and coffers belonging to the eccentric collector William Beckford of Fonthill Abbey. Morrison was also sufficiently confident to engage dealers to bid for him on a regular basis at Christie's and in other salerooms. He bought a number of pieces at three Beckford sales (1841, 1845 and 1848), using William King. At the first sale, King reported, the prices for the paintings were too high, but he purchased a pair of carved oak cabinets, the 'Holbein' or 'Henry VIII' cabinets formerly in the Edward III Gallery at Beckford's Fonthill;[4] also a pair of 'sarcophagus headed coffers and stands of riga and pollard oak,'[5] a console table of ebony and 'beef-woods', the top a slab of *fiore di persico* and a pair of consoles for books, made of ebony and beef-wood with ormolu mouldings, tops of alabaster and jasper, banded with black marble. At the 1845 sale Morrison bought a magnificent Florentine *pietra dura* table for £388 10s. Waagen thought it 'one of the richest and largest I have ever seen'.[6] Over six feet long, it weighed nearly seven hundredweight. The centre was formed of a 'large oval slab of beautiful Oriental alabaster, and the exquisitely designed borders and devices are composed of lapis lazuli, hero antico, and other costly marbles'.[7] Morrison and Beckford shared a passion for ornate decoration and outstanding craftsmanship.

The dealer Peter Norton attended many sales at Christie's on Morrison's behalf, and was also engaged 'to look after my pictures' at fifteen guineas a year. Robert Hume, who worked for Beckford and the Duke of Hamilton, was both a dealer and a conservator. Morrison paid him £100 in 1853 for cleaning pictures; he also knew how to cure 'Evil' grubs. In Italy, Morrison commissioned a number of copies of marble vases in the Vatican and the Villa Borghese to be made by a carver Giuseppe Leonardi while the architect David Brandon paid a carver called George Howitt, incarcerated in the debtors' prison in Devizes, to supply a statue for the grounds. This was a challenge: 'the fact is I have nearly done it, but as I am obliged to work at it entirely by candlelight I can proceed but slowly with it'.[8]

The most colourful of the dealers was William Buchanan (1777–1864). In July 1838 Morrison had bought Rubens' *The Miracles of St Paola* from Buchanan, a 'bluff Regency character, with a racy manner, a vile tongue and a taste for hair-raising speculations'.[9] On 31 December, shortly after the contract was signed for Basildon, Buchanan called in person and proposed that Morrison buy the entire collection of Edward Gray, recently deceased, of Harringay House, Hornsey. Buchanan had made an offer of £15,000 for the 134 paintings, but calculated that, if sold privately, they might raise a total of £19,505. He needed Morrison to provide the initial investment. Gray had built up his collection with the help of Buchanan, who had acquired for him many Dutch paintings, including Rembrandt's lovely portrait of his mistress Hendrickje Stoffels.

After viewing the collection with Buchanan on 1 January 1839, Morrison took to Harringay, on consecutive days, his wife Mary Ann, Papworth, the artists Henry Pickersgill and Charles Eastlake and the sculptor Francis Chantrey. Morrison had perhaps been warned about Buchanan's 'almost total ignorance about works of art, which enabled him to turn a deaf ear and blind eye to any criticism of his wares, and an utter contempt for his clients and indeed for picture lovers of every kind, institutional, aristocratic or nouveau-riche'.[10] Their verdicts were presumably favourable because on 30 January Morrison agreed 'to stand in the shoes of Buchanan' and to take the pictures for £15,000. Although payment was delayed until the end of the year, Morrison immediately began selling some of the pictures for profit. Aelbert Cuyp's *View of Dordrecht*, for example, was sold to the Marquess of Lansdowne for £1,250, Morrison pocketing the profit of £200.[11]

Morrison and Buchanan's complicated, often acrimonious financial dealings lasted for many years as each tried to make money through the other, Morrison advancing the cash and Buchanan locating and selling the pictures. The first floor gallery in Harley Street (see Chapter 9) was partly used as a temporary location for paintings intended either for Basildon or to be sold privately by Buchanan or through Christie's; Papworth also appears to have kept some paintings, presumably at his home in Caroline Street, Bloomsbury.

Buchanan was always behind with payments to Morrison, but always ready with a new deal.

I have yours of the 13th [January 1841] this morning, mentioning the Bill of £400 to be due yesterday … I had considered it due much later in the month … could [it] be renewed for 2 months at the rate of 10 per cent … as by that time I shall have made Sales of some very valuable property, which is coming home to me by various Vessels. … You are probably aware that Mr Papworth holds some very valuable property in Security for the payt of this sum, in particular a very capital picture by Guido, which was val[ue]d in Lucien [Bonaparte's] collection at 1000gns. Altho' I cannot command at this particular Season of the year Cash for my property, yet if my property were put to the test, I am in reality more solvent in its result than one half of the London Bankers [17 January 1841]. I shall send you the Beckford Jan Steen which cost me 500 gns – the Both from Lady Stuart's sale – the Domenichino St Cecilia of the Cambruso Palace valued at 500£ – and the Guido – Lucien's – valued at £400 – in security of my debt to you of £1213 until you receive payt. thereof. … In addition to the Hogarth and Sir Jos. Reynolds now on your hands [8 June 1841].

Buchanan relied on Morrison buying paintings from him, thus avoiding the trouble of finding another buyer; his commission would gradually cancel out his debts. However, as Morrison's collection grew in size his personal taste became more assured. On one occasion, he went ahead on his own initiative and exchanged the 'large ugly Rubens' (*The Flight into Egypt*) and Veronese's *St Cecilia*, 'a fat lady playing the guitar' for Rubens' 'beautiful' *Holy Family*. When Buchanan offered him paintings rather than cash Morrison replied crossly, 'There must be no mistake. I agree to nothing but payment in Cash and that at once. None of the Pictures mentioned by you will suit me. Don't let us have an interminable correspondence in this business. ... You should hand over the £120 at once.' For all his roguery, Buchanan significantly increased Morrison's art collection. Yet it was Papworth who created the overall concept at Basildon, making the rooms into a 'gentlemanly & very useful suite of apartments'.

The *piano nobile* (first floor) of Basildon contained a number of elegant reception rooms opening off the central staircase hall and each eventually presented a different aspect and interpretation of Morrison's collection, in some a theme (Etruscan, Chinese), in others a period (Old Masters, Dutch, Contemporary British). Morrison's own bedroom and dressing room were also on the first floor and incorporated into the decorative scheme. Papworth planned the colours of the walls, ceilings and carpets to complement one another, making adjustments as work progressed: 'the ceiling of the saloon makes the staircase & dining room look fade[d] – these will need a little strong color & the latter some gilding'.

Basildon's original architect John Carr had shown his daughters around soon after the shell of the building was complete. They thought the entrance 'very singular and beautiful. You ascend into the principal storey by a double flight of steps under a beautiful Loggio [sic] of Columns.'[12] From the loggia there was a dramatic view of the estate and (looking up) the massive columns of soft golden Bath stone soaring up to Carr's decorated ceiling. Papworth added large bronze torchères on tripod pedestals decorated with bas-reliefs of classical figures, used to spectacular effect in the evenings as flambeaux burning colza oil.[13]

From the loggia a door opened into the entrance saloon, called the pink drawing room by the Morrisons. Carr's original neo-classical decorations covered the walls and ceiling – diamond pattern bands, griffins and military trophies.[14] These were painted by Papworth in buffs, pink, lilac and green, and plenty of gilding. The carpet, supplied by Jackson and Graham, was patterned in green, brown and silver, and the Seddons made curtains of crimson silk trimmed with gold, the valances of green satin and the cornices 'richly carved & gild'.[15] They also covered the easy chairs with crimson silk. These colours were used throughout the house: pinks, reds, greens and gold. While Mary Ann despaired of her husband's and Papworth's love of gilding ('I own I always dread Mr Papworth's love of gold and loading in decoration'), she had to be advised by Papworth against too much green.

The pink drawing room was dedicated to musical entertainments for family and friends (there was a Broadwood grand piano and an Evard harp) and the priorities were warmth and light. Papworth put glass in the front door to provide more light, then designed a special blind: 'the wind sometimes gets into the Portico with great force & without giving notice of its approach, & I, having observed its power there, feel it right to avoid much Canvas & provide means for its rolling up – in the way of Parasols of Shop windows.'[16] Along with fine Sèvres Bleu-de-Roi vases,[17] ebony cabinets decorated with lapis and jasper,[18] half-columns of red Egyptian porphyry, candelabra of bronze girls set on marble plinths, bookcases of yellow marble and lapis lazuli, boulle tables and, above the mantelpiece, a carved relief in ivory and ebony of Bacchanalian children playing with two goats,[19] Morrison displayed just one painting on an easel, his 'Leonardo'.

According to his own inventory, Morrison bought *Flora* in 1846 for £772, after Robert Hume confirmed it was a genuine work by Leonardo da Vinci. Gustave Waagen was careful when he published his views after visiting Basildon: 'I am inclined to attribute this head really to the hand of Leonardo himself [but] other portions [are by] Luini.'[20] Luini is now considered the painter of the entire canvas. Buchanan was the vendor on behalf of Sir Thomas Baring of Stratton Park (Baring's wife had a 'prejudice to its nudity').[21] Apparently Buchanan also decided to make extra money by commissioning the sculptor Richard Lucas to produce a bust of 'Leonardo's' portrait before the painting was auctioned at Christie's. In 1907 Dr Bode, the German art expert, bought the sculpture in London, proudly announcing that he had discovered a Leonardo bust. He then exhibited it as such in the Kaiser Friedrich Museum in Berlin, before the correct provenance was revealed.[22] Shortly after, *Flora* was replaced by Charles Morrison's choice of artwork, a less controversial painting by Greuze.

A door opened from the pink drawing room into the central staircase hall; from the central hall, doors opened into the dining room and the octagon room. These formed a suite of three richly decorated reception rooms at the centre of the building.[23] The walls of the central staircase hall were painted a warm red, and the stone stairs and floor covered with a green and gold Wilton carpet. The hall is a double-height space lit from above and the only place Papworth considered large enough to hang Turner's 10-foot-long painting *Thomson's Aeolian Harp*, even though it would cover some of Carr's plasterwork of griffons. Turner was a guest at Basildon, bringing his fishing tackle with him, and a family story recounts his working on *Rain, Steam, and Speed* while in the house (the painting completed in 1844 depicts a Great Western Railway train crossing the Thames). The furniture maker Morant made a special sofa for Mary Ann, to be placed under the *Aeolian Harp*. 'I have considered what you observed about wishing to introduce the fine carved wood frieze or pannel that stands in the library and think it could be made to form a tablet to the back of the proposed large sofa for the Hall.'[24] Chantrey's bust of Morrison was given a place of honour in the hall after being exhibited at the Royal Academy.[25]

The dining room was the only room in Basildon that had apparently been fully completed for the Sykeses, according to the 1829 sales catalogue: it was 'furnished and fitted up in the *most costly and elaborate Manner*', with a 'Screen of Corinthian Columns and Pilasters of Porphyry, executed in Scagliola, on statuary Marble Bases', the lunettes and medallions on the ceiling and walls classical allegories in grisaille (shades of grey) by Theodore de Bruyn. Disraeli was impressed: 'a subdued tint pervaded every part of the chamber – the ceiling was painted in grey tinted frescoes of a classical and festive character, and the side table, which stood in a recess supported by four columns, was adorned with choice Etruscan vases.'[26] Morrison, however, disliked both the paintings and the overall effect of the decorations. He first rejected the scheme of Leonard W. Collmann, head of a large firm of decorators, then David Brandon engaged Ludwig Gruner in 1851 to design polychrome scenes from Dante's *Divine Comedy* for the lunettes and medallions. Charles Moxon completed the painting, using sombre Pompeian colours on the walls.[27]

Gruner was more of an artistic adviser than artist, serving Prince Albert for fifteen years, first, in 1844, on the renovations of rooms at Buckingham Palace, then supervising the interior decorations and construction of terraces at Osborne on the Isle of Wight and later designing a new ballroom and Promenade Gallery at Buckingham Palace (working throughout with Moxon).

He was at ease in artistic society in London, and took a house in Fitzroy Square close to Charles Eastlake (who was responsible for introducing Gustave Waagen to Morrison). In the library at Basildon Morrison had copies of Gruner's lavishly illustrated books *Descriptions of the Plates of Fresco Decorations and Stuccoes of Churches and Palaces in Italy* (1844) and *The Decorations of the Garden Pavilion in the Grounds of Buckingham Palace* (1845).[28]

Gruner was still working at Basildon when Waagen visited in 1854 and helped him measure the paintings. Even though Gruner came with royal credentials, Morrison was, as usual, concerned at the cost of the project. Brandon reassured him: 'The plaster decoration of the walls is exceedingly beautiful and required very careful painting. It is such as is very seldom to be seen & I think you will in this respect be very much satisfied with the effect produced – Grunner's [*sic*] designs have been adopted as the key for the colouring of the Walls and I have endeavoured to prevent Mr Moxon from indulging in any attempts at colour much at variance with them. ... My own opinion of the room is that the <u>effect produced justifies the labour that has been expended upon it</u>, and I sincerely hope the style of decoration will meet your wishes.'[29] The paintings, Carr's chimneypiece, doors and door-cases and sections of the plasterwork were removed in 1929 to be sold along with other fixtures and fittings from the house, and found their way to the United States; the paintings and chimneypiece can now be seen in the Basildon Room of the Waldorf Astoria Hotel in New York.

The Library at the north-west corner, traditionally a masculine domain, was reached from both the pink drawing room and Morrison's dressing room. It was lavishly furnished in the Morrisons' favourite colours, green, crimson and gold. The Seddons used Morrison's own 'embossed green pattern' velvet for the curtains;[30] the chimneypiece, installed in 1850, was made of green marble with white veins; a Persian carpet covered the floor. When the architect Charles Cockerell was designing the stable block in 1844 he cast doubts on the attribution of Morrison's bronze *Bacchante and the Medusa*: 'you will excuse my frankness in saying – it is just possible that it may be an artistic Fraud by some ... French artist. My judgment in sculpture cannot be conclusive tho not a mean one, but if antique it is one of the most precious discoveries of modern times – the identity of the features the né[z] retroussé excited my suspicion.'[31] Waagen was also suspicious of her 'modern look'; for once, it would seem, Morrison had been poorly advised. However, Waagen considered other objects in the room 'few, but very remarkable'. They included four great paintings: Rembrandt's portrait of Hendrickje Stoffels, Poussin's *Triumph of Pan* from the collection of Lord Ashburnham, Rubens' *Virgin and Child with St Joseph*, from the collection of Sir Simon Clarke, and the small Parmigianino, *The Triumph of Cupid* from the Palazzo Barberini.[32]

Morrison commissioned David Brandon to design a peculiar bookcase in walnut of an 'architectural design' for the library, the front part of very 'beautiful brown marble with shells, which is enframed in black marble'. The Snells made the piece, also another dwarf bookcase with a marble top, a centre table and set of chairs, all in walnut. Brandon's 'architectural' bookcase was perhaps inspired by the Holbein cabinets from Fonthill Abbey also on display in the library. Morrison's collection of books at Basildon covered similar topics to Harley Street, with little duplication, indeed books migrated back and forth (at his death volume I of Sir Joshua Reynolds' works was in Harley Street, and volumes II and III in Basildon). There were the works by and about friends, colleagues and acquaintances, political economists, politicians and artists (including his partner John Dillon's son Frank), runs of journals (the *Quarterly Review* and the *Annual Register*), more poetry than novels (Byron, Pope, Cowper, Thomson, Scott and Thackeray), serious parliamentary reports (*On the Training of Pauper Children, On the Employment of Women and Children in Agriculture*), descriptions of royal and aristocratic collections in Britain and Europe and the design of palaces and country houses, studies of Renaissance artists and architecture. Morrison created two impressive libraries, one in town and one in the country, both reflecting the interests of a well-educated and well-travelled gentleman: politics, economics, agriculture, travel, anthropology, literature, art and architecture. Classical literature in Greek and Latin was the only obvious omission.

The oak room, also known as the green room, at the south-east corner was part of the family suite of rooms. Here there was a concentrated hang of Morrison's Dutch pictures including intimate landscapes and genre scenes, by Teniers, Dujardin, Van der Neer, Hobbema, Van de Velde, Geysels, Backhuysen, Jan Both, Pynacker, Paul Potter, Van Ostade. There were also the two pretty Watteaus, brought from Harley Street, three Poussins, Van Dyck's double portrait of the Countesses of Leicester and Carlisle (formerly at Strawberry Hill) and one of their few Italian paintings, Guercino's *St Sebastian with Angels*. The room was richly furnished with velvet-covered chairs, a mantelpiece of fine 'brown red' marble, a cabinet of ebony and purple-wood containing oriental and Sèvres china,[33] a rosewood portfolio stand, Venetian glass and agate cups. It was a room in which to recline, and contemplate the Old Masters.

Papworth obviously had some fun with Morrison's dressing room, designing the whole room 'in the style of the Etruscan Chambers ... in accordance with the Baths of Titus at Rome. ... I know of nothing, at all like it ... it is a good style and a new one, at least in this country. ... It would be executed in Washable paper.' He also designed a special piece of furniture, a 'bath sofa' which disguised the bath. It was six feet long: 'the Cover will be open framed work, & girth web, to take the Horsehair stuffing & mahogany rim & sides – to receive the stamped velvet or other covering. ... The Cover when so made & having a sort of folding Tressel Leggs, will make the convenient Dresing Soffa.' This was a bathroom to linger in, with boulle furniture, bookcases of oriental alabaster, *rosso* and *giallo antico* and black marble, bronze statues and Etruscan vases displayed on a table of white agate, and another with elaborate Chinese decorations.

When Papworth proposed that the family breakfast room (at the southeast corner) be Chinese, then, on second thoughts, Indian, Morrison was delighted. 'The more I think of your new Indian notion for the so-call'd Chinese Room, the more I like it. May you be as happy as you were in the Etruscan.'[34] Papworth was fashionably eclectic, agreeing with his contemporary Thomas Hopper that 'it is an architect's business to understand all styles and to be prejudiced in favour of none'.[35] He regularly sought inspiration in the British Museum, which was conveniently located a few minutes from his home in Caroline Street: 'my idea for the Curtains in the india style – much of fringe & Tassel is avoided and there is fair authority for the design – in the British Museum but nothing for the Lounging chair'.[36] Undeterred, he came up with a chair design for the Seddons in 'mother of pearl & japan & gold', also a table in ebony and mother-of-pearl and he proposed making Morrison's jasper-topped tables brought from Fonthill 'the key note of the whole'. Thomas Seddon, however, was worried by the designs Papworth was providing, writing directly to Morrison:

I hope you will not require a fixed estimate for that drawing because it is so completely different to anything that has been executed & will require great attention & perhaps many alterations before it can be carried out so as to make it perfect that it is scarcely possible to estimate it correctly. I should be sorry to name an exorbitant price & at the same time I am sure you would not wish me to work without some profit indeed you kindly named when I was at Fonthill that you wished me to have a fair profit and I assure you I do not deceive.[37]

Papworth obligingly changed the design to reduce the cost.

At Morrison's death in 1857 the room was described as being Chinese rather than Indian, although even this was a general term. Furniture and *objets d'art* included a Chinese stool inlaid with pearl, a Chinese screen, Chinese metal vases and a bronze incense pot and cover, but there were also Japan china jars, black and old Japan bottles, a Japan table, a boulle commode and a boulle and tortoiseshell armoire. The white marble chimneypiece was possibly by the sculptor Richard Westmacott the elder.[38] Morrison also liked to collect English furniture lavishly decorated with Chinese images: in Basildon he owned a green-japanned bureau cabinet, while at Fonthill he had similar bureau cabinets of red and black lacquer.

The climax was the octagon room, now the only room where National Trust visitors still get a sense of how Basildon was in the mid-nineteenth century. Here Morrison and Papworth indulged their passion for texture, pattern and colour on every surface. On the ceiling and frieze W.B. Simpson[39] painted an exuberant design adapted by Papworth from the Italian sixteenth century. Papworth carefully explained the cost of the work, knowing Morrison always demanded detailed accounts of money and time spent and would often dispute mere shillings and pence. The gilding of the ceiling alone was £80;[40] Simpson's total bill for all the decorative painting and gilding at Basildon was £2,101, a princely sum.

The walls were covered in purple fabric specially dyed at Fore Street to match the ceiling (10 to 12 shillings per yard) and thick bands of gilt papier mâché ornament were placed in the angles of the room. The curtains, designed by Papworth and made by the Seddons, incorporated a tapestry fabric bought by Morrison.[41] 'Two pair of curtains of your tapestry cloth, lined with merino, and trimmed with gold silk & worsted gymp, looped up with rich tassel'd embraces, with deep twine fringe valans with silk trimmings'.[42]

Morrison was both critical and admiring of displays and decoration he observed in the palaces and country houses he visited. At Hamilton Palace (home of William Beckford's son-in-law) Waagen found 'a more numerous display of tables and cabinets of the richest Florentine mosaic than I had seen in any other palace'.[43] Morrison, visiting for the second time in the summer of 1841, wrote to Papworth, 'There is nothing but the Cabinets to envy, and the best of these have been made up by [Robert] Hume. The Dining-room is the only one of the new rooms which is finished (except, by the way, the Library, which is a great failure).' However, he was impressed by the use of marbles, adding, 'it suggests more marble and scagliola for the Octagon Room at Basildon.'[44]

Papworth was already at work designing the marble chimneypiece carved by the sculptor W.G. Nicholls (also much employed by Robert Smirke and Charles Cockerell), an elaborate steel and ormolu fire-grate made by W. Slark & Son, and a marble-topped 'window table'. The fireplace has been removed but the window table remains, with a top of breccia marble called 'sea green polyeverra' from a quarry near Mount Cenis, supported on a structure of 'wood carving gilt and with parts burnished' with silvered glass beneath. The room was also filled with magnificent furniture, including one of Morrison's boulle library tables,[45] and a boulle commode noted by Waagen. There were two large sofas, a centre ottoman and five carved ebony chairs all covered in purple Utrecht Velvet (Seddon called it violet) trimmed with gold. And in the centre, below Papworth's vibrant ceiling, was Beckford's equally ornate and colourful mosaic table.

Once the decorations were completed, Morrison decided to use the octagon room to display most of his British paintings (resulting in a rehang in Harley Street). The twenty-six paintings provide an extraordinary over-view of British art from Hogarth to Turner.[46] Waagen referred to the display as being by 'the most distinguished modern British painters': landscapes (Constable's *Lock*, Clarkson Stanfield's *The Mola de Gaeta*,[47] Turner's *Pope's Villa*), sentimental genre (William Collins' *Fisherman's Farewell*, Wilkie's *The Confessional*), illustrations to literature (Hilton's *Penelope Recognising Ulysses*, Henry Howard's scene from *Paradise Lost*), historical dramas (Eastlake's *Escape of the Carrara Family from the Duke of Milan*). Hilton's *Una Bound by the Spells of Comus* had pride of place over the fire above green china crackle vases from Beckford's collection.[48]

When Morrison turned sixty in 1849 Basildon was almost finished. William Theed had sculpted his bust when he visited Italy in 1847 and A.E. Chalon painted Mary Ann the prevous year. In 1850 he bought two of his most important paintings, Claude Lorrain's *Golden Calf* and the Poussin, *Triumph of Pan*, for a total of over £2,300. And his copies of 'Alcibiades's Dog' arrived from Giuseppe Leonardi in Rome. When Robert Hume completed a major rehang in both Basildon and Harley Street in 1851, he took advice from Morrison and Mary Ann. He wrote to Morrison: 'I believe that when I last had the pleasure to see you it was proposed that I should meet Mrs M at Harley Street to decide which pictures should be set aside to make room for the Claude [*Golden Calf*]. I have last week prepared an arrangement of the pictures upon paper.'

The year 1851 marked the end of Morrison's collecting. He replied to a dealer keen to sell him some pictures, 'I have no more room for paintings.' He had already switched his interest to buying more land to share out among his sons; ill health and the tragic loss of two of his children was focusing all his attention on his legacy.

CHAPTER FIFTEEN

✢✢✢✢✢

The Final Decade

Which of us will death seize as his victim to break the fourfold tie of natural
Union ... Is it I?

> Martha Morrison to her brother James, on hearing the news of
> the death of their sister Maria in Australia, 1849

The acquisition of the Basildon estate and the Gray picture collection gave
James Morrison a social position far above his rival haberdashers and many
merchant bankers: the distance travelled from the Lower George Inn, Middle
Wallop, was immense. However, as he entered his seventh decade, both his
personal and his professional life were plagued with failures and loss:
suddenly his horizons were limited. His long fruitful relationship with J.B.
Papworth had ended in an acrimonious court case, his last spell as a Member
of Parliament had ended in ignominy, Alfred failed to win Wallingford for the
Liberals, his own health and that of his children were giving cause for
concern. He took no more trips to the continent; instead he took the waters
in Cheltenham and sea air at Brighton. He spent an increasing amount of
time at home, with his family, in his town and country houses.

Unlike Augustus Melmotte, the monstrous speculator in Trollope's *The
Way We Live Now*, his wealth really was certain: 'of the certainty of his money
... there could be no doubt.'[1] The annual turnover of Fore Street was a
respectable £1.5 million and Morrison withdrew about £35,000 every six
months, his share of the profits plus interest on his capital of £350,000.[2] With
additional interest from investments in North America and in European railways, from mortgages and loans and rents from his London and country

properties, Morrison's total annual income by 1850 was some £150,000 (about £14 million in today's values). He calculated he was 'worth' about £2 million. However, he was well aware of the risks attached to trade. He would have agreed with the novelist Nathaniel Hawthorne, who observed on visiting the City of London that 'nobody else runs such risks as a man of business, because he risks everything. Every other man, into whatever depths of poverty he may sink, has still something left, be he author, scholar, handicraft man, or what not; the merchant has nothing.'[3]

The City's position as an 'upmarket shopping centre'[4] was beginning to be challenged by the West End, while the economic situation in the United States was only just stabilising (Morrison's dealings with the collapse of the Bank of the United States continued well into the 1850s). As his own health deteriorated, his anxiety to provide for his wife and all his children increased and he decided to invest in more land.

The phenomenon was not unusual in the 1840s: 'Income from accumulated capital could have a greater ability to pay, on the grounds that it offered a steady income regardless of the risks of trade or personal circumstances, and the underlying asset survived for dependants and heirs. By contrast, income from trade and professions was disrupted by ill-health or economic depression, and it disappeared at death.'[5] But Morrison did nothing on a small scale. With access to credit as well as a large annual income, he went on an extraordinary spending spree, acquiring 80,000 acres of land in just four years between 1849 and 1853 at a cost of almost three-quarters of a million pounds. At his death his portfolio of land rivalled the holdings of some of the oldest and grandest landowners in the country. He, however, was less interested in the totality than the desire to give each of his sons their own self-contained estate.

He began by buying an estate in Kent. Hole Park, near Rolvenden, comprised a Jacobean-style house and 3,000 acres of fine hop farms and woodland. He had been lending large sums of money over five years to the hapless owner Captain Thomas Gybbon Moneypenny, MP for Rye. Unable to pay the interest, feed his children or pay their school bills, Moneypenny was forced to sell the whole property to Morrison for just under £14,000, the difference between the value (£92,500) and the debt.[6]

Alfred was named on the conveyance, perhaps because his father thought running a country estate might provide him with a focus. After Morrison retired from the House of Commons in 1847, Alfred had been persuaded by his father to take up the Liberal cause, and he stood for Wallingford, the agricultural town close to the Basildon estate. Morrison paid his election expenses and handed out considerable sums of money as bribes but Alfred still lost by twelve votes.[7] He then declined to take on Hole Park, and instead was given (perhaps he asked for) the Fonthill Park estate in Wiltshire.

The Pavilion had been a building site since 1846, when Morrison's agent James Combes reported on progress, or rather lack of it:

> The work at the House progresses <u>very slow – alteration upon alteration</u>. I am apprehensive that Mr Brandon had not well matured his Plan before he began – tho' it is generally the case with those <u>high Architects</u>, they generally do things twice before it suits. Don't tell Mr Brandon what I say, for I know nothing is ever got by offending such Gentry – for they will do as they like, or do nothing.[8]

Alongside his work at Basildon, David Brandon was involved in a major transformation of the surviving wing of Fonthill Splendens. At a cost of £8,000 he added a tower, a portico, a servants' wing, a morning room and a conservatory to create a large and fashionable, if rather unattractive, Italianate mansion.[9]

Morrison's plan in enlarging the Pavilion may have been to provide an appropriate country house for his eldest son Charles who turned thirty-three in 1850 and was making his own way in the City. However, Charles was a self-professed 'Cockney', his passion the City of London, not the English countryside. Alfred, on the other hand, was an avid sportsman and would become a successful landowner and prize-winning breeder of sheep. His sister Emily was confident he would look after the estate when she commiserated with their mother: 'I dare say you felt very much about giving up Fonthill for good. I believe Alfred is likely to spend his money well & to look after the poor there, & if you see him happily settled & well employed, I am sure you will not regret your self sacrifice.'[10]

Morrison's next purchase was agricultural land, close to his Basildon estate. He snapped up nearly 3,000 acres around Hillesden, part of the 2nd Duke of Buckingham's estate at Stowe, for £106,000. As with Hole Park, he was again benefiting from poor estate management. The Duke's dire financial and marital affairs had been public knowledge for some years. In 1847 he was declared bankrupt with debts of over £1 million. The furniture dealer Robert Hume wrote to Morrison: 'I have been with the Duke who pleads rotten insolvency. He cannot get to the cellar nor the Duchess to her wardrobe. Kensington Lewis has bought Pall Mall House, and a Mr Shelly has bought the estate at Ovington. There will be a sale of goods at Winchester before Christmas. Twenty keepers are discharged and the farmers are to have all [the] sporting and to pay higher rents.'[11]

Sales particulars were regularly sent to Morrison, confirming not only that his wealth was common knowledge but also the high turnover of agricultural estates, some with sizeable mansions included. Many landowners regularly exchanged parcels of land on outlying properties for land closer to their main estates, but others were forced to sell up to raise moneys for dowries and annuities, because of unwise speculation in railway shares, to pay off gambling debts or, quite simply, through living beyond their means. Apart from his high-risk strategy with the Bank of the United States, Morrison could never be accused of living beyond his means. His only extravagance was steadily and remorselessly increasing his capital to safeguard his family's future. He always paid off his debts. In 1852 Morrison paid £90,250 for the Malham estate in Yorkshire; in 1853 he bought the Hebridean island of Islay for the astonishing amount of £451,000 (about £40 million by today's values).

The Malham estate consisted of 10,400 acres of some of the most dramatic upland limestone landscape in the country including a grouse moor, the mountains of High Craven and Gordale Scar. Thomas Lister, 3rd Baron Ribblesdale, was the owner; the sale provided him with much-needed capital to invest in his principal seat, Gisburn Park, just a few miles away. Together with farms, cottages and inns, Morrison also acquired Tarn House, a fine sandstone house which was originally a hunting box occupied by Baron Ribblesdale's agent and called Malham Water House. It is situated on a man-made ledge above Malham Tarn.[12] Morrison's Abingdon solicitor Graham (who helped him with land purchases in Berkshire and Buckinghamshire) wrote to him: 'I thought you would fix upon Malham. It must be a magnificent thing. Should you go there in the Summer and want a companion I shall be glad to treat myself with a view of it. I would rather see it than the [Great] Exhibition.'[13]

For the present, Morrison let Tarn House for shooting. His tenant was Titus Salt, the Bradford textile manufacturer and philanthropist. He had just conceived building an entirely new town, Saltaire, for his employees and also initiated the regular practice of works trips; the first trip was a day's outing to Malham and Gordale Scar.[14] When it came to raising money for a new harmonium the churchwardens of Kirkby Malham Church skilfully played one wealthy businessman against the other:

> In consequence of the singing of Kirkby Malham Church being of late very defective, we have recently held a meeting in the Vestry & the unanimous conclusion was to procure a musical Instrument called a Harmonium by voluntary subscription. Mr Salt of Bradford, at present your tenant at the Tarn House, Malham Moor, has been of great assistance, & has kindly condescended to purchase one for us in London, cost price 45 guineas, but we find our funds as yet insufficient for the payment, consequently your contribution will much oblige.[15]

Morrison first became interested in Islay when he visited with his family in 1849. The 'Queen of the Isles' was developed in the eighteenth century by Daniel Campbell of Shawfield and his heirs; Islay is thus distinguished from other Highland and Hebridean areas by its numerous villages, from Bowmore, created in 1768, to the fishermen's settlements of Port Ellen (1821), Port Charlotte (1828) and Port Wemyss (1833), many with their own whisky distillery.[16] Islay House, a fine Georgian mansion with a large Victorian wing by William Playfair, along with pleasure grounds and hothouses, was the only property of any size on the island.

In 1846 the potato blight reached Islay, leaving about a third of the population facing starvation.[17] The following year the owner Walter Frederick Campbell revealed debts exceeding £750,000, the estate was sequestrated and he left for France with his wife, younger children and a quantity of silverware. When Morrison visited, the estate was being administered by an Edinburgh accountant. Morrison's wealth was so well known that Campbell's son expected that he would buy the island:

> I heard tonight from good authority that Morrison who bought Fonthill Abbey [Campbell's information was incorrect] was going down to buy

Islay ... I am told he is dour and a good man of business, so if he goes as he intends, he will probably succeed in adding to his fortune perhaps at the expense of the present inhabitants. ... Don't talk much about this for reports spread quickly in Islay, and I don't want to spread the news till I am sure that he has made up his mind – at present it seems that he had only determined on looking: I take it however that he won't hesitate long, for by all accounts he has the means at his disposal.[18]

However, the asking price of £540,000 was too much, even for Morrison. An attempt by the Tontine Association to divide up the estate into 3,000 lots to be sold to the tenants failed, and Morrison instructed his son Charles in 1853 to offer £451,000. In 1726 Daniel Campbell had paid £12,000 for the island.

Morrison's friend John Black, now retired from the *Morning Chronicle*, was on holiday in Scotland when the sale was announced:

Wherever I was the topic of conversation in Highlands & Lowlands, was your purchase and the wonder was naturally expressed, how in all the world you could have so much money. When I happened to mention that Islay was only one of your Estates, and that you had Estates also in Wiltshire, Berkshire, Buck, Kent, Essex, Suffolk, Oxford and Yorkshire, people were lost in amazement.[19]

Morrison was no romantic when it came to his Scottish island; Islay was purchased as an investment not a philanthropic venture, as his son Charles explained to the factor. '[My father] does now wish, never to be troubled at all about the place, and only looks at his investment ledger to see how much of his capital he has spent on it.'[20] This was very different to the expectations circulated on the island, where Morrison was regarded as 'one who has the will and the power to do good and who will not fail to seek to promote the moral and physical well being of the people'. Islay House was let to a succession of tenants, Charles again explaining, 'we must make all arrangements as if we were never going to visit the island except in flying visits and at long intervals and ... we shd in all probability always use the Inn'.[21]

Charles did eventually take a considerable interest in Islay, albeit after his father's death and from London (see Chapter 16). Meanwhile he was taking more responsibility in Fore Street, and in the family's investment house,

Morrison, Sons & Co. James Morrison was suffering increasing bouts of ill health so had no choice but to rely on Charles.

Morrison was not just physically sick; family events were causing him increasing grief too. He was used to regular letters warning him of the 'Certain Solemn Change', sent by his God-fearing sister Martha from Bristol where she lived with their uncle George Barnard. In 1849 she wrote that their uncle had died, then soon after she sent more unexpected news: their sister Maria Cope had died in Australia. 'Maria is no more.' Martha had a powerful way with words: 'which of us will death seize as his victim to break the fourfold tie of natural Union. ... Is it I?' Probably thinking it would bring comfort, she let James know their brother Samuel was 'thinking about eternity'.

There was worse to come. Morrison's son Henry hurt his leg playing sport while at university in Edinburgh (he had been sent north under the care of Professor Pillans at the end of 1848).[22] After six weeks of immobility during which Henry optimistically described the injury as 'nothing more than a severe sprain', there was no improvement and the decision was taken to amputate his leg. Mary Ann, Charles and Alfred travelled to Edinburgh from where Mary Ann sent news south to her husband and the rest of their children:

At one oclock to day [21 March] there was a consultation of three of the most eminent men, two of the finest Surgeons, & one Physician ... not the doubt in the minds of either as to the absolute necessity of acting ... without this in two or three weeks he must sink   he will not suffer the least under the influence of Chloroform ... I thank God for his merciful support afforded me thro' this great trial ... Charles also tells me he feels so much better satisfied with the prospect before us than he did yesterday. ... Tomorrow I take up my abode at Mr Pillans ... dear Mr Pillans is all goodness ... Charles will remain with me until Alfred comes ... I know you will all pray for our dear afflicted one & find a consolation in it & may our Heavenly F. hear & answer it.

One of the surgeons was the eminent James Syme (1799–1870), Professor of Clinical Surgery at the University of Edinburgh, an early advocate of ether anaesthesia (which was fortunate for Henry) and renowned for his innovative surgical procedures. Mary Ann continued her letter the following morning: 'Dearest Children. Our dear Henry has borne the amputation well & under the influence of C[hloroform] had no pain. Charles has seen him calm. ... [Henry] thought he was in the Highlands [during the operation].' Unfortunately, the leg suppurated, and Henry had to suffer a second operation. This was not successful and he died on 10 April; he was seventeen years old.

The Morrisons' grief was intense but their mourning had to be put aside for the first family wedding, which had already been arranged for August 1850. Emily was to marry Captain John Grant, the second son of the laird of Glenmoriston and Moy. Morrison had struck up a close friendship with James Murray Grant of Glenmoriston during the 1840 election campaign at which he became MP for Inverness and the Burghs. Grant advised him on political matters in the north and also helped him acquire properties around Inverness (as usual Morrison built up his electoral support through offering loans and mortgages).[23]

There is no evidence that James and Mary Ann Morrison exerted any pressure on their children regarding suitable marriage partners or went out of their way to find appropriate brides and grooms. At the same time the children appear to have been in no hurry to exchange the comforts of Basildon and Harley Street for new homes. The girls would be heiresses, their marriage settlements of £25,000 (with another £25,000 at their father's death) more than those of many aristocrats. The three who did marry before Morrison's death chose husbands from within the relatively small circle formed through the family and business connections of their parents. The Grant connection brought an ancient lineage but neither a fortune nor the expectation of an estate. Emily's description of early married life suggests her father-in-law was unable to provide his son with a settlement comparable to her own.[24]

Emily was married at Basildon by the Revd John Downes (who had married Mary Ann Morrison's half-sister Lucy Todd in 1833).[25] By November the young couple had moved into their new home, Moy Hall, 'an old fashioned house, very warm and very comfortable'[26] on the edge of Loch Moy and a few miles south of Inverness. Emily immediately launched herself into her role as chatelaine, following her mother's example by visiting the poor, distributing broth and commissioning pairs of warm socks to send to her friends in the south. However, as she struggled through her first Scottish winter, the subject of her health began to dominate her letters home. 'I never was stronger & better than I am here, I have got thus far thro' the winter without one cold in the head! Tell Mary that. Yet I have no fire in my room like most ladies in this country.' Her cough was mentioned frequently and she tried to put on weight. 'I dare say the cod-liver oil is beginning to tell upon me. I now take it three times a day, & it seems to agree well. The last two nights I have passed in comparative comfort, as my cough is much less troublesome.' A visit to Lady Lovat ended badly. 'Felt very miserable during the journey, when I got home took a furious dislike to beef-steak tea & toast. Lay down on the floor with my head on John's knees & groaned. John very kind as usual, after a little petting I got better.' In June 1851, less than a year after their marriage, Captain Grant brought Emily back to Basildon for an extended stay; she never returned to Scotland. Moy Hall was let and in October she moved to rented accommodation in Torquay. Tuberculosis was finally diagnosed.

With its fresh air and mild climate Torquay had been attracting the sick for nearly twenty years; visitor numbers rose dramatically after the arrival of the railway in 1850. Tuberculosis (better known as consumption) was the major killer in Europe through the eighteenth and nineteenth centuries, with a high mortality rate among young adults. It had killed Morrison's friend James Mill, whose son John Stuart Mill also suffered from it but recovered. It was not realised that it was contagious until the experiments of Jean-Antoine Villemin in 1869. Emily shared her new home with fellow sufferers though she wrote bravely to her mother, 'my case is a very fortunate one, beside those of some of my neighbours'. The treatment was barbaric: '[The doctor] does not feel apprehensive of the lungs, but he says a delicate bronchial membrane is more sensitive to cold than even a diseased lung. I am still doomed to the oil & a milder form of blisters, & frequent applications of caustic to the throat.'

She struggled on in Torquay for a further two years, then she was moved to Hastings but died there in the spring of 1854. She was twenty-six years old. Morrison gave Charles the difficult task of arranging the financial settlement of the young widower Captain Grant,[27] while he commissioned two stained-glass windows for the church at Lower Basildon, one in memory of Henry, the other to Emily. He approached William Wailes, a prolific designer who worked for the best Gothic revival architects including G.E. Street, Pearson and Butterfield.[28]

From this period Morrison, who had never seemed to be an ardent Christian (his mother's family were Nonconformists), appears to turn to the Church in search of comfort. Perhaps Mary Ann, who was of a stronger evangelical persuasion, influenced him? He kept letters from priests, one, for example, sent to him after Emily's death: 'Religion does not teach us to be Stoics – it comforts us by the assurance that our dear departed Xtian relatives have gone to their Father's house above – and entered into the rest & inheritance of the people of God. Let us prepare to follow them.'[29] Another was a reply to his own despairing letter: he was unable to pray and wondered if God had left him. 'Often after reading God's word I have no particular sensation – no feeling of comfort – should it be so? ... I am unhappy because I am not more unhappy.' The Revd Guest replied: 'I feel certain that the Lord is working a work in your heart, but at present he does not see fit to give you assured experience. Often times our strength is to sit still. How long had Job to wait! – How long Jacob! Yet it came at last!'[30]

Morrison had always assisted the clergy on his estates (Protestants, Catholics, Nonconformists), restoring churches and chapels, supplementing the incomes of poor curates, subscribing to organ funds. Now, however, he gave increasing sums of money to good causes, using a small number of friends to recommend possible projects. Two were of a High Church persuasion: Samuel Wilberforce, Bishop of Oxford (brother-in-law of Cardinal Newman), and his friend the solicitor Henry Pownall. Over the years Wilberforce received several thousand pounds from Morrison towards the founding of a theological college at Cuddesdon outside Oxford. Pownall received smaller sums to distribute to a number of London-based charities. He provided Morrison with details of his approved 'worthy' causes.

> I do not expect that any of them are new to you as your knowledge of London is far beyond mine, my occupations being confined within a small depraved & lamentable circle such as our Prisons and Lunatic Asylums afford. To relieve whom I aided last week Lord Robt Grosvenor and other magistrates to form a Society for the temporary Assistance and employment of discharged Prisoners from our Middlesex Society. ... There is a valuable Socty called the Female Aid Society, which affords a Home to Female Servants. ... Female Refuge at Chelsea for discharged Female Prisoners – the Elizabeth Fry Refuge also for discharged Prisoners ... in

Middx nearly 30,000 pass thro' our Prisons Annually. St Marys Hospital Paddington and the Consumptive Hospital at Brompton have both a large Ward which I think cannot be opened for want of means to pay for Beds.[31]

Pownall's selection overlapped with the Quaker Samuel Gurney's recommendations. When Morrison gave several hundred pounds to his British and Foreign Bible Society (to send bibles to China) Gurney thanked him for 'a surrender of a portion of that which has been so largely bestowed upon thee for the good of thy fellow creatures and for the promotion of Christianity on the earth'.[32]

Morrison's charitable giving was never excessive, particularly when set against his planning for the distribution of his estate. He drew up his will in July 1852, shortly after hearing the confirmation of Emily's tuberculosis. It was a large document: '[in Doctors Commons] it is the longest document upon record. Upon its production were engaged conveyancers and barristers of eminence, and during its progress to completion the testator evinced much anxiety'.[33] He chose neither primogeniture nor 'partible inheritance' – a roughly equal division of property between the wife and children, favoured by the middle classes.[34] Instead, he left £300,000 in investments and land to each of his younger sons, Frank, Walter, George and Allan, and £50,000 to each of his daughters, Lucy, Mary and Ellen. The legacies for Mary Ann, Charles and Alfred were much larger. Charles inherited investments and land to the value of £1 million, the Basildon estate and his father's pictures and papers. This reflected his seniority but also the responsibility he would be sharing with his mother to support and educate his younger brothers and sisters (in 1852 Allan was only ten years old). Alfred's ownership of the Fonthill estate was confirmed, and his inheritance was worth three-quarters of a million pounds. Mary Ann had the use of Basildon and the house in Harley Street for her lifetime, £5,000 in cash and an annual income of £10,000 derived from estates inherited by Charles and Alfred.

Though Morrison still drew an income from Fore Street he had relied for several years on his manager John Dillon and the other partners to run the business effectively; his visits were infrequent and Charles provided the latest news. Now, however, Morrison was told by his doctor to give up managing his agricultural estates. Charles immediately turned to Alfred for assistance.

Father wants you to undertake the management of his land. The physicians agree that he must give up business – and although I have until recently been averse to his giving up the management of his land because I thought the occupation desirable, I now see that both the opinions of his physicians and his own wishes are so decided that I have changed my views. Although, therefore, there are objections to you undertaking it, there seems to be no other alternative than either my doing it or your doing it – and as I am an unmitigated cockney it will be much better that you should be the man.[35]

Alfred had already recommended James Rawlence of Heale near Salisbury to value his father's Berkshire farms: 'his name stands very high as a farmer. ... I should think he was what is called a pleasant man to do business with – there is none of the pretence about him which is common to the race of land agents.'[36] Rawlence and his partner Elias Squarey of Odstock agreed to manage Morrison's estates as a six-month experiment from the beginning of 1854. Their practice was one of the most important in Wiltshire, Hampshire and Dorset.[37]

The arrangement was not without problems as Morrison's tendency to think he was being cheated increased as his health declined. He constantly questioned their charges and accounts, forcing them to write defensive responses. This is one example from many:

Your letter of the 28th inst. both vexed and annoyed me, as you say you hope no improper things will be done at the Basildon Audit ... and that no Pipes, tobacco, nor Spirits will be allowed to the Tenants – If you think either Squarey or myself can be guilty of any improper conduct at your Audits, you certainly ought not to employ us, and I do think it is a great pity, that you should deprive the old Tenants of their Pipe, as many of them would quite as soon go without their dinner as their Tobacco, and for the cost, why spirits & water, is quite as cheap as wine – Since we have managed your Property the Tenants have paid their rents well, and conducted themselves creditably and respectably at the Audits, but of course if you choose to say that they must not have any tobacco, they shall not, although I should much regret such a decision – Waiting your reply. ... P.S. I know of no Audit where the Tenants were not allowed Spirits, & but one where they are not allowed to smoke.[38]

Alfred's approach to estate management was quite different, as he preferred to keep his distance from his agents and tenant farmers. He found his father's constant meddling and interference extremely vexatious. He was playing the go-between, typically writing to his father, 'I see no good reason for these complaints – you get the accounts within a week – the money you get immediately … if you wish to break off your connection with these gentlemen it is better to do so amicably than to drift into a quarrel.'[39]

Though Morrison could not refrain from grumbling about the collection of rents (too low) and the charges of the agents (too high), the relationship continued. Rawlence and Squarey even agreed to provide some guidance for Morrison's third son Frank in land management. Frank was the only son who did not attend university, and his preference for music halls and actresses had been of concern for some time. The latest issue involved his conducting a flirtatious relationship with Emily's sister-in-law Harriet Grant, to the concern of both sets of parents. Morrison had to advise his friend James Murray Grant that Frank needed to try a serious occupation before he could be regarded as a suitable son-in-law. Grant replied: 'I have no wish to press for a hasty union giving due weight to what you say of the bearing of Frank's general character and business capacity which you desire to test in Farming.'[40]

With no other option, Frank agreed to be installed on the Hole Park estate to prove his worth as a landowner and husband. The letters he wrote to his father suggest a surprising degree of attention. He writes: 'it is my most earnest wish to know every thing which is done on the estate in order that I may talk with you about such things so as to relieve your mind as much as I possibly can'. 'I have manured two parts of the paddock by the house, one with ashes for wh I have paid 3d, 3½ d & 4d according to their dryness, and the other part with heaps of pig-dung from my pig-stye & heaps of soil.'

Meanwhile Mary Morrison had been quietly conducting her own affair with a young clergyman, George Goodwin Pownall Glossop. Like Emily and Frank, she had found love within the small circle provided by her parents. The Glossops were old family friends of the Todds (in 1841, Mary Ann's half-brother Joseph had married an elder sister of George) and related to Morrison's friend the lawyer Henry Pownall. Even though the young curate had a small income, the alliance was acceptable: the Glossops were thoroughly respectable members of the professional middle class. Mary received her settlement of £25,000, or an annual income of £1,000 and the marriage

took place at Basildon on 7 February 1854. After convincing his father that
he would make a sober landowner, Frank was then allowed to marry Harriet
Grant at Invermoriston on 26 September. Hole was given to him for his life,
plus an income of £1,500.[41]

Lucy Morrison was the only child to choose a spouse with any money.
The tea merchant George Moffatt was a friend of her father's, independently
wealthy (he would make an additional settlement of £25,000 on Lucy),
middle-aged and inclined to pomposity. Lucy had first refused him, but at the
age of thirty-one (Moffatt was fifty), she may have decided marriage was
better than spinsterhood.[42] According to his descendants, Moffatt was 'a
small man of domineering temperament'; his son called him a pious hypocrite. The jokes he exchanged with Morrison were probably wasted on Lucy:
'The statistics of pigs is both interesting & instructive – & to a man in your
shattered pecuniary condition, most useful: as it appears upon a four monthly
outlay of £70 you obtain a clear profit of £16 so that when lands & stocks fail
& business stands still, you can take to pigs.'[43] But the marriage took place at
Basildon on 6 August 1856. Five months later, Mary gave birth to the
Morrisons' first grandchild, Bertha Glossop.

Morrison's health continued to deteriorate. His weight had increased, he
was 'holding water' and had to use a wheelchair. Knowing he was dying, he
made alterations to his will, leaving the capital in Fore Street, £350,000, to
Charles, the only one of his children interested in business: 'the whole of the
capital employed in such business [that] belongs to me exclusively, and parts
of the premises on which the said business is carried on [that] are my freehold property. ... I give [to Charles] all my interest and goodwill of and in
the said business, and all powers for the admission and removal of partners
into and from the same.' He also gave Islay to Charles, and left Harley Street
outright to his wife Mary Ann, not just for her life. He confirmed Frank as the
owner for his lifetime of Hole Park, then gave the Malham estate to Walter.

He continued to organise his vast archive, working with a secretary to list
the contents of the black tin boxes stored in Basildon and Harley Street. If he
intended to write his memoirs, he had left it too late. The boxes would
remain virtually untouched for the next hundred years, but his lists would
guide his biographers.

James Morrison died at Basildon, on 30 October 1857. He was sixty-eight
years old. Three years before, Charles had written an 'Essay on the Relations

between Labor [*sic*] and Capital' in which he defined his ideal businessman. His father was the model:

A man sparing of words – close in disposition – often intuitively seeing what is best to be done without being fluent in explaining to others his reasons for doing it – wary in his choice of men – cautious and balanced in his opinions – careful never to promise as much as he expected to perform – innovating only in a gradual, practical, and tentative manner – averse to tumult and verbal contention – willing to work in obscurity for a result only to be realised after years of patience – instinctively distrustful of everything showy and popular – and punctiliously correct in the minutest pecuniary detail.

CHAPTER SIXTEEN

ᢓᠫ᠖᠖᠖᠖᠖

Charles Morrison, 1817–1909: 'Statesman in Finance'

Sir Peter Vigo had the wisdom to retain his millions, which few manage to do, as it is admitted that it is easier to make a fortune than to keep one.

Disraeli, *Endymion*, 1880

In his lifetime James Morrison amassed a vast fortune, country and town houses, land, stocks and shares and works of art. He was the Napoleon of shopkeepers, the richest commoner of the nineteenth century, a Leviathan of trade and commerce. After his retirement from Fore Street and his increasing ill health, Charles, his eldest son, became the central guiding power behind the family finances as well as building up his personal portfolio. Among his six surviving sons, it was Charles who went on to substantially increase the family wealth through his canny investments. When Charles died on 25 May 1909 at the age of ninety-two he still owned the town and country houses, agricultural estates and works of art left to him by his father over half a century before. But he had also built up an investment portfolio valued at over £12 million; at the time his was 'probably the largest estate in this country of which any one has had absolute disposal'.[1]

Obituaries, not surprisingly, highlighted the size of his fortune: 'such a great accumulation of wealth could only have been made either by gambling speculations or by miserliness and meanness'.[2] *The Times* repeated the story that he 'habitually kept a large sum in gold as a reserve against serious financial loss'.[3] He was also something of an enigma, 'a man who by simplicity of life and financial acumen became probably the wealthiest commoner of our time'; 'a bachelor, with no expensive tastes … he lived a quiet, retired, and save for his immense speculations, an entirely uneventful life, disliking publicity above all things'.[4] And he made no attempt 'to evade death duties by disposing of his wealth in his lifetime'.[5] This chapter focuses on this shy bachelor and his astonishing ability to make money.

Charles was always shy; at Edinburgh University he had been urged by his father to go into society: 'you must learn from men as well as books'.[6] He had been afflicted with debilitating headaches and a boy was engaged to read to him. However, he found like-minded scholars at the Speculative Society, including the classicist John Stuart Blackie, and proved himself an outstanding student, in 1834 winning the 'gold medal for the best scholar in the Humanity Class' of the university.[7] When he had completed his studies, Professor Pillans sent him south with his blessing, a copy of *The Wealth of Nations* and some advice:

> cast aside that extreme reserve which looks more like the suspicion & cautious circumspection of age, than the openness & ingenuousness that are expected in youth. ... Throw off most particularly, all reserve & concealment with a father who deserves all the kindness & confidence you can shew ... take a modest part in ordinary conversation, however trifling it may appear & not consonant with your own thoughts & pursuits, the social ties that are thus knit & the kindly feelings that are thus cherished, contribute no small share to the sum total of human happiness.[8]

It was advice Charles had difficulty following. At Trinity College Cambridge he continued to be plagued by headaches but also found the intellectual quality of the teaching and his fellow students poor when compared to Edinburgh. Letters to his mother (rather than his father) expressed unhappiness, frustration and sickness. 'The College lectures are twaddle ... really for a man of any ability & inclination for study, the course of education, so far as it depends on the College routine wd be below contempt.' '[Send me news of the] monied world ... as I am here in the midst of a set, who know no more of what passes there than of the politics of Timbuctoo'.[9]

After leaving Cambridge without taking his degree, he suffered a mental and physical breakdown, exiling himself on the continent for two years. With only a courier for company, he suffered loneliness and continuous ill health.

Letters became increasingly despairing and guilt-ridden; this, for example, written to his father from Naples, Christmas 1840. 'I must give up the hope of making a fortune for myself or of taking my proper place in your family & in England, & make up my mind to kill time as well as I can on the Continent, till nature shall otherwise dispose of me.' He added that while grateful to his father, he considered the allowance he received of £500 a year too much for such a purposeless life.

Then came the surprising news that Alfred had left Cambridge after only one year to join the newly created merchant house of Morrison, Sons & Co. in Moorgate Street (see Chapter 11). Charles' black mood began to lift as he focused on the 'monied world' rather than his personal situation. He returned to England, 'to learn more correctly than I can do at a distance the future prospects of the new house. Your name & capital are foundations for a splendid business.'[10] The North American experience (see Chapter 12) revealed his outstanding ability as a financier.[11]

His first opportunities in the City were provided by his father, including directorships of the Paris and Strasbourg Railway and the Victoria Docks Company. Morrison's business acquaintance Sir John Easthope was a director of the French railway (he had published some of Charles' letters from America in the *Morning Chronicle*) and his American associate George Peabody was Director of the Docks Company, so Charles was instantly positioned within an established investment network. He and Peabody were soon exchanging information on the financing of North American railways.[12]

Morrison's Canadian interests had been minimal, but Charles decided to involve himself with the country. It was viewed at the time as a 'remote and fragile colony', 'its industry primitive and kept in that state by the dumping of cheap exports from the south, its agriculture hamstrung by inadequate communications'.[13] He began to invest in the Trust and Loan Co. of Upper Canada, which was formed in 1848 with capital of half a million pounds. The trust company was established 'for the purpose of receiving, upon the security of a large subscribed capital, money on deposit at a fixed rate of interest, and lending the same [to fund] mortgages of real estate in Canada'.[14] The depositor could be assured he would 'have the entire investments of share and loan capital in Canada as a collateral security'.[15] Charles was a Director by 1851, Deputy Chairman in 1869 and finally President in 1890, the 'father of the company'. He was relieved to be able to report to the board in 1862 that the Civil War in the United States 'has not been of a prejudicial character; indeed the condition of the agricultural class, with which this company is so intimately connected, is one of marked prosperity'.[16]

All his addresses to the company reveal his natural caution and dislike of risk. There were regular complaints from shareholders that the return was a mere 6% (the company borrowed money at 5%), but Charles patiently explained the increasing competition in Canada, that the company had to seek out mortgagees, that they might venture further west in the territories but 'this was a matter to be proceeded with with very great caution. It must be remembered that in a new country the value of land was liable to great fluctuations, and circumstances might arise in which no one would want to buy it, whereas in an old country land always had some value'.[17] In 1895 he cited the catastrophic collapse in South African mining as a warning: 'a great number of persons, who wanted to get a high rate of interest, instead of being contented with a moderate rate, which was all that could be obtained with really good security, had lost a considerable amount of money'.[18] It was probably as well he kept his much more detailed analysis of the world situation in 1895 to his scrapbook:

[1895] remarkable beyond all years I can remember for the considerable no. of disasters or grave troubles wh have occurred during it 1, the Chino Japanese war, 2 the Armenian massacres, with the attempt of the Powers to stop them ... 3 the check given to the returning prosperity of the US by the continual drain of gold to Europe, 4 the wild speculation in S African mines ... 5 the miserable agricultural season owing to the drought 6 Cleveland's message threatening war on Venezuela ... 7 the alarming aspect of the dispute between the Uutlanders & the burghers of the Transvaal ... the preparations for a little Ashantee War ... 8 the Cuban revolt.[19]

A personal memorial to Charles in the *Agricultural Economist and Horticultural Review* confirmed his (and his father's) cautious approach to investments:

The late millionaire [Charles Morrison] had nothing of the gambler in his nature. He, or his celebrated father before him, had once tried a scientific experiment of investing in all sorts of speculations from solid land holding

to 'wild cat' ventures, and had worked out the results with careful watchful-
ness. It was found that the ventures which promised so much merely ended
in equalising an average of four per cent all round. The losses balanced the
gains and left the speculator with simply a fair low return on his capital.
This gave Mr Charles Morrison his lesson. He became a statesman in
finance.[20]

In 1863, six years after Morrison's death, Charles and his father's old friend
and partner John Dillon took the momentous decision to retire from
Morrison, Dillon & Co., to dissolve their partnership and form a limited
company with an injection of new capital. Charles had no wish to remain
head (however nominal) of a large wholesale warehouse; neither did any of
his brothers. He was only forty-six years old but a plaque given to him as a
farewell from Fore Street refers to his recurring ill health. It was the end of an
era. From this moment the family no longer had any 'hands on' involvement
in trade.

The house was one of the first in the City to make the transition from
family capitalism to a 'more modern, corporate form of enterprise'[21] while
textiles were still 'a flourishing, integral part of the commercial city'[22] (the
accounts of Morrison, Dillon & Co. up to July 1863 reveal the turnover as
holding at just over £1.5 million). The following year the Fore Street
Warehouse Company was formed. Ten thousand shares of £1 were offered to
the public plus 30,000 shares of £20, to 'purchase the goodwill, stock-in-
trade, leasehold and freehold premises, and entire business of Messrs
Morrison, Dillon & Co.'[23] George Brown became the only new Director with
experience of the shop floor (he had been in charge of French lace).[24]
Charles received £600,000, to be paid in half-yearly instalments.[25]

A few months after, John Dillon wrote to Mary Ann acknowledging that
her family had made his fortune: 'Other arrangements have been made in
Fore Street but they do not in any manner lessen my wish to do any thing
on my own, during the probably short remainder of my life, to manifest
my warm feelings towards the business there, and towards your family – and
(if you will allow me to say to yourself, what I have already written to
Mr Charles Morrison) that it will give me great pleasure to attend, in any way,
to your interest & your wishes – for the promotion of which you may always
command me.'[26] He died three years later.

The Morrisons' solicitors handled the transformation of the textile business in Fore Street. John Morris (1823–1905) had joined Ashurst's at 6 Old Jewry in 1841, becoming a partner in 1854.[27] His advice was valued by all the Morrisons; Walter eulogised: 'we all appreciate Mr Morris' resource, his tact and his diplomatic ability. If you were ever to get into a tight place, I do not know anyone better in the City of London to get you out of it.'[28] Morris' legal brain was essential to Charles when he began to take an interest from the mid-1870s in South America, and Argentina in particular, a 'new frontier' that offered investment potential as 'rates of interest in European and US investments fell in the last third of the century'.[29]

British influence in Rio de Janeiro, Valparaiso and Buenos Aires had been strong since the beginning of the nineteenth century; hides, skins and wool were bought from the River Plate area, while the Argentinians purchased British textiles and hardware.[30] James Morrison's merchant bank, Morrison, Cryder & Co., had invested in goods travelling between Canton (tea), London, North America and Valparaiso. Barings was the major British bank lending money from 1850 to the governments of Chile, Mexico, Venezuela and Argentina; Brazil was 'Rothschild country'.[31] 'The coffee of Sao Paolo, the wheat and cattle of the River Plate, the minerals of Mexico, and the nitrates and copper of Chile were moved to the seaports along railway lines partly or wholly financed by British capital.'[32]

The advent of joint-stock enterprises in the early 1860s had provided the ideal vehicle for developing South America, but not all companies were successful. Charles began to buy shares in the Mercantile Bank of River Plate (established in 1872) because their value had collapsed. According to one of his obituaries he 'was said to have exerted a beneficial contracyclical influence on the stock market by buying up securities of sound companies which had fallen disproportionately at times of general panic'. By 1880 he was the second largest shareholder and the following year he was behind the formation of a new company, the River Plate Trust, Loan & Agency Co., which acquired the assets of the Mercantile Bank.[33] John Morris handled the deal.[34]

The omens were good, General Roca became President in 1880, Buenos Aires was 'forcibly and finally integrated with the country' and British investment in joint-stock enterprises soared.[35] The company was to become one of the most profitable of all Anglo-Latin American ventures. The new agency positioned Charles, his brother Walter (also a major shareholder) and their

solicitor at the centre of a 'network of Anglo-River Plate mortgage, investment, utility and railway companies ... linked by directorships, common
management services, and overlapping investment patterns'.[36]

The company was modelled on Charles' other venture, the Trust and
Loan Co. of Upper Canada. The prospectus drawn up for British investors
stated the business of the company as 'the raising of money here on debentures and lending it again in the River Plate at the much higher rates of
interest prevailing there, thus occupying the position of middleman between
lender and borrower'.[37] By 1887, the company had acquired agencies for
drainage companies, railways and tramways, gas and telephones;[38] it also
offered a wide range of management services 'from issuing bonds to bribing
politicians'.[39] The list of interests is reminiscent of James Morrison's investments in North America forty years before, but railways and canals have been
replaced with new forms of communication: the tram, the telegraph and the
telephone.[40] By 1895 Charles owned half a million pounds' worth of shares
in two dozen British-registered Anglo-River Plate companies.[41]

Charles was also able to advise his youngest brother Walter, who began to
take an interest in Argentina from the mid-1870s. He first joined the board of
the Central Argentine Railway, becoming Chairman in 1887, then, the
following year, Chairman of the Argentine Land and Investment Co., which
invested in the land across which the railway was constructed.[42] Walter
considered himself personally involved: 'I am the Chairman of a very humble
Railway ... in South America and in that Railway we have some fifteen thousand shareholders.' He was also clear about the economic significance of the
railway being 'domiciled' in Britain, where 'I know that we spend an enormous amount of money for railway material and plant'.[43]

Construction of the railway began in 1863 but, inevitably, there were difficulties in raising capital. The railway was part of a trans-Andean line
connecting Rosario and Cordoba, financed and built by the British (the
contractor was Thomas Brassey). The intention was to open up the interior
of Argentina, gaining access to the valuable copper and silver mines. Cordoba
was reached in 1870 but the railway only began to make a profit in the
1880s.[44] Accounts of the ordinary general meetings in London reveal
fluctuating profits vulnerable to the effects of the weather on the wheat
and maize harvests, although in 1893 'insurgent forces held a large part of
the line'.[45]

Unlike Charles, Walter enjoyed travelling and his position provided a perfect excuse to sail to South America. In February 1891 he was in Buenos Aires.[46] His sister-in-law Mabel Morrison marvelled at his stamina: 'he likes the climate immensely & says it just suits him, he weighs 12 st 2lb takes no medicine of any kind & says he is up to work of all sorts'.[47] The Central Railway was being challenged by the rival Buenos Aires and Rosario Railway Co. and Walter successfully negotiated their amalgamation, to form the Central Argentine Railways Co. Ltd. He also formed a partnership with George Drabble, establishing the River Plate Fresh Meat Co. which used ground-breaking refrigeration to transport beef across the country. At his death in 1921 Walter had several million pounds invested in companies all over the world but half a million pounds remained in South America.[48] A street in Rosario and a station and town in Cordoba were renamed Morrison in his honour. He and Charles were major River Plate capitalists.[49]

Business interests brought the two bachelor brothers together but neither was particularly sociable; they enjoyed their own company. As a confirmed bachelor, Charles was comfortable moving between 57 Harley Street and Basildon, head of the family but sharing responsibilities with his mother. London, especially the City of London, was his home. Once in the City he could stroll between his own office, board meetings, his lawyers, the Fore Street warehouse, the banks handling his money, finance houses and the Stock Exchange. He would have agreed with T.H.S. Escott, 'If England be the heart of international trade and cosmopolitan finance, and London be the heart of England, the City is the heart of London.'[50] His commitment can be measured in the number and range of his investments, including railways, industrial dwellings, docks, markets, breweries and hotels.[51]

He was not a traveller; he probably never left Britain after his return from North America in 1843 and even though he spent thousands of pounds on improvements he rarely visited Islay. He never accompanied his widowed mother and younger brothers and sisters on their annual trips through Europe and the Near East. But he travelled through time and space in his reading, favouring history, exploration, anthropology, memoirs, biography and religion. 'He loved books and hated show.'[52] And at board meetings, on committees of inquiry, planning the formation of new companies, he was transported for a few hours across Europe, the Americas, Africa, India and Asia; his understanding of economics and his personal investments were on a global scale.

His pleasures were mostly cerebral. He attended lectures, for example at the Royal Statistical Society; in 1889 Mr Giffen discussed the accumulation of capital in Britain between 1875 and 1885, a topic he would have found riveting. His brother Walter's lectures on banking systems delivered to the Co-operative Society would have been equally interesting. Presumably he attended exhibitions at the Burlington, the Grosvenor and the New Gallery, to all of which he lent paintings. He was, however, always interested in new inventions: 'Saw at the side of the Polytechnic, exhibition of the Kinematographe. On a sheet picture with a number of figures in motion. Was struck with the numerous figures moving in different direction & at different speeds, with a RW [railway] train approaching station, small at first, growing.' He invested several million pounds in telegraph and telephone companies (his lawyer John Morris was one of the promoters of the Telephone Company which set up the first exchange in the City in 1879) and he kept a press cutting on the phonograph being introduced to Tibet.[53]

Charles was an avid reader, but also devoted considerable time to writing, completing the draft of a book on the Gospels and publishing two books, one on the relationship between labour and capital,[54] and the other entitled *Doubts about Darwinism*. He also exchanged opinions on books, authors and current affairs with close family and friends.[55] He thought deeply, and as he got older he found himself looking both forward and back, exercising clear judgement and some prophecy. In July 1897, shortly before his 80th birthday, and as the nation celebrated Queen Victoria's Jubilee, he looked forward sixty years to 1947:

> That the struggle between capital and the workmen will continue & be intensified appears certain – that our Government will become more democratic & that steps in the direction of Socialism, or at least of relieving the poor at the expense of the rich equally certain. Also, a great further progress towards equalizing the position of men & women also certain. Whether our exports can continue to grow notwithstanding trades unionism & the development of other countries is more doubtful. The US & Russia will be 2 monsters of Prophetic growth unless they break up. ... Will the continuous increase in the consumption of coal bring the UK by the end of 60 years to the point at wh we shall certainly be inferior in this respect to US certainly & perhaps to some other countries. I guess that a

beginning of decay from this cause may occur. Will there be a great revival
of our Agriculture? I think not. Will the Steam Engine become obsolete? I
think not. Will Electricity be used to a far greater extent than now? Yes. ...
Will belief in a God & a world to come decline? I think unbelief or agnosti-
cism & secularism will continue to spread for a time. But I conjecture that
after a time there will come a reaction in favour of belief, tho this reaction
will fail to reach a large proportion of mankind. ... Shall we be masters of
India 60 years hence? Or will Russia be there? I doubt the former, & dread
the latter. ... We shall have arrived at completely Democratic Government,
including, most probably, female suffrage. Shall we have a Monarch! This
will, I think depend on the conduct of our sovereign & in the occurrence
of events wh may throw the monarchical principle into discredit. Already
we have made some progress towards Socialism with graduated taxation of
the rich, the acceptance of pensions for all on attaining a certain age, free
education for all. ... My father sent me to see the Coronation of William
IV, lest there shd never be another. Perhaps our grandchildren [will] be in
time to see one, though purged of all mediaval [sic] & aristocratic features,
60 years hence.

The eminent obstetrician Dr James Black (who attended his sister-in-law
Mabel: see Chapter 17) was one of his closest friends; Black provided him
with medical advice and unusual pieces of 'medical' information: 'some
female monkeys menstruate, some not. ... Female monkeys have the hymen.
No other animals have it.' The copious notes Charles made on his reading
reveal a particular interest in sexual practices. For example, when reading
J.A. Simond's study of Walt Whitman in May 1894 (published 1893) he
notes: 'friendship between men shd be a passion equally strong, based in
great measure on admiration of physical beauty, contact, kisses'. Two months
later he tried reading Lady Burton's life of Sir Richard Burton, and the first
volume of the *Thousand and One Nights*. 'Other translations give no idea ...
coarseness ... towards ladies of good position, & the constant wearisome
introduction of mahometan pious ejaculations intermixed with vice &
obscenity'. He was also interested in apparitions, ghosts and sea serpents,
strange customs and exceptional individuals. A biography of Arthur
Macmurrough Kavanagh, for example, revealed he was born without legs or
arms. Charles commented: 'A keen sportsman in India & Albania, salmon

fisher in Norway, bold rider to hounds in basket strapped to saddle, active MP in support of Irish landowners. ... I think I was told or read that he drove 4 in hand, but book does not mention this. Unluckily book gives no acct of the ways in wh he contrived to do all these things. Married, had at least one son.'

For a millionaire, Charles lived a relatively modest life, keeping between four and five servants in Harley Street after his mother's death in 1887. Alice Nash cooked his dinner in his final years: 'I am writing to ask you if I might go for my holiday next Friday evening after I have cooked your dinner.'[56] He may have remained a bachelor simply because he never met anyone he wished to marry, or who wished to marry him. And any desire for 'the decent monotony of the domestic hearth'[57] could easily be found at Basildon with his mother (who died when he was seventy), his sister Ellen, who outlived him by just a few months and his niece Bertha Glossop, who was raised by them from infancy after the death of her mother. However, according to the family biographer, he was afflicted by serious inflammation of the bladder: 'so far as he could Charles always sought to keep himself and his business activities out of the public eye. One reason for this was the simple one that for the last 50 years of his life and more he suffered from chronic cystitis, which made appearance in public far from easy.'[58] By the 1870s, cystitis was known to be caused by stones, prostatic disease, stricture or gonorrhoea. If true, this may have contributed to his reluctance to marry.

Charles first began to consider the distribution of his wealth after the sudden death of his brother Allan in 1880 (Allan died as a result of a serious nosebleed). He began by drawing up a fund for nine of his Todd cousins, investing £40,000 to provide each of them with an annual income of around £200. By 1906, twenty-six cousins were benefiting from a fund of £160,000. And on 6 September 1907, the anniversary of his father's baptism, and just before his 90th birthday, he gave his cousins a further several thousand pounds each. H.H. Asquith was about to introduce inheritance tax of 11% payable on estates of £1 million or more.

He also increased his charitable donations, mostly linked to the Church of England. His favourite charity was the Bishop of London's Fund, established in 1863 to build churches in a rapidly expanding London. Charles gave £5,000, then £1,000 almost every year, reaching a total of £36,000 by 1900. Thereafter he increased the annual donation to £1,200.[59]

He added to his property portfolio by building offices in the City of London, including two blocks, Finsbury House, on the corner of Finsbury Circus and Bloomfield Street (1892), which cost £43,000 and the much larger Basildon House in Moorgate (1898). He used the architects Gordon, Lowther and Gunter. Basildon House cost over £120,000: in a 'free Renaissance turning Baroque style', it was 'opulent' but also 'rather vulgar.'[60] It was built to last: 'In the house I am building at Kings Arms Yard the Foundation will go down 30 ft below level of street, mud of a brook & piles of wharf found 10 ft below that level.'[61] The buildings were divided up into dozens of small offices, let to companies with interests all over the world from mining to communications.[62]

Building work on the Basildon estate and Islay was on a much smaller scale, though always with the aim of adding value to the property and at the same time improving the lives of his tenants. Not everyone agreed. A resident of Islay was critical of Charles' 'bachelor life, devoting himself to business in the city; and as he is no sportsman or agriculturalist, the administration of the estate is given over to factors.'[63] However, the surviving correspondence with his principal factor John Dickson reveals his close involvement in the island, even though he rarely visited: 'the minutiae of estate business dealt with, such as harvests, sales, rents and arrears, construction and ornamentation, as well as the perennial problems of steamer provision.'[64] He invested for the long term, paying for repairs and the building of schools, churches and cottages and contributing several thousand pounds towards a new paddle steamer to carry livestock and other island produce to Glasgow. When a proposal was made in the early 1870s that the users of the shipping service should subscribe to a new company, Charles was in favour of only the major landowners investing; he believed the farmers should not divert capital from their farms.

His approach to his estates in Berkshire and Oxfordshire followed a similar pattern with a programme of building schools, cottages and a church. His greatest contribution was possibly reducing rents, year after year, as the agricultural depression coupled with extreme weather took its toll.[65] In 1893 he noted the effect of severe drought in the south of England and the Midlands: 'no year of equal drought since I think 1817. ... Straw very short. Food for stock terribly scarce. Farmers obliged to sell immature animals. Prices of all farm produce very low. ... I wonder there were not much louder [complaints] & that the no. of bankruptcies & abandonment of farms were not far more numerous, the failures to pay rent much more numerous.' And in 1897, after reading a piece in the *Graphic* on the growth of the British Empire under Queen Victoria, he noted, 'There is of course one great & deplorable exception to the general expansion of our industries Agriculture, which has been declining during about the last 20 years ... food dependent on foreign countries.'

In 1906, at the age of eighty-nine, he prepared a speech 'On Building Cottages for Working Men', his response to concerns about rural depopulation led by young men deserting the countryside for better lives in cities:

> There is at present a chorus of voices calling on landowners to cut up a good portion of their land into areas of a few acres building a cottage on each area, which are to be offered to more of the working class, who are presumed to be ready to take them & pay rent.

Charles was critical of the proponents of such a scheme for knowing 'little of agricultural matters'. Not only would the costs fall solely on the landowner, but where would the man be found 'willing to work hard & long, without wanting an occasional visit to London or the nearest great town,' and able to find 'sufficient amusement in watching the progress of his crops'?

Charles was a curious man, who appears to have led 'an entirely uneventful life', or rather a life devoted solely to the accumulation and management of investments. He was very different to some of the more colourful City financiers, for example the corrupt Baron Grant (whose real name was Abraham Gottheimer), who raised a fortune on joint-stock companies which promised but never delivered huge profits:

> There was a time when all persons speculatively inclined came to believe that Grant held the Philosopher's Stone, that everything he touched turned to gold, but the gold eventually turned out to be nothing but dross. He had a very great following of people who wanted to get rich quickly. In consequence, he had the command of very large sums of money, and thinking his riches had come to stay, he committed great extravagances.[66]

There was the talented and flamboyant Harry Panmure Gordon, 'probably the most enviably connected of all late-Victorian stockbrokers',[67] who indulged in a new pair of trousers every day of the year. Charles knew Gordon well enough to include his recipe for the prevention of gout in his scrapbook: 'drink every night before going to bed, a teaspoonful of Effervescent Citrate of Lithia in a glass of water mixed with a teaspoonful of Citrate of Potash'.[68] In fiction, there is the monstrous financier Augustus Melmotte. Trollope presents an unforgettable image of the City and the allure of money:

> Of the certainty of [Melmotte's] money ... there could be no doubt. There was the house. There was the furniture. There were the carriages, the horses, the servants with the livery coats and powdered heads, and the servants with the black coats and unpowdered heads. There were the gems, and the presents, and all the nice things that money can buy. ... The tradesmen had learned enough to be quite free of doubt, and in the City Mr Melmotte's name was worth any money, – though his character was worth but little.[69]

Charles was no swindler; no illegitimate family has emerged, no lover (male or female), no addiction to opium or visits to prostitutes. As the years passed and his wealth increased, he became more and more fascinated by the lives and deaths of millionaires, filling his scrapbooks with comments on new biographies, evidence of philanthropy, the comments in obituaries and the contents of wills. On hearing of Ruskin's death in 1900 he wrote: 'Ruskin died recently. Inherited £200,000. Left little except some land. Was it art or partly mismanagement?' He preferred Samuel Lewis, who died the same year; the 'great money lender ... said to leave 1 m to have received the best society. Began with nothing, or nearly nothing, & to have been much liked by many of those out of whom he made his wealth.' He was impressed by honesty and a sense of honour in business, admiring, for example, the principles of the iron and steel magnate Andrew Carnegie, who 'had not even the ordinary school education'. He kept his workers 'always employed, even at some loss ... [and employed] promising young men, giving them a share in business however <u>small</u>'.[70] One of Charles' obituaries summed up his own personal relations: '[Charles] was most generous to all he employed, and most just to all with whom he had dealings. He was kind, considerate and accessible to those who did not want to prey on him.'[71]

In 1908 he added up his fortune; it was £13,952,770 16s. 6d.[72] His port-folio of investments (the capital account) was over £12 million. There was plenty left, after death duties had been paid, to make his surviving brother and sister and all of his nieces and nephews very rich indeed. However, he could not control what they chose to do with their fortunes.

❧❧❧❧

CHAPTER SEVENTEEN

Alfred Morrison, 1821–1897: 'Victorian Maecenas'[1]

To surround his interior with a sort of invidious sanctity, to tantalise society with a sense of exclusion, to make people believe his house was different from every other, to impart to the fact that he presented to the world a cold originality – this was the ingenious effort of the personage [Gilbert Osmond] to whom Isabel had attributed a superior morality.

Henry James, *The Portrait of a Lady*, 1881

Alfred was thirty-six years old when his father died in 1857. He had been leading a bachelor existence at Fonthill for the previous seven years, attended to by a middle-aged housekeeper and three servants, and taking responsibility for the majority of his father's estates with the assistance of the land agents Rawlence and Squarey. He was already extending his own estate, building cottages and breeding prize-winning horses and sheep. His personal address book is littered with the names and addresses of blacksmiths, wheel-wrights, dealers in animals and animal feed, gamekeepers and nurserymen, notes on North American farming techniques and the pedigrees of his horses. He also supported the churches on his own and neighbouring estates, paying for restoration work and internal fittings.

He had tried again in 1852 to win the parliamentary seat of Wallingford, standing as a free-trader against Richard Malins, a London lawyer. The campaign was lively, both sides combining printed insults with bribes. Alfred was accused of favouring foreign labour over British while his weakness as a public speaker (the family shyness) was a gift to the Tories who depicted him 'always experiencing a painful difficulty in giving utterance to his political opinions – if indeed he possess any'.[2] One hundred special constables were sworn in to keep order during the poll, three men died after being carried from their sickbeds to vote and Alfred was accused of paying farm labourers to carry bludgeons and frighten Tory horses with fireworks.[3] Nevertheless he lost by four votes. There is no evidence that Alfred was particularly disappointed;[4] his overwhelming passions lay elsewhere.

Alfred's travels in North America and Europe had provided him with a deep and wide knowledge of the fine arts, interiors and architecture; he could appreciate the quality and range of his father's collections. Paintings remaining at Fonthill included a Van Dyck and a Rembrandt, there were exquisite marbles and Etruscan vases from Italy, examples of fine Sèvres porcelain and ornate furniture.[5] While enjoying his inherited treasures, Alfred also wanted to own much more: paintings, autographs, porcelain, engravings, textiles, gems, coins, medals, contemporary metalwork, glass and enamels. His approach to collecting (and he became one of the most important collectors of his day) was an addiction.[6]

One of his earliest obsessions was with famous men and women. He surrounded himself with paintings, engravings, medals and autographs of royalty, aristocrats, distinguished politicians, men of letters, soldiers and beautiful women. Society in the second half of the nineteenth century was certainly more exclusive than in his father's day: 'the admission of manufacturers and businessmen of the first and even second generation was problematical'.[7] However, it is possible only to imply, not to prove, that his collecting was linked to a desire for status, for pedigree.

In 1852 he acquired a portrait of Queen Henrietta Maria through a dealer called Walter Tiffin. Seven years later he bid successfully for two Bronzino portraits and another by Amberger at the twenty-two-day sale of John Rushout, Baron Northwick.[8] At Northwick's sale, however, he was competing for pictures with the much richer Marquess of Hertford; even Charles Eastlake, trying to acquire works for the National Gallery, was disappointed.[9] As a consequence, Alfred turned his attention to engraved portraits. He was following the advice of Walter Tiffin: 'What a variety of natural thoughts are conjured up by the sight of a portrait! Tender, pathetic, grave, gay, humorous, every feeling of the heart, every quality of the mind, may be excited by portraits.'[10] Even more significant for a collector like Alfred who preferred to buy in bulk but had limited means, 'engraving allowed those who had not a very long purse to indulge their tastes in this respect'.[11]

Once Alfred was 'hooked' he was never going to be satisfied with a few fine engravings, he wanted to build up a significant collection. This would be repeated whenever he discovered a new area in which to collect. He turned to one dealer in particular, Marseille Middleton Holloway of 20 Bedford Street, Covent Garden,[12] and in less than ten years had amassed 3,000 engraved portraits, including works by Rembrandt, Hogarth and Dürer. Holloway was then commissioned to write descriptions of the portraits for a catalogue.[13]

What makes Alfred's collecting so unusual, even at this early stage, is the scale – so many portraits in a few years – and his desire to publish his achievement in a scholarly catalogue.[14] The pattern is repeated later with his autograph letters. He was also willing to lend, to international exhibitions, to the Royal Academy, the New Gallery and regional museums and galleries. Though shy and self-conscious (shooting off one of his fingers in his twenties only increased his inherited diffidence), he was also proud. Owning the Fonthill estate gave him the status of the landed gentleman but collecting gave him access to a different circle of deference and the exchange of knowledge among equals. He wanted to be taken seriously by scholars as well as being envied by rival collectors. And his achievements were considerable. As Tiffin wrote, 'let us think of the "Collector" with respect, notwithstanding that he may be occasionally afflicted with a "mania" '.[15]

In town, Alfred kept bachelor lodgings at 34 St James's Square; his neighbours included a retired major and a lieutenant colonel. The Reform Club and Brooks's were a short stroll away, also the auction rooms of Christie, Manson and the shops of St James's and Mayfair. His address book reads like a guide for the wealthy 'shopaholic': Purdeys (314 Oxford Street) for guns; Thomas Goode & Co. (19 South Audley Street) for 'examples of all the better classes of Ceramic Art';[16] Mr Asprey (166 Bond Street), 'dressing-case and travelling-bag manufacturer to the Queen'.[17] Mr Bailes at 433 Oxford Street had made his walnut table; his brother-in-law the Revd George Glossop recommended Blackburn, Temple & Robinson (58 Old Bond Street) for 'old West Indian madeira'; Fowell & Co. (106 New Bond Street) supplied his Château-Latour 1848. The name of Mr Durlacher (113 New Bond Street), the major dealer in Chinese porcelain and 'articles of vertu', provides a clue to his next obsession.

James Morrison's collections of porcelain at Fonthill, Basildon and Harley Street included magnificent pieces of Sèvres and Dresden, and fine Chinese and Japanese pieces.[18] But a chance meeting early in 1861 between Alfred and Henry Brougham Loch, recently returned from China, took the scale of his collecting into an entirely different realm to anything his father had achieved.

The Second Opium War between Britain, France and China ended in 1860 with the sacking of the old Summer Palace or Yuanming Yuan (Gardens of Perfect Brightness) outside Peking (now Beijing). The Yuanming Yuan covered 347 acres and comprised hundreds of buildings, including pavilions, temples and galleries. It was exclusively for the use of the Imperial family; the pavilions and temples were filled with rare bronzes, porcelain and other treasures. The French were the first to loot the complex. Ten days later, the British General Lord Elgin ordered the Yuanming Yuan to be burnt. He was retaliating for the imprisonment, torture and execution of four British prisoners, including Mr Bowlby, correspondent of the London *Times*. Captain George Gordon of the Royal Engineers later recalled his own part in the British action:

> We accordingly went out, and, after pillaging it, burned the whole place, destroying in a vandal-like manner most valuable property which would not be replaced for four millions. ... You can scarcely imagine the beauty and magnificence of the places we burnt. It made one's heart sore to burn them; in fact, these places were so large, and we were so pressed for time, that we could not plunder them carefully. Quantities of gold ornaments were burnt, considered as brass. It was wretchedly demoralising work for an army.[19]

One of the men who survived three weeks' imprisonment and torture was Lord Elgin's private secretary Henry Brougham Loch, who returned to London in December 1860.[20] Some time early in 1861, so the story goes, Loch was in the Travellers' Club describing his escapades in China and how much loot he had come away with. When he called out 'Who is the richest man in the room?' all eyes turned to Alfred Morrison (a guest in the club), who agreed there and then to buy Loch's treasure, sight unseen, literally a shipload of Imperial porcelain. In another version, it is claimed Alfred paid Loch '£400 over a glass of port'.[21]

The facts were probably much more prosaic. Loch was no stranger to the Morrisons; his father, like James Morrison, had been a member of the Whig Party and they had sat on committees together. Perhaps the offer of porcelain was made in a private meeting. However it was done, Alfred acquired possibly over a thousand pieces. They had been packed so carefully that hardly any pieces were chipped or cracked; some were still filled with straw. They bore the Imperial marks and were of outstanding quality.[22] Many dated from the eighteenth-century Emperors Yung Cheng and Ch'ien Lung, the period when *famille rose* decoration, with its distinctive 'bright, piquant rose-colour'[23] was used on Chinese porcelain for the first time. Alfred's addiction was lifelong. He spent a further £40,000 in just five years acquiring hundreds more pieces through the Bond Street dealer Durlacher, and by the time of his death he had amassed nearly 2,000 bowls, vases and plates.[24]

The porcelain presented a new challenge to Alfred: where and how to display such delicate objects to be enjoyed but also studied by connoisseurs. The 1862 International Exhibition in London provided an inspirational solution.[25] The furniture makers Messrs Jackson & Graham were 'among the largest and most important exhibitors of cabinet-work'.[26] Alfred spent a total of £7,500 at the exhibition, buying hundreds of pieces, including three cabinets of ebony and ormolu by Jackson & Graham.[27] He then approached the firm to provide appropriate fittings at Fonthill for his porcelain; Jackson & Graham turned to Owen Jones for the designs.

Jones had achieved international fame as Director of Decorations for the Crystal Palace when it reopened on its new site in Sydenham in 1854. He designed the Greek, Roman, Egyptian and Alhambra courts and was awarded the Gold Medal of the Royal Institute of British Architects in 1857. Also, just by chance, he already had a connection with the Morrisons. At the beginning of his career he had worked with William Wallen,[28] surveyor to James Morrison at Fore Street;[29] his Alhambra drawings shown at the Royal Academy between 1835 and 1841 brought him to the attention of Morrison and he was one of those invited to Mary Ann's special 'at home' in 1839.[30] In 1845, Morrison had commissioned a design for an 'Ornamental Dairy and Cottage', unfortunately never built.[31] Christopher Dresser, reviewing the 1862 exhibition, wrote of Jones that his 'skill as an ornamentalist surpasses that of any other with whom we are acquainted'.[32] Alfred could be assured he was paying for the best.

Jones, Jackson & Graham were engaged at Fonthill from 1862 until about 1867.[33] They decorated the staircases with 'the purest Greek forms … united with the delicate tones of colour in the finest specimens of egg-shell pottery', and the dining room was 'built, decorated and fitted up … in the Cinque-cento style. … The chimney-piece and fittings are entirely of ebony, inlaid with ivory, and the ceilings of wood, panelled and inlaid, the mouldings being black and gold.'[34] Once completed, the ebony and ivory cabinets were lined with yellow silk and eventually filled with over 300 pieces of porcelain.[35]

Working with Alfred's collection of porcelain had a dramatic effect on Jones, opening his mind 'to a new world of ideas with regard to colouring in the practice of decorative art'. His *Grammar of Chinese Ornament*, published in 1867, drew on the Fonthill collection; he wrote in the preface of the pieces, 'which are remarkable, not only for the perfection and skill shown in the technical processes, but also for the beauty and harmony of the colouring, and general perfection of the ornamentation.'[36]

While engaged at Fonthill, Jones also designed the interior decorations of the new Langham Hotel in Portland Place, using diapers of a 'late Mooresque character'. The rooms were 'very novel and striking', as were the 'judicious assortments of tints in the various carpets, which have evidently also been designed expressly for the situation.'[37] Alfred was obviously struck by the unusual decorations and decided to provide Jones with a much grander commission than at Fonthill: to transform the interior of a brand-new house in the most fashionable part of London into a palace of art.

James Morrison's town house in Upper Harley Street had been in keeping with his position in society; many of his neighbours were successful tradesmen, bankers, merchants, members of the East India Company and Members of Parliament (including the fictional Mr Merdle in *Little Dorrit*). Charles was content to remain there with his mother, spinster sister and younger brothers. When Walter and Frank Morrison purchased their own town houses, both chose new properties in the Cromwell Road, South Kensington; their neighbours were of similar social and financial status, of independent means, many with links to trade and banking. Alfred's choice of a London residence reveals rather different ambitions.

In 1863 he applied for a lease on 16 Carlton House Terrace, one of the last 'Dwelling-Houses of the First Class'[38] designed by John Nash and adjacent to the former site of Carlton House, the luxurious residence of the Prince Regent. Nash's references included the Louvre, the Pantheon and 'ultimately Imperial Rome';[39] the first western section of the terrace was completed by 1833, the eastern section in 1864 by Samuel Morton Peto.[40]

Alfred was positioning himself in an imposing stuccoed property, resplendent with Corinthian capitals, overlooking St James's Park and the Mall and close to the London clubs and shops of the West End. His closest neighbours included the Earl of Lonsdale at numbers 14 and 15, Earl Grey at number 13 and the banker Russell Sturgis at number 17. Gladstone, the Chancellor of the Exchequer, was at number 11; however, he was forced to move to Harley Street in 1876 when he lost the election and his salary as Prime Minister; he complained that everyone else in the terrace had an annual income of £25,000 (Alfred's income was considerably more).[41]

From the outside, 16 Carlton House Terrace looks nothing out of the ordinary: 'one of those large, square, lead-colored buildings, of which so many thousands exist in London ... characteristically characterless. It repeats the apparent determination of ages that there shall be no external beauty in London ... a blank fortress'. However, 'pass through this heavy doorway, and in an instant every fair clime surrounds you, every region lavishes its sentiment; you are the heir of all the ages.'[42]

The impact of Owen Jones' decorations was (and is) overwhelming; the interiors were one of his most important commissions. Nothing else Alfred did as a collector and patron was so imaginative and enlightened. The overall impression is of colour and pattern – multicoloured coffered geometrical ceilings, enamelled mantelpieces, inlaid woods. *The Builder* provided a general description in its obituary for Jones:

Here the woodwork of the panelling, dado, doors, architraves, and window-shutters in the outer and inner hall, staircase, and all the rooms on the ground and first floors, is inlaid from designs by Mr. Jones, with various woods of different kinds, the colours of which were carefully selected by him, with a view to perfect harmony of colouring. The walls are hung with the richest Lyons silks, all specially designed by him, and coloured to harmonise with the ceilings, which may be described as perfect, in the proportions of their geometrical divisions and the designs and colouring of their decorations. The chimney-pieces, too, grates, and fenders; the carpets, and the furniture, which is all marquetrie, were designed by Mr Jones.[43]

Henry Cole, Director of the South Kensington Museum, was one of the first of the distinguished visitors whose views Alfred would have welcomed. In his diary for 22 May 1870 he noted: 'To Mr Morrison's … his house filled with marquetrie designed by Owen Jones … mixture of Greek & Moorish, perfect mechanical work.'[44] The *Magazine of Art* also noted the marquetry produced by machine: 'it is so accurately produced as to almost overpower one with a sense of hopelessness of escape from never-changing precision. We may search for some flaw, some mistake; we can find none.'[45] Faint praise indeed. Moncure Conway, however, visiting in 1881 was overwhelmed by the combination of ebonised and many-coloured woods:

> Trees belonging to every land and clime of the earth have sent here their hearts, and, without a particle of pigment being used on any one of them, they gather to form rosettes on the chimney-pieces cappings for the dados, and finest featherings around the doors – white, golden, red, cream-colored, brown.[46]

Three rooms opened off the umber-toned hall dominated by H.W.B. Davis' bronze of a bull.[47] The study or morning room had walls covered with silk of 'reddened gold and blue steel hue',[48] the ceiling was a 'massive Oriental arrangement of beams, golden crosses, and grooved golden cupolas, each set in a bright blue ground'; the carpet of a 'greenish-yellow hue'.[49] The ceiling of the dining room was 'of a pure Moresque type' with 'interchanging star-shaped forms of deep red ornament on a golden ground, and of deep blue ornament on a golden ground'. The mantelpiece and fireplace were enriched with grey and green marbles, 'the lower portions of the marble columns on each side of the mirror on the mantelpiece … encased in bronze-work' by F. Barbedienne.[50] The table of amboyna and purpleheart with the monogram AM was by Jackson & Graham's other talented designer, Alfred Lormier.[51]

In the library, the inlaid ebony bookcases made by Jackson & Graham[52] displayed Alfred's growing collection of miniatures, metalwork and porcelain, Roman and Phoenician glass. The library ceiling was covered in white stars, with gold tracery, the walls were 'brilliant with golden-green silk hangings'.[53]

Alfred acquired a small number of important contemporary paintings. Frederic Leighton's *Summer Moon* hung in the library.[54] 'Suffused with poetry and mystery', two sleeping girls are 'suspended between life and death, night and day'.[55] Alfred also owned work by Richard Dadd, 'unhealthy nightmares of grey, ghostly hues'.[56] The dealer Holloway acquired five paintings for Alfred at the sale in 1870 following the death of Dr William Charles Hood, physician superintendent of Bethlem Hospital, where Dadd was an inmate. *Contradiction* was the most striking: 'This eccentric painter … has contrived ingeniously to blend his forms together so that there is a pleasing composition of lines; the ideas, however, with which the composition of lines is inevitably associated, are unquestionably weird, if not hideous and inexplicable.'[57] Alfred's taste for Dadd was no passing whim; in 1891 he acquired *The Fairy Feller's Master-Stroke*, also 'Elimination of a Picture & its Subject', the 'autograph poem' in which Dadd explained the creation of the painting. Both had been given by Dadd in 1865 to G.H. Haydon, steward of Bethlem Hospital.[58]

There were three reception rooms on the first floor. The east drawing room, with windows overlooking St James's Park, of 'cold yet luxurious opalescence and pale orange-wood marquetry',[59] had an alabaster chimneypiece with enamel decoration by the French enamellist and jeweller Charles Lepec. The second morning room was 'a yellow satin-hung or golden room' and the third boudoir was 'a silvery-blue room'.

Alfred had developed a close relationship with Lepec after first buying an enamel piece at the 1862 Paris Exhibition.[60] The chimneypiece took Lepec two years to complete. By 1867, at the Exposition Universelle,[61] almost everything on display made by Lepec was lent by Alfred, revealing both his taste and his wealth, but also the maniacal side to his collecting. It seems as if he wanted to stop his rivals possessing pieces by Lepec. The exhibition pieces included three-feet-high ormolu pilgrim bottles 'rich with an Oriental profusion of conventional flowers done in opaque and translucent red, blue, and green enamels'[62] and a sumptuous gold and enamel 'nef' (boat-shaped) tazza, with a figure of Cupid riding a winged dragon.[63] The *Magazine of Art* offered faint praise: 'here again, in the effort to be original, subservience of decoration to construction or utility would appear to have been set aside by the producer. On reflection, this disregard of utility is an element in these articles *de luxe*. It occurs to one that they must solely be regarded as precious and costly works of modern art.'[64]

Alfred revealed the same excessive behaviour when he began to collect the paintings of John Brett. His address book for 1864 included the names of three artists: Brett, John William Inchbold and Henry William Banks Davis. Brett was his favourite, and he eventually owned nearly thirty paintings and sketches. The first Brett that Alfred bought was *Massa, Bay of Naples* which was exhibited at the Royal Academy in 1864. When he paid 250 guineas rather than the £250 price tag, Brett was touched and a friendship was formed. 'Hitherto I have found people mostly forget what a guinea means and pay a pound instead, but you on the contrary have sent me guineas when I only asked pounds.'[65] The following year the Royal Academy rejected *Capri in the Evening* but Alfred had already bought it for £300.[66] He then acquired one of Brett's most striking portraits *Lady with a Dove (Jeannette Loeser)* for £100.[67]

After Alfred bought a 'little sea drawing' in 1866, Brett wrote of his appreciation: 'to know that my work is sincerely liked is an intense pleasure to me. I think of acting on your suggestion and trying the effect of that little sea subject or something like it on a larger scale next winter.'[68] The result was *Lat. 53 Degrees 15' N Long. 5 degrees, 10' W (Rainbow at Sea)*, Brett's first substantial painting of the open sea.[69] Alfred immediately commissioned something much larger, paying £150 in advance and £400 on completion. Brett replied: 'With the view of doing justice to your commission to paint a large sea picture, I propose in the first place to make a few voyages. These will occupy two or three months, and at the end of that time I shall be in a much better position to submit a subject for your approval than now, so that if you want to have the best work I can produce I should recommend you to leave the subject an open question for the present.'[70]

Brett's best paintings represented far from conventional seascapes and their symbolic content may have appealed to Alfred. Gustave Waagen noted the English – and Alfred's – passion for animal paintings: 'In no country is so much attention paid to the races of different animals as in England, and, although a mercenary reason may be assigned in the case of horses, oxen, and sheep, yet a feeling for the beauty of these animals is also very general.'[71] H.W.B. Davis specialised in very large paintings of sheep and cows and Alfred acquired several. *A Panic*, shown at the Academy in 1872, was eight feet high and 16 feet long, the largest painting of cattle in the world;[72] it completely filled the end wall of the music gallery. When Philip Burne-Jones was commissioned to paint Alfred's portrait in 1892 he worked in the music gallery beneath the vast canvas of stampeding cattle.

> Their gallery of pictures was the most depressing thing of all. I had never quite realised what unlimited wealth – combined with bad taste – could achieve. Do you remember that vast canvas, of life-size cows coming full tilt at one, with a thunderstorm raging in the background? It got on my nerves – & I wondered whether my portrait wd look like the Cow picture when it was done. But they were kind & hospitable – & everyone needn't have good taste, need they?[73]

At the beginning of 1866, Alfred was forty-four years old, single and very rich, his days occupied in Wiltshire with rural matters, improving his estate, indulging in country sports, collecting prizes for his sheep. In London he followed the progress of his palace of art, while continuing to buy engravings, autographs, *objets d'art* and paintings, visiting artists' studios, engaging dealers to bid on his behalf at auctions. He may have met his brothers at the Reform Club, but he rarely visited Basildon, where he did not get on with his sister Ellen;[74] his life was singularly self-contained.

Alfred's type, the wealthy, obsessive, self-centred connoisseur and collector, was depicted in contemporary fiction, usually as unpleasant and sometimes villainous. While there is no hard evidence that George Eliot or Henry James used Alfred as a source, his activities were known to them. Eliot and her partner G.H. Lewes shared Owen Jones as a decorator, they visited Alfred's London house and entertained him and his wife at the Priory (Leighton was a fellow guest the year Alfred bought his *Summer Moon*). A friend of Henry James lived next door in Carlton House Terrace.

When so little of Alfred's personal archive survives, these fictional versions provide colourful and perceptive substitutes. For example, Gilbert Osmond, the connoisseur in *The Portrait of a Lady*, exhibits similar characteristics to Alfred:

> He was certainly fastidious and critical; he was probably irritable. His sensibility had governed him – possibly governed him too much; it had made him impatient of vulgar troubles and had led him to live by himself,

in a sorted, sifted, arranged, world, thinking about art and beauty and history. He had consulted his taste in everything – his taste alone perhaps.[75]

By the time James wrote the novel (it was published in 1880–81), he had been settled in London several years; he would have known of Alfred through a number of sources, but most probably through his friend the banker Russell Sturgis who lived at 17 Carlton House Terrace.

Gilbert Osmond had secretly kept a mistress, Madame Merle, the mother of his daughter Pansy. It would have been easy for Alfred to keep a mistress. Perhaps he had already had a relationship with a servant in Fonthill, the elusive Louisa Farley? In the census for 1861 John Farley, aged twenty, is a servant at Fonthill House. Louisa Mold, aged nineteen, is an under-housemaid at the Rectory close by. From 1863 Alfred sent gifts and money to a Mrs Louisa or Louie Farley at various addresses, beginning in the Isle of Wight, then in Kent and London (Lower Clapton). While it has not been possible to find evidence of Louisa's marriage to John Farley, the circum-stances fit. Alfred continued to send Louisa £75 approximately every six months. In 1881 Mrs Farley became Mrs Alkins (presumably she remarried) but she continued to live in the same house, and to receive payments from Alfred for another ten years. Year after year, for thirty years, Alfred kept a note of her address (mostly Clapton and finally Brixton with three years at the Queen's Hotel, Brixham, Devon). The amount of money was not insignifi-cant: £150 per annum provided a comfortable living, particularly if Louisa owned her own house. But why did Alfred provide for her, what was his debt? Perhaps his missing correspondence held the answer.

Alfred's bachelor state was not unusual. Statistics from the mid-century reveal increasing numbers of professional men and men with independent incomes marrying late or never. Contemporary commentators blamed the avoidance of marriage on 'the scourge of prostitution' and 'surplus women'.[76] The writer Samuel Butler met 'his own sexual needs as a middle-aged bachelor … by a commercial arrangement with a mistress over many years'.[77] In Trollope's contemporaneous novel *The Belton Estate* the young ambitious MP Captain Aylmer, second son of a baronet and already in possession of a small estate, is advised by his father not to marry: 'in the way of comfort, you can be a great deal more comfortable without a wife than you can with one. What do you want a wife for?' [78]

Alfred was also a second son in possession of a considerable estate. However, he may have wondered who would inherit not only his, but also his brothers' properties. What would happen to his and his father's collections of art? Charles and Walter were confirmed bachelors, Allan and Frank were invalids and unlikely to have children. George might have a family, but in 1866 he was only twenty-seven years old and single. Of his sisters, Ellen was a spinster, apparently contented to help her mother run Basildon and Harley Street for Charles. Mary had died in 1859 leaving her baby daughter Bertha Glossop to be brought up at Basildon. Only Lucy had a male heir, Harold Moffatt.

If Alfred was seriously considering the necessity to marry, his mind was made up when he met Mabel Chermside, the eighteen-year-old daughter of the Rector of Wilton in Wiltshire, a few miles from Fonthill. Though twenty-six years older, Alfred proposed marriage and was accepted.[79] While it was thought normal, at the time, for grooms to be older than their brides, the 'ideal age' difference was around three to seven years. Upper-class girls may have hoped to be engaged by twenty, but the reality was nearer twenty-five.[80] Marriages to much older men were acceptable only if the man was a widower with children to raise. Alfred was, however, very rich and Mabel was an unusual young woman.

Wilton was one of the most desirable livings in the country, under the patronage of the Herbert family, Earls of Pembroke, since the sixteenth century. It was only offered to exceptional clergymen: 'a squire ... would look for someone who was socially congenial to him and his own family ... a man whose family would be welcome in the drawing-room of the Hall'.[81] The Rectory, a 'broad, beneficent Georgian building of deep red brick',[82] was immediately next door to Brandon & Wyatt's extraordinary Italian Romanesque church.

Dr Chermside was an appropriate choice as rector. He was the son of a distinguished physician, Sir Robert Alexander Chermside (1792–1860), who had served in the Peninsular War and at Waterloo before studying medicine at Edinburgh University and becoming a fashionable society doctor; one of his patients was the Duchess of Kent, mother of Queen Victoria. He eventually settled in Paris as physician to the English Embassy but was also the personal doctor of the elderly Lady Hertford, member of an unconventional family now famous for creating the Wallace Collection in London.

After Oxford, Dr Chermside began his ministry in Leeds, where he married Emma Dawson, daughter of a London merchant with Jamaican plantations; Mabel was still a baby when the family moved to Wilton in 1848. While ministering to the Wilton congregation, Chermside continued his scholarly activities; he was also an able artist and amateur geologist, writing for *Macmillan's* and the *Dublin University Magazine*.[83] Mabel was sent to Paris for part of her childhood to stay with her grandfather, and here she enjoyed easy access to the Hertford treasures and the unusual company in the Rue Taitbout. She also had 'exotic' connections in England: through her aunt Isabelle Walter,[84] Mabel was familiar with Byron's ancestral home, Newstead Abbey, and its owner Colonel Wildman, another friend of her grandfather's.[85] At Wilton the Chermside children were permitted to play with the young Herberts. Mabel became a lifelong friend of Lady Maud who married the composer Hubert Parry.

Mabel was consequently an unusually sophisticated young woman, with a knowledge of languages and personal experience of French culture. She was comfortable in the company of aristocrats, eccentric connoisseurs and collectors; Richard Wallace (1818–90), the illegitimate son of the 4th Marquess of Hertford, was just three years older than Alfred. The Hertfords' taste was similar to that of both James Morrison and Alfred. Mabel was renowned, all her life, for making an immediate impression:

> At sixteen Mabel was a singular and beautiful figure to come upon in a country rectory. All her life she had her own peculiar style of dressing, and already she enjoyed collecting amusing costumes in the various countries she visited. She brought back strange headdresses, shawls, and jewels, to add their foreign flavour to her own lavish movements, to the beauty of her face, and to the brilliancy of her speech. The Chermsides were not rich, but Mabel had always her own splendour.[86]

Alfred, however, was rich. As his wife, Mabel would be able to indulge to the full her passion for exotic clothes and precious jewels. She must have believed an alliance with the shy middle-aged millionaire would 'assure her a future of beautiful hours.'[87] Chaperoned visits to Fonthill would have presented to Mabel a life of incomparable comfort and style.

However, two letters written shortly before the marriage suggest the engagement was sudden and a little awkward for both sides. Dr Chermside first visited Basildon without his daughter, early in 1866, to meet Alfred's mother Mary Ann. He received a letter soon after from Ellen, who was corresponding on behalf of her mother:

> When you [Dr Chermside] were sitting on the sofa with me you spoke so affectionately of your daughter hoping that we should receive her kindly amongst you that I send you one line just to say how pleased we shall [be] to be connected with you & how glad we should be to be intimate with Mabel shd she on a nearer acquaintance grow to like us. We have not asked her to come & see us here because we live very quietly & Alfred is not fond of staying at Basildon, but I dare say some day he will bring her down to us himself.[88]

Was Ellen warning Dr Chermside that Mabel could not expect an immediately warm welcome from the larger Morrison family because relations were strained between Alfred and his sister and brother at Basildon? Later, Mabel wrote of feeling sorry for Ellen 'for I see how lonely she will be some day, & I would have done every & anything to make her happy if she would have cared to pay us visits but no she <u>never</u> would'.[89]

In February Mary Ann and Ellen called at the Rectory, presumably driving over from Fonthill, and met Mabel for the first time. It was customary for female members of the groom's family to welcome a prospective bride.[90] After they left, Dr Chermside wrote to Ellen:

> I will own I was anxious as to your mother's reception of her, and your own; but when I had the pleasure of looking into the eyes of you both, that anxiety dwindled forthwith. ... I remember how young my child is, and how much discipline of life it takes to form character and to clothe it with true grace, no less than to train it into noble force.[91]

Dr Chermside's anxiety was real: Mabel was about to marry a man three years *his* senior. Also he was already seriously ill and would be unable to conduct their wedding service which took place very soon after, on 11 April, at St James's, Piccadilly.

The marriage settlement and Alfred's will (signed immediately after the wedding ceremony) reflected the wealth of the groom but also the different ages of the happy couple: Mabel would appear to be well supported as a widow. A trust of £50,000 worth of consolidated stock of the East India Railway was established for her, Alfred receiving the dividends in his life-time.[92] This amount was typical of the upper limit of substantial marriage settlements made by wealthy industrialists and aristocrats at the time, £50,000 yielding £2,000 per annum (invested at 4%).[93] Alfred, however, provided the entire settlement. Alfred's sisters had received personal settle-ments of £25,000 capital on marriage, with a further £25,000 at the death of their father. On Alfred's death, Mabel would have a lifetime interest in Fonthill House and 300 acres of surrounding parkland, the house in Carlton House Terrace, the household effects in both properties, and stables in Duke Street.[94] She would also receive an annuity of £150,000, to keep even if she married again; invested at 4% this would yield a further £6,000 per annum.

The Fonthill treasures were treated as a special item. An inventory was to be made immediately after Alfred's death listing 'pictures prints statues busts bronzes marbles antiquities and other articles of art or vertu' which were to be deemed heirlooms. They could be enjoyed by Mabel in her lifetime but would then pass with Fonthill to the heir. Alfred was anticipating the need to safeguard the best pieces he had inherited or acquired for himself. If they had no children everything would go to his sister Lucy's son Harold Moffatt.[95]

After honeymooning in the south of France, Alfred and Mabel set up temporary home at 2 Harley Street while the decorations of Carlton House Terrace were completed. Mabel had become pregnant soon after their wedding, but the baby, christened Rachel, died at ten months (when Mabel was again pregnant). Unfortunately this was all too common, even among the rich. Between 1860 and 1900 over 14% of infants in England and Wales died before their first birthday.[96] Dr Chermside also died in July 1867. He was only forty-four.

Alfred commissioned Brett to paint Mabel just a month before their second child was born.[97] Mabel's face is wistful, reflecting, no doubt, the loss of a father and a daughter as well as anxiety over her approaching confine-ment. A healthy boy, Hugh, was born on 8 June 1868 but there were compli-cations with the next pregnancy, two doctors attending Mabel a month before Katharine was born on 21 August 1869; the gap between the babies was just fourteen months. Almost immediately Alfred and Mabel moved into 16 Carlton House Terrace, the palace of art created for Alfred by Owen Jones.

Few personal letters survive between Alfred, Mabel, their family and friends and as Mabel outlived her husband by thirty-six years the assumption is that she destroyed the correspondence. It is consequently difficult to judge what Mabel thought of the appearance of their London house or its contents. It is distinctly possible she thoroughly disliked both, because within months of Alfred's death she sold the house and a large quantity of paintings, sculpture, textiles, porcelain, autographs, lace, jewels, metalwork, glass and enamels, in the end almost everything not deemed an 'heirloom'.

Certainly her involvement in Alfred's obsessions and his almost maniacal acquisition of objects was limited. After Lepec and Brett, Alfred discovered the Spanish craftsman Placido Zuloaga, and began to buy examples of his metalwork.[98] A surviving letter to Mabel confirms that Zuloaga was first commissioned at the end of 1867 to make a necklace for her and 'other small pieces which you ordered'. Alfred, however, also commissioned very large pieces. Size (like Davis' painting of the stampeding cattle) mattered to him. Zuloaga continued: 'I have sent with all possible haste to your house in London a large life sized drawing of the large tray as Mr Morrison wishes to see a drawing of it ... I hope it will be to your taste.'[99] The tray, or iron salver, was over five feet long, damascened in gold and silver; it was displayed in the dining room. Zuloaga's claim that 'it is a piece that no one dared to make in times gone by because of the difficulty of construction' would have appealed to his patron.[100]

Zuloaga was commissioned by Alfred to make a massive cassone.[101] The chest was over six feet long by three feet high, of 'forged iron and chiselled and engraved iron repousse, silver with niello, gold and silver damascening'[102] Alfred apparently boasted that he had advanced Zuloaga £1,000 '... and told him to begin something on that. Zouloaga [*sic*] worked at the coffer for four years, and its owner saw at once that he had but paid an instalment of the real value of this marvellous work.'[103] The *Magazine of Art* was less impressed: 'undoubtedly it is a triumph of skilled workmanship. The ornament is elegant and delicate, but has no symbolism. ... Undoubtedly this important piece of fine art metal-work is primarily to be gazed at – to use it would entail much trouble on the user – including possible injury.'

Alfred eventually acquired over forty pieces by Zuloaga, though there is no proof that he responded to the craftsman's plea to provide financial support for his workshop in Spain.[104] There were large vases in the inner hall of gold and dark steel,[105] golden Moorish amphora-shaped vases in the dining room,[106] and a pair of tripod stands of dark blue steel, ornamented in silver, supporting damascened iron vessels. There was a hall table (with the monogram AM) designed in the Renaissance Revival style made of iron with gold and silver damascene, including classical columns and masks, acanthus foliage and egg-and-dart mouldings.[107] Zuloaga also made an elaborate chest to hold Alfred's coins and medals, veneered in tortoiseshell, the drawers lined with mahogany, and 'enamelled in intricate baroque floral patterns in red, green and gold over a silvered ground'.[108]

Zuloaga performed a rather more dubious function for Alfred, obtaining paintings originally from Spain. The portrait of Charles III of Spain by Goya had apparently been looted from the Prado in Madrid and taken to Paris where it was 'found' by Zuloaga and brought to England. The triptych *The Madonna and Child with Angels and Saints*, believed to be by Memling, had been walled up in a monastery during the war, then brought to England by Zuloaga, presumably with Alfred already lined up as the buyer.

Either Zuloaga or Lepec may have introduced Alfred to the French craftsman Lucien Falize.[109] In about 1880 Falize began to make him a fantastic clock of gold, silver, enamels and gems, in the shape of a late Gothic church tower.[110] It was an object of marvel, 'a work in which the opulence of the materials has been exceeded twenty times over by the work of the artist'; 'a masterpiece evoking the marvels of the Louvre Museum'.[111] The monogram AM is displayed on the front, so there is no chance the identity of its owner (and Falize's patron) will be forgotten.[112]

Alfred's generosity to artists such as Brett, Zuloaga, Lepec and Falize is unquestionable, but his eagerness to own the entire output of an artist must on occasion have appeared stifling. It appears that Mabel found living amongst his collection was also stifling, while visitors questioned the sheer quantity of objects which were said to detract from Owen Jones' initial design. The tea-room, for example, was 'choked by lace, old *Oriental* plates and vases, and cabinets of *Boule* work in silver and tortoise-shell, and *Oriental* ivory gilt in lace-like patterns'. The boudoir was similar, with 'more lace, more embroideries, covering every vacant space, and themselves covered with pots and ornaments, ivories and bronzes, some of great age, some modern'.[113]

Some of Alfred's critics were unfair and probably envious of his wealth. However, his approach to collecting appears both excessive and obsessive.

32 Inlaid marble table top, Rome, *c*. 1580. This may be the pietre dura table acquired by James Morrison for £388.10s at the Lansdown Tower sale, 20–29 November 1845, lot 416, and displayed in the Octagon Room. The centre was formed of a 'large oval slab of beautiful Oriental alabaster'. It was sold by Morrison's descendants from Fonthill House.

33 Coffer on stand, probably designed by H.E. Goodridge and William Beckford, manufactured possibly by Robert Hume Junior *c*. 1831–41. This may be one of the pair of coffers acquired by James Morrison at the Lansdown Tower sale, 4–5 May 1841; 'a pair of sarcophagus headed coffers and stands of riga and pollard oak', lot 27.

34 Rembrandt, *Portrait of Hendricke Stoffels*, 1654–6, oil on canvas. Purchased in 1839 by James Morrison as part of the Edward Gray collection.

35 Nicolas Poussin, *The Triumph of Pan*, 1636, oil on canvas. Purchased by James Morrison, 1850, from Lord Ashburnham. This and the Rembrandt hung in the library at Basildon Park.

36 The Oak Room, Basildon Park. In the photograph the Hobbema is surrounded by works by Poussin, Teniers, Dujardin, Van de Velde, Pynacker, and Guercino.

37 Meindert Hobbema, *Wooded Landscape*, c. 1662–3, oil on canvas.

38 Giovani Francesco Barbieri (Guercino), *St Sebastian succoured by two angels*. One of James Morrison's few Italian paintings.

39 Claude Lorraine, *The Adoration of the Golden Calf*, 1660, oil on canvas. Purchased by James Morrison, 1850. Robert Hume rehung the gallery in Harley Street in 1851 to make room for the Claude.

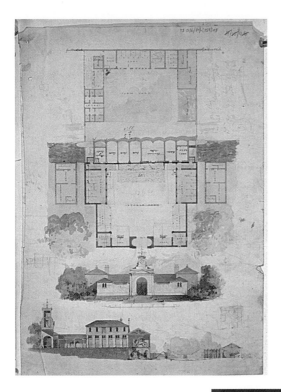

40 J.B. Papworth, design for Great Stables at Basildon. Papworth and James Morrison's long relationship came to a bitter end in 1844 over the design for the stables.

41 Mary Ann Morrison photographed at Basildon Park after James Morrison's death in 1857.

42 Hole Park, near Rolvenden, Kent. The estate was purchased by James Morrison in 1849 and given to Frank Morrison on his marriage.

43 Islay House, Islay, Argyll. James Morrison bought the Islay estate in 1853 for £451,000. Hugh Morrison commissioned Detmar Blow to add the large wing to the right of the original Georgian mansion.

44 Alfred Morrison was 48 when John Brett painted his portrait in 1870.

45 Agnolo Bronzino, *Cosimo I de' Medici in armour*, oil on canvas.

46 John Brett, *Lady with a Dove: Madame Loeser,* 1864. Alfred Morrison bought the painting from Brett in 1865 for £100.

47 Photograph of Mabel Morrison, taken at Fonthill House shortly after her marriage to Alfred in 1866. She was 26 years younger than Alfred.

48 Richard Dadd's *The Fairy Feller's Master-Stroke* was acquired by Alfred Morrison in 1891. He already owned five Dadd paintings, including *Contradiction*.

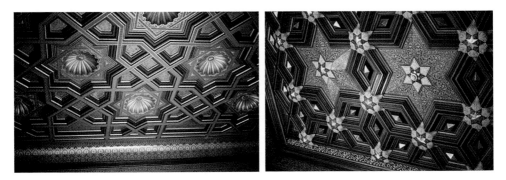

49 Examples of Owen Jones' decorations of the ceilings of 16 Carlton House Terrace. Jones' designs for the interiors, furnishings and some of the furniture were extraordinary; nothing else Alfred Morrison did as a patron was so imaginative and enlightened.

50 Lucien Falize was commissioned in 1880 to make this fantastic clock of gold, silver, enamels and gems, in the shape of a late Gothic church tower.

51 Placido Zuloaga was first commissioned by Alfred Morrison in 1867 to make a necklace for Mabel. His massive cassone of 'forged iron and chiselled and engraved iron repousse, silver with niello, gold and silver damascening', took four years to make and cost Morrison £1000.

52 The Saloon was one of three rooms added by Alfred Morrison to Fonthill House in around 1890 to display some of his treasures. He eventually owned several thousand pieces of Imperial Chinese porcelain.

53 This is an important and very rare yellow-ground *famille rose* vase, Jiaqing iron-red six-character sealmark and of the period (1796–1820). Sold at Christie's Hong Kong, 1 December 2010, lot 2981, it is now in a private collection.

54 Placido Zuloaga's portrait, *c.* 1880, reveals Alfred Morrison's shy and fastidious nature.

55 These are a very rare and important pair of Imperial cloisonné enamel double crane censers of the Yongzheng period (1723–35). Sold at Christie's Hong Kong, 1 December 2010, lot 2983, they are now in a private collection.

56 The Music Gallery, Fonthill House. John Brett's *Christmas Morning*, 1866, hangs above the fireplace; the lights are by W.A.S. Benson.

57 H.W.B. Davis, *A Panic*, shown at the Royal Academy in 1872. Reputedly the largest painting of cows in the world.

58 In 1902 Detmar Blow was commissioned by Hugh Morrison to build Little Ridge across the lake from Fonthill House (the old Pavilion). He moved a ruined manor-house from Berwick St Leonard, then added wings after Hugh inherited money and Islay from his Uncle Charles.

59 Hugh Morrison's only son John Granville was born in 1906; he was created the 1st Lord Margadale by Sir Alec Douglas-Home in 1964 and demolished Little Ridge in 1972.

60 Fonthill House (formerly the Pavilion) was demolished by Hugh Morrison in 1921.

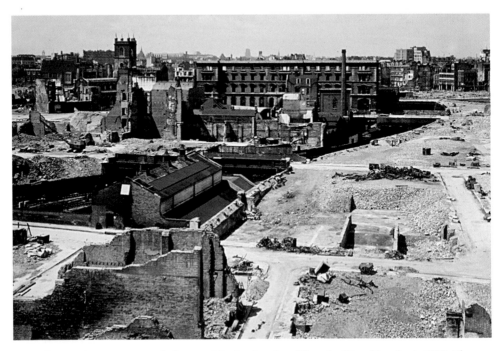

61 A plaque in Fore Street records the site of the first bomb to fall on the City of London in 1940. The Fore Street and Milton Street complex of warehouses was obliterated. The view is across Milton Street towards St Giles' Cripplegate, taken by City police photographers Fred Tibbs and Arthur Cross, 1942.

His monogram was everywhere, on clocks, tables and bookcases. Charlotte, Baroness Lionel de Rothschild, was particularly unkind:

> He, you know, is enormously rich, is building a most beautiful house and filling it with wonders, chiefly Japanese and Chinese, hitherto, to which he has no objection to add others of an entirely different origin. The gentleman did not seem to me to understand much he is ... very commonplace looking.[114]

George Eliot was also unimpressed. When she and G.H. Lewes were invited to Carlton House Terrace to look at a bust of Voltaire by Houdon,[115] they found Alfred's manner insufferable. They were 'bored by being shown all their Splendours and rarities ... each the "finest in the world" '.[116] They concluded that their wealthy acquaintance was not willing to part with his money for anything other than his own pleasure. Attempts to interest him in saving the Swiss Cottage fields from development proved embarrassing, as Eliot explained to her friend Barbara Bodichon (who was trying to raise money for Girton College, Cambridge): 'I lately gave an introduction to Gertrude [Bodichon's sister] that she might try to interest him [Alfred] in keeping open the Hampstead fields, and she found the interview a great crux.' Eliot added that Alfred was 'a most unsympathetic mortal'.[117] She would have agreed with the Duke of Westminster who visited Fonthill in 1878: 'Mr A [Alfred Morrison] is an eccentric individual with peculiar views on most things, one being never to give away a farthing in "charity" ... another to denounce all art and artists except those of which he himself approves and there [sic] are a queer lot.'[118]

In *The Portrait of a Lady*, when Gilbert Osmond says 'I don't object to showing my things – when people are not idiots', he sounds remarkably as Alfred might have done. And Isabel Archer finds Osmond's Italian 'palace of art' a house of 'darkness ... dumbness ... suffocation'.

One of Mabel's cultural activities independent of Alfred was her support for the Royal School of Art Needlework. A group of aristocratic friends, including two daughters of Queen Victoria, had established the school in 1872 to provide employment for gentlewomen. Leading artists including Leighton, Poynter, William Morris and Burne-Jones provided original designs to be copied. Mabel became a member of the council in 1875. She also interested herself in lacemaking, not it would seem making it herself, but collecting examples, which she lent for exhibitions,[119] and joining a committee in 1885, with Richard Wallace, to promote the survival of the industry in Ireland. Her involvement with needlework and lacemaking was not strenuous, nor did it require much travel. This suited her well because following the birth of her fifth and last child she spent many years condemned to rest on a sofa or in bed.

According to Edith Olivier, daughter of the new Rector of Wilton, 'for twelve years after the birth of her last child ... she endured very great pain from an internal illness, and was condemned to be nearly always on her back'.[120] Her illness, possibly a prolapsed womb, forced almost constant rest from about 1874, until 1886 when she was thirty-nine. Alfred would then have been sixty-five. She was attended by Dr James Watt Black, a distinguished obstetrics physician and lecturer on midwifery at the Charing Cross Hospital. He also looked after Mabel's Wilton neighbour Lady Maud Herbert and was a friend of Alfred's brother Charles. He was responsible for her recovery in the mid-1880s[121] and also commissioned paintings from Brett after seeing his work during visits to Carlton House Terrace.[122]

It is impossible to know the impact of such a condition on Mabel and Alfred's marriage. Olivier claimed, 'Mabel's independent mind was an unfailing delight to her husband in whose eyes she remained the most unique among all the treasures he had collected.'[123] Mabel herself wrote early in the 1880s, 'I fretted dreadfully at first for fear my being ill should spoil my husband's or children's life, but I see it doesn't & that is everything.'[124]

Certainly there is no evidence that Alfred's collecting diminished. He also pursued his own male-centred social life away from the family. In 1868 he was a founder member of the Savile Club, which aimed to elect men 'widely differing from each other in occupations, tastes, accomplishments and interests'.[125] Some were rich: 'Herbert, Goschen and Goldsmid were members of wealthy families, and the two Morrisons [Alfred and Walter] were among the richest men in England.'[126] The majority, however, reflected the cultural interests of the club: artists, explorers, scientists, philosophers, engineers, journalists, historians, lawyers, a few politicians and aristocrats; many were Fellows of the Royal Society. They included the philosophers Leslie Stephen (father of Virginia Woolf) and Henry Sidgwick; Tom Hughes, author of *Tom Brown's Schooldays* and friend of Walter Morrison; and the explorer Stanley Baker.

The artists were almost all patronised by Alfred: John Brett, H.W.B. Davis, Andrew Maccallum and Thomas Woolner (who sculpted Mabel's bust). Members met in the evenings, twice weekly and the club quickly earned a reputation for 'simple and well-worn furniture ... plain and sufficient meals'. Alfred was a member for the rest of his life. He was obviously at ease with men who would understand and appreciate his collecting (if not always his taste), and his dedication to the patronage of contemporary art. He would have enjoyed the view of the Savile that began to circulate: 'It's an awful swell club. They won't elect you unless you're an atheist or have written a book.'[127]

Some time around 1890 Alfred extended Fonthill by building three top-lit galleries.[128] Space was an increasing problem in Carlton House Terrace where the silk wall-coverings seriously limited the display of pictures. John Brett referred to Alfred's dilemma in a lecture to the Architectural Association in 1892: 'I know a man whose house was finished by Owen Jones. He's very fond of pictures but has to keep them piled up in stacks for fearing of spoiling his walls.'[129] A number of key paintings were moved from London, including Leighton's *Summer Moon*, as well as works by Zuloaga, Lepec and Falize, and chandeliers were commissioned from the young designer W.A.S. Benson.[130] The saloon was devoted to Chinese porcelain, marble statues and engraved portraits, while contemporary works were displayed in the Music and Picture Galleries against blue and white wallpaper chosen by Mabel.

Alfred's final obsession was the publication of his collection of autograph letters of famous men and women.[131] He had begun in the 1860s with the help of Holloway, acquiring a large number of autograph letters (he spent £1,284) at a Sotheby's sale on 10 June 1869 of the collection of John Dillon, his father's partner in Fore Street. Then the archivist and palaeographer A.W. Thibaudeau, of 382 Oxford Street,[132] became his buyer and collaborator. Not surprisingly, Alfred's 'special penchant [was] for distinguished recipients as well as writers',[133] for example Queen Elizabeth I to Henry IV of France, Keats to Fanny Brawne, Robespierre to Danton. Some of his purchases were connected to Beckford and Fonthill Abbey. He acquired, for example, the letter-books of Beckford's lawyer Thomas Wildman expressing concerns about the demolition of Fonthill Splendens and expenses attached to building the Abbey. He also bought the correspondence of Sir William Hamilton, his wife Emma and her lover Nelson.[134] Alfred's obituary summed up the collection: 'it is hardly an exaggeration to say that every reigning Sovereign and every first-rate statesman whose name is to be found in the French or English history of the last three centuries, and nearly all the great names of literature, science, and art, are represented in this collection.'[135]

Alfred was keen to reveal the extent of this aspect of his collecting to public gaze. He lent examples to exhibitions[136] and conceived a series of luxurious publications which included lengthy extracts and facsimiles of some of the most significant letters. In 1883, he and Thibaudeau published the first of six folio volumes of the *Catalogue of the Collection of Autograph Letters and Historical Documents formed between 1865 and 1882 by Alfred Morrison*.[137] Scholars were welcome to handle the original documents and a wave of biographies appeared at the end of the century drawing on his collection, including lives of the Duke of Marlborough, Lady Hamilton and Lord Nelson, and the poets Byron, Burns, Coleridge and Shelley. 'Writers upon almost every question of a biographical character sought his kindly permission – never refused – to study the letters in his possession.'[138]

In 1895 Alfred underwent a major operation on his nose and made a good recovery. Charles was impressed: 'Alfred tells me he shot 120 head in 180 minutes. Very good for a man over 74 & who has recently suffered much from great haemorrhage & other effects of an infection in the nose.' Two years later, on 22 December 1897, Alfred died and to the consternation of his family, it was discovered he had made no changes to the will drawn up on his marriage. Mabel was still the main beneficiary, inheriting Fonthill House and 300 acres of parkland, the London house and all Alfred's treasures for her lifetime. She was only fifty (and lived to eighty-six), so her eldest son Hugh had to wait a long time.

Probate was granted in June 1900 at just under £1 million with death duties amounting to £10,000. To pay these, Mabel turned to Christie's auction house: embroideries and rugs, intagli, gold rings and Greek vases went under the hammer at three sales in 1898, raising over £11,000. And this was only the beginning. Mabel continued to sell her husband's collections, as if nothing held any emotional or artistic value for her, including Owen Jones' palace of art. Number 16 Carlton House Terrace, with a remaining sixty-three-year lease, was valued at £20,650 but disposing of it saved her little money, because she immediately bought a house in Bruton Street which required thirteen servants (Carlton House Terrace had required sixteen).[139]

Mr Cox of Christie's drew up the list of heirlooms as requested in the will, 'having regard to their artistic and intrinsic value or merit and their suitability in their surroundings'. He excluded pieces 'of no art value, or which, in his opinion, were of but trifling intrinsic value and of small or no artistic merit'.[140] However, Mabel was accused by her surviving brothers-in-law of taking a number of heirlooms from Fonthill to Bruton Street. She was taken to the High Court in June 1900, before agreeing to return the items. Charles and Walter, acting on behalf of their nephews and nieces, were concerned that she might try to sell off the 'family silver'.

Sotheby's, where most of Alfred's autographs had been acquired, was keen to snap up his collection; again Mabel was content to sell, disposing of the Hamilton–Nelson letters in 1900. Sotheby's then began a campaign to purchase the rest of the collection in its entirety, offering Mabel £200,000 in 1903 if she would sell through them to J. Pierpoint Morgan. Mabel demanded £250,000, 'exclusive of Sotheby's commission as their approach had been totally unsolicited'.[141] Pierpoint Morgan withdrew and the sale collapsed.

She claimed her actions were the result of poverty and in 1909 she gave Fonthill House and the heirlooms to Hugh and moved out. It was no coincidence that her brother-in-law Charles died the same year leaving her a mere £20,000, much less than she had expected. She wrote to Hugh:

I hope with all my heart you will pull the house I live in down. ... For years I have lived on the margins of debt & of debt incurred through [no] fault of my own but by my being placed in a position too large for my income – I tried to hide from Katharine & Dorothy how distasteful the life was to me but the bitterest thought was the uselessness of my sacrifice & the positively sinful waste of money! When I think of the thousands of pounds wasted, electric light, water supply galleries etc etc I wring my hands in sheer despair.[142]

Her interpretation of poverty was of course relative. She was left with sufficient to buy a substantial country house near Winchester where she outlived her eldest son.

Epilogue

It is the diligent hand and head alone that maketh rich – in self-culture, growth in wisdom, and in business. ... Riches are so great a temptation to ease and self-indulgence, to which men are by nature prone, that the glory is all the greater of those who, born to ample fortunes, nevertheless take an active part in the work of their generation – who 'scorn delights and love laborious days'.

Samuel Smiles, *Self-help*, 1859

James and Mary Ann Morrison had only nine grandchildren, six girls and three boys. All inherited fortunes. However, the two who bore the Morrison name, Hugh and Archie, not only benefited from the collecting addiction of their father Alfred, but also acquired most of their grandfather's remaining properties via their uncles Charles and Walter. Hugh, as the eldest, got Fonthill, then Uncle Charles left him Islay. Archie inherited Basildon from Uncle Charles and Malham from Uncle Walter.

Charles and Walter had followed the example of their father, scorning delights and loving 'laborious days.' However, neither Hugh nor Archie was remotely interested in 'making money', either through trade or finance; quite the opposite. Both chose to spend their fortunes with a recklessness that would have horrified their grandfather. Hugh was the first Morrison to marry into the aristocracy although his wife Lady Mary Leveson-Gower had no fortune. Her father, the 2nd Earl Granville, had lived almost next door, at 18 Carlton House Terrace, but he was virtually bankrupt when he died in 1891. Gladstone helped to raise a subscription of £18,000 for the surviving family,[1] while Alfred settled £50,000 on Hugh and a further £50,000 on Lady Mary when they married the following year.[2]

After Alfred's death, Mabel still had Fonthill for life, so Hugh decided to build himself a new country house on the eastern edge of the estate. The first stage was relatively modest, as it involved merely the removal of a ruined manor house from Berwick St Leonard, only a few miles away, to the new site. Hugh engaged the Arts and Crafts architect Detmar Blow in 1902 to 're-vivify and re-clothe' the old building, renamed Little Ridge.

Archie's career began well enough. He survived the Sudan campaign and the Boer War with distinction, was elected the Conservative Unionist MP for Wilton and married the Hon. Mary Hill-Trevor, another member of the aristocracy. They had a son Simon, born in 1903, and took up farming on part of the Fonthill estate. Meanwhile Hugh and Mary were receiving embarrassing, sometimes painful medical treatment for their apparent infertility.[3] If they remained childless, Archie and his son would inherit everything.

After fourteen years of treatment, in 1906 Mary finally gave birth to a son, John Granville. Writing to his cousin Hugh, Harold Moffatt expressed a dynastic sigh of relief.

> It really looked at one time as though there was a chance that the Morrison name would become extinct in the male line with you and Archie, and I used to be rather sad about it as it was too good a stock to die out for lack of boys to carry on ... I do trust the little fellow will grow up to inherit the family physique, the brains of Uncle Charles, row in the Varsity VIII, and otherwise distinguish himself [4]

Three years later Uncle Charles died leaving Islay to Hugh, and Mabel gave up Fonthill. Hugh went on a spending spree: Blow was commissioned to extend Little Ridge, design a substantial house in Belgravia and add an enormous wing to Islay House.[5] The old Pavilion beside the lake at Fonthill was demolished.

Archie meanwhile inherited Basildon and James Morrison's contemporary and Old Master paintings. He may have intended to make Basildon his family home: running for re-election in East Nottingham in 1910, his occupations were listed in the *Nottingham Guardian* as 'Soldier, politician, agriculturalist, member of Parliament, Poor Law guardian, rural councillor, churchwarden, and co-operative farmer'.[6] However, over the next two years he was divorced by his wife, named as the co-respondent in the divorce of his mistress and accused of bribing the voters of Nottingham. Harold Spender wrote a scathing attack during the 1911 election: 'It is now, therefore, declared to be part of the law of the land that a member of parliament – and therefore a candidate also – may establish a bureau of "charity" in his constituency, and may drench the place in gold. It therefore becomes clear that a new power is given to wealth in British politics by this as by other recent decisions ... happily there are not many members so rich as Capt. Morrison.'[7]

Archie resigned his seat and retreated to Kenya to shoot big game. Out on safari he suddenly decided 'he would like, amongst other things, to develop a modern residential suburb [of Nairobi] with a Country Club and a nine-hole golf course'. He paid £60,000 towards the creation of the Muthaiga Club, to become notorious in the 1920s and 1930s through its association with the scandals of Happy Valley. Plans to settle in Kenya were ended by the outbreak of war, Archie returned to active service, and a hospital for the Grenadier Guards was established in Basildon. He survived with honours and the rank of major and set about engaging Edwin Lutyens to design an extraordinary Byzantine church, almshouses, a village institute and communal services at Basildon.[8] He married again in 1920.

The following year Archie inherited Malham. However he decided to sell it almost immediately. Within ten years he was divorced again, Lutyens' plans for Basildon were never realised and the Basildon estate was sold, along with the few remaining commercial properties in London. Archie established himself in Kensington with his third wife, thirty years his junior. When he died in 1934 his estate was valued at a mere £5,459.[9] His obituary in *The Times* referred to the enormous sums of money he had lavished on farming, but the payments to ex-wives and lovers, to his children, to lawyers, to prop-ping up the Muthaiga Club, and to prolonged hunting and fishing expedi-tions across Africa and Canada all contributed to the dramatic reduction in his fortune. Nicknamed 'Jumbo', he had lived life to the full, but also reduced his inheritance by disposing of land, country houses and family treasures. He was the nearest to a 'black sheep' in the family.

Hugh's only excess was building. Consequently his son John Granville managed to live a lavish lifestyle at Fonthill and on Islay until well after the Second World War. He served as an MP for Salisbury and Chairman of the

1922 Committee, confirming the family's political shift towards the right, and was rewarded with a hereditary peerage by Sir Alec Douglas-Home in 1964. However, the economic climate was no longer supportive of the life of a landed gentleman: agricultural rents were falling, but labour costs and taxes were rising. Blow's house in Belgravia was sold (it is now the Caledonian Club). The commercial properties in London were also sold, together with Islay House and part of the Scottish estate. The nadir was reached at the end of the 1960s with 'rampant inflation, falling production, collapsing land prices, rising unemployment; tax on investment income at 98 per cent; a sliding stock market; Capital Gains Tax, Capital Transfer Tax, Value Added Tax, and to crown everything the threat of a Wealth Tax'.[10] The decision was taken to sell most of the contents of Little Ridge (the remains of Alfred's collection) and, to the horror of architectural historians and conservationists, to demolish Blow's 'masterpiece of the Arts and Crafts tradition', building a much more convenient neo-Georgian box within the floor plan.

No one could have foreseen the late twentieth-century desire, once again, to buy country estates, or the emergence of new fortunes from steel, oil, gas, advertising, computers, telecommunications, transport and fashion. The 3rd Lord Margadale continues to live at Fonthill, but several nearby estates have been acquired by new men. 'New money has resumed its primordial role as the elixir of the English country house.'[11] James Morrison, a lifetime supporter of free trade, could not but approve.

Notes

INTRODUCTION

1. W.D. Rubinstein was the first to place the Morrisons firmly within the 'rich list', proposing James as the richest commoner of the nineteenth century and one of the 250 richest Britons ever. See Philip Beresford and W.D. Rubinstein, *The Richest of the Rich* (Petersfield, 2007). Also see W.D. Rubinstein, *Men of Property: The Very Wealthy in Britain since the Industrial Revolution* (London, 1981).
2. Samuel Smiles, *Self-Help* (London, 1860), first published 1859.
3. Unless separately noted, all Morrison material (letters, diaries, ledgers) is from a private collection. Enquiries can be made to archives@fonthillfarms.co.uk regarding consulting the collection.
4. Roy Porter, *English Society in the 18th Century* (Harmondsworth, 1991), p. 39.
5. See Stanley Chapman, *Merchant Bankers. The Rise of Merchant Banking* (London, 1984) and *Merchant Enterprise in Britain: From the Industrial Revolution to World War One* (Cambridge, 1992); Stanley Chapman examined the activities of James and Charles as merchant bankers, and their involvement with the Bank of the United States in the 1830s and 1840s. See Charles A. Jones, *International Business in the Nineteenth Century: The Rise and Fall of a Cosmopolitan Bourgeoisie* (Brighton, 1987) and *Great Capitalists* (London, 1980). Charles Jones focused on the second generation, and the effect in Argentina of the investments of Charles and Walter, supported by the family solicitors, Ashurst, Morris and Crisp. See David Kynaston, *The City of London Volume 1: A World of its Own 1815–1890* (London, 1994). Several generations of Morrisons feature in David Kynaston's three-volume history of the City of London; James is simply the 'kingpin' of textiles.
6. Martin Daunton, *Progress and Poverty: An Economic and Social History of Britain 1700–1850* (Oxford, 1995), p. 318.
7. James Morrison and his descendants are not related to the Scottish Morrison supermarket owners.
8. See Roy Strong, *The Destruction of the Country House* (London, 1974), Giles Worsley, *England's Lost Houses* (London, 2002).
9. John Tosh, *A Man's Place: Masculinity and the Middle-Class Home in Victorian England* (New Haven, CT, and London, 1999), p. 4.

10. Beverley Southgate, *History meets Fiction* (Harlow, 2009), p. 8.
11. Smiles, p. 229.
12. Disraeli, *Endymion* (New York, 1880), p. 12.

CHAPTER 1: MIDDLE WALLOP

1. Choosing to marry Mary Ann Todd on 6 August may be evidence that this was his birthday; a gap of one month between birth and christening was commonplace.
2. John Morrison, born and died in 1787, may have been a twin of Samuel.
3. B. Critchett, *A New Guide to Stage Coaches, Waggons, Carts, Vessels … for the Year 1808* (London, 1808), lists eleven locations in London from where to catch a coach to Salisbury.
4. Porter, p. 191.
5. Mr Etwall's account book, Hampshire Record Office, Winchester, ref. 5M52/TR8, details the annual repairs (£45) carried out on a stretch of road through Middle Wallop. Notices of repairs to the road and widening were regularly reported, for example in the *London Gazette*, 20 March 1764 and 2 July 1785, also the *Dublin Gazette*, 30 May 1797.
6. See Richard Gatty, *Portrait of a Merchant Prince* (Northallerton, 1976), p. 2: 'old folk in Wiltshire told a tale about the Morrisons that is still remembered – that the first one in those parts had been a Scottish drover, whose calling had often taken him to Wilton Fair. Now the old folk in Wiltshire have a way of being right.'
7. Porter, p. 35.
8. The Clan Morrison was scattered by the beginning of the seventeenth century, the last Brieve of the Clan having been executed in 1613. In the 1861 census only 1,500 Morrisons were living in the Highlands. In 1909 a Clan Morrison Society was founded; Hugh Morrison was granted arms in 1927 and adopted the ancient motto.
9. *Inverness Courier* February 1840, quoted in Gatty.
10. Dorothy Beresford, *Nether Wallop in Hampshire* (Over Wallop, 1973), p. 5.
11. See John Chandler, *Endless Street: A History of Salisbury and its People* (Salisbury, 1983), pp. 94, 105. A day book for 1796–1815 records 21,000 sheep sold each year at Salisbury.
12. George Morrison will signed 4 February 1743, Hampshire Record Office, Winchester, ref. 1744A091.
13. It was not at all unusual, during the eighteenth and early nineteenth centuries, for a woman, particularly a widow, to run an inn; it became less common in the nineteenth century. See L. Davidoff and C. Hall, *Family Fortunes: Men and Women of the English Middle Class 1780–1850* (London, 1987), pp. 299–300.
14. See Daunton 'investment in better roads raised the productivity of horses, permitting the replacement of pack-horses by carts, and an increase in the size and speed of wagons and coaches. … a dense, interconnected network of carriers' services emerged in the eighteenth century' (pp. 305, 307).
15. Margaret Morrison will signed 17 May 1762, Hampshire Record Office, Winchester, ref. 1767A079.
16. See Porter, pp. 366–7, quoting Joseph Massie's 'Estimate of the social structure and income 1759–1760'.

17. *Hampshire Allegations for Marriage Licences granted by the Bishop of Winchester* (London, 1893). Marriage of Joseph Morrison, Nether Wallop, Victualler, to Mary Wheeler, Little St Swithuns Winchester, 26 December 1768.

18. Anon., *Reminiscences of an Old Draper* (London, 1878), p. 51. The lease of the Old George was renewed on 1 June 1777 and again on 1 August 1795 when Fifehead Manor was sold to Mr Sutton.

19. Ibid., p. 51.

20. Details of baptisms, marriages and deaths in Hampshire Record Office, Winchester, reveal a bewildering number of Morrisons with similar names, but few details of the maiden names of their wives. Mary Wheeler of Winchester married Joseph Morrison 'vintner' in 1768; died 1773; daughters Mary born 1772 died ? and Elizabeth born 1773 died 1804. They may also have had a son William, born 1769, who died in 1799. A second Joseph Morrison was married to Elizabeth *c.* 1779; they had at least five children before he died in 1795 and she in 1804.

21. Mary Morrison will, Hampshire Record Office, Winchester, ref. 1803A079. She left her property to her niece Margaret Hillary.

22. In 1768 the Red Lion was established in Somerton, to meet the needs, like the Lower George, Middle Wallop, of increasing commercial and private traffic.

23. Jane Austen, *Emma* (London, 1938), p. 23. First published 1816. While the Morrisons and Barnards possessed the 'independence' which irritated Emma, they were not yet of the 'genteel' or 'polite' class identified by Amanda Vickery in *The Gentleman's Daughter: Women's Lives in Georgian England* (New Haven, CT, 1998), which consisted of lesser landed gentlemen, attorneys, doctors, clerics, merchants and manufacturers.

24. Paul Langford, 'The uses of eighteenth-century politeness', *Transactions of the Royal Historical Society*, 6th ser., XII (2002), pp. 318–19.

25. 'Death of Mr James Morrison', *The Times*, 2 November 1857.

26. R.H. Sweet, 'Topographies of politeness', *Transactions of the Royal Historical Society*, 6th ser. XII (2002), p. 359.

27. Robert Baldick (ed.), *The Memoirs of Chateaubriand* (London, 1961), p. 109.

28. Leigh Hunt, 'Coaches', *The Indica, and the Companion* (London, 1834), Part II, p. 14.

29. Beckford described her as 'Lord Nelson's Lady Hamilton or anybody else's Lady Hamilton'; H.A.N. Brockman, The *Caliph of Fonthill* (London, 1956), p. 118.

30 Joseph Morrison will, Hampshire Record Office, Winchester, ref. 1805A060. His brother George and Sarah's brother James Barnard were executors.

31 Conflicting evidence provided by Joseph Gilchrist, haberdasher, who worked for Morrison, Dillon & Co. in the mid-nineteenth century and by J.L. Mallett, fellow member of the Political Economy Club.

32. The *London Post Office Directory* (London, 1808): S. Barnard haberdasher and hosier, 16 and 40 Fore Street; *Johnstone's London Commercial Guide* (London, 1817): Barnard & Co., wholesale linen drapers, 129 Cheapside; G. & J. Morrison, tailors and mercers, 15 Craven Street.

33. When Owen first came to London as a boy, he lodged with his brother. His father had written in advance 'to his friend, a Mr Heptinstall, of No. 6 Ludgate Hill, who was a large dealer in lace foreign and British; and Mr Moore had written in my favour to Mr Tilsley, of No. 100 Newgate Street, who then kept what was deemed to be a large draper's shop'. See J. Butt, *The Life of Robert Owen written by himself* (London, 1971), p. 12.

34. John Chandler, *Endless Street: A History of Salisbury and its People* (Salisbury, 1983), pp. 91–2.
35. Kynaston, p. 58.
36. Telba [Ablet], *A Few Every-day Hints, addressed to the Youth and Young Men of the Drapery Trade* (London, n.d. [1878]), p. 15.
37. Kynaston, p. 9, quoting *Picture of London*, 1815.

CHAPTER 2: THE TODDS OF FORE STREET

1. Morrison archive, James Morrison's handwritten account of his early years in Fore Street. The same date is recorded in Joseph Todd's earliest ledger; also in a notebook kept in the Morrison estate office, Coleman Street, until the late twentieth century.
2. He also kept among his personal papers a highly inaccurate newspaper version of his first meeting with the Todds, published several years after he was recognised to be one of the wealthiest men and largest landowners in the country. 'On his arrival in London, he was walking along the pavement of a certain street, looking about him, but not where he should have looked: he stumbled into an open cellar, and, in his fall, either broke or very severely injured one of his limbs. The people to whom the house and shop belonged were much concerned at the accident, and the more so when they found he was a poor, friendless, and penniless adventurer in London. They got surgical assistance to him; kept him in their own house until well; and after that, being pleased with his amiable disposition, took him into their linen drapery as an apprentice. He advanced successively to be journeyman [then] foreman.' See Adam Brown, 'Travels of Adam Brown, Salisbury, November 20, 1842', *The League*, 9 December 1843, pp. 169–70.
3. According to Richard Gatty, Joseph Todd worked first as a clerk in Penrith; however, it is most likely he was apprenticed in the textiles trade. Like James Morrison, he would have had to spend between three and seven years apprenticed, then spend a period as journeyman and shopman before setting up his own retail business in 1793. Carleton Cowper family papers (ref. DCC2) in Cumbria Record Office, Carlisle, include complex property transactions between three brothers, William, Thomas and Joseph Todd, skinners, linen merchants and linen drapers working in Penrith, Manchester and London.
4. When Joseph Todd applied for arms in 1823, Lucy is described in the grant and exemplification of arms as 'daughter and coheir of William Plowes of Wakefield Yorkshire': see Morrison archive. They married in 1792. John Plowes of Wakefield, dealer and chapman (merchant), was declared bankrupt 12 April 1768; the *London Post Office Directory* for 1817 includes John Plowes & Co., merchant, Gracechurch Street.
5. Morrison archive, the lease was obtained from John Shibblehill.
6. No. 154 Cheapside, assignment of lease from Radford and Grant. The 1808 Directory lists: 105 Fore Street haberdashery and 154 Cheapside lace; other Morrison records suggest that Fore Street dealt with wholesale orders and Cheapside retail. Todd took out insurance with the Royal Exchange for Fore Street, the Globe for Cheapside.
7. Kynaston, p. 9, quoting *Picture of London*, 1815.
8. Hugh Thomas, *The Slave Trade: The History of the Atlantic Slave Trade, 1440–1870* (London, 1997), p. 447; J.H. Parry, *Trade and Dominion* (London, 2000), p. 278.
9. Parry, p. 286.
10. Ibid., p. 287.

11. S.D. Chapman and S. Chasagne, *European Textile Printers in the Eighteenth Century* (London, 1981), pp. 4, 84.

12. See ibid., also Adrian Forty, *Objects of Desire: Design and Society 1750–1980* (London, 1986); John Styles, 'Manufacturing, Consumption and Design in Eighteenth-century England', in John Brewer and Roy Porter (eds), *Consumption and the World of Goods* (London, 1993).

13. Thomas p. 320; also pp. 318–20. A range of woollen cloths were sold in West Africa, 'then and now a protection against the fierce cold wind of the Gulf of Guinea', including says (a fine woollen cloth mixed with silk), perpetuanas (a tough cloth like tweed) from Devon, bays (baize), bridgwaters (from Bridgwater) and Welsh plaines (from Wales and the Midlands). The cottons included coarse annabasses, particularly desired by Portuguese and French captains, and the 'Guinea' cloth.

14. Beresford and Rubinstein, p. 359.

15. Ibid., p. 235.

16. Kynaston, p. 25. Of 131 houses in Wood Street, 78 were devoted to textiles; many of the houses in Fore Street were also involved in the textiles trade, including hosiers, linen drapers, hatters, haberdashers and lace manufacturers.

17. R. Phillips, *Picture of London for 1803* (1803), p. 32.

18. A. Adburgham, *Shops and Shopping* (London, 1964), p. 8.

19. Butt, p. 21.

20. Anon., *Draper*, p. 32.

21. Graham Wallas, *The Life of Francis Place 1771–1854* (London, 1918), p. 30.

22. The staff in the wholesale concern in Fore Street included Mary Dann, Misses Paul, Downing, Jenkins and Richards, Mr Woolsey and Mr Bassett. Mr Caulier became Todd's partner and ran the Cheapside business, William Cope was his shopman, Mr Luck and Henry Dicks the apprentices.

23. The Danns owned a small estate in Bexley but both Laetitia and her younger sister Mary served apprenticeships in the textiles trade while their brother studied law. It was no more unusual for women to work in the textile trade, as shopwomen and also proprietors, than it was for them to own and run public houses, like Morrison's grandmother Margaret in Middle Wallop. And it was extremely common for wives to act as 'junior partners' to their husbands, working alongside them at the shop counter. See Tosh, pp. 14–15.

24. Anon., *Draper,* p. 44.

25. The articles of partnership were signed on 12 March 1812, Morrison's salary rising to £70 for the first year, £80 for the second, and £50 for the final six months before the partnership began on 29 September 1814. His income for the first year of the partnership was to be £500.

26. Clare Walsh, 'Shop Design and the Display of Goods in Eighteenth-Century London', *Journal of Design History*, 8, no. 3 (1995).

27. D. Alexander, *Retailing in England during the Industrial Revolution* (London, 1970), p. 132.

28. *The Book of English Trades* (London, 1821), p. 192.

29. Alexander, p. 133.

30. Lewin B. Bowring, *Autobiographical Recollections of Sir John Bowring* (London, 1877), pp. 58–9.

31. Butt, p. 21.

32. Joseph Todd also acquired a 31-year lease at Christmas 1813 for 106 Fore Street from the Vicar and Churchwardens of St Giles and the Churchwardens of St Luke, at a rent of £92.

33. 'We had quite determined on a start, Mr Beaston (now Bridges & Beaston) had applied to Cope to join us & a House in Fleet Street among others in which a Mr Hall (a great Rascal, a friend of the Theobalds & I suspect of Mr Kinneas) a Boot & Shoe maker had just failed was talked of', James Morrison's account, Morrison archive.

34. [Warren], *Ten Thousand-a-Year* (Edinburgh, 1841), vol. I, p. 29.

35. *The Examiner*, 21 June 1835.

36. Gatty, p. 11.

37. Butt, p. 19.

38. Anon., *Draper*, pp. 10–11. And see Styles 'Manufacturing', p. 170 on a draper's shop on Ludgate Hill in 1808 – presumably Waithman's – through which 600 customers passed in a day, 50 or 60 at a time served by eight or nine shopmen.

39. [Warren], vol. I, p. 2.

40. *New Dictionary of National Biography*. In his *Memoirs*, published in 1794, James Lackington noted the general increase in reading to which his business contributed: 'I suppose that more than four times the numbers of books are sold now than were sold twenty years since. … If John goes to town with a load of hay, he is charged to be sure not to forget to bring home *Peregrine Pickle's* adventures; and when Dolly is sent to market to sell her eggs, she is commissioned to purchase *The History of Pamela Andrews*. In short, all ranks and degrees now READ.'

41. Volney, *Ruins of Empire*, was published in a cheap edition pocket book for artisans. See E.P. Thompson, *The Making of the English Working Class* (Harmondsworth, 1975), pp. 107–8 on the influence of Paine, Godwin and Volney.

42. [Sam Dobell], *A Brief Description of the Principles of the Freethinking Christians* (Cranbrook, Kent, 1824).

43. Iain McCalman, *Radical Underworld Prophets, Revolutionaries and Pornographers in London 1795–1840* (Oxford, 1988), p. 74.

44. While denying the divinity of Christ's person, the Freethinking Christians did 'believe in the divine character or nature of his mission as a teacher of religion': see *The Freethinking Christians' Quarterly Register* (London, 1823), vol. I, p. 114.

45. McCalman, p. 74.

46. See Allan Nevins (ed.), *America through British Eyes* (Oxford, 1948), pp. 53–4.

47. Judy Slinn, *Ashurst Morris Crisp: A Radical Firm* (Cambridge, 1997), p. 4.

48. Speech by Walter Morrison, 'Report of proceedings at the banquet, on Saturday, the 12th December, 1903 in commemoration of the eightieth birthday of Mr John Morris', privately circulated, copy in Morrison archive.

49. Nigel Cross, *The Common Writer* (Cambridge, 1985), p. 20.

50. John Dillon, *Retribution, or the Chieftain's Daughter* (1818), Dedication to John Symmons and Mary Dillon.

51. *The Monthly Repository of Theology and General Literature* (London, 1818), vol. XIII, p. 365.

52. Joseph Todd acquired a 17-year lease of a house in Paradise Row, Lambeth, close to Lambeth Palace and St Mary's Church, in July 1811 for £350.

53. W.M. Thackeray, *Vanity Fair* (New York, 1962), p. 12.

54. Possibly Melmoth's, *Shenstone-Green; or, the New Paradise Lost being a history of human nature* (1799), 3 vols; Vol. I, chapter 10, 'The Effusions of Enthusiasm'.

55. Gatty mistakenly believed Rosa to be another woman. James' language is similar to Rosa Matilda's in Charlotte Dacre's *The Passions* (1811), likely reading for the couple. 'Perhaps it may be a misfortune to possess a disposition such as mine, for though keenly alive to

pleasure, and, in the ardor of imagination, exalting it to rapture, still am I no less suscep-
tible of pain or disappointment: the measure is equal and if I *enjoy* more exquisitely than
the common lot of mankind, I likewise *suffer* more severely.'

56. In his address James misquotes Goldsmith's poem 'The Traveller': 'Creation's heir, the
world, the world is mine', also Gray's 'Elegy written in a Country Churchyard'. See John
Brewer, *The Pleasures of the Imagination* (London, 1997), p. 489 on mass production
providing access for 'modest' people to quality literature: 'at the dawn of the nineteenth
century it had become possible to imagine, to hold and even to own the works of literature and art, or at least copies of them, which had been enshrined by London critics,
commercial booksellers and art dealers as Britain's cultural heritage.'

57. Marriage certificate, Morrison archive.

58. W.M. Thackeray, *The Newcomes* (Ann Arbor, Michigan, 1996), p. 12.

59. New articles were drawn up on 8 June 1816.

60. Gatty, p. 15.

CHAPTER 3: FORE STREET AND THE TEXTILES TRADE

1. James Morrison to John Dillon, July 1826. According to family tradition, the commercial
traveller, or 'Brummagem Bagman', who came upon Wellington in the middle of the
battle without an ADC and who rode off to deliver a vital message before disappearing
from the battlefield, was travelling on behalf of Fore Street: see Gatty, p. 18.

2. See Thackeray, *Vanity Fair*, chapter 18. The merchant John Sedley lost everything: his
'fortune was swept down with that fatal news.'

3. Daunton, *Progress*, p. 433. And on end of taxes see Daunton, *Trusting Leviathan*, p. 51.

4. R. Davis, *The Industrial Revolution and British Overseas Trade* (Leicester, 1979), p. 40.

5. S. Chapman, *Merchant Enterprise in Britain. From the Industrial Revolution to World War I*
(Cambridge, 1992), p. 168.

6. Ibid., p. 168.

7. W.H. Hillyer, *James Talcott, Merchant, and his Times* (New York, 1937), pp. 92–3, quoted
in Chapman, p. 185.

8. D. Puseley, *Commercial Companion* (1860), p. 125.

9. Anon., *Draper*, p. 29. Later in the century, the buyers at Fore Street were significant and
well rewarded. William Cross, chief buyer of silks, could afford to buy a comfortable villa
in Blackheath and send two sons to private schools.

10. Butt, pp. 18, 13.

11. *Economist and General Adviser*, 1825, quoted in Alexander, p. 163.

12. Richard Rush, quoted in Kynaston, p. 29.

13. See Records of the Sun Fire Office, 30 March 1820, MS 11936, Guildhall Library, City
of London, now London Metropolitan Archive, Clerkenwell, London.

14. See Styles, pp. 530–1. 'Factory production of textiles in England between 1760 and 1850
was associated with an increasingly diverse range of final products, often customised for
particular markets and subject to frequent changes in character according to constant and
rapid changes in clothing and furnishing fabrics.'

15. Lucy Johnston's *Nineteenth-Century Fashion in Detail* (London, 2005) uses the collections of the Victoria and Albert Museum to examine surviving examples of dress, for men
and women.

16. Celina Fox (ed.), *London–World City 1800–1840* (New Haven, CT, 1992), p. 109.

17. Wyatt Papworth, *John B. Papworth Architect to the King of Württemberg: A Brief Record of his Life and Works* (London, 1879), p. 31. For the involvement of Auguste Pugin with the Repository, see Rosemary Hill, *God's Architect: Pugin and the Building of Romantic Britain* (London, 2007).

18. R. Ackermann (ed.), *The Repository of Arts, Literature, Commerce, Manufactures, Fashions, and Politics* (London, 1809–1815), August 1813; April 1814.

19. See Morrison's comments about one of Todd's apprentices, Mr Dicks, established in Dover: 'Dicks exactly what a pupil of old Fore Street should be leading cheap goods Hdkfs, Hose, braces, Caps &c all hung all along the front of the house with large tickets & cotton lace & cheap Thread Lace tickets in the window, he is full of bustle & will keep his head above water.' James Morrison travel diary for June and July 1823, Morrison archive.

20. Turnover was always highest during March, April, May and June, coinciding with Easter, Whitsun and the demands of the London Season.

21. Anon., *Draper*, p. 221.

22. Charles Morrison born 20 September 1817.

23. Anon., *Draper*, pp. 157, 54, 159.

24. Old Bailey Records, 10 November 1819: t18191201–165.

25. Old Bailey Records, 10 July 1821: t18210718–37. Recommended to mercy by the prosecutors, so presumably they were not hanged.

26. Ibid., 6 September 1832: t18320906–70.

27. Alexander Galloway (1776–1847), President of the London Corresponding Society (his brother-in-law Thomas Evans was Secretary), imprisoned in Newgate without trial 1798–1801, he then joined Place's campaign to elect Sir Francis Burdett to Parliament and in 1813 campaigned with Place for the abolition of the apprenticeship clauses which they believed prevented flexibility in the labour market. He was a cool, cautious and methodical man of business, and as his business expanded he became one of London's largest employers with over a hundred men working in his factory in Smithfield. He was courted by 'literary and scientific men of all parties and all professions', McCalman, p. 29.

28. Papworth, *John B. Papworth* pp. 25, 55.

29. Select Committee on the Copyright of Designs, Minutes of Evidence, *Parliamentary Papers*, 1840, vol. VI, para. 3062.

30. The loan was in the form of a mortgage on Galloway's property in Holborn, 95 and 97 Chancery Lane, 1 and 2 Three Arrow Court and 2 Academy Court, together with a warehouse, counting house and smith shop behind Star Yard, Carey Street. Galloway wrote to Papworth, 13 June 1821, 'we shall want some of your assistance to-morrow; and I want particularly to consult you about making the Roofs of the Buildings of iron, as such roofs promise considerable advantages': Papworth, *J. B. Papworth*, p. 52.

31. Johnston, p. 154.

32. Anon., *Draper*, p. 84. See also William Hull, *The History of the Glove Trade* (London, 1834).

33. Kynaston, p. 41. See Daunton, *Progress*, p. 539 on 'the Petition of the London Merchants': 'less a united commercial plea for free trade than a traditional complaint by particular interests for favour. North European merchants were protesting against preferences to Canadian timber; the East India Co. was urging free trade in sugar against West Indian

interests while defending its own monopoly of tea for China. Free trade was another weapon to be used by commercial and industrial interests in a battle to shape policy for their own ends.'

34. E. Gaskell, *Cranford* (Oxford, 1960), p. 44.

35. Lady Strachey (ed.), *Memoirs of a Highland Lady. The Autobiography of Elizabeth Grant of Rothiemurchus* (London, 1898), p. 260.

36. The main producers were Hinde & Hardy and Grout & Bayliss of Saffron Walden; Samuel Courtauld became a major competitor from the 1820s.

37. Lou Taylor, *Mourning Dress: A Costume and Social History* (London, 1983), p. 204.

38. Bombazine had a silken warp, worsted weft and twilled finish, but with the worsted surface uppermost, thus making the fabric as dull as possible when worn: see ibid., pp. 202–3, 191.

39. There were a number of deaths marked in the accounts: Princess Charlotte 1817 ('P.Charlotte'), Queen Charlotte 1818 ('Roy. Burial'), King George III ('King buried'), Queen Caroline 1821, Duke of York 1827 ('D Y buried').

40. Thea Holme, *Prinny's Daughter: A Life of Princess Charlotte of Wales* (London, 1976), p. 240. And see Lou Taylor, p. 128. Official court mourning was announced: 'the Ladies to wear black bombazines, plain muslins or long lawn crape hoods, shammy shoes and gloves and crape fans. The Gentlemen to wear black cloth without buttons on the sleeves or pockets, plain muslin or long lawn cravats and weepers [white cuffs] shammy shoes and gloves, crape hatbands and black swords and buckles.'

41. James Morrison to George Crow, 6 January 1827; James Morrison to John Dillon, 15 January 1827.

42. Puckler Muskau, *Puckler's Progress: The Adventures of Prince Puckler-Muskau in England, Wales and Ireland as Told in Letters to His Former Wife 1826–1829* (London, 1987), p. 83.

43. James Morrison to John Dillon, 23 February 1827.

44. Old Bailey Records, t18170219–68. William Everington of Ludgate Hill was another retailer who bought from Levick. Everington also acquired shawls from a number of ladies returning from India, who had the sudden need, once in London, to dispose of their personal property (no duty liable) for cash. Everington did well as the ladies then used their cash to buy his table linen, cheaper shawls and other articles to take out to India. 'Of course no consideration of Custom-house duty entered into these calculations', Anon, *Draper*, p. 83.

45. Edwin Chadwick, 'Opening Address of the President of Section F (Economic Science and Statistics) of the British Association for the Advancement of Science, at the Thirty-Second Meeting, in Cambridge, in October, 1862', printed in the *Journal of the Statistical Society of London*, December 1862, and in Russell D. Roberts, *The Invisible Heat: An Economic Romance* (London, 2001), p. 260. Smiles, p. 210, lists the qualities requred 'for the efficient conduct of business of any sort' as 'attention, application, accuracy, method, punctuality, and despatch', all practised by James Morrison.

46. James Morrison to John Dillon, 1827.

CHAPTER 4: JAMES MORRISON, 'THE NAPOLEON OF SHOPKEEPERS'

1. Gatty, p. 28.
2. Transcript by Ashurst's firm of material relating to James Morrison's dispute with John Edward and Joseph Todd and eventual acquisition of his father-in-law's business, Morrison archive. All quotations following are from this source unless otherwise cited.
3. He would retire immediately (1818) from managing the Cheapside concern, paying £400 per annum for his replacement, then he would receive his capital when he retired completely in 1822. Accounts reveal him receiving £77,673 between 1821 and 1824.
4. Joseph Todd agreed to delay his own retirement until 1826, keeping at least £30,000 capital in the business which Morrison would pay off 'at one, two and three years with interest till paid at 5 per cent', and become sole owner. A memo of 7 February 1826 details Joseph Todd receiving a total of £187,489 and John Edward Todd receiving £84,841, Morrison archive.
5. The partnerships were 1/32nd.
6. James Morrison reply to Bill of Chancery 28 May 1824, included in transcripts of dispute.
7. 'To attendance and making plans of buildings in Grub Street as executed by Sowler and others' £150, Morrison archive. Morrison had bought 33 and 34 Grub Street in 1820 for £2,000 and, the following year, 31 and 32 for £950. Two years later he acquired the Greyhound Inn and Yard, also in Grub Street, for another £950.
8. See John Styles, *The Dress of the People* (New Haven, CT, 2007), p. 209 and language applied to clothes and appearance – neat, clean.
9. Papworth, *John B. Papworth*, p. 58.
10. Charles Knight, 1851, quoted in Adburgham, p. 96.
11. See H.J. Dyos, *Exploring the Urban Past. Essays in Urban History*, ed. D. Cannadine and D. Reeder (Cambridge, 1982), and Akira Satoh, *Building in Britain. The Origins of a Modern Industry*, trans. Ralph Morton (Aldershot, 1995).
12. Charles Dickens, *Sketches by Boz* (Harmondsworth, 1995), p. 214.
13. Charles Dickens, *Nicholas Nickleby* (London, 1986), p. 464.

CHAPTER 5: THE EDUCATION OF A GENTLEMAN (PART ONE)

1. Joseph Todd acquired the Twickenham Park estate in about 1817 from Francis Gosling, a London banker: see R.S. Cobbett, *Memorials of Twickenham: Parochial and Topographical* (London, 1872), p. 233, and Alan C.B. Urwin, *Twicknam Parke* (Hounslow, 1965). Thomas Hofland painted the view of Richmond from Twickenham Park for Todd in 1821–2. Papworth worked on the mansion, adding a conservatory for Thomas Todd who appears to have taken over the property before the death of his father. Joseph Todd acquired Molesey House and estate in about 1821. Horace Walpole visited in 1795, declaring that 'the situation seems handsome, the house extremely pretty, there is a lovely little gallery', Rowland G.M.Baker, *The Book of Molesey* (Buckingham, 1986), p. 89. In 1823 Todd paid £125 for a grant of arms, 'being desirous of bearing armorial ensigns with lawful authority', including ensigns 'in memory of his late wife Lucy daughter and Co-heir of William Plowes of Wakefield'.

2. Benjamin Disraeli, *Vivian Grey* (London, 1853), first published 1826–7, p. 16.
3. In 1821 the population of Balham was 712, living in 97 dwellings. Balham history is taken from Graham Power, *Balham: A Brief History* (Wandsworth, 1996), and from material in the local history section of Battersea Public Library.
4. John Ruskin, *Praeterita* vol. 35 of *The Works of John Ruskin*, ed. E.T. Cook and Alexander Wedderburn, 29 vols, London, 1903–12. p. 11. And see T. Hilton, *John Ruskin, The Early Years 1819–1859* (New Haven, CT, 2000). Ruskin's father was a partner in a firm of wine merchants; their semi-detached villa in Herne Hill had previously been occupied by a linen draper from Cheapside.
5. Five acres, 19 poles and 2 messuages bought freehold from Thomas Puckle for £1,500; two houses bought leasehold from Mr Bish for £2,500. See papers relating to history of Balham, Battersea Local History Library, London.
6. *The Times*, 3 February 1808.
7. Papworth's work at Balham included designs for the grounds and the farmyard, as well as the addition of a porch and internal decorations, see RIBA.
8. Papworth, *John B. Papworth*, p. 56, 13 February 1823.
9. See Walter Leaf, *Some Chapters of Autobiography* (London, 1938). Park Hill later became the London residence of Sir Henry Tate of Tate & Lyle, founder of the Tate Gallery (now Tate Britain).
10. Wyatt Papworth, *John B. Papworth*, p. 73.
11. Ibid., p. 25. And see Morrison to Papworth: 'I regret very much being obliged to trouble you so frequently – but I do so only in matters of Arts, and you have brought all the trouble upon you by leading me into temptation', pp. 57–8.
12. Gatty, p. 11.
13. Perhaps he thought he was similar to the traveller in Revd John Chetwode Eustace's *Classical Tour through Italy* (1821), who believed 'that it becomes a man of a liberal and active mind to visit countries ennobled by the birth and the residence of the Great; who, with the same Roman [Cicero], finds himself disposed by the contemplation of such scenes to virtuous and honourable pursuits'. In Dibdin's *Library Companion*, he would have appreciated the 'moral' guidance offered on how to avoid the 'mischievous application of superfluous wealth' when building a library. He owned both publications. See Eustace, *Classical Tour*; and the Revd Thomas Frognall Dibdin, *The Library Companion; or, the Young Man's Guide, and the Old Man's Comfort, in the Choice of a Library* (1824).
14. W.A. Speck, *Robert Southey: Entire Man of Letters* (New Haven, CT, 2006), p. xvi.
15. On 3 September 1823, James' diary entry reads: 'Saddle back. & Skiddaw wet morning. could not go to Buttermere & Crommack lakes. call'd on Mr Southey & had a conversation of 2 hours – on the effects of the Manufacturing system – fortunes from conquest & the Spinning Jenny. on Mr Owens plan. Unitarians in America. on the improvement in the distribution of Church Patronage in last reign & present. never reads Don Juan or Edinboro Review. Brays village Libraries & Society for Promoting Xian Knowledge. Went again to Tea & stop'd 4 hours. present Mrs S & family. a sister. & Mrs & Miss Coleridge. Fearons book. guess in New England & reckon in Virginia Mr Everett Freethinking Xians. thought their profession of Religion a moral disguise, confounded them with Bible Xians at Manchester & only book he had seen their Cookery Book. admired the system of internal discipline & wish'd such in the church. Unitarian version of Testament unfair. we excel all other nations in everything but Physiology & Criticism (the Germans beat us in these). Americans follow Echhorn lamented that some articles

should have appeard in Quarterly Review against America. thinks the Americans will fail in the experiment now going on in that Country. of seeing with how little of power in the Government they can do with. dont like Calvinism and quoted Warburton against them. thinks some people have too high an opinion of Bible Societys. Is about to publish the Book of the Church. or English Ecclesiastical History. has some thoughts of another on the history of dissent – has now in hand. Dialogues on the progress of Society. thinks the English Poor are as bad of as they were the day Julius Ceaser landed in England. Effects of dissolution of monasteries. read a part, to shew his opinion of Owens system & of the present state of society in England. thinks we are sleeping on gunpowder. dreads a Servile War. we are just about to feel the effects of the modern discoveries in Science. & of the art of Printing people will read. 'a little learning is a dangerous thing'. we are at Sea without a compass. no period in history furnishes a parallel, a crisis will come. Savoyard Boy & his monkey. Mr Barrow. Croker. Gifford Monk. Wordsworth lives at Rydal recommended me to read. Turners 'Anglo Saxons' Souths sermons Millers Bampton lectures Bensons Hulsean Lectures. Berkleys minute Philosopher. Butlers analogy. Mr S thought poor Martin would have done as much good in England as in India shew'd me 'a New System of Vegetable Cookery' Salford 1821 By a Society of Bible Christians. Can be had at Souters. Holy Alliance wrong in Spain. Historical blunder in prospectus of Godwin's intended work. Mary Woolstencroft Shelly. don't like public Education would if possible educate at home certainly girls. preparatory schools bad. proper place for a young child is its mothers side. too many brought up to professions. gentility the evil immediately threatening us. Medical profession fears is now tricky. Lawyers certainly an evil.'

16. Southey to Lightfoot, 23 September 1823, letters published 1849, quoted in Gatty, p. 53.
17. And in fact never finished.
18. J.L. Mallet, [Diary] *Political Economy Club* (London, 1921), p. 206.
19. *The Times*, 1 April 1809. See Francis Haskell, *The Ephemeral Museum* (New Haven, CT, 2000), chapters 3 and 4, also Brandon Taylor, *Art for the Nation* (Manchester, 1999), chapter 2. The mission of the British Institution was 'to raise the standard of morality and patriotism; to attract the homage and respect of foreign nations, and to produce those intellectual and virtuous feelings, which are perpetually alive to the welfare and glory of the country', Brandon Taylor, p. 30.
20. J. Carey, *A Descriptive Catalogue of a Collection of Paintings by British Artists in the Possession of Sir John Fleming Leicester Fleming, Bart* (London, 1819), p. x.
21. Walter Thornbury, *The Life of J.M.W. Turner, RA* (London, 1970), repr. of 1877 edn, pp. 320–1.
22. Papworth worked on Pickersgill's house, 18 Soho Square.
23. The archive contains a number of charming watercolours of the children as babies, though none, apart from Alfred's, are signed. Behnes' commission for a marble bust of Princess Victoria was completed in 1829. Morrison wrote to Papworth in December the following year: 'Mr Behnes call'd yesterday to say the Bust is now finish'd, and will be sent home in a day or two. Will you oblige me by calling to look at the finish and suggest any final touches which you may think it wants.'
24. Papworth, *John B. Papworth*, p. 58. William Hilton's *Comus with the Lady in the Enchanted Chair* was exhibited at the RA in 1823 (no. 196) but Morrison only bought it from Christie's in 1841. Henry Howard's *Hesperus Leading the Starry Host* was also shown in 1823 at the RA (no. 21).

25. Constable, 'Pickersgill is an honourable man, and his art is sound and good', see *New DNB*. *A Boat Passing a Lock*, RA 1824, no. 180.
26. Now in the Thyssen-Bornemisza collection in Madrid.
27. Constable to Fisher, 8 May 1824, in C.R. Leslie, *Memoirs of the Life of John Constable* (London, 1951), p. 121.
28. Papworth, *John. B. Papworth*, p. 57.
29. RA 1826, no. 268.
30. Papworth, *John. B. Papworth*, pp. 57–8.
31. RA 1825, no. 465.
32. Now in Manchester City Art Gallery.
33. Wilkie Collins, *Memoirs of the Life of William Collins Esq, RA* (London, 1978), repr. of 2-vol. edn of 1848, pp. 266–8. Morrison had a copy of the memoirs in his library.
34. Edward T. Joy, *English Furniture 1800–1851* (London, 1977), pp. 176–7. And see introduction to RIBA catalogue of drawings of Papworth by George McHardy. For details of the furniture trade see Geoffrey Beard and Christopher Gilbert (eds), *Dictionary of English Furniture Makers 1660–1840* (Leeds, 1986), and Pat Kirkham, *The London Furniture Trade 1700–1870* (Leeds, 1988).
35. Maria Edgeworth, *The Absentee* (Oxford, 1988), pp. 13–14; first published 1812.
36. Wyatt Papworth, *Memoir of Alfred Whitehead Morant*, reprinted from 'Additions' for the *Builder*, 20 August 1881.
37. Kirkham, pp. 67, 76–7.
38. Papworth, *John B. Papworth*, pp. 57–8.
39. Madame Venturi's life of W.H. Ashurst, written for the *DNB*, reprinted in the 'Report of proceedings at the banquet, on Saturday, the 12th December, 1903 in commemoration of the eightieth birthday of Mr John Morris', privately circulated.
40. See Flora Fraser, *The Unruly Queen: The Life of Queen Caroline* (London, 1996), p. 464. Richard Honey, carpenter and George Francis, bricklayer, were shot by Life Guards at Cumberland Gate.
41. See George Holyoake, *The History of Cooperation* (London, 1906), quoted Gatty, p. 54.
42. 'My father was one of the last representatives of the ancient woollen trade of Exeter, and saw its final decay and departure to the north', Bowring, p. 54.
43. There is no evidence, however, that Morrison made use of Place's famous library, 'a sort of gossiping shop for such persons as were in any way engaged in public matters having the benefit of the people for their object', Wallas, p. 177.
44. 'Since you [Morrison] called on me this morning I have thought much on your proposal to print small tracts for distribution among the working people in the manufacturing districts. You said, that, many Manufacturers were desirous of a better understanding with the workmen than had ever existed, and were willing to do much towards so desirable an end. ... Small tracts, which should clearly yet shortly, and in plain language explain the nature of wages, and employment, the modes of accumulating capital, its nature, and such other matters relating to Political economy. ... No vituperative language – no epithets – no imputation of motives, nothing abusive should be inserted, its tone should be mild and conciliatory. ... If you can pursuade [*sic*] the manufacturers to subscribe their money for the purpose named, you will be the means of conferring many important blessings on a large number of human beings', Francis Place to James Morrison, 8 December 1824. Place suggested that manufacturers subscribe £500, tracts to be priced at a penny halfpenny.

45. *Morning Chronicle*, 12 January 1824, quoted in F. Rosen, *Bentham, Byron, and Greece. Constitutionalism, Nationalism, and Early Liberal Political Thought* (Oxford, 1992), p. 106.
46. See H. Hale Bellot, *University College London 1826–1926* (London, 1929), and Negley Harte and John North, *The World of UCL 1828–1990* (London, 1991).
47. Between 1818 and 1831, 25% of MPs were connected with trade, see Gerrit P. Judd, *Members of Parliament 1734–1832* (New Haven, CT, 1955), p. 57.
48. 'I [Bowring] should be very sorry to see you involved in a contest of which the expense would be great & the risk considerable – but if Hume's representation be correct, neither of these evils would be to [us?] anticipated at Dover. That I have very much at heart your entering "honorable house" you very well know – I have a portion of spite against the aristocracy – but a stronger & a better feeling is the conviction that you would really & truly be of great value to the popular cause. ... I want to see good sense pitted against eloquent discourse – a knowledge of facts weighted in the balance against oratorical decorations – an acquaintance with – an interest in the welfare of the many. ... Rotten boroughs seem less & less obtainable. If you succeed at Dover – & that connection becomes in any respect an undesirable one, I am persuaded you will have paved the way to a seat for some other place – and then the next parliament will probably be one in which the liberal commercial policy of the government will be yet more developed – & surely you could do much here & do much for which ministers themselves would feel indebted to you – much that would give you at once a respectable standing even in their eyes.' Bowring to Morrison, 28 July 1825.
49. Joseph Hume to the Chairman of a Meeting of the Freemen of Dover, 15 September 1825, published as a leaflet, Morrison archive.
50. James Grant, *Random Recollections of the House of Commons* (London, 1836), pp. 6–7.
51. Valerie Chancellor, *The Political Life of Joseph Hume 1777–1855* (Stratford upon Avon, 1986), pp. 7, 18.
52. *New DNB.*
53. Morrison and Poulett Thomson to the Independent Freemen of the Town and Port of Dover, 16 September 1825, Morrison archive.
54. Copy of song in Morrison archive.
55. *The Times*, 29 September 1825.
56. *Morning Chronicle*, 29 September 1825.
57. See Ben Wilson, *Decency and Disorder: The Age of Cant 1789–1837* (London, 2007), pp. 320–3.
58. Kynaston, p. 65.
59. *Kent Herald*, 27 April 1826.
60. *New DNB.*
61. Gatty, p. 66. From the *Buckinghamshire, Bedfordshire and Hertfordshire Chronicle.*
62. *The Times*, 20 June 1826.
63. The Morrison archive has a list of voters and their votes for Marlow dated 1826, also a booklet dated 1827 listing the occupiers of properties and the owners of their properties.
64. *The Times*, 26 March 1827.
65. James A. Jaffe, *'The Affairs of Others', the Diaries of Francis Place 1825–1836* (Cambridge, 2007), Camden Soc., 5th ser., no. 30, p. 109 (4 July 1826).

CHAPTER 6: THE EDUCATION OF A GENTLEMAN
(PART TWO): THE GRAND TOUR

1. The family of Mary Ann Morrison's stepmother. Morrison's partners John Dillon and George Crow also paid regular visits, writing of the children's well-being.
2. See Brian Dolan, *Exploring European Frontiers. British Travellers in the Age of Enlightenment* (London, 2000).
3. Morrison was charged 1%.
4. James Morrison to James Croft, Rome, 5 December 1826.
5. Quoted in Gatty, p. 69. Morrison had by this time heard that Wethered had bribed the wife of one voter and paid the rates of another so they would support the Williamses. He continued (to Dillon): 'I wish Wethered could be got at. ... It might first be attempted to neutralize him by saying I shan't be likely to look to M [Marlow] hereafter, having Norwich, Worcester etc in my power – that he would be popular now and carry his man hereafter only by being quiet now – but the cash is your last resort. I should like to succeed if possible – all engines should be used. By the way it just occurs to me that Hudson Gurney is a leading partner in Barclay's Brewery, and they employ Florence Young (the loyal chairman of Barclay's committee in the Borough you will recollect) who is their cooper – and the son of Florence Young married Wethered's daughter – now cannot this be turned to account? ... Hudson knows a man pays "in meal or malt", and could perhaps set Florence to see Wethered. You of course in my name may see any of these, including Hume ... better no bribe in my name.'
6. James Morrison to John Dillon, Rome, 11 December 1826.
7. See *Cobbett's Weekly Register*, 4 November 1826, pp. 366–7: 'Burdett, Hobhouse, Ellice, Hume, Bowring, Rump Galloway, have been cramming their fingers into this [Greek] pie.' Also see Rosen. Hume's own financial mishandling of the arrangements with the Greek representatives would have cost him his political career if Place and James Mill had not come to his aid.
8. Thomas Galloway Bey also dealt in Egyptian artefacts, and sold three mummies to Morrison which he gave to London University in 1828; Papworth was commissioned to design a railway station and tombstone in Alexandria through the Galloways.
9. James Morrison to John Dillon, 30 November 1826.
10. King's Arms Yard also operated from 1828 as a money-lending concern: see chapter 8.
11. James Morrison to John Dillon, 11 August 1826: 'The discovery of error in stock is a pleasant incident – if you are rich you will of course, & as a matter of course, give the surplus to Gurney.' Over a six-month period in 1827, Morrison paid back Gurney £53,000.
12. James Morrison to John Dillon, 30 July 1826; 27 January 1827; [September] 1826.
13. James Morrison to John Dillon, 23 September 1826.
14. James Morrison to John Dillon, 24 December 1826.
15. James Morrison to John Dillon, 23 November 1826; and see Derek Wilson, *Rothschild* (London, 1994), p. 80.
16. James Morrison to John Dillon, 30 November 1826.
17. James Morrison to James Croft, 14 March 1827. John Henning 1771–1851. See John Wall, *John Henning, That Most Ingenious Modeller* (London, 2008).
18. David Wilkie to James Morrison, Madrid, 27 November 1827.
19. James Morrison to John Dillon, 19 February 1827.

20. Mussolini lived in the Villa Torlonia from 1925 until 1943. It has recently been restored as a museum.
21. James Morrison to John Dillon, 21 February 1827.
22. Nicolas Demidoff 1773–1828. His son Anatole completed the Villa, adding to his father's collection. A large number of paintings, furniture, porcelain and metalwork were acquired by Lord Hertford and are now in the Wallace Collection in London. See *Anatole Demidoff, Prince of San Donato (1812–70)*, exhibition catalogue (Wallace Collection, 1994), with biographical essay by Francis Haskell.

CHAPTER 7: INTO PARLIAMENT

1. Collins, *Memoirs*, pp. 285–6.
2. John Landseer, *Review of Publications of Art*, June 1808, in Martin Butlin and Evelyn Joll, *The Paintings of J.M.W. Turner* (New Haven, CT, 1977), pp. 47–8.
3. Gatty, p. 103, quoting from the *Buckinghamshire, Bedfordshire and Hertfordshire Chronicle*, 4 August 1827.
4. See Jeremy Bentham Papers, University College London, xviii, 179. The prospectus proposed its plan of education would 'best fit a young man for pursuing the study of a learned profession at the Universities, entering the army or the navy, or engaging in agricultural or commercial pursuits'.
5. See Mrs Thomas Geldhart, *Memorials of Samuel Gurney* (London, 1857); also entry in *New DNB*. At Gurney's death deposits in his bank totalled £8 million. In 1865, Overend Gurney became a joint-stock company but the following year it collapsed with liabilities of £11 million.
6. Wyatt Papworth, *John B. Papworth*, p. 68.
7. See Walsh.
8. Pevsner, p. 569.
9. See Political Economy Club, *Minutes of Proceedings 1821–1882, Roll of Members, and Questions Discussed* (London, 1882), vol. IV.
10. D.P. O'Brien, *The Classical Economists Revisited* (Princeton, NJ, 2004), p. 13.
11. Mallet, pp. 255–6.
12. R. Moody, *Mr Benett of Wiltshire* (East Knoyle, 2005), p. 53, quoting from An Observer, *Kaleidoscope Wiltoniensis: or, A Literary and Moral View of the County of Wilts during the Contested Election for its Representation, in June 1818* (London, 1818), pp. 311–12.
13. See Davidoff and Hall, p. 22, for the effect of such a scandal on the middle classes – and presumably Morrison. 'In a blaze of publicity, the wife and young family were deserted, and soon after died, reputedly of a broken heart. Such a case received maximum local and national publicity and enhanced middle-class determination to build their homes into havens of comfort, stability and morality where wives and children would be protected and controlled.'
14. Moody, p. 84. Long-Wellesley's campaign in Wiltshire in 1818 had cost him between £30,000 and £40,000.
15. Gatty, p. 106, quoting *West Briton and Cornwall Advertiser*, 23 July 1830.
16. A lawsuit followed between Wellesley and Hawkins.
17. Keith Alton, 'Municipal and Parliamentary Politics in Ipswich 1818–1847', PhD dissertation, University College London, October 1987, p. 187.

18. Denis Le Marchant (ed.), *John Charles, Viscount Althorp Third Earl Spencer* (London, 1876), pp. 237–9. While most Whigs regarded Poulett Thomson as 'an ultra political communist' or 'a City man suspected of using his office for personal profit', Althorp made him Vice-President of the Board of Trade and Treasurer of the Navy. See Peter Mandler, *Aristocratic Government in the Age of Reform* (Oxford, 1990), pp. 91, 112. Althorp was also a founder and supporter of the Society for the Diffusion of Useful Knowledge, President of the Smithfield Club and first President of the Royal Agricultural Society. He became 3rd Earl Spencer in 1834.

19. James Morrison to John Dillon, 27 and 28 September 1826.

20. Though the budget was rushed and Althorp inexperienced, it did succeed in abolishing 260 unnecessary government offices and repealed a number of duties, including that on printed cotton. 'A printed dress, of good materials and neat pattern, with fast colours, may now be bought for two shillings [instead of four]', see Baines, *History of the Cotton Manufacture* (1835), p. 285, quoted in Le Marchant, p. 275.

21. Gatty, p. 123.

CHAPTER 8: FONTHILL

1. James Morrison to J.B. Papworth, 8 and 10 August 1830.

2. Philip Hewat-Jaboor, 'Fonthill House', in D.E. Ostergard (ed.), *William Beckford 1760–1844: An Eye for the Magnificent* (New Haven, CT, 2001), p. 51.

3. See Bet Mcleod, 'Treasures of England's Wealthiest Son', *Country Life*, 7 February 2002, p. 41.

4. *Gentleman's Magazine*, 28 December 1800.

5. J. Lees-Milne, *William Beckford* (Tisbury, 1976), p. 49.

6. See unpublished essay, *c.* 1946, by the late Colonel Stephen Scammell of East Knoyle, copy in possession of the author.

7. Phillips, *The Valuable Library of Books in Fonthill Abbey ... The Unique and Splendid Effects of Fonthill Abbey ... The Pictures and Miniatures at Fonthill Abbey* (London, 1823).

8. Fonthill Park sale particulars, 29 October 1829: 'one of the most compact and valuable Clothing Establishments in the kingdom'.

9. Lees-Milne, p. 76.

10. Megan Aldrich, 'William Beckford's Abbey', in Ostergard, p. 117.

11. *Country Life*, 28 December 1901, p. 845.

12. Moody, p. 158.

13. George, James, Charlotte and Mary Mortimer; John Frazer; Elizabeth Trezevant, née Frazer, and Charlotte Temple Pole, née Frazer.

14. In 1830, when Mortimer signed a contract with Morrison, he, Mortimer, was entitled to the Park estate only when he paid a balance of £18,000 and the interest which had accrued since the 1826 contract with his uncle. Consequently Morrison's initial payment of £14,000, which he made on 18 September 1830, was a mortgage 'to pay off balance of purchase money to Farquhar's Estate so as to get the legal estate of the property into his own name'. A further two payments of £1,500 were made by Morrison before Mortimer died in 1832. Morrison then agreed with Mortimer's brother James to advance the widow Ann Mortimer £1,000 plus £200 per quarter until the legal situation was resolved. The final settlement was made on 6 December 1838.

15. James Everard, Baron Arundell and Sir Richard Colt Hoare, Bart, *The History of Modern Wiltshire* (London, 1829), p. 28; John Rutter, *Delineations of Fonthill and its Abbey* (London, 1823), p. 107.

16. Isaac Sewell to James Morrison, 31 August 1830.

17. Wyatt Papworth, *John B. Papworth*, pp. 79, 239.

18. Edward Boykin (ed.), *Victoria, Albert and Mrs. Stevenson* (New York, 1958), pp. 25–6.

19. T. Mowl, 'A Biographical Perspective', in Ostergard, p. 23.

20. John Britton, *Graphical and Literary Illustrations of Fonthill Abbey, Wiltshire* (London, 1823), pp. 32–3.

21. Now at Manchester City Art Gallery.

22. John Landseer, *Review of Publications of Art* (1808), quoted in Martin Butlin and Evelyn Joll, *The Paintings of J.M.W. Turner* (New Haven, CT, 1977), vol. 1, p. 48. See also description by John Britton, *The Fine Arts of the English School* (London 1812): 'the mind is alternately soothed and distressed, delighted and provoked. ... Sacred spot ... now desecrated: the dwelling of the poet has been levelled to the ground, and his favorite haunts have been despoiled of their local charms' (p. 19). *Pope's Villa at Twickenham* sold by descendants of James Morrison, Sotheby's, 9 July 2008, now in a private collection in the USA.

23. There were further connections. Morrison's father-in-law's estate at Twickenham Park was close to Turner's house, Sandycombe Lodge, and after Todd's (and Turner's) death Morrison became the owner of the lodge for a brief period. He took the opportunity of visiting the site of Pope's Villa, finding it a 'poor & tasteless House'.

24. Cyrus Jay, *Recollections of William Jay, of Bath* (London, 1859), p. 202.

25. Eric Richards, 'The Land Agent', in G.E. Mingay (ed.), *The Victorian Countryside*, (London, 1981), vol. II, p. 440. Richards provides a clear analysis of the importance of the land agent in the nineteenth century.

26. The Combeses were related to a number of prominent families; James Combes' wife Anna Maria was the daughter of Edward Bracher, whose family had for generations tenanted the medieval Place Farm which Morrison eventually bought. As an unhappy reflection of the closeness of these families, James and Anna Maria Combes, who were first cousins, had, out of five children, two blind and idiot sons. Combes' uncle was the celebrated Congregationalist preacher William Jay of Bath. Research on Combes and Brachers by Nigel Cross

27. See Judd.

28. The Seddons reduced its height by cutting pieces off the legs and refitting the ormolu ornaments. It was inherited by Alfred Morrison and sold by his grandson at Christies', 7 May 1936, for 330 guineas to Wildenstein; sold Christies', 15 December 2005, lot 225.

29. See Papworth to Morrison, 8 August 1833 (Morrison archive): 'The Tables that were Cosways have tops that do not fit them nor indeed belong to them – but these I find on examination are <u>solid</u> verdantique & therefore valuable – when cleaned these would be effective furniture for Fonthill.'

30. See Ian Bristow, *Architectural Colour in British Interiors 1615–1840* (New Haven, CT, 1996), p. 167; elevation and ceiling in Pompeian style by Roos, 1833, p. 169. Also Richard Garnier, 'Alexander Roos (c.1810–1881)', *Georgian Group Journal*, 15 (2006).

31. Boykin (ed.).

32. Benett began desultory building works in the early 1830s, 'connecting the Brown parlour, and Yellow rooms into a residence by the addition of offices and other buildings – but

these proceed very gradually and no part is at present inhabited': see J.B. Nichols, *Historical Notes of Fonthill Wiltshire* (London, 1836), p. 39.

33. See Sarah Rutherford, 'Draft Basildon Park Framework Garden Conservation Plan' (National Trust, 2006), p. 17. Morrison also knew of Loudon's work as editor of the *Gardeners' Magazine*, calling on him in 1835, possibly to discuss Fonthill. Loudon had described a visit to the ruins of Fonthill Abbey in 1833 in the magazine (September 1835).

34. Pevsner, p. 249.

35. James Combes to James Morrison, 2 May 1838.

36. Papworth enlarged Job's 'Garden Milk House' in 1837. He also designed at least two cottages, the Keeper's Lodge and Berwick Hall, the latter to be used for refreshments by shooting parties.

37. *The Times*, 5 October 1826.

38. James Combes to James Morrison, 23 June 1837. Mr Harben is the same clergyman who painted the Abbey ruins and a number of watercolours of country houses (now in the collection of the National Trust) – information from Martin Wood.

39. James Combes to James Morrison, 29 November 1836.

40. Pevsner, p. 249.

41. James Combes to James Morrison, 25 June 1837.

42. James Combes to James Morrison, 27 March 1839.

43. From Beckford, *Modern Novel Writing* (1796), quoted in T. Mowl, 'Inside Beckford's Landscape of the Mind', *Country Life*, 7 February 2002, p. 62.

44. James Combes to James Morrison, 4 May 1837.

45. Coade stone is an artificial stone, invented by Mrs Coade in the eighteenth century. Its 'secret formula' included white china clay from Cornwall and finely ground quartz or glass which formed easily moulded acid and frost-resistant pieces. See www.vauxhallsociety.org.uk/Coade.html.

46. Morrison spent a total of £137, also acquiring 40 Gothic heads to decorate the tunnel and grottos. One head has been recovered; the majority, it is feared, were broken or stolen during the Second World War when soldiers were billeted in the park. See also Mowl, for further discussion of the landscape and grottos.

47. James Combes to James Morrison, 21 May 1837.

48. Collins, *Memoirs*, p. 335.

49. Lucy Morrison to Mary Ann Morrison, 19 [June] 1840.

50. Boykin (ed.), p. 32.

51. William Cobbett, *Rural Rides* (Harmondsworth, 1985), p. 337. Morrison owned a copy of Cobbett's *Cottage Economy*.

52. J.L. and Barbara Hammond, *The Village Labourer* (London, 1948), vol. II, p. 63; first published 1911.

53. Full account of the incident in Robert Moody's biography of John Benett, chapter 6. For report of the trial see *The Times*, 3 January 1831.

54. In their 1911 survey of agricultural labourers, the Hammonds were eloquent in their depiction of the world of the rural poor in 1830. 'This world has no member of Parliament, no press, it does not make literature or write history; no diary or memoirs have kept alive for us the thoughts and cares of the passing day. It is for this reason that the events of the winter of 1830 have so profound an interest ... we have the mind of this class hidden from us through all this period of pain, bursting the silence by the only power at its command', Hammond and Hammond, vol. II, p. 44.

55. 2001 census: population of Fonthill Gifford 120; Fonthill Bishop 83.

56. James Combes to James Morrison, 2 January 1837.
57. RIBA, Papworth plan for Fonthill School. Papworth also designed a school at Cholsey for Morrison.
58. Boykin (ed.), p. 29.
59. Penuel Cross remained just ten years in Fore Street. He discovered his true vocation, music, in London, through singing with the Sacred Harmonic Society. He obtained a position in the choir of Winchester Cathedral and became lay clerk at Winchester College. However, he obtained a place for his son William in Fore Street (after it became a limited company); William rose to become chief buyer of coloured silks. He earned sufficient to purchase a large villa in Blackheath and send his two sons to public school.
60. James Combes to James Morrison, 20 May 1837.
61. Rollo Russell (ed.), *Early Correspondence of Lord John Russell*, 6 October 1835, Melbourne to Lord John Russell.
62. Henry Petty-Fitzmaurice, 3rd Marquess of Lansdowne (1780–1863), was one of the most powerful of the Whig grandees, opposing the slave trade and discrimination against Catholics, dissenters and Jews. Another of his protégés was Thomas Spring Rice, a parliamentary colleague of Morrison. The Bowood House circle mixed 'Benthamite utilitarianism and laissez-faire economics with traditional constitutional Whiggism': see *New DNB*.

CHAPTER 9: 57 HARLEY STREET

1. Mary Ann Morrison to Charles, quoted in Gatty, p. 123, and dated March 1831.
2. Morrison had taken a three-year lease on 63 Portland Place in 1828 which Papworth worked on for him, but he appears not to have moved in. He does give Portland Place as his address when first elected to the Council of London University.
3. Auctioned by Mr James Denew of Charles Street, Berkeley Square, 'on the premises', 16 June 1831. Morrison completed the purchase at the end of November 1831.
4. See Lord Howard De Walden Estate Papers, Marylebone, London.
5. Disraeli, *Tancred*, quoted in Rachel Stewart, *The Town House in Georgian London* (New Haven, CT, 2009), p. 120.
6. Charles Dickens, *Dombey and Son* (Harmondsworth, 1987), p. 74.
7. Charles Dickens, *Our Mutual Friend* (Harmondsworth, 1977), p. 176.
8. Charles Dickens, *Little Dorrit* (Oxford, 1979), p. 240.
9. See Stewart, pp. 172–94, who describes the town house as the 'container' for the interior.
10. Estimate in Morrison archive:

> Burton work to house and premises, furniture and fittings, dining room ceiling and hall, wardrobe, whitewashing basement and stables £1029 19s. 7d.; Brine green chimneypiece and red chimneypiece £115 2s.; Croggen scagliola, chimneypiece boudoir, pedestals in library £171; Leschallas £791; Morant £492 for painting, papering, gilding and various decorative work to gallery, back drawing room, boudoir, library, dining room, front bedroom, dressing room and attic, also bathroom and housekeeper's and butler's rooms; Pots furniture £56; Seddon furniture made, two couches, cases, dining tables £631; Snell furniture made, tables for library, furniture for back drawing room, Earlstoke glass, curtains £517; Stephens copper pipe, kitchen range, bell hanging; plumbers, bricklayers, ironmongers, fenders, fireirons, grates, cleaning and polishing stoves £151; Murray blinds £4.

11. Alton, p. 8.
12. His obituary in the *Morning Chronicle* was damning: 'redeemed by no single virtue, adorned by no single grace, his life has gone out without even a flicker of repentance; his "retirement" was that of one who was deservedly avoided by all men.'
13. Alton, p. 183.
14. Balham Hill was let for £230 per annum; Morrison rarely sold any of his properties.
15. Gustave Waagen, *Treasures of Art in Great Britain: Being an Account of the Chief Collections of Paintings, Drawings, Sculptures, Illuminated Mss; &c &c* (London, 1854), 3 vols, vol. II, p. 23. Papworth's drawings, letters and invoices, Morrison's diaries and record of his art purchases and the inventories made after his death provide an unusual level of detail about the appearance of the rooms.
16. 'Curtains of your scarlet cloth for the 2 windows in the dining room with rosettes & pendant tassels to draw wh [*sic*] line & pullies with large brass wings, on brass poles & 4 carved & gilt ends valances covered with cloth & gold mouldings', Morrison archive. Beckford used reds and crimsons lavishly in his Harley Street house.
17. See Vanherman, *The Painter's Cabinet and Colourman's Repository* for 1828, recommending crimson for libraries, referenced in Bristow, p. 203.
18. Thomas and George Seddon to J.B. Papworth, 26 July 1832.
19. Thomas and George Seddon, April 1832.
20. Morrison also bought from aristocratic collections. When Lady Lansdowne sold a few unwanted objects at auction in July 1833, Papworth acquired for him a pair of oriental china jars, 'a pair of fine Italian bronzes – Mercury and the Vestal Virgins 13 guineas', a 'magnificent & exquisitely modelled bronze figure of Neptune £39.18s', and the 'companion bronze figure representing David in the act of slinging the stone at Goliath £34.13s'. J.B. Papworth to James Morrison, 18 July 1833. The latter two bronzes may have been reductions of the famous statues by Bernini.
21. Charles Morrison to Mary Ann Morrison, 12 February 1840, Naples.
22. See design by Papworth, R.I.B.A. Prints and Drawings collection at the Victoria and Albert Museum, London.
23. 'India green silk damask' £37 16s. 'cutting & making silk curtains for the 3 windows in Gallery edged with brocade silk lace to the sides & bottoms, crimson plush bands with brocade silk face, deep twine fringe valance with silk tassel hangers drawn by French pulley rods with openings complete with brass pole cornices & 6 carved & gilt end ornaments rings &c' £55 4s.
24. J.B. Papworth to George Crow, 29 January 1833, 'Mr Morant has been with me respecting the Blue Silk or Blue Tabouret which he finds can be obtained according to the enclosed pattern [at Mr Lynes, Silk Manufacturer, 25 Milk Street Cheapside]. 4/3pr yd – perhaps it may be got else where but there it certainly can – Mrs M will want 33 yards of it.'
25. Snells 'Cornices to continue over the 2 windows door & pier with carved end ornaments & mouldings with pelmet valance formed in wood with ... ornaments richly gilt, with silk tassel hangers & lath made wide enough to receive Muslin ... & 6 pr of blue silk tassels wh. rope' £99 10s.
26. J.B. Papworth to James Morrison, 12 August 1832.
27. The catalogue for the 21-day-long sale at Erlestoke compared Watson Taylor's collection to Beckford's, 'of superior elegance and taste as that which adorned the Abbey of Fonthill', but it could also have been describing the emerging collection of Morrison: 'Fine marble busts and statues, 2 noble porphyry busts of Caesar and Nero, a lion and

bull in Sienna marble ... magnificent cabinets and tables of the choicest Florentine mosaic, enriched with agates, precious stones, and Sèvres porcelain, painted in an exquisite manner; the finest japan marqueterie and buhl cabinets ... an infinity of articles of taste and virtu.' See *The Times*, 4 July 1832, notice by Mr George Robins of Erlestoke sale by auction.

28. Charles Ely to Mr Brine, 19 June 1832: 'On behalf of Mr Morrison I hereby agree to give you Seventy Pounds for Mr Westmacott's Red Chimney Piece including the cost of conveying it to Mr Morrison's house in Upper Harley Street and fixing it there complete.'

29. Papworth had a particular interest in chimneypieces and looking glasses, focusing on their changed role in his 1826 edition of Chambers' *Treatise:* 'the fashion for chimney-pieces has undergone a complete revolution, for they are now treated rather as pieces of furniture than as integral portions of the edifice, and which character they formerly maintained. Immense looking-glasses, with gilt frames, have superseded the carved and painted superstructure of the fire-place, and the chimney-piece is now reduced from its late magnificence, to the duty of supporting clocks, girandoles, vases, and bijoutry.' Sir William Chambers, *A Treatise on the Decorative Part of Civic Architecture* (London, 1826), ed. J.B. Papworth, p. 146. Papworth's observation was out of date by over half a century.

30. Waagen, *Treasures of Art*, vol. II, p. 263. Morrison acquired another piece from Erlestoke for the drawing room, a purple wood cabinet or sideboard, which Papworth thought 'the most beautiful piece of Furniture I have ever seen'; also a pair of Verd Antique Vases mounted in ormolu which were displayed in the gallery.

31. Morrison's diary, 19 April 1833.

32. Wyatt Papworth, *John B. Papworth*, p. 82.

33. Ibid.

34. Bought in 1834 for 37 guineas.

35. J.B. Papworth to James Morrison, 20 August 1834.

36. J.B. Papworth to James Morrison, 12 August 1832: 'The British Artists Gallery is closed, & looking for furniture pictures or Drawings for Fonthill – I find a good & interesting one a view in Wales painted by Marshall that he would now sell for 25 pounds with a good handsome frame – fresh gilt ... it would quite answer your purpose for over the fire place in the Green room.'

37. Morrison archive note: 'Claude b. from Lanerville 17 Sept 1831'. See Gatty, p. 246, painting 'recently imported into England by M. Laneuville'.

38. See Francis Haskell, *Rediscoveries in Art* (New Haven, CT, 1976), p. 57. Watteau was also represented in the collection of Samuel Rogers, see David Solkin (ed.), *Turner and the Masters* (London, 2009), p. 192. Turner copied Watteau and exhibited his own *fête galante (What you Will!)* at the Academy in 1822: see Solkin, p. 159. Another Watteau imitator was Thomas Stothard, who contributed to the revival of the *fête galante* imagery in Britain after Waterloo. His and Watteau's works were collected by the poet Samuel Rogers; Morrison (who knew Rogers' collection) also acquired a Stothard in the style of Watteau.

39. Two Teniers that Morrison acquired in 1845 came from the collections of Sir Thomas Baring and Lord Ashburton (Alexander Baring).

40. Solkin, p. 143.

41. Norton lived at 22 Soho Square near Morrison's portraitist Henry Pickersgill.

42. Peel's collection in Whitehall Gardens contained paintings by Rubens, Rembrandt, Dow, Jan Steen, Teniers, Adriaen and Isaak van Ostade, Van de Velde, Dujardin, Wouwermans, Wynans, Ruysdael, Hobbema and Backhuysen. Morrison carefully kept his admission ticket signed by Peel; within a few years he would have examples by all Peel's artists.
43. Solkin, p. 152.
44. Dickens, *Little Dorrit*, pp. 543–4.
45. Sold 1834. It had hung in the Palazzo Barberini in Rome until the second half of the eighteenth century when it was sold by Cardinal Antonio Barberini to Gavin Hamilton on behalf of Sir John Taylor of Jamaica, father-in-law of Watson Taylor of Erlestoke. See Elizabeth Gardner, 'Provenance Notes: Parmigiano', *Burlington Magazine*, 125, no. 968 (November 1983), pp. 691–2. It was included in the background of Pieter Christoffel Wonder's oil sketch (1826–30) of an imaginary gallery hung with pictures from famous British collections. Watson Taylor is depicted kneeling in front of Titian's *Bacchus and Ariadne* (which was in the collection of the jeweller Thomas Hamlet). Wonder, who stands in the background holding his palette, also included Sir John Murray, who commissioned the painting and the Revd William Holwell-Carr, benefactor of the newly formed National Gallery.
46. Hamlet's sale, 19 May 1836.
47. Mr Finden borrowed the painting at the end of 1836 for five weeks for Frederick Bacon to make an engraving for the publication *Royal Gallery of British Art*, 1845. Eastlake produced a second version of the painting in 1849 for Robert Vernon, exhibiting it at the RA in 1850 (this version is now in the Tate collection).
48. Edward Morris, *French Art in Nineteenth-century Britain* (New Haven, CT, 2005), p. 30.

CHAPTER 10: IN PARLIAMENT

1. *Report from the Select Committee on the Silk Trade, with Minutes of Evidence*, printed 2 August 1832, no. 678.
2. Wyatt Papworth, *John B. Papworth*, p. 106.
3. Charles Badham, *The Life of James Deacon Hume* (London, 1859), pp. 138–9.
4. John Bowring to James Morrison, 1 May 1832.
5. Badham, pp. 146–7. Morrison's views did not go down well when he stood for the Sudbury by-election in 1837: the town's silk industry had been adversely affected by foreign competition. Morrison lost the election.
6. Christopher Frayling, *The Royal College of Art: One Hundred & Fifty Years of Art & Design* (London, 1987), p. 13. Also see Forty, chapter 3, 'Design and mechanisation'. And Taylor, p. 67, on the Whig politicians' 'exasperation at the cultural level of the population'.
7. John Orbell, *Baring Brothers & Co., Ltd, A History to 1939* (Frome, 1985), pp. 26–7.
8. Gillian Darley, *John Soane: An Accidental Romantic* (New Haven, CT, 1999), p. 303.
9. HC Deb, 1 April 1833, vol. 16 cc 1333–43 in Hansard on-line (http://hansard.millbank-systems.com/commons/1833/apr/01/sir-john-soanes-museum).
10. Frayling, p. 13.
11. 27 July 1835, see RIBA, *Transactions* I, 1835, pp. 111–14. Papworth was Vice-President 1835–7, 1844–5.
12. Papworth, *John B. Papworth*, p. 107.

13. See J. Mordaunt Crook, 'The Pre-Victorian Architect: Professionalism & Patronage', *Architectural History*, 12 (1969), pp. 62–78, for discussion of the link between architectural and design training.

14. Mark Goodwin, 'Objects, Belief and Power in mid-Victorian England – the Origins of the Victoria and Albert Museum', in Susan M. Pearce (ed.), *Objects of Knowledge* (London, 1990), p. 38.

15. Crook, p. 73, quoting from the Select Committee on Arts and Manufactures, 1835.

16. Frayling, p. 14

17. Ibid.

18. See Edward Morris p. 30; Frayling, p. 17; C. Gere and C. Sargentsen (eds), *Journal of the History of Collections*, 14, no. 1 (2002), a special edition on the making of the South Kensington Museum.

19. HC Deb, 4 February 1834, vol. 21 cc 33–108 in Hansard on-line.

20. Gatty, p. 131.

21. Speech sent to James Brown, Worthington, Joseph Todd, T. Wiggins, S. Gurney, Easthope, Pearson, H. Dann, C. Smith, H. Seymour, John Todd, Thomas Todd, Dillon, C. Lear, R. Southey, Bowring, Coulson, James Mill, S. Morrison, Barrington, Charles Morrison, J. Combes, John Downes, W.H. Ashurst, J.B. Fearon, C.F. Williams, Notcutt, G. Barnard, McCulloch, Papworth and N. White.

22. James Morrison to Charles Morrison, 14 December 1834.

23. *Suffolk Chronicle*, 10 January 1835, quoted in Alton, p. 193.

24. Mary Ann Morrison to Charles Morrison, 16 January 1835. Charles had his own example of bribery, writing to his mother on 20 January 1835 that the Tory victory in Midlothian was won through 'active intimidation, corruption, & whiskey. Where they could not get a man to vote for them, the next thing was to prevent him from voting at all. As a specimen of their dexterity I heard that two Whig canvassers were bringing up a man, who had already had a drop too much, to the poll, when they stopt in the street to speak for a couple of minutes to one of their own party. When they turned round, lo! & behold, their man was gone! the Tory canvassers had got hold of him, given him 2 or 3 glasses of whiskey, laid him comfortably in a cellar, & locked the door.'

25. Gatty, p. 143, quoting findings of 10 June 1835.

26. P. Fitzgerald, *Bozland: Dickens' Places and People* (London, 1895), p. 16.

27. Charles Morrison to Mary Ann Morrison, 12 June 1835.

28. For contemporary views see John A. Francis, *A History of the English Railway: Its Social Relations and Revelations 1820–1845* (London, 1851), 2 vols, and William Galt, *Railway Reform: Its Importance and Practicability* (London, 1865). Morrison's specific significance is covered in detail in Robert S. Sephton, 'Small Profits on a Large Trade: James Morrison, parts 1 and 2', *Journal of the Railway and Canal Historical Society*, 34, part 6 (November 2003), no. 186.

29. Speech sent 17 May to Dillon, Cryder, McCulloch, Wilkins RA, Norton, Pickersgill, Papworth, Humphrey, Wood, H.B. Ker, W. May, M.D. Hill, Brandt, Chapman, Hume MP, Ashurst, Glynn, J.A. Smith, R. Stewart, Ewart, Frazer, Talfourd, C.F. Wiliams, John Todd, Sir A. Carlisle, O'Connell, Holland MP, Bagshaw and Lord Churchill.

30. Francis, vol. 2, p. 279.

31. *Ipswich Journal*, 28 May 1836.

32. George Woodbridge, *The Reform Club 1836–1978* (Bradford, 1978), p. 15; J. Mordaunt Crook, *The Reform Club* (London, 1973), p. 11, quoting *The Times* 1844.

33. Crook, *Reform Club*, p. 1. Morrison's eldest sons Charles, Alfred and Walter were also lifelong members; Alfred served on the Club General Committee, and Walter as a Liberal MP upheld the political connection. It was the next generation of Morrisons that switched political allegiance and joined the Carlton Club.
34. Alton, pp. 198–9, quoting the *Suffolk Chronicle*, December 1836.
35. See Daunton, *Progress*, p. 500: 'the Reform Act of 1832 had extended the vote to members of the propertied middle class, but removed it from many artisans and workers. … The reform of the poor law, the creation of a police force, the Coercion Act in Ireland in 1833 which suppressed political activity, the transportation of the "Tolpuddle martyrs" in 1834 and the leaders of the Glasgow spinners' strike in 1837 caused disquiet. "What have we had since the Whigs passed the Reform bill?" asked a workman in Yorkshire in 1833. "We have had nothing but cruelty and hypocrisy." '

CHAPTER 11: THE AMERICAN PROJECT

1. Agricultural estates in addition to Fonthill: Porton, Wallasea, Ton Mawr, Wallop, Mendlesham, North Waltham, Cholsey, Seckford, Bexley. London properties in addition to Harley Street: Balham Hill, Holborn, Pitt Street, Newington, Whitechapel, Vine Street. Loans and mortgagees (larger): St Ives (Long-Wellesley), Marquess of Headfort, Earl Grey, Major Crosse, Alexander Galloway, Thomas Todd.
2. Edward Boykin (ed.), *Victoria, Albert and Mrs. Stevenson* (London, 1958), p. 29.
3. Stanley Chapman provides a useful definition of the sort of merchant bank Morrison formed: 'though they pass under the names of merchants, all their pecuniary affairs are of the nature of banking commissions charged for affording credit facilities', S. Chapman, *Merchant Bankers*, p. 39.
4. Walter Buckingham Smith, *Economic Aspects of the Second Bank of the United States* (Cambridge, MA, 1953), p. 183; Kynaston, p. 106.
5. Kynaston, p. 104.
6. James Morrison's diary entry for 20 June 1840: 'Black [editor of the *Morning Chronicle*] ask'd me how Easthope had better go to work to get the Baronetcy he wishes. I said let him go to Palmerston or Duke of Sussex at once.'
7. Kynaston, pp. 93, 103.
8. Bates was the mastermind behind the bank's resurgence in the 1830s.
9. Kynaston, p. 93.
10. Smith, p. 28.
11. Mira Wilkins, *The History of Foreign Investment in the United States to 1914* (Cambridge, MA, 1989), p. 56.
12. Walter Barrett, *The Old Merchants of New York City* (New York, 1863), p. 295.
13. Ibid.
14. Kynaston, p. 104.
15. Wilkins, p. 60.
16. See Kynaston, p. 99. Abolition of the monopoly in 1833 'in theory [threw] open the Cantonese tea trade, and in October there took place the City's first sale of "free trade tea". Yet for several years the playing field of the London tea market remained distinctly unlevel, as the East India Comapny retained control of its Canton exchange until the end of the decade and the long-established tea brokers fought hard to prevent new entrants.'

17. Kynaston, p. 102.

18. Smith, pp. 21–2.

19. Norman Sydney Buck, *The Development of the Organization of Anglo-American Trade 1800–1850* (Newton Abbott, 1969), p. 41.

20. Smith, pp. 32, 92, 93 quoting Consul Buchanan of New York.

21. Charles Morrison, 10 January 1843, Guildhall Library 11718, now in London Metropolitan Archive.

22. Chapman, *Merchant Bankers*, p. 40.

23. Kynaston, p. 104.

24. Disraeli, *Endymion*, pp. 63–4.

25. Gloucester Lodge, Regent's Park (1836).

26. See Buck, pp. 157–9.

27. Morrison, Cryder & Co., Letter Books, Morrison archive.

28. Wilkins, pp. 55–6.

29. Smith, p. 183.

30. Wilkins, p. 67.

31. Bank of England, G8/29, 26 October 1836.

32. Philip Ziegler, *The Sixth Great Power: Barings, 1762–1929* (London, 1988), p. 148.

33. Northern and Central Bank applied for emergency aid in November, but it was granted only on condition that it liquidated.

34. Kathleen Burk, *Morgan Grenfell 1838–1988: The Biography of a Merchant Bank* (Oxford, 1989), p. 2.

35. His capital invested in Morrison, Cryder & Co. now amounted to £235,763; Cryder's was £50,725, his own American stocks £56,000. The company held £85,000 bonds of the Morris Canal and Banking Co. of New Jersey (special bonds endorsed by the Bank of America and made payable at Morrison, Cryder & Co.) and £100,000 shares in the Bank of America.

36. Ralph Hidy, *The House of Baring in American Trade and Finance* (New York, 1949), p. 84.

37. Kynaston, p. 110. The loan from the Bank of England was secured against almost all Morrison's property, including Fore Street and Milton Street, and his loans to Long-Wellesley and the Marquess of Headfort: see Article of Agreement dated 9 June 1837, 11718 Box 1, Morrison, Cryder & Co. papers, formerly Guildhall, London now LMA.

38. 1 August 1836, Dillon's analysis of 14 years of Fore Street trading in Morrison archive. 'The 1st of August 1836 being a kind of epoch in the business, as completing a term of *14 years* from 1st August 1822 – my attention has been directed to the calculating certain totals & marking certain results, with regard chiefly to the counting house. Purchases £22,929,657. Sales £23,942,555 … . 14 yrs Bills of Exchange received by us £17,556,270.0.2. 14 yrs cas[1] [cash] checks etc received by us £6,332,842.19.10.'

39. Morrison diary entry 9 June 1837; MS 11,720, folder one, 9 June 1837, Morrison Cryder papers, Guildhall Library, now London Metropolitan Library, London.

40. James Morrison to Richard Alsop, 17 July 1837, 11718 Box 1, Morrison, Cryder & Co. papers, Guildhall Library, now Metropolitan Library, London.

41. Thomas C. Cochran and William Miller, *The Age of Enterprise: A Social History of Industrial America* (New York, 1961), p. 46.

42. Joshua Bates, February 1836, in Kynaston, p. 105.

43. Samuel Gurney wrote to Gurney & Co. on 10 February 1838 'Morrison Cryder & Co's funds have completely come round. They have paid the Bank off all they had borrowed

... and the wiley Scotchman [Morrison] will never I think accept another bill excepting where the funds for its discharge are completely under his own control'. See Gurney & Co. MSS 0003–2144, Barclays Bank PLC Archive.

44. By August 1838 Morrison's capital invested in Broad Street was £235,287, and his holding of American securities £131,418.

45. See Charles Pugh, *Basildon Park* (National Trust, 2002); Clive Williams, *Basildon Berkshire* (Reading, 1994).

46. The 2nd Baronet gambled and fought a duel before dying of scarlet fever in Germany.

47. For sale by auction at the Mart near the Bank of England, 23 September 1829.

48. Robert Blake, *Disraeli* (London, 1969), p. 96.

49. Ibid., p. 141.

50. Wyatt Papworth, *John B. Papworth*, p. 90.

51. Richard Benyon de Beauvoir of Englefield married Elizabeth, daughter of Sir Francis Sykes, in 1798; he owned the Grotto House close to Basildon Park.

52. Charles had no desire to stand for Parliament, writing from Turin on 3 June 1841, 'the Whigs, who you say want me for Wallingford, must wait for another year, when Alfred will be of age'. Alfred, who did want to be an MP, tried twice to represent Wallingford, but failed.

53. Morrison asked Henry Dann of Bexley (the family of Mary Ann's stepmother) to carry out a valuation of the timber in December 1840 to confirm that £21,000 was the correct price to pay.

54. Washbourne to Morrison, 25 September 1838.

55. Morrison did not have to pay the first instalment until November 1839: '£25,000 to be paid on acct with Int on the purchase money & Timber from Xmas last. The remainder of the purchase money at two months notice on either side or at any fixed period you may name. Possession to be given you of the Mansion Shooting &c without prejudice.' Isaac Sewell to James Morrison, 4 October 1839. Basildon was finally conveyed to Morrison in 1844.

56. Isaac Sewell to James Morrison, 19 July 1839.

57. Isaac Sewell to James Morrison, 3 August 1839.

58. Morrison's diary, 26 March 1838.

59. Disraeli, *Sybil* (Harmondsworth, 1985), p. 139. Morrison noted in his diary, 20 June 1840, the advice he gave the journalist John Black who enquired how the owner of the *Morning Chronicle* John Easthope might acquire a baronetcy: 'I said let him go to Palmerston or Duke of Sussex', presumably with the offer of money. Easthope became Sir John in 1841.

60. Charles Morrison had to attend Cambridge for three years to obtain a degree with honours. The sons of peers were entitled to honorary degrees after merely attending for two years. See *Pelham*: 'I suppose the term [honorary] is in contradistinction to an honourable degree, which is obtained by pale men in spectacles and cotton stockings, after thirty-six months of intense application', Anon. [E. Bulwer Lytton], *Pelham; or, The Adventures of a Gentleman* (London, 1828), vol. I, p. 12.

61. *The Inverness Courier*, 19 February 1840, quoted in Gatty, p. 200.

62. See Simon Martin to Samuel Gurney, 8 February 1818, Barclays Bank PLC Archive, Gurney & Co. MSS 0003–2654, 'The history of the bills drawn by Hall & Co on Morrison is not satisfactory. ... I would caution you against permitting the wiley Scotchman again to throw his net over you.'

63. Charles Morrison had written to his mother Mary Ann on 29 January, 'I am sorry that the present dimensions of no 10 [George] are such as to have earned for him the name of Tiny – as it wd be a sad thing if he shd turn out a specimen of the Todd race, & so have to bring up the rear of his long legged brothers & sisters.' Morrison nicknamed him Bull-nose.

64. Wilkins, p. 62.

65. Smith, p. 14.

66. Kynaston, p. 116.

67. Burk, p. 6.

68. Richard Alsop of Philadelphia provided Morrison with notes on Samuel Jaudon. Jaudon was a brilliant cashier when he worked in a counting house in Philadelphia, and then in Canton. He joined the North American Insurance Company in Washington where he shared lodgings with the rising politician Daniel Webster who, 'finding Jaudon a very clever & useful fellow … recommended him strongly to N Biddle who in consequence employ'd him in the Bank'.

69. James Morrison to Charles Morrison, 5 April 1840.

70. Listed in Guildhall papers (new London Metropolitan Archive):
American Life Insurance Trust 120,000
Farmers Loan and Trust Co. 50,000
Ohio Life Insurance & Trust Co. 112,500
Commercial Bank of Natchez 225,000
Reading Railroad 50,000

71. Charles to James Morrison, 9 October 1840.

72. On 1 January 1841 Morrison wrote to Gabriel Shaw, who continued to take a salary, 'I beg to acquaint you, that I have taken into partnership, my two Sons Mr Charles Morrison and Mr Alfred Morrison, under the Firm of "Morrison, Sons & Co", – who are charged with the liquidation of the business of "James Morrison;" the House I established, on the dissolution of "Morrison, Cryder & Co.", Morrison anticipated making a profit of £20,000 in the first year, with Charles and Alfred receiving a quarter-share.

73. Wilkins, pp. 69–70.

74. Smith, pp. 225–6.

75. Cutting from *Morning Post*, January 1841, 11718 Box 1, Morrison, Cryder & Co. papers, Guildhall, London Metropolitan Archive.

76. Smith, p. 227.

77. Burk, p. 6.

78. Wilkins, p. 70.

79. William E. Bowen of the great Philadelphia bankers Brown, Shipley & Co. writing to Joseph Shipley in Liverpool in January 1841. See John A. Kouwenhaven, *Partners in Banking. An Historical Portrait of a Great Private Bank: Brown Brothers Harriman & Co. 1818–1968* (New York, 1968), p. 75.

80. Hidy, p. 301.

81. R.G. McGrane, *Foreign Bondholders and American State Debts* (London, 1935), p. 59, and Wilkins, p. 71.

82. Gatty, p. 214.

CHAPTER 12: LETTERS FROM AMERICA, 1841–1845

1. Sailing packets could take from 16 to 83 days to cross the Atlantic in the 1840s; steamships averaged 15 days, see G.R. Taylor, *The Transportation Revolution* (New York, 1957), p. 145.
2. See Fred M. Leventhal and Roland Quinault, *Anglo-American Attitudes from Revolution to Partnership* (Aldershot, 2000).
3. Charles to James Morrison, 9 October 1842.
4. Howard Bodenham, *A History of Banking in Antebellum America* (Cambridge, 2000), p. 85.
5. Gatty, p. 161.
6. John Forster, *The Life of Charles Dickens* (London, 1927), 2 vols, vol. I, p. 183. The Tremont was opened in 1829, one of the first Greek Revival style hotels designed by Isaiah Rogers.
7. Alfred to Charles Morrison, 29 October 1841.
8. See Thomas Dublin, *Lowell: The Story of an Industrial City* (Washington, n.d.), p. 15; also Robert C. Winthrop, *Memoir of the Hon. Nathan Appleton* (1861). Appleton, Francis Cabot Lowell, Patrick Tracy Jackson and Paul Moody developed first at Waltham, Massachusetts, the unique centralised operations which brought several processes under one roof to produce cotton cloth. British visitors, including Dickens and Harriet Martineau, were astonished by the setting and the contrast with British mills, particularly in Lancashire.
9. Dickens, *American Notes* (Oxford, 1987), first published 1842, p. 66.
10. Leventhal and Quinault, p. 111.
11. Charles to James Morrison, 14 April 1843.
12. John Jacob Astor had bought the land, commissioning Isaac Rogers to design bigger and better than the Tremont in Boston. The austere and monumental exterior was built of Quincy granite; beggars found shelter under the grand portico. Catherine Hoover Voorsanger and John K. Howat, *Art and the Empire City: New York 1825–1861* (New Haven, CT, 2000), pp. 32, 175.
13. Alfred to Mary Ann Morrison, 22 November 1841.
14. Dickens, *American Notes*, p. 82.
15. Charles to Mary Ann Morrison, 15 April 1843.
16. Barrett, p. 299.
17. 'It was notorious for many years, that Alsop & Co., every five years, made a profit of over a million of dollars', ibid., p. 295.
18. Alfred to Mary Ann Morrison, 20 February 1842, Morrison archive.
19. Dickens, *American Notes*, p. 98.
20. John Tyler became President after the death, while in office, of W.H. Harrison on 4 April 1841.
21. Alfred to Mary Ann Morrison, 20 March 1842.
22. Charles to Mary Ann Morrison, 9 March 1843.
23. Dickens, *American Notes*, p. 115.
24. See Garrison's newspaper, *Liberator*, 21 April 1843. Charles was not impressed: 'Another very ill-judged act of this Abolitionist deputation was the bringing to the meeting a coloured person as one of their speakers. This Speaker, happening to take offence at something wh occurred, held forth in a harsh, censorial tone, wh wd have alienated the audience even from a white speaker, & taking into account the deeply engrained feelings

& associations of all Americans with respect to the coloured race, must have excited in the minds of many of his male auditors, even those sincerely hostile to slavery, a strong desire to kick him off the platform.'

25. Dickens, *American Notes*, p. 134.
26. Philadelphia & Reading; Norristown & Valley; Philadelphia, Wilmington & Baltimore; Camden & Amboy; Philadelphia, Germanton & Norristown; Stonington; North Hudson.
27. Alfred to Mary Ann Morrison, 9 April 1842.
28. Charles to Mary Ann Morrison, 23 May 1842.
29. Dickens, *American Notes*, pp. 62–4.
30. Forster, vol. I, p. 216.
31. Alfred to Mary Ann Morrison, 9 April 1842.
32. Alfred to Charles Morrison, 19 April 1842.
33. Ibid.
34. Gatty, p. 217, letter dated 22 March 1842.
35. Dickens disliked the crowded steamboat; Alfred, however, found the cooking good and the black waiters excellent: 'The negro appears to me to have been specially created for the purpose of attending whites on board steamboats; you cannot imagine how infinitely superior a jet-black woolly-headed negro in a white jacket & apron is to a slovely unclean-looking white – In the manners too of the negro there is a civility & even politeness which reminds me of the French & which I need hardly say is very seldom met with among white servants.'
36. See Andrew Wilton and Tim Barringer (eds), *American Sublime Landscape Painting in the United States 1820–1880* (London, 2002): 'the artistic exploration of the area bordered by the Hudson was both a cause and a symptom of a boom in tourism from the mid-1820s' (p. 48). The Catskill Mountain House Hotel opened in 1822 and was extended in 1824–25. Its location became popular with artists, particularly the sunrise viewed from its front bedrooms. Thomas Cole, who influenced Cropsey, moved to the village of Catskill in 1836.
37. Alfred to Mary Ann Morrison, 27 April 1842.
38. Alfred to Mary Ann Morrison, 1 May 1842.
39. Ibid. Grand Island had passed through a number of speculators. Alfred noted Mordecai Manuel Noah, recently made judge of the New York Court of Sessions, who, in 1823, had planned that the island would become a resting place for persecuted Jews, 'a second Jerusalem in fact & Noah was to have been High Priest – The scheme of course never got beyond the concoction & failed entirely & the only trace of it is a stone with a very absurd inscription partly Hebrew & partly English which was placed on the Island & which remains there to this day.'
40. Charles to James Morrison, 18 May 1842.
41. Charles to Mary Ann Morrison, 23 May 1842.
42. Charles to James Morrison, 11 November 1842.
43. The fortunes of the Reading line were turned around through the efforts of their director, and James Morrison's business partner John Cryder, who in a secret partnership with Wetmore and Peabody raised $3.5 million in 1843–44 in London: see Wilkins, pp. 72–3, and Buck, p. 8.
44. The brothers' investigations into railroads coincided with James Morrison's investing in French railroads, from Paris to Rouen and Rouen to Le Havre (see chapter 14).

45. Charles to James Morrison, 19 July 1842.
46. James Morrison to Daniel Webster, 9 March 1841, see Gatty, p. 161.
47. See Norma Lois Peterson, *The Presidencies of William Henry Harrison and John Tyler* (Lawrence, KS, 1989).
48. Cf. Dickens' notice of an article in a Cleveland newspaper: 'very strong indeed upon the subject of Lord Ashburton's recent arrival at Washington, to adjust the points in dispute between the United States Government and Great Britain: informing its readers that as America had "whipped" England in her infancy, and whipped her again in her youth, so it was clearly necessary that she must whip her once again in her maturity; and pledging its credit to all True Americans, that if Mr Webster did his duty in the approaching negotiations, and sent the English Lord home again in double quick time, she should, within two years, sing "Yankee Doodle" in Hyde Park, and Hail Columbia in the scarlet courts of Westminster,' *American Notes*, p. 190.
49. Charles to Mary Ann Morrison, 9 September 1842.
50. Charles to James Morrison, 21 November 1842.
51. Audubon's *The Birds of America* was published 1827–38.
52. Alfred to Charles Morrison, 23 September 1842.
53. Charles to Mary Ann Morrison, 30 October 1842.
54. Charles to Mary Ann Morrison, 30 December 1842.
55. Alfred to Mary Ann Morrison, 11 January 1843.
56. Charles Dickens, *Martin Chuzzlewit* (Oxford, 1984), pp. 304–7.
57. Alfred to Mary Ann Morrison, 11 January 1843.
58. Ibid.
59. 'Banks served the Americans as a lever … to cover the country with roads, canals, factories … with everything that goes to make up a civilization': see Bodenham, p. 84. Louisiana chartered the New Orleans Canal and Banking Company to build a canal (Morrison had £11,000 stock), also the Exchange and Banking Company and the New Orleans Improvement and Banking Company to build and operate hotels.
60. Charles to Morrison Sons & Co., 3 January 1843.
61. Alfred to Mary Ann Morrison, 13 March 1843.
62. Peterson, pp. 158–9.
63. Alfred to Mary Ann Morrison, 11 March 1844.
64. Charles to James Morrison, 5 December 1842.
65. Charles to James Morrison, 14 January 1843.
66. Charles wrote to his father about New York City Stock on 18 October 1842 and whether money was to be made from investing in the new water supply. 'I am told that the introduction of it, even into the houses of the better classes, proceeds slowly. Families have other means of supplying themselves with water, to wh they have become accustomed. Such as live in the upper part of the City have in many cases bored wells, from wh they obtain good water – but the usual resource is rain water of wh a supply is preserved in large tanks, & purified for use by filtration. Still there can be little doubt that the great proportion of the better classes will ultimately be willing to pay their $10 or $12 a year, with the farther expence of introducing the water into their houses, for the advantages they will derive from it. But among the poorer, & therefore more numerous class of inhabitants the liberty wh is afforded of obtaining the water gratis from the hydrants in the streets will greatly interfere with its general introduction into the houses. At the best we must expect a delay of 2 or 3 years, before the introduction of the water into the

houses in all parts of the City can become general – & even then a very large no of houses will remain without it.'

67. Charles to James Morrison, 26 September 1842.

CHAPTER 13: BASILDON: PAPWORTH'S LAST COMMISSION

1. Sale particulars 23 September 1829, National Trust.
2. Disraeli, *Endymion* (New York, 1880), p. 5.
3. Morrison's diary, 29 January 1840.
4. G. Jackson-Stops, *Basildon* (National Trust 1995), p. 8.
5. Thomas Burton to James Morrison, 26 September 1839.
6. Disraeli, *Henrietta Temple: A Love Story* (London, 1853), first published 1837, pp. 97, 95.
7. J.B. Papworth to James Morrison, 28 November 1840.
8. Rutherford, p. 18. On 8 December 1842 Papworth had submitted designs to Morrison for his approval: 'my motive for liking the Vase last submitted to you better than the first is that it is more classic and not too large – the other is in George II stile [*sic*] approaching the grotesque'. The 'Italian chimnies for lodge, ornaments boys and vases' were eventually supplied by Austin and Seeley in summer 1843.
9. Rutherford, p. 17.
10. J.B. Papworth to James Morrison, 25 April 1842.
11. J.B. Papworth to James Morrison, 3 July 1842.
12. Papworth also renovated Orleans House in Twickenham and Cally in Scotland for Lord Lucan's son-in-law.
13. W.H. Ashurst to James Morrison, 12 February 1841.
14. James Morrison to J.B. Papworth, 23 October 1842.
15. Henry Burton to James Morrison, 150 Aldersgate Street, 6 December 1841.
16. J.B. Papworth to James Morrison, 27 January 1849.
17. Demolition was delayed by Morrison deciding he liked the part-dismantled block: 'he thought a bit he saw left of the older part would become picturesque with a little care as a ruin', 19 April 1842. It would appear Papworth persuaded him against his picturesque ruin.
18. J.B. Papworth to James Morrison, 1 February 1844.
19. See Gatty, p. 186.
20. Brandon and Wyatt designed a number of churches in Wiltshire, including the magnificent north Italian Romanesque St Mary and St Nicholas, Wilton, commissioned by Sidney Herbert in 1841.
21. Sephton, 'Small Profits', p. 366.
22. The Marquess of Lansdowne to James Morrison, [January 1845].
23. James Morrison, *Speech on Moving Resolutions Respecting Railings*, 20 March 1845, privately printed, London, 1846, Morrison archive.
24. Sephton, 'Small Profits', p. 366.
25. The major railways were the Paris and Rouen, Rouen and Le Havre, Paris and Strasbourg, Paris and Lyons, Orleans and Bordeaux, and Nantes. Morrison had very few shares in English railways. His view that they offered less security was not unique: 'a solicitor or two, a civil engineer, a Parliamentary agent, possibly a contractor, a map of England, a pair of compasses, a pencil, and a ruler, were all that were requisite to commence the

formation of a railway company', Edward Callow of the Stock Exchange, quoted in Charles Duguid, *The Story of the Stock Exchange* (London, 1901), pp. 148–9, and Kynaston, p. 153.

26. Sephton, 'Small Profits', p. 367. Morrison hoped to gain support now by 'presenting the fostering of enterprise as something which should be preserved at the same time as protecting the interests of the public. In this way he was hoping to gain the support of both providers and users of the service'.

27. Melmotte in Trollope's *The Way We Live Now*, first published 1875; Merdle in Dickens' *Little Dorrit*, first published 1855–6. Unlike George Hudson, both Melmotte and Merdle commit suicide when their swindles are uncovered.

28. Joseph Hume to James Morrison, 10 April 1846.

29. James Morrison to Edwin Chadwick, 29 July 1846, University College London archive.

30. The Board was to consist of a paid President, two MPs and two members of the Lords, and clerks employed in the Railway Department of the Board of Trade would be transferred to it.

31. John Delane to James Morrison, 31 August 1846.

32. James Morrison, *The Influence of English Railway Legislation on Trade and Industry* (1848), p. 97. See David Salomons, *Railways in England and in France; being suggested by Mr Morrison's Pamphlet, and by the Report drawn up by him for the Railway Acts Committee* (1847), for contemporary criticism of some of Morrison's views.

33. J.R. McCulloch, *The Principles of Political Economy* (London, 1849), p. 301.

34. Edward Strutt to James Morrison, 26 June 1847.

CHAPTER 14: BASILDON: 'WHAT A CASKET TO ENCLOSE PICTORIAL GEMS'

1. Alfred had served as a cornet in the Royal Wiltshire Yeomanry Cavalry. Mary Ann's sister-in-law Jane Todd shared her concerns about Alfred's future writing: 'you mentioned in your letter there were no tidings of a Commission for Alfred. I must hope he may receive it soon as I am sure he would be better for permanent employment, he is learning Italian & oil painting, that and hunting forms his chief business, but as his Father and him seem to not always agree it would be very desirable to get him settled from home', n.d. [1847].

2. See guidebooks produced for the National Trust: Gervase Jackson-Stops, 1995, and Charles Pugh, 2002.

3. With references to Morrison's inventory, letters from Papworth, Brandon and the dealers who worked for him, Waagen's description of the collection, also a small number of black-and-white photographs taken in about 1909. At Morrison's death Christie's and the solicitors Farrer's both valued the paintings in Basildon and Harley Street. Christie's was higher for Basildon (£18,920 to Farrer's £16,570) but lower for Harley Street (£12,075 to £15,045), both totals equivalent to some £3 million in today's values. But Morrison's paintings that have been sold recently have reached far higher prices at auction, Turner's *Pope's Villa* selling for £5.4 million in 2009 and Constable's *The Lock* for £12 million in 1990. The combination of sound advice, personal wealth and good taste created an exceptional collection.

4. 4 January 1841, Lot 24, 'pair of cabinets of oak, most elaborately carved in the richest style of Holbein; with folding doors, – an upper shelf, with most elaborately carved frieze

and cornice, rests upon oval carved supports; and the cabinets stand on columns of very original and striking design.'

5. Beckford sold two pairs of coffers at the 1841 sale, then changed his mind and bought back one pair (Lot 26). William King explained to Morrison on 5 January 1841: 'the second pair I gave £71.8 for. The party who bought the first pair wishes to have yours.' When Morrison declined to give his up, King informed him that 'Mr Beckford ... writes this Morning to Mr Hume thus "thank God I have two of the coffers safe here" ', 7 January 1841.

6. Gustave Waagen, 'Catalogue of Pictures, Sculpture and Other Works of Art at Basildon Park' (n.d.), p. 9, Morrison archive.

7. '[Lansdowne Tower] Sale', *Illustrated London News,* 6 December 1845, p. 364, reprinting an account previously published in the *Bath Chronicle.*

8. George Howitt to David Brandon, 1 January 1851.

9. Hugh Brigstoke, *William Buchanan and the 19th Century Art Trade: 100 Letters to his Agents in London and Italy,* published privately for the Paul Mellon Centre for Studies in British Art, 1982, p. 38. Morrison owned a copy of Buchanan's *Memoirs,* published in 1824 when his business was in the doldrums.

10. Brigstoke, p. 11.

11. Ibid., p. 31.

12. According to John Carr's nieces who visited after the house was finished: see Pugh, p. 7.

13. The torchères were based on the celebrated Barberini candelabrum in the Vatican Museum and illustrated by C.H. Tatham in his *Ancient Ornamental Architecture,* 1799; see Jackson-Stops, p. 11.

14. The decorations were derived from the *Book of Ceilings* published by Robert Adam's draughtsman George Richardson in 1776, the year Carr began Basildon. They were probably executed by William Roberts: see Jackson-Stops, p. 12.

15. Mary Ann Morrison made last-minute alterations to their design. The Seddons wrote on 18 February 1843: 'The three windows of the Saloon we quite agree will be beautiful with your India silk worked to the drawing as amended and approved by Mrs Morrison.'

16. J.B. Papworth to James Morrison, 17 June 1843.

17. See Waagen, *Catalogue of Pictures*: 'superbly decorated ... with two very delicately executed pictures after Adrian van der Werff – one of them Hagar presented to Abraham by Sarah, the other Hagar sent into the wilderness.' Bought by Robert Hume for £445.

18. Morrison's inventory lists two cabinets of ebony with lapis and jasper panels for the saloon bought 20 November 1839 for £220 through King.

19. The carved relief by François du Quesnoy was bought by Norton at Lady Mansfield's sale at Richmond, May 1844, for £56 14s.

20. Waagen, 'Catalogue of Pictures'.

21. Morrison inventory; bought August 1846 for £772 at Christie's, Buchanan the vendor. 'Affidavits concerning the wax bust of Flora', *Burlington Magazine,* 17, no. 87 (June 1910), p. 182.

22. Gatty, p. 251. And see article in *Burlington Magazine* of 1910.

23. See Jackson-Stops, p. 12.

24. Morant to Mary Ann Morrison, 10 March 1845.

25. Allan Cunningham to James Morrison, 11 August 1842: 'I write to say that your Bust in marble from the hand of your friend Sir Francis Chantry [*sic*] – the last piece of Bust

Sculpture alas! Which will come from his hand – is now in his Studio and as the Executors are anxious to have all finished work off their hands I am requested to require to which of your residencies you wish the Bust to be sent and to inform you that the price – the customary price for all such works – is Two hundred guineas.'

26. Pugh, p. 16, quoting from Disraeli, *Henrietta Temple* (1837).
27. Jackson-Stops, p. 20. Moxon's decorations cost £410; see Morrison's inventory March 1852.
28. For further information about Ludwig Gruner see Jonathan Marsden (ed.), *Victoria & Albert: Art & Love* (London, 2010).
29. David Brandon to James Morrison, 31 August [1851].
30. 'Mr Seddon has this moment been here and he agrees with me that your embossed green pattern is quite right for the Library', J.B Papworth to James Morrison, 18 February 1843.
31. C.R. Cockerell to James Morrison, 10 September 1844.
32. The Poussin was bought through Christie's on 22 July 1850 for 1,180 guineas and hung in Basildon by Robert Hume in 1851; the Rubens was bought 22 August 1846 for £250, Buchanan claiming Clarke paid Holford £945 for it.
33. Could this be the long ebony and gold cabinet Morrison acquired at the 1841 Beckford sale lot 23, for 75 guineas? William King was concerned about its condition, writing on 7 January 1841: 'When the Furniture arrives let them be put into a Room of moderate heat that they may dry gradually. Mr Bs servants have been very neglectful in letting the place get damp and you will see the Plinth of the large Ebony Cabinet is injured by it & therefore requires care I gave the Man strict charge about it – therefore if there is any pieces off it [they] must be in the Van.'
34. J.B. Papworth to James Morrison, 7 February 1843.
35. See Neil Burton, 'Regency Eclecticism', in *The Regency Great House* (Oxford, 1998), p. 78.
36. J.B Papworth to James Morrison, 28 November 1843.
37. Thomas Seddon to James Morrison, 30 October 1843.
38. See Jackson-Stops, p. 24.
39. John Crace had written to Morrison on 21 May 1842 asking to tender for the decorating contract but presumably he was turned down.
40. 'Gilding to the Ceiling & Cornice of Octagon Room Eighty Pounds – the woodwork of doorcases & caps – also the window dressings & Skirtings Twenty Pounds – Four panels (No X) which are called decorations 12:10 each of 50£ – The 4 others instead of the decoration merely – seventy pounds', Papworth to Morrison 9 July 1842.
41. The fabric was bought on 7 September 1843 for £34 6s. 11d.
42. Details from the Seddons' bill covering March to June 1844.
43. Waagen, *Treasures*, vol. III, p. 295.
44. James Morrison to J.B. Papworth, 21 July 1841, in Papworth, *John B. Papworth*, p. 86.
45. Illustrated in sale catalogue of Basildon contents 1920.
46. Hogarth's *The Punch Club, the Modern Midnight Conversation*, acquired from Buchanan in lieu of debts.
47. Stanfield's *Italian Sea Coast* also called *Ischia* or *The Mola de Gaeta*, bought in 1847 for £262 10s.; Stanfield was a guest at Basildon in 1844.
48. Hilton's *Una and Comus* bought by Peter Norton at Christie's June 1841, £237 1s. Now private collection.

CHAPTER 15: THE FINAL DECADE

1 Anthony Trollope, *The Way We Live Now* (Harmondsworth, 1993), pp. 33–4.

2 The highest annual turnover was achieved in 1830 – £1,883,391. Morrison's four partners John Dillon, John Kersop, George Brown and Robert Slater withdrew about £2,500
a year.

3 Nathaniel Hawthorne, *The English Notebooks* (1941), pp. 604–7, quoted in Kynaston,
p. 198.

4 Kynaston, p. 140.

5 Martin Daunton, *Trusting Leviathan: The Politics of Taxation in Britain 1799–1914*
(Cambridge, 2001), p. 139.

6 Cf. the arrangement between Gurney, Morrison and the Marquess of Headfort. The sum
was larger – £190,000 – but Headfort was able to pay regular interest and eventually pay
off the loan.

7 See Robert S. Sephton, *William Seymour Blackstone (1809–1881) a Wallingford M.P.*
(Kennington, Oxford, 2003), for further discussion of Alfred's attempts to get into
Parliament.

8 James Combes to James Morrison, 28 June 1846.

9 It was a rival to the new Fonthill Abbey designed by William Burn in the incongruous
Scottish Baronial style, for the Marquess of Westminster who had purchased the old
Abbey estate. James Combes wrote to James Morrison, 22 May 1846, reporting on the
activities of the Marquess, 'determined to make the place as private as it was in the days
of Beckfords prosperity'.

10 Emily Grant to Mary Ann Morrison, 14 December 1850.

11 Robert Hume to James Morrison, November 1847. The contents of Stowe House were
auctioned the following year, and the Duke and Duchess were divorced by Act of
Parliament in 1850, the same year Morrison acquired Hillesden. By coincidence another
aristocrat on the edge of bankruptcy was the rake Long-Wellesley, Morrison's fellow MP
for St Ives (Chapter 7), who had become 4th Earl of Mornington in 1845. His Irish
estates were temporarily saved in the interests of his son through a mortgage from
Morrison for over £90,000. Morrison's list of investments in 1851 includes a mortgage
with the Earl of Mornington for £92,385 1s. 10d. See also F.M.L. Thompson, *English
Landed Society in the Nineteenth Century* (London, 1963), p. 286.

12 W.R. Mitchell, *Walter Morrison: A Millionaire at Malham Tarn* (Giggleswick, 1990), p. 11.
Tarn House is now a National Trust Field Centre.

13 William Graham to James Morrison, 24 December 1850, in Gatty, p. 291.

14 Jack Reynolds, *The Great Paternalist Titus Salt and the Growth of Nineteenth-century
Bradford* (Hounslow, 1983), p. 167.

15 The Churchwardens to James Morrison, 2 August 1853. But see Thomas Hardy, *Under
the Greenwood Tree*, first published 1872, for the impact of a harmonium on church
'orchestras'.

16 Margaret Storrie, *Islay: Biography of an Island* (Islay, 1997), pp. 3–4.

17 Norman S. Newton, introduction to *Descriptive & Historical Sketches of Islay by William
Macdonald.* (Islay, 1997, first published Glasgow, 1850).

18 John Francis Campbell to John Ramsay, April 1849, quoted in Gatty, p. 289.

19 John Black to James Morrison, 21 September 1853.

20 8 December 1853, see Storrie, p. 165.

21   3 June 1854, see ibid, p. 165. Sporting estates in Scotland attracted high rents. Strathconan, for example, was leased to the Marquess of Bath in 1854 for £1,200: see Grant Jarvie and Lorna Jackson, 'Deer Forests, Sporting Estates and the Aristocracy', http://www.umist. ac.uk/umits_spot/jarvie.html, 2001.

22   Professor Pillans to James Morrison, 31 August 1848, Edinburgh: 'I must intreat Charles to put his brother [Henry] thro' a pretty minute & searching examination as to the present state of his knowledge, especially in the article of Latin & Greek, & to do me the favour of transmitting to me the result with some detail ... board, lodging, tuition and superintendence for the College Session would be charged at £300 [not including class fees]'. Morrison archive. Pillans, with some embarrassment, negotiated a loan of £750 from Morrison at the same time.

23   £3,380 worth of loans and mortgages.

24   See Pat Jalland, *Women, Marriage and Politics 1860–1914* (Oxford, 1988), p. 59. Four per cent was the common rate of interest on a capital sum, hence £25,000 from Emily would bring £1,000 a year. Grant may instead have provided their home, Moy Hall. In a letter to James Morrison, 14 January 1849, he refers to 'our friends Mr Ashurst & Mr Blake' putting the Deeds 'into shape'.

25   Mary Ann Morrison's brother John Edward Todd married Jane Downes; his daughters attended St John's Wood Park boarding school with Ellen Morrison.

26   Elizabeth Grant, *Memoirs of a Highland Lady*, vol. I, (1898), p. 122.

27   Captain Grant's life interest from the marriage settlement was £625 per annum with a further £625 at Morrison's death (from capital invested at 4%).

28   Wailes designed a window in Wyatt and Brandon's church at Wilton in 1847.

29   Revd Thorpe, a friend of Mary Ann Morrison's, writing to James Morrison, 27 April 1854.

30   Revd Benjamin Guest to James Morrison, 28 February 1855.

31   Henry Pownall to James Morrison, 10 March 1856. Morrison also relied on his old friend Mathew Davenport Hill, now retired to Bristol, and the Revd Thomas Garnier for advice on worthy charities.

32   Samuel Gurney to James Morrison, 21 June 1854.

33   See Barrett. The will was signed on 30 July 1852.

34   See Davidoff and Hall, p. 206.

35   Charles Morrison to Alfred Morrison, 7 August 1854, Gatty, p. 300.

36   Alfred Morrison to James Morrison, 12 February 1851.

37   Squarey joined by 1853. In 1898 the firm acted on behalf of the War Department in purchasing Salisbury Plain as a training centre, while Rawlence was also a successful farmer and the founder of the Hampshire Down breed of sheep. The firm is still going strong, becoming Humberts in the twentieth century and Chesterton Humberts in the twenty-first: see Derek Barber, *Humberts into the Eighties: A History of Humberts Chartered Surveyors 1842–1980* (1980).

38   James Rawlence to James Morrison, 30 June 1855.

39   Alfred Morrison to James Morrison, July 1855.

40   James Murray Grant to James Morrison, 12 November 1853.

41   Harriet's settlement included an annuity of £750 if Frank died, and a further £18,750 for any children born to the couple.

42   The *New DNB* described Moffatt as a 'sound and enterprising Victorian businessman who turned his skills to the public good. A descendant, pitching his judgement on the

size of Moffatt's waistcoat, pictured him as a small man of domineering temperament.' His son Harold, perhaps the same descendant, called him a 'pious old hypocrite'. He was portrayed by George Meredith in his novel *Beauchamp's Career* (1876) as the long-winded and non-radical Mr Cougham.

43   George Moffatt to James Morrison, 31 January 1852.

CHAPTER 16: CHARLES MORRISON, 1817–1909: 'STATESMAN IN FINANCE'

1. *The Times,* 10 November 1910.
2. E.O.G., 'Notable Personalities. The late Charles Morrison', *The Agricultural and Horticultural Review,* August 1909.
3. *The Times,* 26 May 1909; W.D. Rubinstein calculates that Charles Morrison was probably the second wealthiest man in Britain at his death, *Elites and the Wealthy in Modern British History* (Brighton, 1987), p. 27. He left the first probated estate in Britain of over £10 million: see Beresford and Rubinstein, p. 389.
4. *The Art Journal* (1909), p. 223; Obituary in Morrison archive.
5. *The Times,* 10 November 1910.
6. James Morrison to Charles, January 1833, quoted Gatty, p. 170.
7. Charles won the 1st prize for his English prose translation of the First Book of Quintilian (April 1833) and the 1st prize for his English essay on 'A View of the Arguments of the different Speakers in the Three Books of Cicero's Dialogue *De natura decorum* with Illustrations and concluding Observations' (April 1834).
8. Professor Pillans to Charles Morrison, Edinburgh, 30 May 1835, Morrison archive.
9. Charles to Mary Ann Morrison, 21 November 1836.
10. Charles to James Morrison, 3 June 1841.
11. Family matters included his purchase of Islay on behalf of his father, handling his siblings' marriage settlements and arranging an annuity for the retired and widowed family solicitor William Ashurst. See Slinn, p. 42. The Morrisons drew up an annuity of £400 for Ashurst, thereby paying off their outstanding debts owed to the firm.
12. Peabody was recommending Bonds of the Illinois Central Rail Road. 'The subject is now under consideration by both Barings & Rothschilds', 20 October 1851, Peabody to Charles Morrison, Morrison archive. See Kynaston, p. 174. By the end of the century Charles had several million pounds invested in railways that criss-crossed the United States from coast to coast: the railroads of Alabama, Alabama & Vicksburg, Baltimore & Ohio, Chicago & E. Illinois, Chicago & Great Western, Chicago & Western Indiana, Cincinnati, Denver & Rio Grande, Detroit, Erie, Great Northern Railway of Minnesota, Kansas City, Louisville & Nashville, Milwaukee, Minneapolis, Missouri Kansas & Oklahoma, Missouri Kansas & Texas, St Louis & San Francisco, Schuylkill Valley, Toledo, Wabash, Pittsburgh, Western Pacific, Western Maryland, White Pass & Yukon.
13. Ziegler, pp. 223–4.
14. *The Times,* 20 September 1869.
15. *Morning Chronicle,* 15 March 1852.
16. *Daily News,* 20 May 1862. Connections to business ventures of Charles and his father are plentiful. The secretary was Fred Fearon, son of James Morrison's friend Henry Fearon, writer on North America and purveyor of wine and spirits. The President in the 1850s

was Thomas Weguelin, a director of the Bank of England, and a fellow director with Charles of the Paris and Strasbourg Railway. Weguelin was also, in 1857, a founder member, with Charles and Gladstone, of a new international bank based in Paris, the International Society of Commercial Credit. The connection with Barings was long – stretching back to James Morrison's troubled dealings with the Bank of the United States. Also, in 1845, Thomas Baring was a trustee for the newly formed Water Supply, Drainage and Towns Improvement Company; James Morrison was a director, along with Edwin Chadwick and Sir John Easthope.

17. *The Times,* 29 November 1892.
18. *The Times,* 29 November 1895.
19. Those who rushed to the Klondike in 1899 in the hope of finding quantities of gold were a grave disappointment to him: 'these were people who ought to have taken land and have borrowed money from the company, but the attraction of gold had proved greater than that of agriculture', *The Times,* 26 May 1899.
20. E.O.G., p. 210.
21. Kynaston, p. 305.
22. Ibid., p. 171.
23. *Birmingham Daily Post,* 16 March 1864.
24. The other directors were Thomas Hankey, John Pender MP, J. Cunliffe Pickersgill, William Smith and James Aspinall Turner MP. Morrison archive.
25. Shortly before his death Charles still owned shares in the Fore Street Warehouse Co. worth *c.* £1,489.
26. John Dillon to Mary Ann Morrison, 27 August 1864.
27. See C. Jones, 'John Morris' in *Dictionary of Business Biography,* eds D. Jeremy and C. Shaw (London, 1985). Morris was fortunate to be bequeathed a 'thriving company business which had grown up around the core provided by the investments of the Morrisons', p. 328. The firm was renamed Ashurst, Son & Morris in 1854, Ashurst & Morris in 1863 and Ashurst, Morris, Crisp & Co. in 1878: see Slinn.
28. 'Report of proceedings at the banquet, on Saturday, the 12th December, 1903 in commemoration of the eightieth birthday of Mr John Morris', privately circulated. See also R. Burnet Morris, *The Morris Family of South Molton, Devon* (Guildford, 1908), C. Jones, 'John Morris'.
29. C. Jones, 'John Morris', pp. 343–4. Charles was Director of the Swedish Central Railway Co. (1878); and Director of the St Lawrence & Ottawa Railway Co. (1882–4).
30. 'The British had cheap, good-quality goods to sell; they could extend long credit at low interest rates, being backed by England's money markets, and their shippers provided competitive costs of carriage', D. Joslin, *A Century of Banking in Latin America* (Oxford, 1963), p. 5.
31. Ziegler, p. 230.
32. Joslin, p. 101.
33. C. Jones, 'Great Capitalists and the Direction of British Overseas Investment in the Late Nineteenth Century: The Case of Argentina', *Business History,* 22 (1980), p. 158. Company name filed at Companies Registration Office London, 6 August 1881. The records of the River Plate Trust Loan & Agency Co. Ltd are held by University College London, ref. GB 0103. They include records of the companies which they administered, revealing the vast network with which Charles was involved. At his death he had shares in most: the River Plate & General Investment Co., the Mortgage Company of the River Plate, the

Compagnie Française des Chemins de Fer de la Province de Santa Fe, the London
Trust Company, the Entre Rios Railway Company, the Montevideo Waterworks, the
Consolidated Waterworks of Rosario, the Rosario Drainage Company, the Consolidated
Debt of Costa Rica, Cucuta Railways, Buenos Ayres Central Railways, the Buenos Ayres
& Belgrano Electric Tramways Co., the Argentine Refinery Company, the Barranquilla
Railway & Pier Co., La Plata Electric Tramways, Buenos Ayres & Lacroze Tramways, the
River & Mercantile Trust, the Rosario & Cordoba Waterworks Co.

34. John Morris handled the purchase of the bank for £335,714; the initial capital of the
    Trust Company was £1.25 million. Morris was the best lawyer for such a deal, with
    particular expertise in Argentina and Uruguay. He published *The Argentine Republic: The
    Forced Currency Law of 1885 and Gold Contracts* (new and revised edn, 1891). Walter
    Morrison could indeed claim 'Mr Morris' name is almost as well known in the Argentine
    Republic and in the United States of America as it is in the City of London.' See Speech
    at John Morris' 80th birthday celebration, Morrison archive.

35. Ziegler, p. 236.

36. Charles Jones, 'Charles Morrison', in *Dictionary of Business Biography* (London, 1984),
    p. 344. The Trust Company describes its financial business thus: 'to hold, work, and
    develop any property so taken over as aforesaid, or of which the Company may become
    possessed in the course of its business as mortgages or otherwise, and to take shares in or
    otherwise to subscribe to any Company, enterprise, or undertaking in which the
    Company may become interested, or which may be calculated to improve or develop any
    property or security of the Company, or to assist it in its business, and to sell, let, or
    otherwise deal with or dispose of any such property or other property of the Company',
    University College London, ref. A4/8.

37. Slinn, p. 80. A report on the company assets was presented to the first London board.
    They included the Montevideo Waterworks, 'capable of large development', the Pando
    Railway which 'runs from Montivideo [*sic*] (where it has the best position for its station)
    to the ... Pando, distant about 22 miles (almost finished)', the Wanklyn Quinta, a large
    country house near Buenos Aires, formerly home of the late Mr Wanklyn and recently let
    to the President of the Republic, a warehouse company in Buenos Aires, and land
    destined for tramways. River Plate Trust, UCL ref. A4/16.

38. Including the Rosario Drainage Company, the Cordoba Central Railway Company, the
    Rosario Telephone Company, the Belgrano Gas Company, the Santa Fe Land Company,
    the Belgrano Tramway Reconstruction, the Rosario Tramway, the Costa Rica Railway
    Company and the Cucuta Railway Company (Compania del Camino a san Buenaventura).
    The Cucuta Railway connected the town of San Jose de Cucuta with the port of Puerta
    Villamizar so that the 'well-known "Maracaibo" brand of coffee' could reach the markets
    of Europe and America. River Plate Trust, UCL ref., A7/5.

39. C. Jones, 'John Morris', p. 329.

40. John Morris claimed to have been one of the men who introduced the telephone into
    Britain; in 1869 he and eleven others subscribed £1,000 each to the National Telephone
    Company. See R. Burnet Morris, p. 34.

41. Charles' 1908 list of assets includes bonds, debentures and shares in the following
    companies: Anglo Argentine Tramways, Argentine Great Western Railway, Buenos Aires
    Central Railway, Electric Tramway, Grand National Tramway, Great Southern Railway,
    Lacroze Tramways, New Tramways, Port and City Tramways, Buenos Aires and Pacific
    Railway (£115,000), City of Rosario loan, Cordoba Central Buenos Aires Extension

Railway, Cordoba Copper, Cordoba Bonds, Cordoba and Rosario Railway, Dorada Extension Railway (£166,000), Entre Rios Railway, Montevideo Gas, Telephone and Waterworks, River Plate Electricity, River Plate Fresh Meat, United River Plate Telephone (£108,249), United Tramways of Montevideo.

42. Such a venture may have been worth investing in 'not as an end in itself but rather as a means of stimulating the local economy and opening up of markets', Colin M. Lewis, *British Railways in Argentina 1857–1914* (London, 1983), p. 21.

43. Speech at John Morris' 80th birthday celebration. Charles Jones suggests that such investment by the Morrisons in transport and communications coincided 'neatly with liberal objectives: the growth of international trade, the development of an international labour market, the extension of political education of the newly enfranchised masses through a cheap daily press, and so on'. See research materials in possession of Charles Jones.

44. The return on investments from 1864 to 1881 was only 5%, thereafter 6%.

45. *The Times*, 3 May 1894. See Lewis, p. 50: 'the railways played an integral role ... in Argentina's incorporation within the world economy'.

46. His visit took place immediately after the momentous collapse of Barings Bank. Their huge investment in the Buenos Aires Water Supply and Drainage Company, coinciding with political unrest in the country, proved calamitous. At the same time the Russian government made huge withdrawals from the Bank, and only intervention by the Bank of England and the City saved the business – though not some of its directors. Charles had £50,000 invested in the company, and was still fighting to get compensation in 1894. See Ziegler.

47. Mabel Morrison to Hugh Morrison, [February 1891].

48. Many of the following duplicated investments of his brother Charles: Antofagasta (Chile) and Bolivia Railway, Argentine Loans, Argentine Great Western Railway, Argentine North Eastern Railway, Bolivar Railway, British & Argentine Meat, Buenos Ayres Central Railway, Southern Railway, Pacifica Railway and Western Railway, Central Argentine Railway, Central Uruguay Eastern Extension Railway, Chile Loan, Cordoba Central Railway, Cordoba Province Bonds, Costa Rica Electric Light & Traction, Costa Rica Railway, Dorada Extension Railway, Esperanza Copper & Sulphur, Interoceanic Railway of Mexico, Land Company of Chiapas Mexico, Mexican Central Railway, Mexican Electric Light, Mexico City Loan, Midland Uruguay Railway, Monterey Railway, Montevideo City Loan, National Railways of Mexico, River Plate Electricity, Rosario City Loan, Salinas Railway, San Paolo Brazilian Railway, San Paolo Tramway, United Tramways of Caracas, United River Plate Telephone Western Railway of Buenos Ayres.

49. See C. Jones, 'Who invested in Argentina and Uruguay?', *Business Archives, The Journal of the Business Archives Council*, 48 (November 1982), pp. 1–23.

50. T.H.S. Escott, *England: Its People, Polity, and Pursuits* (London, 1879), vol. I, p. 190, quoted Kynaston, p. 330.

51. The list included Booths Distillery, Central London Railway, Charing Cross Euston & Hampstead Railway (£48,125), Greenwich Inland Linoleum, Improved Industrial Dwellings, London Central Markets, London Chatham & Dover Railway, London Electrical Suppliers, London India Docks, London Middlesex Freehold Estates, London Tilbury Railway, Metropolitan District Railway, Metropolitan Markets (£43,325), Metropolitan Water & Water Board, Muswell Hill & Alexandra Palace Railway, National Telephone Co. (£35,199), New Cross Brewery, Old Albion Brewery, Olympia, Savoy Hotel, Surrey Commercial Dock, Thornycroft & Co., and Underground Electric Railway. He was Director of the Hounslow & Metropolitan Railway from 1880 until 1904.

52. Obituary, *Agricultural Economist and Horticultural Review,* August 1909. A typical Morrison greeting was sent from Emily to Charles in 1850, thanking him for marriage gifts of a shawl box, shawl and books with special bindings: 'I would say a great deal more about my delight & gratitude, but I remember that you are a Morrison and I was one', Morrison archive.

53. Slinn, pp. 70–2. Allan Morrison was a director of the Telephone Company before his sudden death.

54. When his *Essay on the Relations between Labor and Capital* was published in 1854, his father's friend Matthew Hill wrote to Lord Brougham, 3 May 1854, 'Young Charles Morrison, the son of our money getting friend, and without money saving, has written a first rate book on Capital and Labor, which is just published – He has sent me a copy which I am reading with high gratification', Brougham Collection, University College London, ref. 8808.

55. Unpublished material in Morrison archive includes: 'Opinions &c of Jefferson, taken from his correspondence', April 1839; 'On Love of Novelty and Habit', 21 September 1845; 'On scarcity or abundance of money', n.d.; 'Examination of the objection to the employment of convicts in productive labour', 16 May 1854. When considering the question of whether convicts should contribute to their expenses or be 'paid for' in prison out of taxes, Charles was convinced they should be allowed to work for wages. 'Probably no one would think of objecting to their being employed in increasing the quantity of food in the world instead of serving only to consume the food raised by other people.'

56. Alice Nash to Charles Morrison, 26 June [*c.* 1907].

57. W.R. Greg on the deterrents to matrimony (1869): 'the fetters of a wife, the burden and responsibility of children, and the decent monotony of the domestic hearth', quoted in Tosh, p. 173.

58. Private letter, Richard Gatty to Dr Charles Jones, 14 April 1975.

59. His brothers supported the Fund in the 1860s when it was being used to pay for a curate and build a new church in the parish of St Mary Charterhouse. A population of 6,000, mostly poor, occupied a network of courts and alleys between Whitecross Street and Golden Lane with no access to a Protestant church.

60. Pevsner, p. 563.

61. Charles Morrison scrapbook entry, 1898, Morrison archive.

62. List of limited companies registered at Basildon House in 1908: London and Paris Exchange, White Pass and Yukon Railway, Second Kansas Land, Panhandle Land, United Electric Tramways of Montevideo, Delhi Electric Tramways and Lighting, Shanghai Electric Construction, Aluminium Corporation, Durham Collieries Electric Power, Houghton-le-Spring and District Electric Lighting plus a number of stockbrokers, chartered accountants and foreign bankers.

   And at Finsbury House, 1908: United Mining and Finance, Mines and Banking Corporation, Medapola, Broomassie Mines, Prudeau Wheel Syndicate, Himan Concessions, Roper River Land and Minerals, Heredia Lead Mines, Rogoso Gold Mines, Bengal Mills, Sulphide Corporation, Central Zinc, St John del Rey Mining, European Gas, Elmores German and Austro-Hungarian Metal, Oriental Gas, Bolders Deep Levels plus a number of merchants and the architects Gordon and Gunter.

63. Joseph Mitchell, *Reminiscences of my Life in the Highlands* (Newton Abbot, 1971), p. 300. first published 1883–4, 2 vols.

64 Storrie, p. 165.

65. Twenty per cent reduction of rents in 1871 (the severe drought the previous summer had destroyed the root crops), 50% in 1879 (bad weather), 15% from 1880 to 1885 followed by 25% reduction from 1885 to 1888. See *Jackson's Oxford Journal*, 7 January 1871, 19 December 1879; *The Times*, 8 January 1885.

66. H. Osborne O'Hagan, *Leaves from my Life* (London, 1929), vol. I, p. 32.

67. Kynaston, p. 360.

68. Scrapbook of Charles Morrison.

69. Trollope, *The Way We Live Now*, pp. 33–4.

70. Scrapbook of Charles Morrison.

71. 'Notable Personalities', *The Agriculturalist Economist and Horticultural Review*, August 1909, p. 210.

72. His investments were not all successful in his lifetime or at his death. A trust was established at his death to include his bad holdings, 'all of the unrealised or unrealisable shares that Charles Morrison held at his death'. Known as the Morrison 'fool', it produced profits gradually over the next century. Pamela Gatty letter to Charles Jones, 22 April 1980, in possession of Dr Jones.

CHAPTER 17: ALFRED MORRISON, 1821–97: 'VICTORIAN MAECENAS'

1. *The Times*, 27 December 1897: 'his special interest ... lay in encouraging the finest forms of modern handicraft. ... He loved to be the Maecenas of these men.'

2. *Freedom of Election* leaflet 4 June 1852, Wallingford. Morrison archive.

3. Sephton, *Blackstone*, pp. 53–4, quoting the *Berks and Oxon Advertiser*, 21 January 1921.

4. Alfred was still interested enough in politics to serve on a committee with Joseph Hume, John Dillon, William Ashurst and George Moffatt to secure the return of Lord Robert Grosvenor and Mr Bernal Osborne for Middlesex: *The Times*, 17 July 1852.

5. As no inventory was made of the Fonthill contents at James Morrison's death, it is not easy to ascertain which pieces came to Alfred, and which he bought for himself. Furniture included bureau cabinets of red and black lacquer and a magnificent boulle marquetry bureau plate sold at Christie's 7 May 1936 to Wildenstein and again Christie's 15 December 2005 (lot 225).

6. *Daily Chronicle*, December 1897, from scrapbook of Charles Morrison: 'one of the greatest collectors of pictures, engravings, and autographs of modern times'.

7. Leonore Davidoff, *The Best Circles* (London, 1986), p. 59.

8. Phillips handled the sale from 26 July to 30 August 1859. Bronzino's portrait of a boy, supposedly of the family of Cosimo de' Medici, was noticed at Thirlestaine House by Gustave Waagen as being 'treated with great care and animation', Waagen, *Treasures of Art*, vol. III, p. 197. The second Bronzino was a portrait of Bianca Capella. The Amberger, a portrait of a member of the Froschl Family, is in the National Gallery of Art Washington, and now considered to be by Hans Mielich.

9. See D. Robertson, *Sir Charles Eastlake and the Victorian Art World* (Princeton, NJ, 1978).

10. Walter F. Tiffin, *Gossip about Portraits, including Engraved Portraits* (London, 1867), p. 95. Tiffin's collection of nearly 500 engravings, many with a theatrical theme, was sold by Christie's 12–14 March 1889.

11. Ibid., p. 175.

12. His name first appears in Alfred's address book in 1859. Tiffin, p. 189, refers to Holloway paying £70 for heads of Sir William and Lady Paston at the Marshall sale in 1864, presumably for Alfred.

13. A hundred copies printed in 1868, *The Collection of Engravings, formed between the years 1860–68, by Alfred Morrison. Annotated Catalogue and Index to Portraits by M. Holloway.* Holloway also acquired paintings for Alfred, including, in 1864, *A Village Fair* by Brueghel (110 guineas, Christie's 4 June 1864). Alfred's widow Mabel sold a large number of engravings through Sotheby's, 21–23 November 1927 – 618 lots, some containing several engravings – described as being from 'the Holloway collection'.

14. A surviving bill from Holloway for February to June 1868 lists over 175 items purchased for him totalling £1,340. Morrison archive.

15. Tiffin, p. 8.

16. *The Art Journal Illustrated Catalogue of the International Exhibition* (London, 1862), p. 88.

17. *The Art Journal,* 1862, p. 72.

18. These included a pair of fabulous Bleu-de-Roi Sèvres china vases with mounted ormolu bought from Lord Pembroke for £456 and sea green crackle china vases from William Beckford.

19. Lord Elton, *General Gordon* (London, 1954), pp. 44–5.

20. Henry Brougham Loch, lst Baron Loch of Drylaw (1827–1900), published his *Personal Narrative of Occurrences during Lord Elgin's Second Embassy to China* in 1869. After returning to England in December 1860, he left the army and was made Governor of the Isle of Man, Governor of Victoria, Australia, and Governor of the Cape Colony, South Africa.

21. *The Times,* 3 November 1971.

22. George C. Williamson, *The Book of Famille Rose* (London, 1970), pp. 162–3. Williamson saw the collection when it was owned by Alfred's son Hugh. Examples of such porcelain with the Imperial mark were extremely rare in Europe before the Boxer Rebellion of 1900; Empress Eugénie had a few examples (now in Fontainebleau).

23. Ibid., p. 51.

24. Alfred's passion for oriental treasures was lifelong. Mabel Morrison to Hugh, 12 December 1890: 'Father ... has just bought such a big pair of Japanese vases ... they are certainly handsome & he is enchanted with them', Morrison archive.

25. The Fine Arts section was managed by the wealthy manufacturer and art collector Thomas Fairbairn (Chairman of the 1857 Manchester Art Treasures exhibition). He was known to Alfred; both patronised John Brett.

26. *The Art Journal Illustrated Catalogue,* p. 34. They were already known to the Morrisons, having supplied carpets for Basildon House. Their pieces at the exhibition included a cabinet of ebony, inlaid with ivory, a piano case of amboyna wood inlaid with medallions of painted porcelain by Minton, and a Renaissance buffet designed by Alfred Lormier. Also see Kirkham.

27. The most expensive piece Alfred bought at the 1862 Exhibition was a carved ebony cabinet inlaid with plaques of lapis lazuli and bloodstone with ivory drawers from Fourdinois of Paris for £1,400.

28. See M. Darby, 'Owen Jones and the Eastern Ideal', PhD dissertation, University of Reading, 1974.

29. Wallen was one of the innumerable neighbours and business acquaintances who borrowed money from James Morrison.

30. Listed in James' diary as 'Alhambra Jones'. James could have attended his lecture at the Architectural Association in December 1835, 'on the influence of religion upon art'.

31. Reviewed in *Civil Engineer and Architects' Journal*, July 1845, p. 215, also in *Athenaeum*, 17 May 1845: 'he here gives us a modified version of some Alhambra ideas in a subject that readily lends itself to some play of fancy. Though the design is of unusual character there is nothing extravagant or forced about it, nothing of an exotic look; the composition is simple but effective and picturesque, the two portions well grouped together, the little terrace quite alluring, in short we cannot better express our opinion of it than by terming it a pleasing architectural Anacreonatic.' Quoted in Darby, 'Owen Jones', p. 158. Jones was a fashionable personality at this time, so James may have been showing how 'in touch' he was with current taste by commissioning the dairy. That it was never built suggests he preferred the more conservative designs of Brandon and Wyatt. The design for the dairy was shown at the 1874 exhibition of Owen Jones' work but its whereabouts is unknown.

32. Christopher Dresser, *Development of Ornamental Art in the International Exhibition* (London, 1862), p. 82; *The Art Journal Illustrated Catalogue* …, p. 247.

33. Jackson & Graham invoice 10 February 1868 for £2,500 for the new room at Fonthill House, including ebony cases (£2,000), six marquetry chairs (£300) and a marquetry table (£250). They also supplied a suite of furniture in rosewood for a bedroom, bed curtains of French chintz and an ebony and enamel coffret, invoice dated 1 July 1864, £290 5s. 4d., so presumably for Fonthill. Morrison archive.

34. *Builder*, 9 May 1874, p. 385. And see M. Darby, 'Fonthill House', *Wiltshire Archaeological and Natural History Magazine*, 94 (2001), p. 232: 'Cinquecento is a term often applied misleadingly to Jones's designs which were purely eclectic and made no attempt to imitate or reproduce that style.'

35. Both the fittings and their contents were included in Alfred's list of 'heirlooms' drawn up after his death. The fittings were removed from Fonthill early in the twentieth century, but parts have been appearing at auction and some are now in museums: both the Toledo Museum and the Dunedin Art Gallery, New Zealand, have square upright display cabinets; the fireplace with overmantel and mirror passed through Sotheby's on 17 February 1984 (lot 95) and 19 July 1985 (lot 124); a large curved cabinet was sold by Christie's on 4 March 2004 (lot 209). Jones also designed decorations for the drawing room and free-standing furniture: see *Catalogue of works by the late Owen Jones*, London International Exhibition 1874: No. 64 Details of Drawing Room Inlays, No. 65 Decoration of Drawing Room at Fonthill House, No. 100 Decoration of Drawing Room at Fonthill. One of the carpets (Axminster, 256 points to the inch) was exhibited at the 1867 Paris Exposition Universelle, see G.A. Sala, *Notes and Sketches of the Paris Exhibition* (London, 1868), p. 350. The 1874 catalogue included a list of sofas, couches, chairs, tables and designs for carpets, some of which were for Fonthill. The carpet is referred to in an unidentified newspaper article in Darby, 'Owen Jones'.

36. Owen Jones, *The Grammar of Chinese Ornament. Examples of Chinese Ornament selected from Objects in the South Kensington Museum and Other Collections* (London, 1867), preface.

37. *The Building News*, 16 June 1863, p. 422.

38. Geoffrey Tyack, *Sir James Pennethorne and the Making of Victorian London* (Cambridge, 1992), p. 17. A receipt in the Morrison archive is from Lucas Brothers, 22 February 1864, 'received £4000 further on account of work on building' 16 Carlton House Terrace.

39. Tyack, p. 20.

40. The valuation of the house for insurance with the North British and Mercantile Insurance Company. Charles Morrison was Deputy Chairman of the insurance company. Alfred's 97-year lease, which began on 10 October 1864, with an annual ground rent of £284 8s., was at this stage £5,000 for 'the Building of a House situate in Carlton House Terrace Pall Mall London Brick and Stone built at present in course of erection but intended for the private occupation of the Assured'. In 1869, when work was completed, the insurance was increased to £10,000. Details of lease in Darby, 'Owen Jones', p. 417, and in the Crown Estate Office files 10205, 10282 and PRO LRRO, crest 2 no. 535, crest 1 no. 2367. Insurance details, Morrison archive.

41. R. Jenkins, *Gladstone* (London, 1995), p. 59.

42. Moncure Conway, *Travels in South Kensington. Decorative Art and Architecture in England* (London, 1882), p. 154.

43. 'The late Mr Owen Jones', *The Builder*, 32, no. 1631 (9 May 1874), p. 385. Receipts in the Morrison archive from Jackson & Graham most probably refer to their work at Carlton House Terrace: 9 July 1866 for £5,000 and 16 February 1868 for £2,000.

44. See Darby, 'Owen Jones', p. 422.

45. 'Treasure-Houses of Art – 1', *Magazine of Art*, II (1879), p. 141.

46. Conway, p. 156.

47. Bought RA 1871, eventually moved to the entrance porch at Fonthill.

48. 'Treasure-Houses of Art', p. 141.

49. Ibid.

50. Ibid. Alfred acquired bronze lions from F. Barbedienne in 1863, shown at the 1863 Paris Exhibition (brought back by Jackson & Graham); he bought a cafétière from Barbedienne in 1865 and saw more of his work at the 1867 Exposition Universelle. The dining room was damaged by fire in 1934 and there is no visual record of the chimneypiece.

51. Lormier's table was engraved in the illustrated catalogue of the 1867 Exposition Universelle published by the *Art Journal*. Sold Phillips, 25 October 1988.

52. They were exhibited at the 1867 Exposition Universelle (while the house was still being decorated). G.A. Sala (p. 350), reviewing the exhibition, was struck by their appearance, 'described as Cinquecento, but ... surely more allied by the mother's side to the Gothic, and, by the father's, to the Mauresque'.

53. 'Treasure-Houses of Art', p. 142.

54. Alfred had been approached in 1865 by Mr Pilgeram, secretary to the dealer Gambart, 'about Leightons picture – Mother & Child in the Exhibition'. Entry in Alfred's address book, Morrison archive. And see J. Maas, *Gambart, Prince of the Victorian Art World* (London, 1975), pp. 180–1. *Mother and Child* had not sold at the Academy and was on display in Gambart's Pall Mall Gallery.

55. Leonee and Richard Ormond, *Lord Leighton* (London, 1975), p. 34. However, *Summer Moon* was not sold at Christie's on 24 March 1906 to Ranjitsinhji; it passed to Alfred's son Archie and was sold from Basildon to the Maharajah's collection, where it remains. It was lent by Alfred to the Royal Jubilee Exhibition in Manchester 1887: see *The Times*, 11 May 1887. Davis' *Strayed Herd* was also lent to Manchester. *Summer Moon* was lent by Alfred in 1890 (Guildhall Corporation Art Gallery) and 1897 (Royal Academy). Mabel Morrison lent it in 1911 to the Rome International Exhibition.

56. 'Treasure-Houses of Art', p. 210.

57. Ibid. The sale was at Christie's, 28 March 1870. *Contradiction* (Holloway paid 136 guineas) passed to Alfred's son Archie, sold from Basildon House 1920 (no. 981), now in

collection of Lord Lloyd Webber. Holloway also bought for Alfred *A Reminiscence of Venice*, *The Medway at Chatham*, *A Sea Piece* and *Jael and Sisera*.

58. *The Fairy Feller's Master-Stroke* passed by descent to Alfred's daughter Katharine Gatty, then her daughter Hester who married Siegfried Sassoon, who gave it to the Tate (Britain). The manuscript remained at Fonthill, was sold at Christie's 20 December 1972, and is now in the Bethlem Hospital Museum.

59. 'Treasure-Houses of Art', p. 143.

60. *The Art Journal Illustrated Catalogue*, 1862, p. 22. At the International Exhibition, the Art Journal commended Phillips display, including 'a Greco-Etruscan' necklance, an ornamental casket and two jewels which 'are among the most perfect Art-works of the Exhibition, p. 194. Phillips of 23 Cockspur Street is first mentioned in Alfred's address book in 1861.

61. *The Art Journal*, 1867, vol. VI, New Series, p. 154. Alfred's younger brother Allan Morrison was on the committee for the 1867 exhibition dealing with objects relating to the army and navy. His activities included organising a regatta on the Seine. Morton Peto, builder of Alfred's London house was also on the committee.

62. 'Treasure-Houses of Art', p. 208. See Blairman catalogue 2004, selling Lepec enamelled bottle from the Morrison collection.

63. See Daniel Alcouffe, 'Les Emailleurs Français à l'Exposition Universelle de 1867', *Antologia di Belli Arti*, 13–14 (1980), pp. 102–21. The *nef* tazza was sold by Christie's 20 November 1971 (lot 110) and is now in the Badisches Landesmuseum, Karlsruhe. Another enamelled and gilt tazza and cover, sold Christie's 25–27 January 1899, is in the Fitzwilliam Museum, Cambridge.

64. 'Treasure-Houses of Art', p. 208. Lepec also designed a number of enamelled and gilt tazzas and caskets and a 'startling' enamelled clock of Moorish design almost nine feet tall: 'the like of it is to be seen nowhere else', ibid. Sold Christie's 23 February 1899 for just seven guineas. He carved exquisite frames incorporating Cupids and dragons to contain miniatures of Alfred's wife and children. Lepec carved frame containing his miniature of Mabel Morrison illustrated in E. Olivier, *Four Victorian Ladies of Wiltshire* (London, 1945), p. 53. Some examples remain in the family, others were sold at the Basildon contents sale 1920. At the 1872 International Exhibition in London, Lepec showed three pieces belonging to the Morrisons, an enamelled mirror, a small enamelled jewel box and an enamelled coffer.

65. John Brett to Alfred Morrison, 3 June 1864. Brett sent back to Alfred a cheque for £12 10s.

66. The painting was probably bought by Alfred before it was sent to the RA, see Christiana, Payne, *John Brett* (New Haven, CT, 2010), p. 86. Also see John Brett to Alfred Morrison, 1 July 1865, asking if he can borrow the painting to send to the Royal Academy in 1866 if he is unable to complete a new work over the winter.

67. Brett called it the 'Lady and Pigeon' when asking Alfred if he wanted to buy it, 'for a less sum than I named when you asked me some weeks ago: not that I imagine you want it, but merely that no one may suppose I have two prices for two people', 18 July 1865, Morrison archive. And see Payne, pp. 80–2, for the romantic relationship between Brett and Madame Loeser. The painting is now in the Tate Britain.

68. John Brett to Alfred Morrison, 17 August 1866. The drawing was probably *The Open Sea*, (1865), see Payne, p. 254.

69. Alfred paid £250. The painting is untraced. There is a photograph in a private collection and a reproduction of the photograph in the Witt Library, Courtauld Institute, London.

70. John Brett to Alfred Morrison, 7 June 1867. And see Payne, pp. 96–9.

71. See Waagen, *Treasures of Art*, vol. I, p. 381, on the British passion for paintings of animals: Alfred also acquired a large number of animal and bird studies by James Ward.
72. *The Strayed Herd*, RA 1865, sold 17 June 1899, whereabouts unknown; *Thunderstorm: Flocks Driven*, RA 1866, sold 17 June 1899, now Russell-Cotes Art Gallery & Museum, Bournemouth; *Labourage*, RA 1866, sold 28 January 1899, whereabouts unknown; *A Panic*, RA 1872, bought J.E. Champney and given 1921 to Beverley Art Gallery, Yorkshire.
73. Caroline Dakers, *Clouds: The Biography of a Country House* (New Haven, CT, 1993).
74. Undated letter from Mabel Morrison, written in early 1880s: 'Ellen … has some curious dislike to Alfred & always splashes him plentifully with cold water'.
75. Henry James, *The Portrait of a Lady* (Harmondsworth, 1986), p. 312.
76. Tosh, p. 173.
77. Ibid., p. 183.
78. Anthony Trollope, *The Belton Estate* (Oxford, 1943), p. 353. First published 1865–66.
79. In George Eliot's *Middlemarch*, the proposal by the Revd Casaubon, aged almost fifty, to the nineteen-year-old Dorothea Brooke, is regarded as disgusting and Dorothea's acceptance perverse. She, however, found all the passion she required in his confession of affection: ' My dear Miss Brooke. … Our conversations have, I think, made sufficiently clear to you the tenor of my life and purposes: a tenor unsuited, I am aware, to the commoner order of minds. But I have discerned in you an elevation of thought and a capability of devotedness, which I had hitherto not conceived to be compatible either with the early bloom of youth or with those graces of sex that may be said at once to win and to confer distinction when combined, as they notably are in you, with the mental qualities above indicated', George Eliot, *Middlemarch* (Oxford, 1967), p. 40.
80. Jalland, p. 79.
81. Owen Chadwick, *Victorian Miniature* (Cambridge, 1991), p. 12.
82. Edith Olivier, *Without Knowing Mr Walkley* (London, 1938), p. 15.
83. *Daily News*, 6 August 1867.
84. Isabelle Walter of Papplewick Hall, Nottinghamshire (the Walter family were founders of *The Times*).
85. The connections are complex. Colonel Wildman's father was a prominent London solicitor who had managed the fortune of William Beckford, while the Colonel's uncles ran Beckford's estates in Jamaica to their advantage and Beckford's considerable loss. Newstead was bought from the Colonel by William Frederick Webb, whose daughter Geraldine married Mabel Chermside's brother Herbert. Sir Stephen Gatty, who married Mabel's daughter Katharine in 1905, had previously been married to Alice Rawlinson, daughter of Dr Chermside's sister. Information from Rhoda Bucknill née Gatty, granddaughter of Mabel and Alfred. And see Rosalys Coope, 'The Wildman Family and Colonel Thomas Wildman of Newstead Abbey, Nottinghamshire', *Transactions of the Thoroton Society*, 95 (1991).
86. Olivier, *Four Victorian Ladies*, p. 50.
87. See James, *Portrait of a Lady*, p. 279. Isabel Archer marries the much older Gilbert Osmond against the advice of her friends. She is seduced in part by his carefully constructed apartment. 'The room … was moreover a seat of ease, indeed of luxury, telling of arrangements subtly studied and refinements frankly proclaimed, and containing a variety of those faded hangings of damask and polished oak, those angular specimens of pictorial art in frames as pedantically primitive, those perverse-looking relics of mediaeval brass and pottery, of which Italy has long been the not quite exhausted

storehouse. These things kept terms with articles of modern furniture in which large allowance had been made for a lounging generation; it was to be noticed that all the chairs were deep and well padded and that much space was occupied by a writing-table of which the ingenious perfection bore the stamp of London and the nineteenth century.'

88. Morrison archive.
89. Mabel Morrison, undated letter, early 1880s.
90. Jalland, p. 30.
91. Dr Chermside to Ellen Morrison, 9 February 1866.
92. Indenture signed 11 April 1866 by Alfred Morrison, Mabel Chermside, Charles Morrison and Richard Seymour Conway Chermside.
93. Jalland, p. 65.
94. The rental of the stables in 1910 was £250 per annum.
95. Harold would have been a worthy heir: he inherited Goodrich Court and its contents from his father, and set about adding to the collection buying fine sixteenth- and seventeenth-century English furniture from *c.* 1879 onwards. Like his uncle Alfred, he was also interested in sharing his collection with a wider public, publishing a catalogue of photographs and descriptions of over one hundred examples: *Illustrated Description of some of the Furniture at Goodrich Court, Herefordshire and Hamptworth Lodge, Wiltshire* (Oxford, 1928). He inherited Hamptworth from his uncle George Morrison who had no children.
96. Jalland, p. 180.
97. Brett completed an oil portrait and a couple of drawings (all lost) – the surviving drawing was kept by the artist. See Payne, p. 212.
98. James D. Lavin (ed.), *The Art and Tradition of the Zuloagas: Spanish Damascene from the Khalili Collection* (London, 1997), provides a thorough history of damascene, the decoration of iron with gold and silver.
99. See letter from Zuloaga to Mabel Morrison, 5 February 1868, in the Khalili private collection. Alfred may have met Zuloaga at the 1862 exhibition; they could possibly have been introduced by Owen Jones.
100. Ibid. 27 July 1869, Khalili private collection: 'I have dispatched today by the quickest possible means the large tray ordered by Mr Morrison. I hope that you will be pleased with it.' The enormous tray was illustrated in 'Treasure-houses of Art', p. 209.
101. Ewart piano in case by Jackson & Graham, designed by Jones. Now at Sewerby Museum, Yorkshire.
102. Lavin, p. 71. The cassone was sold at Christie's, 1 November 1971, for 3,000 guineas and is now in the Khalili private collection.
103. Conway, p. 157.
104. See Zuloaga to Alfred Morrison, 13 October 1868, Lavin, p. 54.
105. Now in the Khalili collection, Lavin, p. 88.
106. Sold Christie's 1 November 1971, now in the Khalili private Collection, Lavin, p. 83.
107. See ibid., p. 61. Now in the Royal Collection.
108. Sold Christie's 19 May 1966, now Khalili private collection, Lavin, pp. 106–9. Zuloaga also made a large steel cabinet of blue enamel, damascened in gold and silver to hold over 200 medals, sold Christie's 19 May 1966.
109. Alfred bought two vases by Falize at the 1878 Exposition Universelle, so this could also have formed their connection.

110. 'Falize writes about horloge', Alfred's address book entry 21 December 1881, Morrison archive.
111. Charles Blanc, *Grammaire des arts décoratifs*, quoted Katherine Purcell, *Falize: A Dynasty of Jewelers* (New York, 1999), pp. 94–5. The clock, wrongly attributed to Zuloaga, was sold at Christie's on 8 December 1938, for a mere £65 2s.; it is now in the Metropolitan Museum, New York
112. Soon after, Falize was asked by Mabel to design a much smaller piece, a vase of enamelled gold and carved rock crystal using the Sassanids period for the theme. Falize imagined that Khusro the Great 'had ordered his goldsmith to mount in gold a crystal vase belonging to the royal treasure and hoarded since the capture of Babylon: that he had it inscribed with the story of his father Kavad. The piece took three years to make. After the 1889 Exposition Universelle, at which both the vase and the clock were exhibited, Falize wrote of the significance of Alfred and Mabel: 'it is thanks to his refined taste, the trust he had placed in me, as well as the intelligent advice of Mrs Morrison, whose competence is great in these matters'. See Falize's 'Mémoire explicatif sur une Coupe d'Or et de Cristal de style Sassanide', in Purcell, p. 95. The vase was sold at Christie's on 30 November 1971. And see *Rapport sur l'orfèvreries* in Purcell, p. 73.
113. Mrs Haweis, *Beautiful Houses* (London, 1882), p. 58.
114. Charlotte, Baroness Lionel de Rothschild, to her son, Leopold, 5 August 1866. RAL 000/84. Rothschild archive at www.rothschild archive.org.
115. Sold Christie's 10 February 1900, bought by Duveen for £660, now in National Gallery of Art, Washington.
116. Gordon S. Haight (ed.), *The George Eliot Letters* (New Haven, CT, 1959), vol. VI, p. 162, quoting Lewes' diary, 21 March 1872. The bust of Voltaire is now in the National Gallery of Art, Washington. On a later visit they were shown a fine watercolour by Dürer of the wing of a European roller bird, sold Christie's 6 July 1982.
117. Haight (ed.), vol. IV, p. 161, 13 August 1875. G.H. Lewes wrote to his son Charles on 24 June 1875, also about the Swiss Cottage fields, 'from all we have seen or heard, he [Alfred] is not at all a likely person to be moved in that direction ... and the Mutter [Eliot] feels so little personal sympathy with him that she cannot write to him more fully'. See Gillian Darley, *Octavia Hill* (London, 1990), p. 177.
118. See Dakers, p. 72, Duke of Westminster to Madeline Wyndham, 1878.
119. For example in 1881, when she lent valuable Italian altar cloths to an exhibition at Messrs Hayward, 81 Oxford Street.
120. Olivier, *Four Victorian Ladies*, p. 54.
121. At about the same time Alfred built her the 'Ranch' at Great Ridge on the Fonthill estate, a luxurious cabin, at the cost of £3,000.
122. Dr Black also attended Alfred's funeral.
123. Olivier, *Four Victorian Ladies*, p. 60.
124. Undated letter [early 1880s] from Mabel Morrison, Morrison archive.
125. R. Martin Holland, *The Savile Club* (Edinburgh, 1923), p. 8.
126. Ibid., pp. 7–8.
127. Ibid., p. 35. Several Savile members were on the committee which Alfred joined in 1870, to help the family of the deceased librarian at Windsor Castle; similarly in 1874, when a committee was formed to raise money for a portrait of Lord Derby. Alfred's positioning within the highest artistic circles of society can be traced through such groupings, also through his loans and willingness to be included in prestigious

publications. In 1873, for example, an illustration of one of his Chinese vases was included in *Works of Art in the Collections of England,* published by his own dealer Holloway. His piece appeared alongside works from the collections of the Queen, the British Museum, the South Kensington Museum, Richard Wallace and the Rothschilds. See *The Times,* 28 January 1870, 16 May 1874, 30 August 1873.

128. There is no record of the architect/builder. Alfred had noted in his address book, 29 June 1874, the cost of a plain picture gallery 80 feet long, 30 feet wide and 30 feet high as £2,400 according to Mr Corder. In 1880 he added bedrooms in the attic of 16 Carlton House Terrace for his four children; the architect was Charles Edward Sayer; see Patricia Reed, 'A History of No. 13–15 Carlton House Terrace with a Short Note on No. 16 Carlton House Terrace', prepared for the Crown Estate office, 13 October 2003, p. 8.

129. *The Architect and Builder,* December 1892.

130. See Ian Hamerton (ed.), *W.A.S. Benson, Arts and Crafts Luminary and Pioneer of Modern Design* (Suffolk, 2005).

131. See A.N.L. Munby, *The Cult of the Autograph Letter in England* (London, 1962), p. 77.

132. The first entry in Alfred's address book, 2 August 1875.

133. Munby, p. 79.

134. Sotheby's, 3 March 1886, Sir William Hamilton sale, including 1,050 documents and letters of Sir William Hamilton and Nelson, sold to Peterson for £2,500, then to Alfred. Sotheby's 19–20 July 1887, correspondence of Nelson from collection of Joseph Mayer of Liverpool, bought by Thibaudeau for £510 on behalf of Alfred. Though Alfred was willing to lend from his collection to publicise the launch in 1892 of the Society of Archivists and Autograph Collectors, he refused the offer of President. See Munby, p. 80. H. Saxe Wyndham was the secretary, the society folded in 1900. Instead, Alfred carried on publishing: three volumes (1893–96) covered the letters he had collected between 1882 and 1893; two volumes (1893–94) were devoted to the Hamilton–Nelson Papers; the Blessington Papers appeared in 1895 and the first volume of the Bulstrode Papers the following year. While Sir John Bulstrode was British agent, then envoy at the court of Brussels between 1667 and 1689, he received nearly 1,500 newsletters describing affairs in England. The first volume included about one fifth of the letters owned by Alfred. Part of Bulstrode Papers now at Harry Ransom Center, Austin, Texas.

135. *The Times,* 27 December 1897. Kept in Charles Morrison's scrapbook.

136. For example, 1887, Saltaire Institute; 1891, 450th anniversary of Eton College; 1894, Italian Art at the New Gallery; 1895, Venetian Art at the New Gallery.

137. A.W. Thibaudeau, *Catalogue of the Collection of Autograph Letters and Historical Documents formed between 1865 and 1882 by Alfred Morrison,* vol. I *A–C* (1883), vol. II *D–J* (1885), vol. III *K–L* (1888), vol. IV *M* (1890), vol. V *N–R* (1891), vol. VI *S–Z* (1892).

138. *Standard,* December 1897, obituary notice. Twentieth-century biographers have been less than enthusiastic about the accuracy and use of the publications. Michael Sadleir, biographer of Blessington D'Orsay, attacked the Blessington Papers: 'For the incompetence with which this work was produced no possible excuse can exist. Here was a portion of a magnificent collection of autograph letters, belonging to a wealthy amateur and, at his expense, printed for private issue. If ever there was an occasion for intelligent and informative editing, here was one. Yet what happened? No explanation is given of the source of the papers. ... There is neither contents list nor index. ... It is full of valuable original material; but unless the reader is prepared to do an editor's work for

himself, he will find that material virtually unusable.' See M. Sadleir, *Blessington D'Orsay* (London, 1933), p. 389. And see Kenneth Henriques on mistakes with the transcription of a Samuel Richardson letter: 'The Reliability of Alfred Morrison's Transcriptions', Journal of the Modern Language Association (*PMLA*) 112, no.1 (1997), pp. 120–1. In a Richardson letter of 2,800 words the transcription has '250 errors, inaccuracies, additions, and omissions. ... There must be other researchers who now have reason to wonder about the reliability of Morrison's documents they have used in their work.'

139. The house was valued by Gordon, Lowther & Gunton on 18 February 1898. The same architects designed Finsbury House for Charles Morrison.

140. *The Times,* 22 June 1900.

141. Frank Herrmann, *Sotheby's: Portrait of an Auction House* (London, 1980), p. 123. Mabel eventually sold the collection during the First World War, receiving only £53,151.

142. Mabel Morrison to Hugh, 6 June 1909.

EPILOGUE

1. Jenkins, p. 594.

2. By an odd coincidence Lady Mary's grandfather on her mother's side was Walter Campbell of Islay, whose financial incompetence had led to the sale of his estate to James Morrison.

3. A story circulated among Hugh's employees at Fonthill that Mary conceived only after Hugh was circumcised.

4. Harold Moffatt to Hugh Morrison, 19 December 1906, Morrison archive. Moffatt inherited Goodrich Castle from his father and Hamptworth, in the New Forest, from his uncle George Morrison.

5. See Michael Drury, *Wandering Architects* (Stamford, CT, 2000).

6. *Nottingham Guardian*, 18 January 1910.

7. Press cutting, n.d. [May 1911].

8. Lutyens had misgivings: 'Rural conditions difficult ... There will certainly be a communal kitchen and a communal laundry, but it seems a communal building is impossible in the country. The villager will not be man-handled. As near neighbours the women quarrel.' See Clayre Percy and Jane Ridley (eds), *The Letters of Edwin Lutyens To his wife, Lady Emily* (London, 1985), p. 361, 27 May 1918. In the end Lutyens designed only a few cottages.

9. *New Milton and District Advertiser & Lymington Times*, 18 June 1949.

10. J. Mordaunt Crook, review of Giles Worsley, *England's Lost Houses*, 2002, in *The Times Literary Supplement*, 21 June 2002, p. 20.

11. Ibid.

Select Bibliography

PRIMARY SOURCES

The main source has been the extensive Morrison archive which is in the process of being catalogued (2011). Enquiries can be made regarding the archive to archives@fonthillfarms.co.uk.

County and record offices and local history libraries have provided the following material: Middle Wallop, Nether Wallop and Over Wallop births, deaths and marriages (Hampshire Record Office, Winchester); Basildon estate papers (Berkshire Record Office, Reading), Carleton Cowper family papers (Cumbria Record Office, Carlisle), the early nineteenth-century history of Balham (Battersea Local History Library, London); Fonthill history (Salisbury Local History Library).

The London Metropolitan Archive now has papers formerly in the Guildhall, London, including the business papers of Morrison, Cryder & Co. and the Sun Fire Office. The archives of University College London have the papers of Jeremy Bentham; Edward Chadwick; the history of London University; the River Plate Trust and Agency Company Ltd. Other London archives consulted are the Reform Club, Pall Mall; the Bank of England, Threadneedle Street; the Royal Institute of British Architects in Portland Place and at the Victoria & Albert Museum; the Royal Academy, Piccadilly; the Lord Howard de Walden Estate, Marylebone; Gurney & Co. in the Barclays Bank PLC Archive; the Palestine Exploration Fund, Marylebone; the Crown Estate Office.

The National Trust at Hughenden, Buckinghamshire, has some papers relating to Basildon. The Rothschild archive can be accessed via www.roths-childarchive.org. Nineteenth-century newspapers, Parliamentary Papers, Old Bailey records have been consulted on-line and at the British Library.

PRINTED SOURCES

FICTION

Austen, Jane, *Emma* (London, 1938), first published 1816
Bulwer-Lytton, Edward, *Pelham; or, The Adventures of a Gentleman* (London, 1828)
Collins, Wilkie, *The Woman in White* (London, 1969), first published 1860
Dickens, Charles, *Nicholas Nickleby* (London, 1986), first published 1838–9
——, *Sketches by Boz* (Harmondsworth, 1995), first published 1839
——, *Master Humphrey's Clock* (London, 1840), 3 volumes
——, *Martin Chuzzlewit* (Oxford, 1984), first published 1843–4
——, *Dombey and Son* (Harmondsworth, 1988), first published 1846–7
——, *Hard Times* (Harmondsworth, 1987), first published 1854
——, *Little Dorrit* (Oxford, 1979), first published 1855–6
——, *Our Mutual Friend* (Harmondsworth, 1977), first published 1864–5
Dillon, John, *Retribution, or the Chieftain's Daughter*(London, 1818)
Disraeli, Benjamin, *Vivian Grey* (London, 1853), first published 1826–7
——, *Henrietta Temple: A Love Story* (London, 1853), first published 1837
——, *Sybil* (Harmondsworth, 1985), first published 1846
——, *Tancred* (London, 1847)
——, *Endymion* (New York, 1880)
Edgeworth, Maria, *The Absentee* (Oxford, 1988), first published 1812
Eliot, George, *Middlemarch* (Oxford, 1967), first published 1871–2
Gaskell, Mrs *Cranford* (Oxford, 1960), first published 1853
Godwin, William, *Caleb Williams* (London, 1794)
Hardy, Thomas, *Under the Greenwood Tree* (London, 1872)
Hughes, Thomas, *Tom Brown's Schooldays* (London, 1856)
James, Henry, *The Portrait of a Lady* (Harmondsworth, 1986), first published 1881
Kingsley, Charles, *The Water Babies* (London, 1863)
Thackeray, W.M., *Vanity Fair* (New York, 1962), first published 1847–8
——, *The Newcomes* (Ann Arbor, MI, 1996), first published 1853–5
Trollope, Anthony, *The Belton Estate* (Oxford, 1943), first published 1865–6
——, *The Way We Live Now* (Harmondsworth, 1993), first published 1875
[Warren], *Ten Thousand-a-Year* (Edinburgh, 1841)

NON-FICTION

[Ackermann, R. ed.], *The Repository of the Arts, Literature, Commerce, Manufacturers, Fashions, and Politics* (London, 1808–15) (London, 1816–22) (London, 1823–8) (London, 1829)

Adburgham, A., *Shops and Shopping* (London, 1964)

Alexander, D., *Retailing in England during the Industrial Revolution* (London, 1970)

Alton, Keith, 'Municipal and Parliamentary Politics in Ipswich 1818–1847', PhD dissertation, University College London, October 1987

Anon., *Reminiscence of an Old Draper* (London, 1878)

Anon., 'Treasure-Houses of Art', *Magazine of Art*, II, (1879), pp. 140–4; 206–11

The Art Journal Illustrated Catalogue of the International Exhibition (London, 1862)

Arundell, James Everard, Baron, and Sir Richard Colt Hoare, Bart, *The History of Modern Wiltshire* (London, 1829), vol. IV of Sir Richard Colt Hoare, *The Modern History of South Wiltshire* (London, 1822–37)

Badham, Charles, *The Life of James Deacon Hume* (London, 1859)

Baker, Rowland G.M., *The Book of Molesey* (Buckingham, 1986)

Baldick, Robert (ed.), *The Memoirs of Chateaubriand* (London, 1961)

Barber, Derek, *Humberts into the Eighties: A History of Humberts Chartered Surveyors 1842–1980* (1980)

Barrett, Walter, *The Old Merchants of New York City* (New York, 1863)

Beard, Geoffrey and Gilbert Christopher (eds), *Dictionary of English Furniture Makers 1660–1840* (Leeds, 1986)

Bellot, H. Hale, *University College London 1826–1926* (London, 1929)

Beresford, Dorothy, *Nether Wallop in Hampshire* (Over Wallop, 1973)

Beresford, Philip and William D. Rubinstein, *The Richest of the Rich* (Petersfield, 2007)

Blake, Robert, *Disraeli* (London, 1969)

Bodenham, Howard, *A History of Banking in Antebellum America* (Cambridge, 2000)

The Book of English Trades (London, 1821)

Bowring, Lewin B., *Autobiographical Recollections of Sir John Bowring* (London, 1877)

Boykin, Edward (ed.), *Victoria, Albert and Mrs Stevenson* (London, 1958)

Bradley, Simon and Nikolaus Pevsner, *London I: The City of London* (Harmondsworth, 1997)

Brewer, John, *The Pleasures of the Imagination* (London, 1997)

Brigstoke, Hugh, *William Buchanan and the 19th Century Art Trade: 100 Letters to his Agents in London and Italy*, published privately for the Paul Mellon Centre for Studies in British Art, 1982

Bristow, Ian, *Architectural Colour in British Interiors 1615–1840* (New Haven, CT, 1996)

Britton, John, *The Fine Arts of the English School* (London, 1812)

Britton, John, *Graphical and Literary Illustrations of Fonthill Abbey, Wiltshire* (London, 1823)

Brockman, H.A.N., *The Caliph of Fonthill* (London, 1956)

Brodrick, George, *English Land and English Landlords* (London, 1881)

Buck, Norman Sydney, *The Development of the Organization of Anglo-American Trade 1800–1850* (Newton Abbot, 1969)

Burk, Kathleen, *Morgan Grenfell 1838–1988: The Biography of a Merchant Bank* (Oxford, 1989)

Burton, Neil, 'Regency Eclecticism', in *The Regency Great House* (Oxford, 1998)

Butlin, Martin and Evelyn Joll, *The Paintings of J.M.W. Turner* (New Haven, CT, and London, 1977), 2 volumes

Butt, John (ed.), The *Life of Robert Owen Written by Himself* (London, 1971)

Carey, J., *A Descriptive Catalogue of a Collection of Paintings by British Artists in the Possession of Sir John Fleming Leicester Fleming, Bart* (London, 1819)

Catalogue of Works by the Late Owen Jones, London International Exhibition 1874

Chadwick, Owen, *Victorian Miniature* (Cambridge, 1991)

Chancellor, Valerie, *The Political Life of Joseph Hume 1777–1855* (Stratford on Avon, 1986)

Chandler, John, *Endless Street: A History of Salisbury and its People* (Salisbury, 1983)

Chapman, S., *Merchant Bankers. The Rise of Merchant Banking* (London, 1984)

——, *Merchant Enterprise in Britain. From the Industrial Revolution to World War I* (Cambridge, 1992)

Chapman, S.D. and S. Chasagne, *European Textile Printers in the Eighteenth Century* (London, 1981)

Cobbett, R.S., *Memorials of Twickenham: Parochial and Topographical* (London, 1872)

Cobbett, William, *Rural Rides* (Harmondsworth, 1985)

Cochran, Thomas C. and William Miller, *The Age of Enterprise: A Social History of Industrial America* (New York, 1961)

Collins, Wilkie, *Memoirs of the Life of William Collins, Esq., RA* (London, 1978; repr of 2 vol. edn of 1848)

Conway, Moncure, *Travels in South Kensington. Decorative Art and Architecture in England* (London, 1882)

Critchett, B., *A New Guide to Stage Coaches, Waggons, Carts, Vessels … for the Year 1808* (London, 1808)

Crook, J. Mordaunt, 'The Pre-Victorian Architect: Professionalism & Patronage', *Architectural History*, 12 (1969)

——, *The Reform Club* (London, 1973)

——, *The Rise of the Nouveaux Riches* (London, 1999)

Cross, Nigel, *The Common Writer* (Cambridge, 1985)

Crowley, D.A. (ed.), *A History of Wiltshire: South-West Wiltshire: Chalke and Dunworth Hundreds*, vol. XVIII, *The Victoria County History of Wiltshire* (Oxford, 1987)

Dakers, Caroline, *Clouds: The Biography of a Country House* (New Haven, CT, 1993)

Darby, Michael, 'Owen Jones and the Eastern Ideal', PhD dissertation, University of Reading, 1974

——, 'Fonthill House', *Wiltshire Archaeological and Natural History Magazine*, 94 (2001)

Darley, Gillian, *Octavia Hill* (London, 1990)

——, *John Soane: An Accidental Romantic* (New Haven, CT, 1999)

Daunton, M., *Progress and Poverty: An Economic and Social History of Britain 1760–1850* (Oxford, 1995)

——, *Trusting Leviathan: The Politics of Taxation in Britain 1799–1914* (Cambridge, 2001)

Davidoff, Leonore, *The Best Circles* (London, 1986)

Davidoff, L., and C. Hall, *Family Fortunes: Men and Women of the English Middle Class 1780–1850* (London, 1987)

Davis, R., *The Industrial Revolution and British Overseas Trade* (Leicester, 1979)

Dibdin, Revd Thomas Frognall, *The Library Companion; or, the Young Man's Guide, and the Old Man's Comfort, in the Choice of a Library* (London, 1824)

Dickens, Charles, *American Notes* (Oxford, 1987), first published 1842

[Dobell, Sam], *A Brief Description of the Principles of the Freethinking Christians* (Cranbrook, Kent, 1824)

Dolan, Brian, *Exploring European Frontiers. British Travellers in the Age of Enlightenment* (London, 2000)

Dresser, Christopher, *Development of Ornamental Art in the International Exhibition* (London, 1862)

Drury, Michael, *Wandering Architects* (Stamford, CT, 2000)

Dublin, Thomas, *Lowell: The Story of an Industrial City* (Washington, DC, n.d.)

Duguid, Charles, *The Story of the Stock Exchange* (London, 1901)

Dyos, H.J., *Exploring the Urban Past. Essays in Urban* History, ed. D. Cannadine and D. Reeder (Cambridge, 1982)

E.O.G., 'Notable Personalities. The Late Charles Morrison', *Agricultural and Horticultural Review*, August 1909

Elton, Lord, *General Gordon* (London, 1954)

Escott, T.H.S., *England: Its People, Polity, and Pursuits* (London, 1879)

Eustace, Revd John Chetwode, *Classical Tour through Italy* (London, 1821)

Fitzgerald, P., *Bozland: Dickens' Places and People* (London, 1895)

Flores, Carol A. Hrvol, *Owen Jones; Design, Ornament, Architecture, and Theory in an Age in Transition* (New York, 2006)

Forster, John, *The Life of Charles Dickens* (London, 1927), 2 vols

Forty, Adrian, *Objects of Desire: Design and Society 1750–1980* (London, 1986)

Fox, Celina (ed.), *London – World City 1800–1840* (New Haven, CT, 1992)

Francis, J.A., *A History of the English Railway 1820–1845* (London, 1851), 2 vols

Fraser, Flora, *The Unruly Queen: The Life of Queen Caroline* (London, 1996)

Frayling, Christopher, *The Royal College of Art: One Hundred & Fifty Years of Art & Design* (London, 1987)

The Freethinking Christians' Quarterly Register (London, 1823)

Galt, William, *Railway Reform: Its Importance and Practicability* (London, 1865)

Garnier, Richard, 'Alexander Roos (c.1810–1881)', *Georgian Group Journal*, 15 (2006)

Gatty, Richard, *Portrait of a Merchant Prince* (Northallerton, 1976)

Geldhart, Mrs Thomas, *Memorials of Samuel Gurney* (London, 1857)

Gere, C. and C. Sargentsen (eds), *Journal of the History of Collections*, 14, no. 1 (2002)

Goodwin, Mark, 'Objects, Belief and Power in mid-Victorian England – the Origins of the Victoria and Albert Museum', in *Objects of Knowledge*, ed. Susan M. Pearce (London, 1990)

Grant, James, *Random Recollections of the House of Commons* (London, 1836)

Gumm, Gordon, *Over Wallop in Hampshire* (Over Wallop, 1992)

Haight, Gordon S. (ed.), *The George Eliot Letters* (New Haven, CT, 1959)

Hamerton Ian (ed.), *W.A.S. Benson, Arts and Crafts Luminary and Pioneer of Modern Design* (Suffolk, 2005)

Hammond, J.L. and Barbara, *The Village Labourer* (London, 1948), 2 vols; first published 1911

Hampshire Allegations for Marriage Licences granted by the Bishop of Winchester (London, 1893)

Harte, Negley and John North, *The World of UCL 1828–1990* (London, 1991)

Haskell, Francis, *Rediscoveries in Art* (New Haven, CT, 1976)

——, *Anatole Demidoff, Prince of San Donato (1812–70)*, exhibition catalogue (Wallace Collection, 1994)

——, *The Ephemeral Museum* (New Haven, CT, 2000)

Haweis, Mrs, *Beautiful Houses* (London, 1882)

Herrmann, Frank, *Sotheby's: Portrait of an Auction House* (London, 1980)

Hewat-Jaboor, Philip, 'Fonthill House', in D.E. Ostergard (ed.), *William Beckford 1760–1844: An Eye for the Magnificent* (New Haven, CT, 2001)

Hidy, Ralph, *The House of Baring in American Trade and Finance* (New York, 1949)

Hill, Rosemary, *God's Architect: Pugin and the Building of Romantic Britain* (London, 2007)

Hillyer, W.H., *James Talcott, Merchant, and his Times* (New York, 1937)

Hilton, Timothy, *John Ruskin, The Early Years 1819–1859* (New Haven, CT, 2000)

Hoare, Richard Colt, *History of Modern South Wiltshire* (1822–37), 5 vols

Holland, R. Martin, *The Savile Club* (Edinburgh, 1923)

Holloway, Marseille Middleton, *The Collection of Engravings, Formed between the Years 1860–68, by Alfred Morrison. Annotated Catalogue and Index to Portraits by M. Holloway* (privately printed, 1868)

Holme, Thea, *Prinny's Daughter. A Life of Princess Charlotte of Wales* (London, 1976)

Holyoake, George, *The History of Cooperation* (London, 1906)

Hull, William, *The History of the Glove Trade* (London, 1834)

Hunt, Leigh, 'Coaches', *The Indicator, and the Companion* (London, 1841)

Jackson-Stops, Gervase, *Basildon* (National Trust, 1995)

Jaffe, James A. (ed.), *'The Affairs of Others', The Diaries of Francis Place 1825–1836* (Cambridge, 2007), Camden Society, 5th ser., no. 30

Jalland, Pat, *Women, Marriage and Politics 1860–1914* (Oxford, 1988)

Jay, Cyrus, *Recollections of William Jay, of Bath* (London, 1859)

Jenkins, Roy, *Gladstone* (London, 1995)

Johnston, Lucy, *Nineteenth-Century Fashion in Detail* (London, 2005)

Johnstone's London Commercial Guide (London, 1817)

Jones, Charles A., *Great Capitalists* (London, 1980)

——, 'Who Invested in Argentina and Uruguay?', *Business Archives: The Journal of the Business Archives Council*, 48 (November 1982)

——, 'Charles Morrison', *Dictionary of Business Biography* (London, 1984)

——, 'John Morris', in *Dictionary of Business Biography*, ed. D. Jeremy and C. Shaw (London, 1985)

——, *International Business in the Nineteenth Century: The Rise and Fall of a Cosmopolitan Bourgeoisie* (Brighton, 1987)

Jones, Owen, *The Grammar of Chinese Ornament. Examples of Chinese Ornament Selected from Objects in the South Kensington Museum and Other Collections* (London, 1867)

Joslin, D., *A Century of Banking in Latin America* (Oxford, 1963)

Joy, Edward T., *English Furniture 1800–1851* (London, 1977)

Judd, Gerrit P., *Members of Parliament 1734–1832* (New Haven, CT, 1955)

Kirkham, Pat, *The London Furniture Trade 1700–1870* (Leeds, 1988)

Kouwenhaven, John A., *Partners in Banking. An Historical Portrait of a Great Private Bank: Brown Brothers Harriman & Co. 1818–1968* (New York, 1968)

Kynaston, D., *The City of London Volume I: A World of its Own 1815–1890* (London, 1994)

Langford, Paul, 'The Uses of Eighteenth-century Politeness', *Transactions of the Royal Historical Society*, 6th ser, XII (2002)

Lavin, James D. (ed.), *The Art and Tradition of the Zuloagas: Spanish Damascene from the Khalili Collection* (London, 1997)

Leaf, Walter, *Some Chapters of Autobiography* (London, 1938)

Lees-Milne, J., *William Beckford* (Tisbury, 1976)

Le Marchant, Denis (ed.), *John Charles, Viscount Althorp Third Earl Spencer* (London, 1876)

Leslie, C.R., *Memoirs of the Life of John Constable* (London, 1951)

Leventhal, Fred M. and Roland Quinault, *Anglo-American Attitudes from Revolution to Partnership* (Aldershot, 2000)

Lewis, Colin M., *British Railways in Argentina 1857–1914* (London, 1983)

The London Post Office Directory (London, 1808; 1817)

Maas, J., *Gambart, Prince of the Victorian Art World* (London, 1975)

McCalman, Iain, *Radical Underworld Prophets, Revolutionaries and Pornographers in London 1795–1840* (Oxford, 1988)

McCulloch, J.R., *The Principles of Political Economy* (London, 1849)

McGrane, R.G., *Foreign Bondholders and American State Debts* (London, 1935)

McHardy, G. *Catalogue of the Royal Institute of British Architects Drawings Collection: The Office of J.B. Papworth* (London, 1976)

Mcleod, Bet, 'Treasures of England's Wealthiest Son', *Country Life*, 7 February 2002

Mallet, J.L., [Diary] *Political Economy Club* (London, 1921), vol. VI

Mandler, Peter, *Aristocratic Government in the Age of Reform* (Oxford, 1990)

Marsden, Jonathan (ed.), *Victoria & Albert: Art & Love* (London, 2010)

Middelboe, P. (ed.), *Edith Olivier from her Journals 1924–48* (London, 1989)

Mingay, G.E. (ed.), *The Victorian Countryside* (London, 1981), 2 vols

Mitchell, Joseph, *Reminiscences of my Life in the Highlands* (Newton Abbot, 1971), first published 1883–4, 2 vols

Mitchell, W.R., *Walter Morrison: A Millionaire at Malham Tarn* (Giggleswick, 1990)

Moffatt, Harold, *Illustrated Description of Some of the Furniture at Goodrich Court, Herefordshire and Hamptworth Lodge, Wiltshire* (Oxford, 1928)

The Monthly Repository of Theology and General Literature (London, 1818)

Moody, R., *Mr Benett of Wiltshire: the Life of a County Member of Parliament 1773–1852* (East Knoyle, 2005)

Morris, R. Burnet, *The Morris Family of South Molton, Devon* (Guildford, 1908)

Morris, Edward, *French Art in Nineteenth-century Britain* (New Haven, CT, 2005)

Morrison, James, *Railroads. Speech of James Morrison, Esq., M.P., in the House of Commons, 17th May, 1836, on Moving a Resolution Relative to the Periodical Revision of Tolls and Charges Levied on Railroads and other Public Works* (London, 1836)

——, *Speech of James Morrison, Esq., M.P., March 20th, 1845, On Moving Resolutions Respecting Railways* (London, 1846)

——, *Observations Illustrative of the Defects of the English System of Railway Legislation, and of its Injurious Operation on the Public Interests; with Suggestions for its Improvement* (London, 1846)

——, *The Influence of English Railway Legislation on Trade and Industry* (1848)

Mowl, Timothy, 'A Biographical Perspective', in D.E. Ostergard (ed.), *William Beckford 1760–1884: An Eye for the Magnificent* (New Haven, CT, 2001)

——, 'Inside Beckford's Landscape of the Mind', *Country Life*, 7 February 2002

Munby, N.L., *The Cult of the Autograph Letter in England* (London, 1962)

Nevins, Allan (ed.), *America through British Eyes* (Oxford, 1948)

Newton, Norman S., Introduction to *Descriptive & Historical Sketches of Islay by William Macdonald* ... (Islay, 1997), first published Glasgow, 1850

Nicholls, J.B., *Historical Notes of Fonthill Wiltshire* (London, 1836).

O'Brien, D.P., *The Classical Economists Revisited* (Princeton, NJ, 2004)

Observer, An, *Kaleidoscope Wiltoniensis: or, A Literary and Moral View of the County of Wilts during the Contested Election for its Representation, in June 1818* (London, 1818)

Olivier, Edith, *Without Knowing Mr Walkley* (London, 1938)

——, *Four Victorian Ladies of Wiltshire* (London, 1945)

Orbell, John, *Baring Brothers & Co. Ltd, A History to 1939* (Frome, 1985)

Ormond, Leonee and Richard, *Lord Leighton* (London, 1975)

Osborne O'Hagan, H. *Leaves from my Life* (London, 1929)

Ostergard, D.E. (ed.), *William Beckford 1760–1844: An Eye for the Magnificent* (New Haven, CT, 2001)

Papworth, J.B., *Rural Residences* (London 1818)

——, *Hints on Ornamental Gardening* (London, 1823)

——, (ed.), *A Treatise on the Decorative Part of Civic Architecture* by Sir William Chambers (London, 1826)

Papworth, Wyatt, *John B. Papworth Architect to the King of Württemberg: A Brief Record of his Life and Works* (London, 1879)

——, *Memoir of Alfred Whitehead Morant* (London, 1881)

Parry, J.H., *Trade and Dominion* (London, 2000)

Payne, Christiana, *John Brett* (New Haven, CT, 2010)

Percy, Clayre and Jane Ridley (eds), *The Letters of Edwin Lutyens To his Wife, Lady Emily* (London, 1985)

Peterson, Norma Lois, *The Presidencies of William Henry Harrison and John Tyler* (Lawrence, KS, 1989)

Pevsner, Nikolaus, revised by Bridget Cherry, *Wiltshire* (Harmondsworth, 1975)

Phillips, R., *Picture of London for 1803* (1803)

Phillips, *The Valuable Library of Books in Fonthill Abbey … The Unique and Splendid Effects of Fonthill Abbey … The Pictures and Miniatures at Fonthill Abbey* (London, 1823)

Political Economy Club, *Minutes of Proceedings 1821–1882, Roll of Members, and Questions Discussed* (London, 1882), vol. IV

Porter, Roy, *English Society in the Eighteenth Century* (Harmondsworth, 1991)

Power, Graham, *Balham: A Brief History* (Wandsworth, 1996)

[Puckler-Muskau, Prince], *Puckler's Progress. The Adventures of Prince Puckler-Muskau in England, Wales and Ireland as Told in Letters to his Former Wife, 1826–9* (London, 1987)

Pugh, Charles, *Basildon Park* (National Trust, 2002)

Purcell, Katherine, *Falize: A Dynasty of Jewellers* (New York, 1999)

Puseley, D., *Commercial Companion* (1860)

Reed, Patricia, 'A History of No. 13–15 Carlton House Terrace with a Short Note on No. 16 Carlton House Terrace', prepared for the Crown Estate Office, 13 October 2003

Reynolds, Jack, *The Great Paternalist: Titus Salt and the Growth of Nineteenth-century Bradford* (Hounslow, 1983)

Robertson, D., *Sir Charles Eastlake and the Victorian Art World* (Princeton, NJ, 1978)

Rosen, F., *Bentham, Byron, and Greece. Constitutionalism, Nationalism, and Early Liberal Political Thought* (Oxford, 1992)

Rubinstein, W.D., *Elites and the Wealthy in Modern British History* (Brighton, 1987)

Ruskin, John, *Praeterita,* vol. 35 of *The Complete Works of John Ruskin,* ed. E.T. Cook and Alexander Wedderburn, 39 vols (London, 1903–12)

Russell, Rollo (ed.), *Early Correspondence of Lord John Russell 1805–40* (London, 1913), 2 vols

Rutherford, Sarah, 'Draft Basildon Park Framework Garden Conservation Plan' (National Trust, 2002)

Rutter, John, *Delineations of Fonthill and its Abbey* (London, 1823)

Sadleir, M., *Blessington D'Orsay* (London, 1933)

Sala, G.A., *Notes and Sketches of the Paris Exhibition* (London, 1868)

Salomons, David, *Railways in England and in France; being suggested by Mr Morrison's Pamphlet, and by the Report drawn up by him for the Railway Acts Committee* (1847)

Satoh Akira, *Building in Britain. The Origins of a Modern Industry*, trans. Ralph Morton (Aldershot, 1995)

Sephton, Robert S., 'Small Profits on a Large Trade: James Morrison, parts 1 and 2', *Journal of the Railway and Canal Historical Society* (November 2003), 34, part 6 no. 186

——, *William Seymour Blackstone (1809–1881) a Wallingford M.P.* (Kennington, Oxford, 2003)

Slinn, Judy, *Ashurst Morris Crisp: A Radical Firm* (Cambridge, 1997)

Smiles, Samuel, *Self-help* (London, 1860), first published 1859

Smith, Walter Buckingham, *Economic Aspects of the Second Bank of the United States* (Cambridge, MA, 1953)

Solkin, David (ed.), *Turner and the Masters* (London, 2009)

Southgate, Beverley, *History meets Fiction* (Harlow, 2009)

Speck, W.A., *Robert Southey: Entire Man of Letters* (New Haven, CT, 2006)

Stewart, Rachel, *The Town House in Georgian London* (New Haven, CT, 2009)

Storrie, Margaret, *Islay: Biography of an Island* (Islay, 1997)

Strachey, Lady (ed.), *Memoirs of a Highland Lady. The Autobiography of Elizabeth Grant of Rothiemurchus* (London, 1898)

Strong, Roy, *The Destruction of the Country House* (London, 1974)

Styles, John, 'Manufacturing, Consumption and Design in Eighteenth-century England', in John Brewer and Roy Porter (eds), *Consumption and the World of Goods* (London, 1993)

——, *The Dress of the People* (New Haven, CT, 2007)

Sweet, R.H., 'Topographies of Politeness', *Transactions of the Royal Historical Society*, 6th ser., 12 (2002)

Taylor, Brandon, *Art for the Nation* (Manchester, 1999)

Taylor, G.R., *The Transportation Revolution* (New York, 1957)

Taylor, Lou, *Mourning Dress: A Costume and Social History* (London, 1983)

Telba, [Ablet], *A Few Every-Day Hints, Addressed to the Youth and Young Men of the Drapery Trade* (London, n.d. [1878])

Thibaudeau, Alphonse Wyatt, *Catalogue of the Collection of Autograph Letters and Historical Documents formed between 1865 and 1882 by Alfred Morrison*, vol. I A–C (1883), vol. II D–J (1885), vol. III K–L (1888), vol. IV M (1890), vol. V N–R (1891), vol. VI S–Z (1892) ([London] 1883–92)

Thomas, Hugh, *The Slave Trade: The History of the Atlantic Slave Trade, 1440–1870* (London, 1997)

Thompson, E.P., *The Making of the English Working Class* (Harmondsworth, 1975)

Thompson, F.M.L., *English Landed Society in the Nineteenth Century* (London, 1963)

Thornbury, Walter, *The Life of J.M.W. Turner, RA* (London, 1970), repr. of 1877 edn

Tiffin, Walter F., *Gossip about Portraits, including Engraved Portraits* (London, 1867)

Tosh, John, *A Man's Place: Masculinity and the Middle-class Home in Victorian England* (New Haven, CT, 1999)

Tyack, Geoffrey, *Sir James Pennethorne and the Making of Victorian London* (Cambridge, 1992)

Urwin, Alan C.B., *Twicknam Parke* (Hounslow, 1965)

Vickery, Amanda, *The Gentleman's Daughter: Women's Lives in Georgian England* (New Haven, CT, and London, 1998)

Voorsanger, Catherine Hoover and John K. Howat, *Art and the Empire City: New York 1825–1861* (New Haven, CT, 2000)

Waagen, G., *Treasures of Art in Great Britain: Being an Account of the Chief Collections of Paintings, Drawings, Sculptures, Illuminated Mss; &c &c,* (London, 1854), 3 vols

——, 'Catalogue of Pictures, Sculpture and Other Works of Art at Basildon Park' [1854]

——, *Galleries and Cabinets of Art in Great Britain* (London, 1857)

Wall, John, *John Henning, That Most Ingenious Modeller* (Ely, 2008)

Wallas, Graham, *The Life of Francis Place 1771–1854* (London, 1918)

Walsh, Claire, 'Shop Design and the Display of Goods in Eighteenth-century London', *Journal of Design History*, 8, no. 3 (1995)

[Warren], *Ten Thousand- a-Year* (Edinburgh, 1841)

Wilkins, Mira, *The History of Foreign Investment in the United States to 1914* (Cambridge, MA 1989)

Williams, Clive, *Basildon, Berkshire* (Reading, 1994)

Williamson, George C., *The Book of Famille Rose* (London, 1970)

Wilson, Ben, *Decency and Disorder: The Age of Cant 1789–1837* (London, 2007)

Wilson, Derek, *Rothschild* (London, 1994)

Wilton, Andrew and Tim Barringer (eds), *American Sublime: Landscape Painting in the United States 1820–1880* (London, 2002)

Winthrop, Robert C., *Memoir of the Hon. Nathan Appleton* (1861)

Woodbridge, George, *The Reform Club 1836–1978* (Bradford, 1978)

Worsley, Giles, *England's Lost Houses* (London, 2002)

Ziegler, Philip, *The Sixth Great Power: Barings, 1762–1929* (London, 1988)

Index

Note to index: this index does not cover the endnotes. James Morrison and his wife Mary Ann are not separately listed as references to both appear throughout the book and are roughly chronological. Similarly Charles and Alfred Morrison are not indexed for 'their' chapters (12, 16 and 17). References to textiles and clothing (cotton, silk, ribbons, etc) can be found under textiles; individual railroads are listed under railways.